©Tia Cross 1981

But Some of Us Are Brave

All the Women Are White,
All the Blacks Are Men,

But Some of Us
Are Brave

Black Women's Studies

Edited by Gloria T. Hull,
Patricia Bell Scott, and Barbara Smith

The Feminist Press
at The City University of New York
New York

Published in the United States by The Feminist Press at
The City University of New York, 311 East 94 Street,
New York, NY 10128.

First Edition

02 01 00 98 97 96   13 12 11 10

This work was developed under a grant from the
Women's Educational Equity Act Program, U.S.
Department of Education. However, the content does
not necessarily reflect the position of that Agency, and
no official endorsement of these materials should be
inferred.

We gratefully acknowledge the Muskiwinni Foundation
of New York, N.Y., for a grant which aided in the development and publication of this work, and we offer special thanks to the Polaroid Foundation and to Mary Anne
Ferguson for their contributions toward the publication
of this work.

Library of Congress Catalog Card No. 81–68918
Hull, Gloria et al.
        But some of us are brave.
        Old Westbury, NY: The Feminist Press
        384 p.
        8112   810727

        ISBN 0-912670-95-9 paper

Printed in the United States of America on acid-free
paper by BookCrafters.

Cover photo: French Collection. Library of Congress.

For Beverly Towns Williams
whose commitment and generosity
helped make this book possible.

Woman Seated at Tuskegee Institute, 1906.

Table of Contents

Evicted sharecropper, Butler County, Missouri; November 1939.

WOMEN

They were women then
My mama's generation
Husky of voice-Stout of
Step
With fists as well as
Hands
How they battered down
Doors
And ironed
Starched white
Shirts
How they led
Armies
Headragged Generals
Across mined
Fields
Booby-trapped
Kitchens
To discover books
Desks
A place for us
How they knew what we
Must know
Without knowing a page
Of it
Themselves.

Alice Walker

Foreword

MARY BERRY

Hull, Scott, and Smith have put together a volume that very much needed doing. The education of students has been long bereft of adequate attention to the experiences and contributions of Blacks and women to American life. But practically no attention has been given to the distinct experiences of Black women in the education provided in our colleges and universities. This absence of attention is molded and reflected in the materials made available by scholars.[1]

Black historians and others who focus on Afro-American history are little better than other scholars on this issue. Without the pioneering work of Gerda Lerner and such younger scholars as Rosalyn Terborg-Penn, little would be available in print to begin the quest for knowledge concerning Black women's experiences.[2]

Unfortunately, it is also true that women's studies, which has had to exist on the periphery of academic life, like Black studies, has not focused on Black women. The women's movement and its scholars have been concerned, in the main, with white women, their needs and concerns. However, there are exceptions. For example, in Jo Freeman's *Women: A Feminist Perspective*, two extended essays are devoted to the particular condition of Black women. The feminist perspective, according to Freeman, "looks at the many similarities between the sexes and concludes that women and men have equal potential for individual development. Differences in the realization of that potential, therefore, must result from externally imposed restraints, from the influence of social institutions, and values." The essay she includes by Pauline Terrelonge Stone, "Feminist Consciousness and Black Women," describes the Black woman's condition as differentiated from white women's, "in the peculiar way in which the racial and sexual caste systems have interfaced." Black women, according to Stone, have suffered from "double dependency" on their mates and employers. They have been expected to work while white women have been expected not to. Sexism, however, consigns Black women to lower status jobs, to "female occupations such as nursing and teaching." She believes a feminist consciousness would help Blacks to understand that "many social problems affecting Blacks are in part at least attributable to the operation of sexism in our society."[3] Black women need to understand that sexism and racism impinge on their opportunities negatively.

Hull, Scott, and Smith and their contributors would agree with Stone's analysis as they state that a "feminist, pro-woman perspective" is necessary to understand fully the experiences of Black women in society. However, more importantly, perhaps Black women's studies will help Black women and men understand more about the way in which the Black community is oppressed.

Notes

[1] For example, Anne Firor Scott in her introduction to the modern edition of Julia Cherry Spruill's Women's Life and Work in the Southern Colonies (New York: W. W. Norton Co., 1972), does not note that the book is about white women. William Chafe in The American Woman: Her Changing Social, Economic and Political Roles, 1920-1970 (New York: Oxford University Press, 1972) mentions Negroes twice. Both books, despite their titles, are not about American women but American white women.

[2] For example, the leading history, From Slavery to Freedom: A History of Negro Americans (New York: Alfred A. Knopf, Inc., 1974) by John Hope Franklin pays no specific attention to Black women's roles.

[3] Jo Freeman, Women: A Feminist Perspective (Palo Alto, Ca.: Mayfield Publishing Co., 1979), pp. xxi, 575-588.

Introduction
The Politics of Black Women's Studies
Gloria T. Hull and Barbara Smith

Merely to use the term "Black women's studies" is an act charged with political significance. At the very least, the combining of these words to name a discipline means taking the stance that Black women exist—and exist positively—a stance that is in direct opposition to most of what passes for culture and thought on the North American continent. To use the term and to act on it in a white-male world is an act of political courage.

Like any politically disenfranchised group, Black women could not exist consciously until we began to name ourselves. The growth of Black women's studies is an essential aspect of that process of naming. The very fact that Black women's studies describes something that is really happening, a burgeoning field of study, indicates that there are political changes afoot which have made possible that growth. To examine the politics of Black women's studies means to consider not only what it is, but why it is and what it can be. Politics is used here in its widest sense to mean any situation/relationship of differential power between groups or individuals.

Four issues seem important for a consideration of the politics of Black women's studies: (1) the general political situation of Afro-American women and the bearing this has had upon the implementation of Black women's studies; (2) the relationship of Black women's studies to Black feminist politics and the Black feminist movement; (3) the necessity for Black women's studies to be feminist, radical, and analytical; and (4) the need for teachers of Black women's studies to be aware of our problematic political positions in the academy and of the potentially antagonistic conditions under which we must work.

The political position of Black women in America has been, in a single word, embattled. The extremity of our oppression has been determined by our very biological identity. The horrors we have faced historically and continue to face as Black women in a white-male-dominated society have implications for every aspect of our lives, including what white men have termed "the life of the mind." That our oppression as Black women can take forms specifically aimed at discrediting our intellectual power is best illustrated through the words of a "classic" American writer.

In 1932 William Faulkner saw fit to include this sentence in a description of a painted sign in his novel *Light in August*. He wrote:

> But now and then a negro nursemaid with her white charges would loiter there and spell them [the letters on the sign] aloud with *that vacuous idiocy of her idle and illiterate kind*.[1] [Italics ours]

Faulkner's white-male assessment of Black female intellect and character, stated as a mere aside, has fundamental and painful implications for a consideration of the whole question of Black women's studies and the politics that shape its existence. Not only does his remark typify the extremely negative ways in which Afro-American women have been portrayed in literature, scholarship, and the popular media, but it also points to the destructive white-male habit of categorizing all who are not like themselves as their intellectual and moral inferiors. The fact that the works in which such oppressive images appear are nevertheless considered American "masterpieces" indicates the cultural-political value system in which Afro-American women have been forced to operate and which, when possible, they have actively opposed.

The politics of Black women's studies are totally connected to the politics of Black women's lives in this country. The opportunities for Black women to carry out autonomously defined investigations of self in a society which through racial, sexual, and class oppression systematically denies our existence have been by definition limited.

As a major result of the historical realities which brought us enslaved to this continent, we have been kept separated in every way possible from recognized intellectual work. Our legacy as chattel, as sexual slaves as well as forced laborers, would adequately explain why most Black women are, to this day, far away from the centers of academic power and why Black women's studies has just begun to surface in the latter part of the 1970s. What our multilayered oppression does not explain are the ways in which we have created and maintained our own intellectual traditions as Black women, without either the recognition or the support of white-male society.

The entry entitled "A Slave Woman Runs a Midnight School" in Gerda Lerner's *Black Women in White America: A Documentary History* embodies this creative, intellectual spirit, coupled with a practical ability to make something out of nothing.

> [In Natchez, Louisiana, there were] two schools taught by colored teachers. One of these was a slave woman who had taught a midnight school for a year. It was opened at eleven or twelve o'clock at night, and closed at two o'clock a.m....Milla Granson, the teacher, learned to read and write from the children of her indulgent master in her old Kentucky home. Her number of scholars was twelve at a time and when she had taught these to read and write she dismissed them, and again took her apostolic number and brought them up to the extent of her ability, until she had graduated hundreds. A number of them wrote their own passes and started for Canada....
>
> At length her night-school project leaked out, and was for a time suspended; but it was not known that seven of the twelve years subsequent to leaving Kentucky had been spent in this work. Much excitement over her night-school was produced. The subject was discussed in their legislature, and a bill was passed, that it should not be held illegal for a slave to teach a slave....She not only [re]opened her night-school, but a Sabbath-school.... Milla Granson used as good language as any of the white people.[2]

This document illuminates much about Black women educators and thinkers in America. Milla Granson learned to read and write through the exceptional indulgence of her white masters. She used her skills not to advance her own status, but to help her fellow slaves, and this under the most difficult circumstances. The act of a Black person teaching and sharing knowledge was viewed as naturally threatening to the power structure. The knowledge she conveyed had a politically and materially transforming function, that is, it empowered people to gain freedom.

Milla Granson and her pupils, like Black people throughout our history here, made the greatest sacrifices for the sake of learning. As opposed to "lowering" educational standards, we have had to create our own. In a totally antagonistic setting we have tried to keep our own visions clear and have passed on the most essential kind of knowledge, that which enabled us to survive. As Alice Walker writes of our artist-thinker foremothers:

> They dreamed dreams that no one knew—not even themselves, in any coherent fashion—and saw visions no

one could understand.... They waited for a day when the
unkown thing that was in them would be made known;
but guessed, somehow in their darkness, that on the day
of their revelation they would be long dead.[3]

The birth of Black women's studies is perhaps the day of revelation these
women wished for. Again, this beginning is not unconnected to political
events in the world outside university walls.

The inception of Black women's studies can be directly traced to
three significant political movements of the twentieth century. These are
the struggles for Black liberation and women's liberation, which
themselves fostered the growth of Black and women's studies, and the
more recent Black feminist movement, which is just beginning to show
its strength. Black feminism has made a space for Black women's studies
to exist and, through its commitment to all Black women, will provide
the basis for its survival.

The history of all of these movements is unique, yet interconnected.
The Black movements of the 1950s, '60s, and '70s brought about
unprecedented social and political change, not only in the lives of Black
people, but for all Americans. The early women's movement gained
inspiration from the Black movement as well as an impetus to organize
autonomously both as a result of the demands for all-Black organizations
and in response to sexual hierarchies in Black- and white-male political
groupings. Black women were a part of that early women's movement, as
were working-class women of all races. However, for many reasons—
including the increasing involvement of single, middle-class white
women (who often had the most time to devote to political work), the
divisive campaigns of the white-male media, and the movement's serious
inability to deal with racism—the women's movement became largely
and apparently white.

The effect that this had upon the nascent field of women's studies
was predictably disastrous. Women's studies courses, usually taught in
universities, which could be considered elite institutions just by virtue of
the populations they served, focused almost exclusively upon the lives of
white women. Black studies, which was much too often male-dominated,
also ignored Black women. Here is what a Black woman wrote about her
independent efforts to study Black women writers in the early 1970s:

> ...At this point I am doing a lot of reading on my own
> of Black women writers ever since I discovered Zora
> Neale Hurston. *I've had two Black Lit courses and in
> neither were any women writers discussed.* So now I'm
> doing a lot of independent research since the Schomburg
> Collection is so close.[4] [Italics ours.]

Because of white women's racism and Black men's sexism, there was no room in either area for a serious consideration of the lives of Black women. And even when they have considered Black women, white women usually have not had the capacity to analyze racial politics and Black culture, and Black men have remained blind or resistant to the implications of sexual politics in Black women's lives.

Only a Black *and* feminist analysis can sufficiently comprehend the materials of Black women's studies; and only a creative Black feminist perspective will enable the field to expand. A viable Black feminist movement will also lend its political strength to the development of Black women's studies courses, programs, and research, and to the funding they require. Black feminism's total commitment to the liberation of Black women and its recognition of Black women as valuable and complex human beings will provide the analysis and spirit for the most incisive work on Black women. Only a feminist, pro-woman perspective that acknowledges the reality of sexual oppression in the lives of Black women, as well as the oppression of race and class, will make Black women's studies the transformer of consciousness it needs to be.

Women's studies began as a radical response to feminists' realization that knowledge of ourselves has been deliberately kept from us by institutions of patriarchal "learning." Unfortunately, as women's studies has become both more institutionalized and at the same time more precarious within traditional academic structures, the radical life-changing vision of what women's studies can accomplish has constantly been diminished in exchange for acceptance, respectability, and the career advancement of individuals. This trend in women's studies is a trap that Black women's studies cannot afford to fall into. Because we are so oppressed as Black women, every aspect of our fight for freedom, including teaching and writing about ourselves, must in some way further our liberation. Because of the particular history of Black feminism in relation to Black women's studies, especially the fact that the two movements are still new and have evolved nearly simultaneously, much of the current teaching, research, and writing about Black women is not feminist, is not radical, and unfortunately is not always even analytical. Naming and describing our experience are important initial steps, but not alone sufficient to get us where we need to go. A descriptive approach to the lives of Black women, a "great Black women" in history or literature approach, or any traditional male-identified approach will not result in intellectually groundbreaking or politically transforming work. We cannot change our lives by teaching solely about "exceptions" to the ravages of white-male oppression. Only through exploring the experience of supposedly "ordinary" Black women whose "unexceptional" actions enabled us and the race to survive, will we be able to begin to develop an overview and an analytical framework for understanding the lives of Afro-American women.

Courses that focus on issues which concretely and materially affect Black women are ideally what Black women's studies/feminist studies should be about. Courses should examine such topics as the sexual violence we suffer in our own communities; the development of Black feminist economic analysis that will reveal for the first time Black women's relationship to American capitalism; the situation of Black women in prison and the connection between their incarceration and our own; the social history of Black women's domestic work; and the investigation of Black women's mental and physical health in a society whose "final solution" for us and our children is death.

It is important to consider also that although much research about these issues needs to be done, much insight about them can be arrived at through studying the literary and historical documents that already exist. Anyone familiar with Black literature and Black women writers who is not intimidated by what their reading reveals should be able to develop a course on rape, battering, and incest as viewed by Black female and male authors. Analysis of these patriarchal crimes could be obtained from the substantial body of women's movement literature on the subject of violence against women, some of which would need to be criticized for its conscious and unconscious racism.

In addition, speakers from a local rape crisis center and a refuge for battered women could provide essential firsthand information. The class and instructor could work together to synthesize the materials and to develop a much-needed Black feminist analysis of violence against Black women. Developing such a course illustrates what politically based, analytic Black feminist studies can achieve. It would lead us to look at familiar materials in new and perhaps initially frightening ways, but ways that will reveal truths that will change the lives of living Black women, including our own. Black feminist issues—the real life issues of Black women—should be integral to our conceptions of subject matter, themes, and topics for research.

That politics has much to do with the practice of Black women's studies is perhaps most clearly illustrated by the lack of positive investigations of Black lesbianism in any area of current Black scholarship. The fact that a course in Black lesbian studies has, to our knowledge, yet to be taught has absolutely nothing to do with the "nonexistence" of Black lesbian experience and everything to do with fear and refusal to acknowledge that this experience does in fact exist.[5] Black woman-identified-women have existed in our communities throughout our history, both in Africa and in America. That the subject of Black lesbianism and male homosexuality is greeted with fearful silence or verbalized homophobia results, of course, from the politics of institutionalized heterosexuality under patriarchy, that is, the politics of male domination.

A letter written in 1957 by Black playwright and political activist Lorraine Hansberry to *The Ladder*, a pioneering lesbian periodical, makes clear this connection between homophobia and the sexual oppression of all women. She wrote:

> I think it is about time that equipped women began to take on some of the ethical questions which a male-dominated culture has produced and *dissect and analyze them quite to pieces in a serious fashion.* It is time that 'half the human race' had something to say about the nature of its existence. Otherwise—without revised basic thinking—the woman intellectual is likely to find herself trying to draw conclusions—*moral conclusions*—based on acceptance of a social moral superstructure which has never admitted to the equality of women and is therefore immoral itself. As per marriage, as per sexual practices, as per the rearing of children, etc. *In this kind of work there may be women to emerge who will be able to formulate a new and possible concept that homosexual persecution and condemnation has at its roots not only social ignorance, but a philosophically active anti-feminist dogma.* But that is but a kernel of a speculative embryonic idea improperly introduced here.[6] [Italics ours.]

Hansberry's statement is an amazingly .prescient anticipation of current accomplishments of lesbian-feminist political analysis. It is also amazing because it indicates Hansberry's feminist and lesbian commitments, which have previously been ignored and which will best be investigated through a Black feminist analysis of Black women's studies. Most amazing of all is that Hansberry was speaking, without knowing it, directly to us.

An accountable Black women's studies would value all Black women's experiences. Yet for a Black woman to teach a course on Black lesbians would probably, in most universities, spell career suicide, not to mention the personal and emotional repercussions she would inevitably face. Even to teach Black women's studies from a principled Black feminist perspective might endanger many Black women scholars' situations in their schools and departments. Given the difficulty and risks involved in teaching information and ideas which the white-male academy does not recognize or approve, it is important for Black women teaching in the white-male academy always to realize the inherently contradictory and antagonistic nature of the conditions under which we do our work. These working conditions exist in a structure not only elitist and racist, but deeply misogynist. Often our position as Black women is dishearteningly tenuous within university walls: we are literally the last hired and the first fired. Despite popular myths about the advantages of being "double-tokens," our salaries, promotions, tenure, and general level of acceptance in the white-male "community of scholars" are all quite grim. The current backlash against affirmative action is also disastrous for all Black women workers, including college teachers.

As Black women we belong to two groups that have been defined as congenitally inferior in intellect, that is, Black people and women. The paradox of Black women's position is well illustrated by the fact that white-male academics, like Schockley and Jensen—in the very same academy—are trying to prove "scientifically" our racial and sexual inferiority. Their overt or tacit question is, "How could a being who combines two mentally deficient biological identities do anything with her intellect, her nonexistent powers of mind?" Or, to put it more bluntly, "How can someone who looks like my maid (or my fantasy of my maid) teach me anything?" As Lorraine Bethel succinctly states this dilemma:

> The codification of Blackness and femaleness by whites and males is seen in the terms "thinking like a woman" and "acting like a nigger" which are based on the premise that there are typically Black and female ways of acting and thinking. Therefore, the most pejorative concept in the white/male world view would be that of thinking and acting like a "nigger woman."[7]

Our credibility as autonomous beings and thinkers in the white-male-run intellectual establishment is constantly in question and rises and falls in direct proportion to the degree to which we continue to act and think like our Black female selves, rejecting the modes of bankrupt white-male Western thought. Intellectual "passing" is a dangerously limiting solution for Black women, a non-solution that makes us invisible women. It will also not give us the emotional and psychological clarity we need to do the feminist research in Black women's studies that will transform our own and our sisters' lives.

Black women scholars must maintain a constantly militant and critical stance toward the places where we must do our work. We must also begin to devise ways to break down our terrible isolation in the white-male academy and to form the kinds of support networks Black women have always formed to help each other survive. We need to find ways to create our own places—conferences, institutes, journals, and institutions—where we can be the Black women we are and gain respect for the amazing depth of perception that our identity brings. To do the work involved in creating Black women's studies requires not only intellectual intensity, but the deepest courage. Ideally, this is passionate and committed research, writing, and teaching whose purpose is to question everything. Coldly "objective" scholarship that changes nothing is not what we strive for. "Objectivity" is itself an example of the reification of white-male thought. What could be less objective than the totally white-male studies which are still considered "knowledge"? Everything that human beings participate in is ultimately subjective and biased, and there is nothing inherently wrong with that. The bias of Black women's studies must consider as primary the knowledge that will save Black women's lives.

Black Women's Studies as an Academic Area

Higher education for Black women has always been of serious concern to the Black community.[8] Recognition that education was a key mechanism for challenging racial and economic oppression created an ethic that defined education for women as important as education for men. Nearly 140 Black women attended Oberlin College between 1835 and 1865, prior to Emancipation, and Mary Jane Patterson, the first Afro-American woman to receive a B.A., graduated from Oberlin in 1862. The only two Black women's colleges still in existence, Spelman in Atlanta, Georgia, founded in 1881, and Bennett in Greensboro, North Carolina, founded in 1873, played a significant role in the education of Black women, as did those Black colleges founded as co-educational institutions at a time when most private white colleges were still single-sex schools.

Although Black women have long been involved in this educational work and also in creating self-conscious representations of ourselves using a variety of artistic forms, Black women's studies as an autonomous discipline only began to emerge in the late 1970s. At the moment, it is impossible to gauge definitely how much activity is going on in the field. There have been few statistical studies which have mapped the growth of women's studies generally, and there have been no surveys or reports to establish the breadth and depth of research and teaching on Black women.

One of the few sources providing some documentation of the progress of Black women's studies is *Who's Who and Where in Women's Studies*, published in 1974 by The Feminist Press. This book lists a total of 4,658 women's studies courses taught by 2,964 teachers. Approximately forty-five (or less than one percent) of the courses listed focus on Black women. About sixteen of these are survey courses, ten are literature courses, four are history courses, and the rest are in various disciplines. The largest number of courses taught on Black women was in Afro-American and Black Studies departments (approximately nineteen) and only about three courses on Black women were being taught for women's studies departments. Approximately nine Black colleges were offering women's studies courses at that time. None of the forty-five courses used the words "feminist" or "Black feminist" in the title.

More recent relevant comment can be found in Florence Howe's *Seven Years Later: Women's Studies Programs in 1976*.[9] She states:

> ...Like the social movement in which it is rooted, women's studies has tended to be predominantly white and middle-class, in terms of both faculty and curriculum, and there is a perceived need for a corrective....The major strategy developed thus far is the inclusion of separate courses on Black Women, Chicanas, Third World Women, etc. Such courses, taught by minority women, have appeared on most campuses with the cooperation and cross-listing of various ethnic studies programs. For the most part, it is women's studies that has taken the initiative for this development.

However, as Howe proceeds to point out, more seriously committed and fundamental strategies are needed to achieve a truly multiracial approach.

Clearly, then, if one looks for "hard data" concerning curriculum relating to Black women in the existing studies of academic institutions, we are seemingly nonexistent. And yet impressionistically and experientially it is obvious that more and more study is being done about Black women and, even more importantly, it is being done with an increasing consciousness of the impact of sexual-racial politics on Black women's lives. One thinks, for instance, of Alice Walker's groundbreaking course on Black women writers at Wellesley College in 1972, and how work of all sorts by and about Black women writers has since blossomed into a visible Black female literary "renaissance."

It seems that after survey courses (with titles like "The Black Woman in America") which provide an overview, most courses on Black women concentrate on literature, followed by social sciences and history as the next most popular areas. An early type of course that was taught focused upon "famous" individual Black women. Partly because at the beginning it is necessary to answer the basic question of exactly who there is to talk about, this is the way that materials on oppressed people have often been approached initially. Printed information written about or by successful individuals is also much more readily available, and analytical overviews of the field do not yet exist. Nevertheless, such focusing on exceptional figures is a direct outgrowth of centuries of concerted suppression and invisibility. When the various kinds of pedagogical resources which should exist eventually come into being, teachers will be able to move beyond this ultimately class-biased strategy.

The core of courses on Black women at colleges and universities has grown slowly but steadily during the 1970s. And increasing interest in Black feminism and recognition of Black women's experiences point to the '80s as the time when Black women's studies will come into its own. Perhaps this may be seen less in teaching than in the plethora of other activity in Black women's scholarship. Some essential books have begun to appear: the Zora Neale Hurston reader, *I Love Myself When I Am Laughing...* (Old Westbury, N.Y.: The Feminist Press, 1979); and Sharon Harley and Rosalyn Terborg-Penn's *The Afro-American Woman: Struggles and Images* (Port Washington, N.Y.: Kennikat, 1978), to name only two. Special issues of feminist magazines—like *Conditions* and *Heresies*—are being devoted to Black/Third World women. Workshop sessions and entire conferences on Black women (e.g., The Third World Lesbian Writers Conference in New York City and the National Council of Negro Women's national research conference on Black women held in Washington, D.C.—both in 1979) have been organized.

Other indications that Black/Third World women are talking to each other and carving out ways of thinking, researching, writing, and teaching include the founding of *Sojourner: A Third World Women's Research Newsletter*, in 1977, and the founding, in 1978, of the Association of Black Women Historians, which publishes the newsletter *Truth*. Finally, research and dissertations by young Black female scholars for whom the developments of the past few years have opened the option of studying Black women have begun to produce the knowledge that Black women's studies will continue to need. These scholars—many of them activists—are working on a wide range of subjects—including revising the Black woman's role in slavery, recovering Black female oral and popular culture, and revamping the reputations of earlier Black women authors.

At this point, we are on the threshold—still in our "Phase One," as it were. There are still far too few courses and far too few Black women employed in institutions where they might have the opportunity to teach them. Although people involved in women's studies are becoming increasingly aware of issues of race, the majority of white women teachers and administrators have barely begun the process of self-examination which must precede productive action to change this situation. The confronting of sexism in Black studies and in the Black community in general is a mostly unfought battle, although it is evident from recent Black publications—e.g., *Black Scholar's* Black Sexism Debate issue—that the opposing anti-Black-feminist and pro-Black-feminist forces are beginning to align.

Ideally, Black women's studies will not be dependent on women's studies, Black studies, or "straight" disciplinary departments for its existence, but will be an autonomous academic entity making coalitions with all three. Realistically, however, institutional support will have to come from these already established units. This will be possible only in proportion to the elimination of racism, sexism, and elitism.

Black Women's Studies: The Book Itself

Assembling this volume was a challenging task. It appears at an appropriate historical moment when Black women are consciously manifesting themselves culturally, spiritually, and politically as well as intellectually. The book illuminates and provides examples of recent research and teaching about Black women. We hope, too, that in true harbinger fashion, it will be a catalyst for even greater gains in the future.

The publication of this book fulfills a long-term need for a reference text and pedagogical tool. Those visionary women who pioneered in teaching courses on Black women can attest to the interest generated among other colleagues, friends, and even far-flung strangers—as shown by numerous requests for syllabi, reading lists, and other helpful information. Heretofore, those desiring access to such learning and teaching aids have had to rely largely on growing informal networks and the lucky acquisition of a syllabus here or there. Given this kind of hunger and wealth of materials already existing to satisfy it, it seems particularly important to facilitate the necessary sharing. This becomes imperative when one further considers that Black women's studies is at a crucial initial stage of development where the first flurry of excited discovery must be sustained and deepened if it is not to become just another short-lived enthusiasm or thwarted possibility.

This book is, in essence, the embodiment of "things hoped for, yet unseen." Beyond this, it owes its existence to the dedicated labor of many individuals and a fortuitous confluence of circumstances. When Barbara Smith became the first Black member of the Modern Language Association Commission on the Status of Women in the Profession, she suggested a book on Black women's studies as a publication idea. Gloria Hull, who was later appointed to the Commission, assumed primary responsibility for it as a CSW project. During the first half of 1977, a prospectus was drawn up and a call for contributions issued. That same spring, with the assistance of Florence Howe, Pat Scott became a third editor, thus adding some clearly needed expertise in the social sciences. Responses and contributions continued to trickle in, augmented by specific solicitations. The Feminist Press, having always expressed a commitment to the volume, formally accepted it for publication in the winter of 1977-78, and *Black Women's Studies* was given near-final shape in an editorial meeting in May 1978.

Pulling the book together was a struggle—for reasons which are not unrelated to the politics of our lives as Black women/scholars. Why did our call for papers not yield at least one essay on teaching about Black women? Why don't more Black women write up their research and critical insights? Why do contributors and possible contributors fail to meet deadlines? Why are people reluctant to send so innocuous a piece as a syllabus for inclusion in the book? Why was it nearly impossible to arrange "one simple little" editorial meeting?

The answers appear in many forms. One woman admitted that the death of feminist energy in her essay was caused by her having been recently traumatized by a well-known Black male critic who consistently made misogynistic statements both about Black women writers and about the women in the seminar of which she was a part. Another young woman, isolated at a Big Ten university where she had newly accepted an appointment, wrote:

> ...There's not much I can say to compensate for the inexcusable lateness of this response, but I have really had my hands full just staying above water. You might say that I haven't adjusted to my new environment very well. All of my writing—including my essay *and* the dissertation—are at a virtual standstill. No poetry coming forth either. It's cold as hell out here—and as lonely.
> ...Perhaps I'll get myself together and write, but I just haven't been able to do anything. Seems like some kind of crazy block—some indication, perhaps, of the intense isolation I feel. And there is nothing romantic about it either.

And then, too, one wonders about the accumulated generations of psychic damage which the descendants of Faulkner's nursemaid must heal before being able to put pen to paper, thinking, acting, (and writing) like the wonderful Black women we are. Finally, for a Black woman/feminist intellectual who is trying to live the various aspects of her identity and be a whole person amidst the contradictions and negations of this society, *nothing* is ever simple.

As a finished product, *Black Women's Studies* does not reveal these myriad complications. What it does openly reflect is the "state of the art" at the present time. The book's two opening sections provide materials essential to establishing the framework in which Black women's studies can most successfully be taught, that is, from a pro-Black-feminist and anti-racist perspective. Materials on Black feminism have only recently begun to be available, and Pat Bell Scott's annotated bibliography is a particularly useful resource for encouraging readers in this area. The section on racism contributes to an ongoing and essential dialogue between/about Black and white women. It is significant that several of the contributors to this section are not academics, but feminist activists. The deplorable increase in neo-racist backlash in the country as a whole makes this dialogue among women not only timely, but critical.

In the social sciences, revaluations are needed—new definitions, conceptions, and methodologies which encompass the reality of Black women's experiences. The three essays of this section have all have such "debunking" recasting as their primary motivation. Stetson's article also illustrates how an interdisciplinary approach encourages new uses and interpretations of already-existing materials on Black women.

The book's fourth section offers often-inspiring examples of the various strategies Black women have used to survive. In particular, the articles concerning Black women's health, Black women's music, and Black women in religion are characterized by a sense of Black women's remarkable spiritual vision as well as providing concrete information about struggle and achievements.

The fifth section indicates that much of this beginning work originates in literature and literary study, as was the case with women's studies in general. Even though this in itself is not surprising, one *is* struck by the variety of people's interests and hence their submissions. They range from broad, descriptive investigations of genres and issues to treatments of more specialized subjects and approaches. The literature section which results may not look like anyone's *a priori* dream, but it is representative, useful, and even provocative.

The variety of multidisciplinary bibliographies are meant to encourage integrated work and lively classroom teaching and are a uniquely useful gathering of resources on Black women. The course syllabi (perhaps the most valuable part of the book for many readers) should begin to suggest some possibilities.

We regret that there is no essay here which scrutinizes Black women from the perspective of the pure, or hard sciences; which investigates questions like: What impact do the basic concepts of science such as objectivity and the scientific method have on researching Black women? Are there certain proscribed areas of the science profession that Black women are allowed to operate in? What are research priorities as Black women would establish and pursue them? Unfortunately, we were also unable to include essays on Black women written from an historical perspective, although stimulating research is being done is this area. Other disciplines that we would have liked to give more coverage, such as art, had to be limited because of space, money, and other difficulties.

Originally, we had thought to make this book, not "Black Women's Studies," but "Third World Women's Studies." It became apparent almost immediately that we were not equipped to do so. We hope that this one volume on Black women helps to create a climate where succeeding works on American Indian, Asian American, and Latina women can more swiftly come into being.

Not all of those who research Black women are themselves Black women (in this book, Joan Sherman and Jean Yellin, who contributed bibliographies, are both white). Similarly, we expect that many different types of individuals will do research and teach about Black women. Our only hope is that we have provided materials which everyone can use and, moreover, materials which will help to prepare the least prepared as well as enlarge the understanding of even the most well-suited or ideally qualified persons. Some of the inclusions—for example, the "Combahee River Collective Statement"—are so generally applicable that they might be used in any course, at any level. Others—such as the bibliographies on nineteenth-century Black women—could easily lend themselves to upper-division research projects.

Whatever the uses and results of this anthology, they will be satisfactory as long as the combined acts of faith and courage represented in it do indeed help to save Black women's lives and make Black women's studies a greater educational reality.

Gloria T. Hull
Barbara Smith

November 1979

Notes

[1] William Faulkner, *Light in August* (New York: Modern Library, 1932), p. 53.

[2] Laura S. Haviland, *A Woman's Life-Work, Labors and Experiences* (Chicago: Publishing Association of Friends, 1889; copyright 1881), pp. 300-301; reprinted in Gerda Lerner, ed., *Black Women in White America: A Documentary History* (New York: Vintage, 1973), pp. 32-33.

[3] Alice Walker, "In Search of Our Mother's Gardens," *Ms.* (May 1974): 64-70, 105.

[4] Bernette Golden, Personal letter, April 1, 1974.

[5] J. R. Roberts, *Black Lesbians: An Annotated Bibliography* (Tallahassee, Fla.: Naiad, 1981) contains over three hundred entries of books, periodicals, and articles by and about Black lesbians and provides ample material for developing a variety of courses.

[6] Quoted in Jonathan Katz, *Gay American History: Lesbians and Gay Men in the U.S.A.* (New York: T. Y. Crowell, 1976), p. 425.

[7] Lorraine Bethel, " 'This Infinity of Conscious Pain': Zora Neale Hurston and the Black Female Literary Tradition" (this volume, pp. 176-88).

[8] Most of the material in these first two paragraphs about Black women in higher education was gleaned from an unpublished paper by Patricia Bell Scott, "Issues and Questions in the Higher Education of Black Women: Taking a Brief Look Backwards."

[9] This is a report of the National Advisory Council on Women's Educational Programs published in June 1977. Another study sponsored by the National Institute of Education, "Involvement of Minority Women in Women's Studies," promises additional data.

Visions and Recommendations

Our visions and recommendations for the future of Black women's studies are myriad. Countless projects and areas of research concerning Black women have not even been conceptualized. The following are merely examples:

Many of our visions require financial and institutional support. We would like to encourage:

- Funding of individual research by Black women scholars.
- Funding of teaching projects and curricular materials.
- Funding of summer seminars for college teachers, like those sponsored by the National Endowment for the Humanities.
- Funding of a directory of who's who and where in Black women's studies.
- Funding of a Black women's research institute at an institution with significant holdings on Black women.
- Funding of a national interdisciplinary Third World women's studies conference.
- Funding to allow the creation of our own publications, including both academic and Black feminist movement journals.

Already existing institutions can/must respond to the following needs and recommendations:

- That university departments provide a climate open and supportive to the teaching of materials on Black women.
- That universities and individual departments make hiring, promotion, and tenure of Black women faculty a priority and fulfill affirmative action directives.
- That universities implement more programs for "reentry" women, with particular outreach to Third World and working-class communities.
- That Black women's studies programs be made accessible to all Black women, not only those who are in universities.
- That Black women's studies programs be implemented on the elementary and secondary levels.
- That journals make a serious effort to identify and publish the work of Black women scholars, particularly their research on Black women.
- Accreditation of women's studies programs on the basis of their approach/inclusion of Third World women's studies.

- Accreditation of Black and Third World studies programs on the basis of their approach/inclusion of Third World women.

All of our visions require fundamental social, political, and personal change. For Black women's studies to flourish, we call for:

- The eradication of racism in the white women's movement through a serious examination of their own racism and a recognition of Black history and culture.
- The eradication of antifeminism and homophobia in the Black community and particularly among Black women academics.
- A strong Black feminist movement supported both by white feminists and by the Black community.

Two young women, probably somewhere in Virginia, ca. 1910.

Section One

Searching For Sisterhood: Black Feminism

A Black Feminist's Search for Sisterhood

MICHELE WALLACE

When I was in the third grade I wanted to be president. I can still remember the stricken look on my teacher's face when I announced it in class. By the time I was in the fourth grade I had decided to be the president's wife instead. It never occurred to me that I could be neither because I was Black. Growing up in a dreamy state of mind not uncommon to the offspring of the Black middle class, I was convinced that hatred was an insubstantial emotion and would certainly vanish before it could affect me. I had the world to choose from in planning a life.

On rainy days my sister and I used to tie the short end of a scarf around our scrawny braids and let the rest of its silken mass trail to our waists. We'd pretend it was hair and that we were some lovely heroine we'd seen in the movies. There was a time when I would have called that wanting to be white, yet the real point of the game was being feminine. Being feminine meant being white to us.

One day when I was thirteen on my bus ride home from school I caught a brief but enchanting glimpse of a beautiful creature—slender, honey brown, and she wore her hair natural. Very few people did then, which made her that much more striking. *This* was a look I could imitate with some success. The next day I went to school with my hair in an Afro.

On my way out of my building people stared and some complimented me, but others, the older permanent fixtures in the lobby, gaped at me in horror. Walking the streets of Harlem was even more difficult. The men on the corners who had been only moderately attentive before, now began to whoop and holler as I came into view. Becoming exasperated after a while, I asked someone why. "They think you're a whore, sugar." I fixed my hair and was back to normal by the next morning. Letting the world in on the secret of my native naps appealed to my proclivity for rebellion but having people think I was not a "nice girl" was The War already and I was not prepared for it. I pictured myself in a police station trying to explain how I'd been raped. "Come on, baby, you look like you know your way around," sneered an imaginary policeman.

In 1968 when I was sixteen and the term Black consciousness was becoming popular, I started wearing my hair natural again. This time I ignored my "elders." I was too busy reshaping my life. Blackness, I reasoned, meant that I could finally be myself. Besides recognizing my history of slavery and my African roots, I began a general housecleaning. All my old values, gathered from "playing house" in nursery school to *Glamour* Magazine's beauty tips, were discarded.

No more makeup, high heels, stockings, garter belts, girdles. I wore T-shirts and dungarees, or loose African print dresses, sandals on my feet. My dust-covered motto, "Be a nice well-rounded colored girl so that you can get yourself a nice colored doctor husband," I threw out on the grounds that it was another remnant of my once "whitified" self. My mind clear now, I was starting to think about being someone again, not some*thing*—the presidency was still a dark horse but maybe I could be a writer. I dared not even say it aloud: my life was my own again. I thanked Malcolm and LeRoi—wasn't it their prescription that I was following?

It took me three years to fully understand that Stokely was serious when he'd said my position in the movement was "prone," three years to understand that the countless speeches that all began "the Black man..." did not include me. I learned. I mingled more and more with a Black crowd, attended the conferences and rallies and parties and talked with some of the most loquacious of my brothers in Blackness, and as I pieced together the ideal that was being presented for me to emulate, I discovered my newfound freedoms being stripped from me, one after another. No I wasn't to wear makeup but yes I had to wear long skirts that I could barely walk in. No I wasn't to go to the beauty parlor but yes I was to spend hours cornrolling my hair. No I wasn't to flirt with or take shit off white men but yes I was to sleep with and take unending shit off Black men. No I wasn't to watch television or read *Vogue* or *Ladies' Home Journal* but yes I should keep my mouth shut. I would still have to iron, sew, cook, and have babies.

Only sixteen, I decided there were a lot of things I didn't know about Black male/female relationships. I made an attempt to fill myself in by reading—*Soul on Ice, Native Son, Black Rage*—and by joining the National Black Theatre. In the theatre's brand of a consciousness-raising session I was told of the awful ways in which Black women, me included, had tried to destroy the Black man's masculinity; how we had castrated him; worked when he didn't work; made money when he made no money; spent our nights and days in church praying to a jive white boy named Jesus while he collapsed into alcoholism, drug addiction, and various forms of despair; how we'd always been too loud and domineering, too outspoken.

We had much to make up for by being gentle in the face of our own humiliation, by being soft-spoken (ideally to the point where our voices could not be heard at all), by being beautiful (whatever that was), by being submissive—how often that word was shoved at me in poems and in songs as something to strive for.

At the same time one of the brothers who was a member of the theatre was also a paraprofessional in the school where my mother then taught. My mother asked him what he liked about the theatre. Not knowing that I was her daughter, he answered without hesitation that you could get all the pussy you wanted. NBT was a central institution in the Black cultural movement. Much time was spent reaching for the "godlike" in one another, the things beyond the "flesh" and beyond all the "whitewashing." And what it boiled down to was that now the brother could get more pussy. If that was his revolution, what was mine?

So I was again obsessed with my appearance, worried about the rain again—the Black woman's nightmare—for fear that my huge, full Afro would shrivel up to my head. (Despite Blackness, Black men still didn't like short hair.) My age was one thing I had going for me. "Older Black women are too hard," my brothers informed me as they looked me up and down.

The message of the Black movement was that I was being watched, on probation as a Black woman, that any signs of aggressiveness, intelligence, or independence would mean I'd be denied even the one role still left open to me as "my man's woman," keeper of house, children, and incense burners. I grew increasingly desperate about slipping up—they. Black men, were threatening me with being deserted, with being *alone.* Like any "normal" woman, I eagerly grabbed at my own enslavement.

After all, I'd heard the horror stories of educated Black women who had to marry ditchdiggers and get their behinds kicked every night. I had thought the Black movement would offer me much better. In 1968 I had wanted to become an intelligent human being. I had wanted to be serious and scholarly for the first time in my life, to write and perhaps get the chance Stokely and Baldwin and Imamu Baraka (then LeRoi Jones) had gotten to change the world—that was how I defined not wanting to be white. But by 1969, I simply wanted a man. When I chose to go to Howard University in 1969, it was because it was all Black. I envisioned a super-Black utopia where for the first time in life I would be completely surrounded by people who totally understood me. The problem in New York had been that there were too many white people.

Thirty pounds overweight, my hair in the ultimate Afro—washed and left to dry without combing—my skin blue-black from a summer in the sun, Howard's students, the future polite society of NAACP cocktail parties, did not exactly greet me with open arms. I sought out a new clique each day and found a home in none. Finally I found a place of revelation, if not of happiness, with other misfits in the girls' dorm on Friday and Saturday nights.

These misfits, all dark without exception, all with Afros that were too nappy, chose to stay in and watch television or listen to records rather than take advantage of the score of one-night stands they could probably achieve before being taunted into running home to their parents as "fallen women." They came to Howard to get husbands; if you slept around, or if it got out that you had slept with someone you weren't practically engaged to, then there would be very little possibility of a husband for you at Howard.

Such restrictions are not unique in this world, but at Howard, the scene of student takeovers just the previous year, of riots and much revolutionary talk about casting aside Western values, archaic, Victorian morals seemed curiously "unblack." Baffled by my new environment, I did something I've never done before—I spent most of my time with women, often turning down the inevitable humiliation or, worse, boredom of a date (a growing possibility as I shed the extra pounds) even when it was offered to me. Most of the women were from small southern and midwestern communities. They thought me definitely straitjacket material with my well-polished set of "sophisticated" New York views on premarital sex and atheism. I learned to listen more than I spoke.

But no one talked about why we stayed in on Friday and Saturday nights on a campus that was well known for its parties and nightlife. No one talked about why we drank so much or why our hunger for Big Macs was insatiable. We talked about men—all kinds, Black and white, Joe Namath, Richard Roundtree, the class president who earned quite a reputation for driving coeds out on the highway and offering them a quick screw or a long walk home. "But girl, ain't he fine?" We talked about movie stars and singing groups into the wee hours of the morning.

Guzzling gin, cheating at poker, choking on cigarettes that dangled precariously from the corners of our mouths, we'd signify. "If we could only be woman (white) enough" was the general feeling of most of us as we trotted off to bed.

Meanwhile the males on the campus had successfully buried the old standards of light, curly haired young men with straight noses. They sported large, unruly Afros, dashikis, and flaring nostrils. Their coal-black eyes seemed to say, "The nights and the days belong to me," as we'd pass one another on the campus green, a fashionable, thin, colorless little creature always on their arm.

Enough was enough. I left Howard for City College after one term, and the significance of all I'd seen there had not entirely escaped me, because I remember becoming a feminist about then. No one had been doing very well when I had left New York but now it seemed even worse—the "new Blackness" was fast becoming the new slavery for sisters.

I discovered my voice and when brothers talked to me, I talked back. This had its hazards. Almost got my eye blackened several times. My social life was like guerilla warfare. Here was the logic behind our grandmothers' old saying, "A nigga man ain't shit." It was shorthand for "The Black man has learned to hate himself and to hate you even more. Be careful. He will hurt you."

I am reminded of a conversation I had with a brother up at City College one mild spring day. We were standing on a corner in front of the South Campus gates and he was telling me what the role of the Black woman was. When a pause came in his monologue, I asked him what the role of the Black man was. He mumbled something about, "Simply to be a man." When I suggested that might not be enough, he went completely ape. He turned purple. He started screaming. "The Black man doesn't have to do anything. He's a man he's a man he's a man!"

Whenever I raised the question of a Black woman's humanity in conversation with a Black man, I got a similar reaction. Black men, at least the ones I knew, seemed totally confounded when it came to treating Black women like people. Trying to be what we were told to be by the brothers of the "nation"—sweet and smiling—a young Black woman I knew had warmly greeted a brother in passing on Riverside Drive. He responded by raping her. When she asked the brothers what she should do, they told her not to go to the police and to have the baby though she was only seventeen.

Young Black female friends of mine were dropping out of school because their boyfriends had convinced them that it was "not correct" and "counterrevolutionary" to strive to do anything but have babies and clean house. "Help the brother get his thing together," they were told. Other Black women submitted to polygamous situations where sometimes they were called upon to sleep with the friends of their "husband." This later duty was explained to me once by a "priest" of the New York Yoruban Temple. "If your brother has to go to the bathroom and there is no toilet in his house then wouldn't you let him use your toilet?" For toilet read Black woman.

The sisters got along by keeping their mouths shut, by refusing to see what was daily growing more difficult to ignore—a lot of brothers were doing double time—uptown with the sisters and downtown with the white woman whom they always vigorously claimed to hate. Some of the bolder brothers were quite frank about it. "The white woman lets me be a man."

The most popular justification Black women had for not becoming feminists was their hatred of white women. They often repeated this for approving Black male ears. (Obviously the brother had an interest in keeping Black and white women apart—"Women will chatter.") But what I figured out was that the same Black man who trembled with hatred for white men found the white woman irresistible because she was not a human being but a possession in his eyes—the higher-priced spread of woman he saw on television. "I know that the white man made the white woman the symbol of freedom and the Black woman the symbol of slavery" (*Soul on Ice*, Eldridge Cleaver).

When I first became a feminist, my Black friends used to cast pitying eyes upon me and say, "That's whitey's thing." I used to laugh it off, thinking, yes there are some slight problems, a few things white women don't completely understand, but we can work them out. In *Ebony, Jet*, and *Encore*, and even in *The New York Times*, various Black writers cautioned Black women to be wary of smiling white feminists. The women's movement enlists the support of Black women only to lend credibility to an essentially middle-class, irrelevant movement, they asserted. Time has shown that there was more truth to these claims than their shrillness indicated. Today when many white feminists think of Black women, they too often think of faceless masses of welfare mothers and rape victims to flesh out their statistical studies of woman's plight.

One unusually awkward moment for me as a Black feminist was when I found out that white feminists often don't view Black men as men but as fellow victims. I've got no pressing quarrel with the notion that white men have been the worst offenders but that isn't very helpful for a Black woman from day to day. White women don't check out a white man's bank account or stock-holdings before they accuse him of being sexist—they confront white men with and without jobs, with and without membership in a male consciousness-raising group. Yet when it comes to the Black man, it's hands off. A Black friend of mine was fired by a Black news service because she was pregnant. When she proposed doing an article on this for *Ms.*, an editor there turned down the proposal with these words: "We've got a special policy for the Black man." For a while I thought that was just the conservative feminist position until I overheard a certified radical feminist explaining why she dated only Black men and other nonwhite men. "They're less of a threat to women; they're less oppressive."

Being a Black woman means frequent spells of impotent, self-consuming rage. Such a spell came upon me when I recently attended a panel discussion at a women artists' conference. One of the panel members, a museum director and a white feminist, had come with a young Black man in a sweatshirt, Pro-Keds, and rag tied around the kind of gigantic Afro you don't see much anymore. When asked about her commitment to Black women artists, she responded with, "Well, what about Puerto Rican women artists, and Mexican women artists, and Indian women artists?..." But she doesn't exhibit Hispanic women any more than she does Black women (do I have to say anything about Indian women?), which is seldom indeed, though her museum is located in an area that is predominantly Black and Puerto Rican. Yet she was confident in the position she took because the living proof of her liberalism and good intentions sat in the front row, Black and unsmiling, six foot something and militant-*looking*.

In the spring of 1973, Doris Wright, a Black feminist writer, called a meeting to discuss "Black Women and Their Relationship to the Women's Movement." The result was the National Black Feminist Organization, and I was fully delighted until, true to Women's Movement form, we got bogged down in an array of ideological disputes, the primary one being lesbianism versus heterosexuality. Dominated by the myths and facts of what white feminists had done and not done before us, it was nearly impossible to come to any agreement about our position on anything; and action was unthinkable.

Many of the prime movers in the organization seemed to be representing other interest groups and whatever commitment they might have had to Black women's issues appeared to take a back seat to that. Women who had initiative and spirit usually attended one meeting, were turned off by the hopelessness of ever getting anything accomplished, and never returned again. Each meeting brought almost all new faces. Overhearing an aspiring political candidate say only half-jokingly at NBFO's first conference, "I'm gonna get me some votes out of these niggas," convinced me that Black feminists were not ready to form a movement in which I could, with clear conscience, participate. It is very possible that NBFO was not meant to happen when it did, that the time was not yet ripe for such an organization. I started a Black women's consciousness-raising group around the same time. When I heard one of my friends, whom I considered the closest thing to a feminist in the room, saying at one of our sessions, "I feel sorry for any woman who tries to take my husband away from me because she's just going to have a man who has to pay alimony and child support," even though she was not married to the man in question, I felt a great sinking somewhere in the chest area. Here was a woman, who had insisted (at least to me) upon her right to bear a child outside of marriage, trying to convince a few Black women, who were mostly single and very worried about it, that she was really married—unlike them. In fact, one of the first women to leave the group was a recent graduate of Sarah Lawrence, her excuse being, "I want to place myself in situations where I will meet more men." The group eventually disintegrated. We had no strength to give to one another. Is that possible? At any rate, that's the way it seemed, and perhaps it was the same on a larger scale with NBFO.

Despite a sizable number of Black feminists who have contributed much to the leadership of the women's movement, there is still no Black women's movement, and it appears there won't be for some time to come. It is conceivable that the level of consciousness feminism would demand in Black women wouldn't lead to any sort of separatist movement, anyway—despite our very separate problems. Perhaps a multicultural women's movement is somewhere in the future.

But for now, Black feminists, of necessity it seems, exist as individuals—some well known, like Eleanor Holmes Norton, Florynce Kennedy, Faith Ringgold, Shirley Chisholm, Alice Walker, and some unknown, like me. We exist as women who are Black who are feminists, each stranded for the moment, working independently because there is not yet an environment in this society remotely congenial to our struggle—because, being on the bottom, we would have to do what no one else has done: we would have to fight the world.

2

A Black Feminist Statement

THE COMBAHEE RIVER COLLECTIVE

We are a collective of Black feminists who have been meeting together since 1974.[1] During that time we have been involved in the process of defining and clarifying our politics, while at the same time doing political work within our own group and in coalition with other progressive organizations and movements. The most general statement of our politics at the present time would be that we are actively committed to struggling against racial, sexual, heterosexual, and class oppression and see as our particular task the development of integrated analysis and practice based upon the fact that the major systems of oppression are interlocking. The synthesis of these oppressions creates the conditions of our lives. As Black women we see Black feminism as the logical political movement to combat the manifold and simultaneous oppressions that all women of color face.

We will discuss four major topics in the paper that follows: (1) the genesis of contemporary Black feminism; (2) what we believe, i.e., the specific province of our politics; (3) the problems in organizing Black feminists, including a brief herstory of our collective; and (4) Black feminist issues and practice.

1. The Genesis of Contemporary Black Feminism

Before looking at the recent development of Black feminism, we would like to affirm that we find our origins in the historical reality of

Afro-American women's continuous life-and-death struggle for survival and liberation. Black women's extremely negative relationship to the American political system (a system of white male rule) has always been determined by our membership in two oppressed racial and sexual castes. As Angela Davis points out in "Reflections on the Black Woman's Role in the Community of Slaves," Black women have always embodied, if only in their physical manifestation, an adversary stance to white male rule and have actively resisted its inroads upon them and their communities in both dramatic and subtle ways. There have always been Black women activists—some known, like Sojourner Truth, Harriet Tubman, Frances E. W. Harper, Ida B. Wells Barnett, and Mary Church Terrell, and thousands upon thousands unknown—who had a shared awareness of how their sexual identity combined with their racial identity to make their whole life situation and the focus of their political struggles unique. Contemporary Black feminism is the outgrowth of countless generations of personal sacrifice, militancy, and work by our mothers and sisters.

A Black feminist presence has evolved most obviously in connection with the second wave of the American women's movement beginning in the late 1960s. Black, other Third World, and working women have been involved in the feminist movement from its start, but both outside reactionary forces and racism and elitism within the movement itself have served to obscure our participation. In 1973 Black feminists, primarily located in New York, felt the necessity of forming a separate Black feminist group. This became the National Black Feminist Organization (NBFO).

Black feminist politics also have an obvious connection to movements for Black liberation, particularly those of the 1960s and 1970s. Many of us were active in those movements (civil rights, Black nationalism, the Black Panthers), and all of our lives were greatly affected and changed by their ideology, their goals, and the tactics used to achieve their goals. It was our experience and disillusionment within these liberation movements, as well as experience on the periphery of the white male left, that led to the need to develop a politics that was antiracist, unlike those of white women, and antisexist, unlike those of Black and white men.

There is also undeniably a personal genesis for Black feminism, that is, the political realization that comes from the seemingly personal experiences of individual Black women's lives. Black feminists and many more Black women who do not define themselves as feminists have all experienced sexual oppression as a constant factor in our day-to-day existence. As children we realized that we were different from boys and that we were treated differently—for example, when we were told in the same breath to be quiet both for the sake of being "ladylike" and to make us less objectionable in the eyes of white people. As we grew older we became aware of the threat of physical and sexual abuse by men. However, we had no way of conceptualizing what was so apparent to us, what we *knew* was really happening.

Black feminists often talk about their feelings of craziness before becoming conscious of the concepts of sexual politics, patriarchal rule, and, most importantly, feminism, the political analysis and practice that we women use to struggle against our oppression. The fact that racial politics and indeed racism are pervasive factors in our lives did not allow us, and still does not allow most Black women, to look more deeply into our own experiences and define those things that make our lives what they are and our oppression specific to us. In the process of consciousness-raising, actually life-sharing, we began to recognize the commonality of our experiences and, from the sharing and growing consciousness, to build a politics that will change our lives and inevitably end our oppression.

Our development also must be tied to the contemporary economic and political position of Black people. The post–World War II generation of Black youth was the first to be able to minimally partake of certain educational and employment options, previously closed completely to Black people. Although our economic position is still at the very bottom of the American capitalist economy, a handful of us have been able to gain certain tools as a result of tokenism in education and employment which potentially enable us to more effectively fight our oppression.

A combined antiracist and antisexist position drew us together initially and as we developed politically we addressed ourselves to heterosexism and economic oppression under capitalism.

2. What We Believe

Above all else, our politics initially sprang from the shared belief that Black women are inherently valuable, that our liberation is a necessity not as an adjunct to somebody else's but because of our need as human persons for autonomy. This may seem so obvious as to sound simplistic, but it is apparent that no other ostensibly progressive movement has ever considered our specific oppression a priority or worked seriously for the ending of that oppression. Merely naming the pejorative stereotypes attributed to Black women (e.g., mammy, matriarch, Sapphire, whore, bulldagger), let alone cataloguing the cruel, often murderous, treatment we receive, indicates how little value has been placed upon our lives during four centuries of bondage in the Western hemisphere. We realize that the only people who care enough about us to work consistently for our liberation is us. Our politics evolve from a healthy love for ourselves, our sisters, and our community which allows us to continue our struggle and work.

This focusing upon our own oppression is embodied in the concept of identity politics. We believe that the most profound and potentially the most radical politics come directly out of our own identity, as opposed to working to end somebody else's oppression. In the case of Black women this is a particularly repugnant, dangerous, threatening, and therefore revolutionary concept because it is obvious from looking at all the political movements that have preceded us that anyone is more worthy of liberation than ourselves. We reject pedestals, queenhood, and walking ten paces behind. To be recognized as human, levelly human, is enough.

We believe that sexual politics under patriarchy is as pervasive in Black women's lives as are the politics of class and race. We also often find it difficult to separate race from class from sex oppression because in our lives they are most often experienced simultaneously. We know that there is such a thing as racial-sexual oppression which is neither solely racial nor solely sexual, e.g., the history of rape of Black women by white men as a weapon of political repression.

Although we are feminists and lesbians, we feel solidarity with progressive Black men and do not advocate the fractionalization that white women who are separatists demand. Our situation as Black people necessitates that we have solidarity around the fact of race, which white women of course do not need to have with white men, unless it is their negative solidarity as racial oppressors. We struggle together with Black men against racism, while we also struggle with Black men about sexism.

We realize that the liberation of all oppressed peoples necessitates the destruction of the political-economic systems of capitalism and imperialism as well as patriarchy. We are socialists because we believe that work must be organized for the collective benefit of those who do the work and create the products and not for the profit of the bosses. Material resources must be equally distributed among those who create these resources. We are not convinced, however, that a socialist revolution that is not also a feminist and antiracist revolution will guarantee our liberation. We have arrived at the necessity for developing an understanding of class relationships that takes into account the specific class position of Black women who are generally marginal in the labor force, while at this particular time some of us are temporarily viewed as doubly desirable tokens at white-collar and professional levels. We need to articulate the real class situation of persons who are not merely raceless, sexless workers, but for whom racial and sexual oppression are significant determinants in their working economic lives. Although we are in essential agreement with Marx's theory as it applied to the very specific economic relationships he analyzed, we know that this analysis must be extended further in order for us to understand our specific economic situation as Black women.

A political contribution which we feel we have already made is the expansion of the feminist principle that the personal is political. In our consciousness-raising sessions, for example, we have in many ways gone beyond white women's revelations because we are dealing with the implications of race and class as well as sex. Even our Black women's style of talking, testifying in Black language about what we have experienced, has a resonance that is both cultural and political. We have spent a great deal of energy delving into the cultural and experiential nature of our oppression out of necessity because none of these matters have ever been looked at before. No one before has ever examined the multilayered texture of Black women's lives.

An example of the kind of revelation/conceptualization achieved through consciousness-raising occurred at a meeting when we discussed the ways in which our early intellectual interests had been attacked by our peers, particularly Black men. We discovered that all of us, because we were "smart," had also been considered "ugly," i.e., "smart-ugly." "Smart-ugly" crystallized the way in which most of us had been forced to develop our intellects at great cost to our "social" lives. The sanctions in the Black and white communities against Black women thinkers are comparatively much higher than those against white women, particularly ones from the educated middle and upper classes.

As we have already stated, we reject the stance of lesbian separatism because it is not a viable political analysis or strategy for us. It leaves out far too much and far too many people, particularly Black men, women, and children. We have a great deal of criticism and loathing for what men have been socialized to be in this society: what they support, how they act, and how they oppress. But we do not have the misguided notion that it is their maleness, per se—i.e., their biological maleness—that makes them what they are. As Black women we find any type of biological determinism a particularly dangerous and reactionary basis upon which to build a politic. We must also question whether lesbian separatism is an adequate and progressive political analysis and strategy, even for those who practice it, since it so completely denies any but the sexual sources of women's oppression, negating the facts of class and race.

3. Problems in Organizing Black Feminists

During our years together as a Black feminist collective we have experienced success and defeat, joy and pain, victory and failure. We have found that it is very difficult to organize around Black feminist issues, difficult even to announce in certain contexts that we *are* Black feminists. We have tried to think about the reasons for our difficulties, particularly since the white women's movement continues to be strong and to grow in many directions. In this section we will discuss some of the general reasons for the organizing problems we face and also talk specifically about the stages in organizing our own collective.

The major source of difficulty in our political work is that we are not just trying to fight oppression on one front or even two, but instead to address a whole range of oppressions. We do not have racial, sexual, heterosexual, or class privilege to rely upon, nor do we have even the minimal access to resources and power that groups who possess any one of these types of privilege have.

The psychological toll of being a Black woman and the difficulties this presents in reaching political consciousness and doing political work can never be underestimated. There is a very low value placed upon Black women's psyches in this society, which is both racist and sexist. As an early group member once said, "We are all damaged people merely by virtue of being Black women." We are dispossessed psychologically and on every other level, and yet we feel the necessity to struggle to change our condition and the condition of all Black women. In "A Black Feminist's Search for Sisterhood," Michele Wallace arrives at this conclusion:

> We exist as women who are Black who are feminists, each stranded for the moment, working independently because there is not yet an environment in this society remotely congenial to our struggle—because, being on the bottom, we would have to do what no one else has done: we would have to fight the world.[2]

Wallace is not pessimistic but realistic in her assessment of Black feminists' position, particularly in her allusion to the nearly classic isolation most of us face. We might use our position at the bottom, however, to make a clear leap into revolutionary action. If Black women were free, it would mean that everyone else would have to be free since our freedom would necessitate the destruction of all the systems of oppression.

Feminism is, nevertheless, very threatening to the majority of Black people because it calls into question some of the most basic assumptions about our existence, i.e., that gender should be a determinant of power relationships. Here is the way male and female roles were defined in a Black nationalist pamphlet from the early 1970s:

> We understand that it is and has been traditional that the man is the head of the house. He is the leader of the house/nation because his knowledge of the world is broader, his awareness is greater, his understanding is fuller and his application of this information is wiser.... After all, it is only reasonable that the man be the head of the house because he is able to defend and protect the development of his home.... Women cannot do the same things as men—they are made by nature to function differently. Equality of men and women is something that cannot happen even in the abstract world. Men are not equal to other men, i.e., ability, experience, or even understanding. The value of men and women can be seen as in the value of gold and silver—they are not equal but both have great value. We must realize that men and women are a complement to each other because there is no house/family without a man and his wife. Both are essential to the development of any life.[3]

The material conditions of most Black women would hardly lead them to upset both economic and sexual arrangements that seem to represent some stability in their lives. Many Black women have a good understanding of both sexism and racism, but because of the everyday constrictions of their lives cannot risk struggling against them both.

The reaction of Black men to feminism has been notoriously negative. They are, of course, even more threatened than Black women by the possibility that Black feminists might organize around our own needs. They realize that they might not only lose valuable and hard-working allies in their struggles but that they might also be forced to change their habitually sexist ways of interacting with and oppressing Black women. Accusations that Black feminism divides the Black struggle are powerful deterrents to the growth of an autonomous Black women's movement.

Still, hundreds of women have been active at different times during the three-year existence of our group. And every Black woman who came, came out of a strongly felt need for some level of possibility that did not previously exist in her life.

When we first started meeting early in 1974 after the NBFO's first eastern regional conference, we did not have a strategy for organizing, or even a focus. We just wanted to see what we had. After a period of months of not meeting, we began to meet again late in the year and started doing an intense variety of consciousness-raising. The overwhelming feeling that we had is that after years and years we had finally found each other. Although we were not doing political work as a group, individuals continued their involvement in lesbian politics, sterilization abuse and abortion rights work, Third World Women's International Women's Day activities, and support activity for the trials of Dr. Kenneth Edelin, Joanne Little, and Inez Garcia. During our first summer, when membership had dropped off considerably, those of us remaining devoted serious discussion to the possibility of opening a refuge for battered women in a Black community. (There was no refuge in Boston at that time.) We also decided around that time to become an independent collective since we had serious disagreements with NBFO's bourgeois-feminist stance and their lack of a clear political focus.

We also were contacted at that time by socialist feminists, with whom we had worked on abortion rights activities, who wanted to encourage us to attend the National Socialist Feminist Conference in Yellow Springs. One of our members did attend and despite the narrowness of the ideology that was promoted at that particular conference, we became more aware of the need for us to understand our own economic situation and to make our own economic analysis.

In the fall, when some members returned, we experienced several months of comparative inactivity and internal disagreements which were first conceptualized as a lesbian-straight split but which were also the result of class and political differences. During the summer those of us who were still meeting had determined the need to do political work and to move beyond consciousness-raising and serving exclusively as an emotional support group. At the beginning of 1976, when some of the women who had not wanted to do political work and who also had voiced disagreements stopped attending of their own accord, we again looked for a focus. We decided at that time, with the addition of new members, to become a study group. We had always shared our reading with each other, and some of us had written papers on Black feminism for group discussion a few months before this decision was made. We began functioning as a study group and also began discussing the possibility of starting a Black feminist publication. We had a retreat in the late spring which provided a time for both political discussion and working out interpersonal issues. Currently we are planning to gather a collection of Black feminist writing. We feel that it is absolutely essential to demonstrate the reality of our politics to other Black women and believe that we can do this through writing and distributing our work. The fact that individual Black feminists are living in isolation all over the country, that our own numbers are small, and that we have some skills in writing, printing, and publishing makes us want to carry out these kinds of projects as a means of organizing Black feminists as we continue to do political work in coalition with other groups.

4. Black Feminist Issues and Practice

During our time together we have identified and worked on many issues of particular relevance to Black women. The inclusiveness of our politics makes us concerned with any situation that impinges upon the lives of women and those of Third World and working people in general. We are of course particularly committed to working on those struggles in which race, sex, and class are simultaneous factors in oppression. We might, for example, become involved in workplace organizing at a factory that employs Third World women or picket a hospital that is cutting back on already inadequate health care to a Third World community, or set up a rape crisis center in a Black neighborhood. Organizing around welfare or daycare concerns might also be a focus. The work to be done and the countless issues that this work represents merely reflect the pervasiveness of our oppression.

Issues and projects that collective members have actually worked on are sterilization abuse, abortion rights, battered women, rape, and health care. We have also done many workshops on Black feminism on college campuses, at women's conferences, and most recently for high school women.

One issue that is of major concern to us and that we have begun to publicly address is racism in the white women's movement. As Black feminists we are made constantly and painfully aware of how little effort white women have made to understand and combat their racism, which requires among other things that they have a more than superficial comprehension of race, color, and Black history and culture. Eliminating racism in the white women's movement is by definition work for white women to do, but we will continue to speak to and demand accountability on this issue.

In the practice of our politics we do not believe that the end always justifies the means. Many reactionary and destructive acts have been done in the name of achieving "correct" political goals. As feminists we do not want to mess over people in the name of politics. We believe in collective process and a nonhierarchical distribution of power within our own group and in our vision of a revolutionary society. We are committed to a continual examination of our politics as they develop through criticism and self-criticism as an essential aspect of our practice. In her introduction to *Sisterhood Is Powerful* Robin Morgan writes: "I haven't the faintest notion what possible revolutionary role white heterosexual men could fulfill, since they are the very embodiment of reactionary-vested-interest-power."

As Black feminists and lesbians we know that we have a very definite revolutionary task to perform and we are ready for the lifetime of work and struggle before us.

NOTES

[1]This statement is dated April 1977.

[2]Michele Wallace, "A Black Feminist's Search for Sisterhood," *The Village Voice*, 28 July 1975, pp. 6-7; reprinted above, pp. 5-12.

[3]Mumininas of Committee for Unified Newark, *Mwanamke Mwananchi (The Nationalist Woman)*. Newark, N.J., c. 1971, pp. 4-5.

3

Selected Bibliography on Black Feminism

PATRICIA BELL SCOTT

BLACK FEMINISTS: AUTOBIOGRAPHICAL AND BIOGRAPHICAL WORKS

Barnett, E. "Nannie Burroughs and the Education of Black Women." In *The Afro-American Woman: Struggles and Images,* ed. S. Harley and R. Terborg-Penn, pp. 97–108. Port Washington, N.Y.: Kennikat, 1978.

Bass, C. *Forty Years: Memoirs from the Pages of a Great Newspaper.* Los Angeles: Charlotta A. Bass, 1960.

Bates, D. *The Long Shadow of Little Rock: A Memoir.* New York: David McKay, 1962.

Billington, R. *The Journal of Charlotte L. Forten: A Free Negro in the Slave Era.* New York: Dryden, 1953.

Brown, H. *Homespun Heroines and Other Women of Distinction.* Xenia, Ohio: Aldine, 1926.

Chisholm, S. *Unbought and Unbossed.* Boston: Houghton Mifflin, 1970.

Clark, S. *Echo in My Soul.* New York: E. P. Dutton, 1962.

Cooper, A. *A Voice from the South: By a Black Woman of the South.* Xenia, Ohio: Aldine, 1892.

Coppin, F. *Reminiscences of School Life, and Hints on Teaching.* Philadelphia: African Episcopal Book Concern, 1913.

Daniel, S. *Woman Builders.* Washington, D.C.: Associated, 1931.

Dannett, S. *Profiles of Negro Womanhood.* New York: M. W. Lads, 1964.

Davis, A. "Joanne Little—Politics of Rage." *Ms.* 3 (June 1975):74–77.

23

Davis, A. *With My Mind on Freedom: An Autobiography.* New York: Bantam, 1974.

Duster, A. *Crusade for Justice: The Autobiography of Ida B. Wells Barnett.* Chicago: Univ. of Chicago Press, 1970.

Fauset, A. *Sojourner Truth: God's Faithful Pilgrim.* Durham, N.C.: Univ. of North Carolina Press, 1938.

Gilbert, O. *Narrative of Sojourner Truth: A Northern Slave.* Boston: O. Gilbert, 1850.

Gill, G. "Win or Lose—We Win: The 1952 Vice-Presidential Campaign of Charlotta A. Bass." In *The Afro-American Woman: Struggles and Images,* ed. S. Harley and R. Terborg-Penn, pp. 109–18. Port Washington, N.Y.: Kennikat, 1978.

Harley, S. "Anna J. Cooper: A Voice for Black Women." In *The Afro-American Woman: Struggles and Images,* ed. S. Harley and R. Terborg-Penn, pp. 87–96. Port Washington, N.Y.: Kennikat, 1978.

Hedgeman, A. *The Trumpet Sounds: A Memoir of Negro Leadership.* New York: Holt, Rinehart and Winston, 1964.

Holt, R. *Mary McLeod Bethune.* Garden City, N.Y.: Doubleday, 1964.

Kennedy, F. *Color Me Flo: My Hard Life and Good Times.* Englewood Cliffs, N.J.: Prentice-Hall, 1976.

Lawson, L. *Woman of Distinction: Remarkable in Works and Invincible in Character.* Raleigh, N.C.: L. A. Scruggs, 1893.

Lerner, G. *Black Women in White America: A Documentary History.* New York: Vintage, 1972.

Loewenberg, B., and Bogin, R. *Black Women in Nineteenth-Century American Life: Their Words, Their Thoughts, Their Feelings.* University Park: Pennsylvania State Univ. Press, 1976.

Majors, M. *Noted Negro Women, Their Triumphs and Activities.* Chicago: Donohue & Henneberry, 1893.

Mossell, N. *The Work of the Afro-American Woman.* Philadelphia: George S. Ferguson, 1894.

Murray, P. *Proud Shoes: The Story of an American Family.* New York: Harper & Row, 1956.

Pauli, H. *Her Name Was Sojourner Truth.* New York: Appleton-Century-Crofts, 1962.

Peare, C. *Mary McLeod Bethune.* New York: Vanguard Press, 1951.

Sterne, E. *Mary McLeod Bethune.* New York: Knopf, 1959.

Stewart, M. *Productions of Mrs. Maria W. Stewart.* Boston: W. Lloyd Garrison & Knapp, 1832.

Taylor, S. *Reminiscences of My Life in Camp with the 33rd United States Colored Troops.* Boston: S. Taylor, 1902.

Terrell, M. *A Colored Woman in a White World.* Washington, D.C.: Ransdell, 1940.

Truth, S. *Narrative of Sojourner Truth: A Bondswoman of Olden Time.* Chicago: Thompson Publishing, 1970.

GENERAL WORKS:
BLACK FEMINISM BEFORE 1950

Bethune, M. "A Century of Progress of Negro Women." Address delivered before the Chicago Women's Federation, June 30, 1953.

Bethune, M. "Clarifying Our Vision with the Facts." *Journal of Negro History* 23 (1938):12-15.

Bethune, M. "Faith That Moved a Dump Heap." *Who, The Magazine About People* 1 (1941):31-35, 54.

Bowser, R. "What Role Is the Educated Negro Woman to Play in the Uplifting of Her Race?" In *Twentieth-Century Negro Literature: Or a Cyclopedia of Thought on the Vital Topics Relating to the American Negro,* ed. D. Culp, pp. 179-182. Toronto: J. L. Nickols, 1902.

Burroughs, N. "Black Women and Reform." *The Crisis* 10 (1915):187.

Burroughs, N. *Making Their Mark.* Washington, D.C.: The National Training School for Women and Girls, n.d.

Butcher, B. "The Evolution of Negro Women's Schools in the United States." Master's thesis, Howard University, 1936.

Cooper, A. "The Higher Education of Women." *Southland* 2 (1891): 190-94.

Cooper, L. "Listen to the Story of Luanna Cooper." *National Guardian* 1 (1949):3.

Crummell, A. *The Black Woman of the South: Her Neglects and Her Needs.* Washington, D.C.: A. Crummell, 1881.

Cuthbert, M. *Education and Marginality: A Study of the Negro Woman College Graduate.* New York: Columbia Univ. Press, 1942.

Harper, E. "Coloured Women of America." *Englishwomen's Review* 15 (1878):10-15.

Laney, L. "The Burden of the Educated Colored Woman." Paper read at the Hampton Negro Conference, Report III, July 1899.

Lerner, G. "Letters from Negro Women, 1827-1950." *Masses and Mainstream* (1951):24-33.

Logan, A. "Colored Women as Voters." *The Crisis* 4 (1912):242.

Martinez, S. "Negro Women in Organization—Labor." *The Aframerican*
    2 (1941):17.
Miller, K. "Woman's Suffrage." *Crisis* 11 (1915):7-8.
Neverdon-Morton, C. "The Black Woman's Struggle for Equality in the
    South, 1895-1925." In *The Afro-American Woman: Struggles and
    Images*, ed. S. Harley and R. Terborg-Penn, pp. 43-57. Port
    Washington, N.Y.: Kennikat, 1978.
Perkins, L. "Fanny Jackson Coppin and the Institute for Colored Youth:
    A Model of Nineteenth-Century Black Female Educational and
    ⁻Community Leadership, 1837-1902." Ph.D. dissertation, University
    of Illinois at Urbana-Champaign, 1978.
Pettey, S. "What Role Is the Educated Negro Woman to Play in the
    Uplifting of Her Race?" In *Twentieth-Century Negro Literature: Or
    a Cyclopedia of Thought on the Vital Topics Relating to the
    American Negro*, ed. D. Culp, p. 184. Toronto: J. L. Nickols, 1902.
Quarles, B. "Frederick Douglass and the Woman's Rights Movement."
    Journal of Negro History 25 (1940):35-44.
Remond, S. "The Negroes in the United States of America." *Journal of
    Negro History* 27 (1942):216-18.
Sewall, M. *World's Congress of Representative Women.* Chicago: Rand
    McNally, 1894.
Sprague, R. "What Role Is the Educated Negro Woman to Play in the
    Uplifting of Her Race?" In *Twentieth-Century Negro Literature: Or
    a Cyclopedia of Thought on the Vital Topics Relating to the
    American Negro*, ed. D. Culp, p. 170. Toronto: J. L. Nickols, 1902.
Terrell, M. "Progress of Colored Women." Address before the Women's
    Suffrage Meeting, Washington, D.C., 1898.
Terrell, M. "What Role Is the Educated Negro Woman to Play in the
    Uplifting of Her Race?" In *Twentieth-Century Negro Literature: Or
    a Cyclopedia of Thought on the Vital Topics Relating to the
    American Negro*, ed. D. Culp, p. 173. Toronto: J. L. Nickols, 1902.
Terborg-Penn, R. "Discrimination against Afro-American Women in the
    Woman's Movement, 1830-1920. In *The Afro-American Woman:
    Struggles and Images*, ed. S. Harley and R. Terborg-Penn, pp. 17-27.
    Port Washington, N.Y.: Kennikat, 1978.
Terborg-Penn, R. "The Historical Treatment of the Afro-American in
    the Woman's Suffrage Movement, 1900-1920: A Bibliographical
    Essay." *A Current Bibliography on African Affairs* 7 (1974):245-59.
Thorne, J.   *A Plea for Social Justice for the Negro Woman.* Yonkers,
    N.Y.: Lincoln Press Association, 1912.
Williams, F. "Colored Women of Chicago." *Southern Workman* 43
    (1914):564-66.

BLACK FEMINIST GROUPS:
BLACK WOMEN'S CLUBS, SOCIETIES, AND COLLECTIVES

"The Afric-American Female Intelligence Society of Boston." *Genius of Universal Emancipation* 10 (1832):162-63.

Black Panther Sisters Talk about Women's Liberation. Boston: New England Free Press, n.d.

Black Women's Liberation Group, Mount Vernon, New York. "Statement on Birth Control." *Sisterhood Is Powerful: An Anthology of Writings from the Women's Liberation Movement,* ed. R. Morgan, pp. 360-61. New York: Vintage, 1971.

Carter, M. "The Educational Activities of the National Educational Association for College Women, 1923-1960." Master's thesis, Howard University, 1962.

Cleagle, R. "The Colored Temperance Movement: 1830-1860." Master's thesis, Howard University, 1969.

Combahee River Collective, "The Combahee River Collective Statement: A Black Feminist Statement." In *Capitalism, Patriarchy and the Case for Socialist Feminism,* ed. Z. Eisenstein, pp. 362-72. New York: Monthly Review Press, 1978.

Davis, E. *Lifting As They Climb: The National Association of Colored Women.* Washington, D.C.: National Association of Colored Women, 1933.

"First National Conference of Colored Women, Held July 29, 30, 31, 1895, at Boston." *The Women's Era* 5 (1895):14.

Harper, F. "National Woman's Christian Temperance Union." *A.M.E. Church Review* 5 (1889):242-45.

Harper, F. "The Woman's Christian Temperance Union and the Colored Woman." *A.M.E. Church Review* 4 (1888):314.

Lerner, G. "Early Community of Black Club Women." *Journal of Negro History* 59 (1974):158-67.

Milwaukee County Welfare Rights Organization, *Welfare Mothers Speak Out: We Ain't Gonna Shuffle Anymore.* New York: W. W. Norton, 1972.

Paull, J. "Recipients Aroused: The New Welfare Rights Organization." *Social Work* 12 (1967):101-06.

Robinson, P., and Group. "A Historical and Critical Essay for Black Women in the Cities." In *The Black Woman,* ed. T. Cade, pp. 198-210. New York: Signet, 1970.

Robinson, P., and Group. "Poor Black Women's Study Papers by Poor Black Women of Mount Vernon." In *The Black Woman,* ed. T. Cade, pp. 189-97. New York: Signet, 1970.

Washington, M. "Club Work among Negro Women." In *Progress of a Race*, ed. J. Nichols and W. Crogman, pp. 178, 182, 192–95, 209. Naperville, Ill.: J. L. Nichols, 1929.

Williams, F. "Club Movement among Colored Women of America." In *A New Negro for a New Century*, ed. J. MacBrady, pp. 381–83, 427–28. Chicago: American Publishing House, 1900.

Williams, F. "The Club Movement among the Colored Women." *The Voice of the Negro* 1 (1904):101.

Williams, F. "Club Movement among Negro Women." In *Progress of a Race*, ed. J. Nichols and W. Crogman, pp. 220–26. Atlanta: J. L. Nichols, 1903.

"Women Support Panther Sisters." In *Voices from Women's Liberation*, ed. L. Tanner, pp. 118–19. New York: Signet, 1970.

The Young Women's Christian Association among Colored Women in Cities. New York: National Board of the YWCA, 1915.

THE CONTEMPORARY BLACK FEMINIST MOVEMENT: SELECTED ISSUES

Health

Black Women's Community Development Foundation. *Mental and Physical Health Problems of Black Women*. Washington, D.C.: BWCDF, 1975.

Cade, T. "The Pill: Genocide or Liberation." In *The Black Woman: An Anthology*, ed. T. Cade, pp. 162–69. New York: Signet, 1970.

The Minority Woman in America: Professionalism at What Cost? Hyattsville, Md.: Health Resources Administration, 1979.

Economics

Almquist, E. "Untangling the Effects of Race and Sex: The Disadvantaged Status of Black Women." *Social Science Quarterly* 56 (1975): 129–42.

Beale, F. "Double Jeopardy: To Be Black and Female." *New Generation* 51 (1969):23–28.

Epstein, C. "Black and Female: The Double Whammy." *Psychology Today* 7 (1973):57–61, 89.

Glassman, C. "Women and the Welfare System." In *Sisterhood Is Powerful: An Anthology of Writings from the Women's Liberation Movement*, ed. R. Morgan, pp. 102–15. New York: Vintage, 1971.

Hamer, F. "The Special Plight and the Role of Black Women." Speech given at the NAACP Legal Defense Fund Institute, New York City, May 7, 1971.

Herman, A. "Still... Small Change for Black Women." *Ms.* 7 (1979): 96-97.

Lindsey, K. "The Black Woman as Woman." In *The Black Woman: An Anthology*, ed. T. Cade, pp. 85-89. New York: Signet, 1970.

Robinson, P. *Poor Black Women.* Boston: New England Free Press, 1970.

Tillmon, J. "Welfare Is a Woman's Issue." In *Marriage and the Family: A Critical Analysis and Proposals for Change*, ed. C. Perrucci and D. Targ. New York: David McKay, 1974.

Timberlake, C. "Black Women and the ERA." *Journal of Home Economics* 69 (1977):37-39.

Education

Carroll, C. "Three's a Crowd: The Dilemma of the Black Woman in Higher Education." In *Academic Women on the Move*, ed. A. Rossi and R. Calderwood, pp. 173-85. New York: Russell Sage, 1973.

Doughty, R. "The Black Woman in School Administration." *Integrated Education* (July/August 1977):34-47.

Harris, L. "Black Women in Junior High Schools." In *Voices from Women's Liberation*, ed. L. Tanner, p. 216. New York: Signet, 1970.

Harris, P. "Problems and Solutions in Achieving Equality for Women." In *Women in Higher Education*, ed. W. Furniss and P. Graham, pp. 11-26. Washington, D.C.: American Council on Education, 1974.

Irvine, J. "A Case of Double Jeopardy: The Black Woman in Higher Education Administration." In *Emergent Leadership: Focus on Minorities and Women in Educational Administration*, pp. 61-86. Columbus, Ohio: University Council for Educational Administration, 1978.

Johnson, E. "Ethnic Minority Feminism: A Minority Member's View." *Journal of the National Association for Women Deans, Administrators, and Counselors* 41 (1978):52-56.

Malcom, S.; Hall, P.; and Brown, J. *The Double Bind: The Price of Being a Minority Woman in Science.* Washington, D.C.: American Association for the Advancement of Science, 1976.

National Institute of Education. *Conference on the Educational and Occupational Needs of Black Women.* Washington, D.C.: NIE, 1978.

Noble, J. *The Negro Woman's College Education.* New York: Columbia Univ. Press, 1956.

Parrish, D. "A Question of Survival: The Predicament of Black Women." *Integrated Education* (May/June 1976):19-23.

Schletin, E. "Ethnic Minority Feminism: A Majority Member's View." *Journal of the National Association for Women Deans, Administrators, and Counselors* 41 (1978):47-51.

Politics

Apuzzo, G., and Powell, B. "Confrontation: Black/White." *Quest: A Feminist Quarterly* 3 (1977):34-46.
Beale, F., et al. "Women's Rights—Liberation Panel." In *Women's Role in Contemporary Society, The Report of the New York Commission on Human Rights, September 21-25, 1970.* New York: Avon, 1972.
"Black Feminism: A New Mandate." *Ms.* 2 (May 1974):97-100.
"Black Women Will Join Feminist Movement." *Black Times* 1 (February 1971):14.
Blakey, W. "Everybody Makes the Revolution: Some Thoughts on Racism and Sexism." *Civil Rights Digest* 6 (Spring 1974):11-19.
Chisholm, S. "Race Revolution and Women." *Black Scholar* 3 (1971): 17-21.
Chisholm, S. "Racism and Anti-Feminism." *Black Scholar* 1 (1970):40-45.
Cooper, J. "Women's Liberation and the Black Woman." *Journal of Home Economics* 63 (October 1971):521-23.
Davis, A. "Reflections on the Black Woman's Role in the Community of Slaves." *Black Scholar* 3 (1971):2-15.
Dill, B. "The Dialectics of Black Womanhood." *Signs: Journal of Women in Culture and Society* 4 (Spring 1979):543-55.
Dunayevskaya, R. "Two Worlds: The Black Dimension in Women's Liberation." *News and Letters* 21 (April 1976):5.
Eichelberger, B. "Voices of Black Feminism." *Quest: A Feminist Quarterly* 3 (1977):16-28.
Fischer, B. "Race and Class: Beyond Personal Politics." *Quest: A Feminist Quarterly* 3 (1977):2-14.
Gant, L. "Black Women Organized for Action—They Collect Political IOU's." *Essence* 7 (1976):46.
Golden, B. "Black Women's Liberation." *Essence* 4 (1974):35-36.
Jordan, J. "Second Thoughts of a Black Feminist." *Ms.* 5 (February 1977):113-15.
King, M. "Oppression and Power: The Unique Status of the Black Woman in the American Political System." *Social Science Quarterly* 56 (1975):116-28.
LaRue, L. "Black Movement and Women's Liberation." *Black Scholar* 1 (1970):36-42.
Lewis, D. "A Response to Inequality: Black Women, Racism and Sexism."

Signs: Journal of Women in Culture and Society 2 (Winter 1977): 339-61.

Murray, P. "Equal Rights Amendment." In *Women's Role in Contemporary Society, The Report of the New York Commission on Human Rights, September 21-25, 1970*, pp. 612-18. New York: Avon, 1976.

Murray, P. "The Liberation of Black Women." *Voices of the New Feminism*, ed. M. Thompson, pp. 87-102. Boston: Beacon, 1970.

Norton, E. "A Strategy for Change." In *Women's Role in Contemporary Society, The Report of the New York Commission on Human Rights, September 21-25, 1970*, pp. 52-63. New York: Avon, 1976.

Rickman, G. "A Natural Alliance: The New Role for Black Women." *Civil Rights Digest* 6 (1974):57-65.

Scott, P. "Black Female Liberation and Family Action Programs: Some Considerations." In *The Black Family: Essays and Studies*, ed. R. Staples, 2d ed., pp. 260-63. Belmont, Calif.: Wadsworth, 1978.

Shockley, A. "The New Black Feminists." *Northwest Journal of African and Black American Studies* 2 (1974):1-5.

Smythe, M. "Feminism and Black Liberation." In *Women in Higher Education*, ed. W. Furniss and P. Graham, pp. 279-81. Washington, D.C.: American Council on Education, 1974.

Stimpson, C. "Conflict, Probable; Coalition, Possible: Feminism and the Black Movement." In *Women in Higher Education*, ed. W. Furniss and P. Graham, pp. 261-78. Washington, D.C.: American Council on Education, 1974.

Stimpson, C. " 'Thy Neighbor's Wife, Thy Neighbor's Servants': Women's Liberation and Black Civil Rights." In *Women in Sexist Society*, ed. V. Gornick and B. Moran, pp. 622-57. New York: New American Library, 1971.

Weathers, M. "An Argument for Black Women's Liberation as a Revolutionary Force." In *Voices from Women's Liberation*, ed. L. Tanner, pp. 303-7. New York: Signet, 1970.

Religion

Cone, J. "New Roles in the Ministry: A Theological Appraisal." In *Black Theology: A Documentary History, 1966-1979*, ed. G. Wilmore and J. Cone, pp. 389-97. Maryknoll, N.Y.: Orbis, 1979.

Grant, J. "Black Theology and the Black Women." In *Black Theology: A Documentary History, 1966-1979*, ed. G. Wilmore and J. Cone, pp. 418-33. Maryknoll, N.Y.: Orbis, 1979.

Grant, J. "From Brokenness Toward Wholeness." *New Conversation* (Spring 1979):12-16.

Grant, J. "The Status of Women in the African Methodist Episcopal Church." *Voice of Mission* (October 1976):11-12.

Hoover, T. "Black Women and the Churches: Triple Jeopardy." In *Black Theology: A Documentary History, 1966-1979*, ed. G. Wilmore and J. Cone, pp. 377-88. Maryknoll, N.Y.: Orbis, 1979.

Murray, P. "Black Theology and Feminist Theology: A Comparative View." In *Black Theology: A Documentary History, 1966-1979*, ed. G. Wilmore and J. Cone, pp. 398-417. Maryknoll, N.Y.: Orbis, 1979.

Reuther, R. "Crisis in Sex and Race: Black Theology vs. Feminist Theology." *Christianity and Crisis* 34 (1974):67.

Russell, L. "Feminist and Black Theologies. *Reflection: Alumni Magazine of Yale Divinity School* 1 (1974):11-16.

PERSONAL AND SOCIAL RELATIONSHIPS

Cade, T. "On the Issue of Roles." In *The Black Woman: An Anthology*, ed. T. Cade, pp. 101-10. New York: Signet, 1970.

Clark, J. "Motherhood." In *The Black Woman: An Anthology*, ed. T. Cade, pp. 63-72. New York: Signet, 1970.

Grant, L. "Ain't Beulah Dead Yet?" *Essence* 3 (1973):61.

Height, D. "To Be Black and a Woman." In *Women's Role in Contemporary Society, The Report of the New York Commission on Human Rights, September 21-25, 1970*, pp. 82-85. New York: Avon, 1972.

Hemmons, W. "Towards an Understanding of Attitudes Held by Black Women on the Women's Liberation Movement." Ph.D. dissertation, Case Western Reserve University, 1973.

Jackson, J. "Black Women in a Racist Society." In *Racism and Mental Health*, ed. C. Willie. Pittsburgh: Univ. of Pittsburgh Press, 1972.

Kennedy, F. "To Be Black and a Woman." In *Women's Role in Contemporary Society, The Report of the New York Commission on Human Rights, September 21-25, 1970*, pp. 82-85. New York: Avon, 1972.

Ladner, J. *Tomorrow's Tomorrow: The Black Woman*. Garden City, N.Y.: Anchor, 1971.

Mack, D. "Where the Black Matriarchy Theorists Went Wrong." *Psychology Today* 4 (1971):24, 86-87.

Norton, E. "Black Women as Women." *Social Policy* 3 (1972):2-3.

Norton, E. "For Sadie and Maude." In *Sisterhood Is Powerful: An Anthology of Writings from the Women's Liberation Movement*, ed. R. Morgan, pp. 353-59. New York: Vintage, 1971.

Patton, G. "Black People and the Victorian Ethos," In *The Black Woman: An Anthology*, ed. T. Cade, pp. 143–48. New York: Signet, 1970.

Petwey, J. *Black Women: Action Program for Self-fulfillment*. Ph.D. dissertation, Case Western Reserve University, 1975.

Puryear, G., and Mednick, M. "Black Militancy, Affective Attachment, and Fear of Success in Black College Women." *Journal of Consulting and Clinical Psychology* 42 (1974):263–66.

Reid, I. *"Together" Black Women*. New York: Emerson-Hall, 1972.

Wallace, M. *Black Macho and the Myth of the Superwoman*. New York: Dial, 1978.

Ware, C. "The Black Family and Feminism: A Conversation with Eleanor Holmes Norton. *Ms.* (1972):95–96.

Williams, B. "Black Women: Assertiveness vs. Aggressiveness." In *Perspectives on Afro-American Women*, ed. W. Johnson and T. Greene. Washington, D.C.: ECCA, 1975.

The main street on Saturday afternoon, London, Ohio, summer 1938.

Section Two
Roadblocks and Bridges: Confronting Racism

4

One Child of One's Own: A Meaningful Digression Within the Work(s)—An Excerpt

ALICE WALKER

Of a ghastly yet useful joint illness, which teacheth our pilgrim that her child might be called in this world of trouble the least of her myriad obstacles—

Illness has always been of enormous benefit to me. It might even be said that I have learned little from anything that did not in some way make me sick.

The picture is not an unusual one: a mother and small child, new to the harshness of the New England winter, in one of the worst flu waves of the century. The mother, flat on her back with flu; the child, burning with fever. The mother calls a name someone has given her, a famous pediatrician who writes for one of the largest of the women's magazines—in which he reveals himself to be sympathetic, witty, something of a feminist, even—to be told curtly that she should not call him at his home at any hour. Furthermore, he does not make house calls of any kind, and all of this is delivered in the coldest possible tone.

Still, since he is the only pediatrician she knows of in this weird place, she drags herself up next morning, when temperatures are below zero and a strong wind is blasting off the river, and takes the child to see him. He is scarcely less chilly in person, but, seeing she is Black, makes a couple of liberal comments to put her at ease. She hates it when his white fingers touch her child.

A not unusual story. But it places mother and child forever on whichever side of society is opposite this man. She, the mother, begins to comprehend on deeper levels a story she has written years before she had a child, of a Black mother, very poor, who, worried to distraction that her child is dying and no doctor will come to save him, turns to an old folk remedy, "strong horse tea." Which is to say, horse urine. The child dies, of course.

Now too the mother begins to see new levels in the stories she is at that moment—dizzy with fever—constructing: Why, she says, slapping her forehead, all History is current; all injustice continues on some level, somewhere in the world. "Progress" affects few. Only revolution can affect many.

It was during this same period when, risen from her bed of pain, her child well again and adapting to the cold, the mother understood that her child, a victim of society as much as she herself—and more of one because as yet she was unable to cross the street without a guiding hand—was in fact the very least of her obstacles in her chosen work. This was brought home to her by the following experience, which, sickening as it was, yet produced in her several desired and ultimately healthful results. One of which was the easy ability to dismiss all people who thought and wrote as if she, herself, did not exist. By "herself" she of course meant multitudes, of which she was at any given time in history, a mere representative.

Our young mother had designed a course on Black women writers which she proceeded to teach at an upper-class, largely white, women's college (her students were racially mixed). There she shared an office with a white woman feminist scholar who taught Poetry and Literature. This woman thought Black Literature consisted predominantly of Nikki Giovanni whom she had, apparently, once seen inadvertently on TV. Our young mother was appalled. She made a habit of leaving books by Gwendolyn Brooks, Margaret Walker, Toni Morrison, Nella Larsen, Paule Marshall, and Zora Neale Hurston face up on her own desk, which was just behind the white feminist scholar's. For the truly scholarly feminist, she thought, subtlety is enough. She had heard that this scholar was writing a massive study of women's imagination throughout the centuries, and what women's imaginations were better than those displayed on her desk, Our Mother wondered, what woman's imagination better than her own, for that matter; but she was modest, and as I have said, trusted to subtlety.

Time passed. The scholarly tome was published. Dozens of imaginative women paraded across its pages. They were all white. Papers of the status quo; like the *Times*, and liberal inquirers like the *New York Review of Books* and *The Village Voice*, and even feminist magazines such as *Ms.* (for which our young mother was later to work) actually reviewed this work with various degrees of seriousness. Yet to our young mother, the index alone was sufficient proof that the work could not be really serious scholarship, only serious white female chauvinism. And for this she had little time and less patience.[1]

So, Our Mother[2] thought, cradling her baby with one hand, while grading students papers with the other (she found teaching extremely compatible with child care), the forces of the opposition are in focus. Fortunately, she had not once believed that all white women who called themselves feminists were any the less racist, because work after ambitious work issued from the country's presses, and, with but a few shining examples (and Our Mother considered Tillie Olsen's *Silences* the *most* shining), white women feminists revealed themselves as incapable as white and Black men of comprehending Blackness and feminism in the same body, not to mention within the same imagination. By the time Ellen Moers's book on great *Literary Women* was published in 1976— with Lorraine Hansberry used as a token of what was not to be included, even in the future, in women's literature—Our Mother was well again. Exchanges like the following, which occurred wherever she was invited to lecture, she handled with aplomb.

WHITE STUDENT FEMINIST: "Do you think Black women artists should work in the Black community?"

OUR MOTHER: "At least for a period in their lives. Perhaps a couple of years, just to give back some of what has been received."

WHITE STUDENT FEMINIST: "But if you say that Black women should work in the Black community, you are saying that race comes before sex. What about Black *feminists*? Should *they* be expected to work in the Black community? And if so, isn't this a betrayal of their feminism? Shouldn't they work with women?"

OUR MOTHER: "But of course Black people come in both sexes."

(Pause, while largely white audience, with sprinkle of perplexed Blacks, ponders this possibility.)[3]

Of Our Mother's Continued Pilgrimage Toward Truth at the Expense of Vain Pride, or: One More River to Cross.

It was a river she did not even know was there. Hence her difficulty in crossing it.

Our Mother was glad, during the period of the above revelations—all eventually salutary to her mental health—to have occasion to address a large group of educated and successful Black women. She had adequate respect for both education and success, since both were often needed, she thought, to comprehend the pains and anxieties of women who have neither. She spoke praisingly of Black History; she spoke as she often did, deliberately, of her mother (formerly missing from both Literature and History); she spoke of the alarming rise in suicide of young Black women all over America. She asked that these Black women address themselves to this crisis. Address themselves, in effect, to themselves. Our Mother was halted in mid-speech. She was told she made too much of Black History. That she should not assume her mother represented poor mothers all over the world (which she did assume) and, furthermore, she was told, that those to address were Black men, that, though it appeared more Black women than men were committing suicide, still everyone knew Black women to be the stronger of these two. Those women who committed suicide were merely sick, apparently with an imaginary or in any case a causeless disease. Furthermore, Our Mother was told, "Our men must be supported in every way, *whatever they do.*" Since so many of "our men" were doing little at the time but denigrating Black women (and especially such educated and "successful" Black women as those assembled) when they deigned to recognize them at all, and since this denigration and abandonment was a direct cause of at least some of the suicides, Our Mother was alarmed. Our Mother was furious. Our Mother burst into tears. (Which some around her thought a really *strong* Black woman would not do.)

However, Our Mother did not for one moment consider becoming something other than Black and female. She was in the condition of twin "afflictions" for life. And, to tell the truth, she rather enjoyed being more difficult things in one lifetime than anybody else. She even regretted (at times) not being still desperately poor. She regretted (at times) her private sexual behavior was so much her own business it was in no sense provocative. She was, in her own obstacle-crazed way, a snob.

But it was while recuperating from this blow to her complete trust in *all* Black women (which was foolish, as all categorical trust is, of course) that she began to understand a simple principle. People do not wish to appear foolish; to avoid the appearance of foolishness, they were willing to remain actually fools. This led directly to a clearer grasp of many Black women's attitudes about the women's movement.

They had seen, perhaps earlier than she (she was notorious for her optimism regarding any progressive group effort), that white feminists are very often indistinguishable in their attitudes from any other white person in America. She did not blame white *feminists* for the overturned buses of school children from Baton Rouge to Boston, as many Black women did, or for the Black school children beaten and spat upon. But look, just look, at the recent exhibit of women painters at the Brooklyn Museum!

("Are there no Black women painters represented here?" one asked a white feminist.

"It's a *women's* exhibit!" she replied.)

Of the need for internationalism, alignment with non-Americans, non-Europeans, and nonchauvinists and against male supremacists or white supremacists wherever they exist on the globe, with an appreciation of all white American feminists who know more of nonwhite women's herstory than "And Ain't I a Woman?" by Sojourner Truth.

There was never a time when Our Mother thought, when someone spoke of "the women's movement," that this referred only to the women's movement in America. When she thought of women moving, she automatically thought of women all over the world. She recognized that to contemplate the women's movement in isolation from the rest of the world would be—given the racism, sexism, elitism, and ignorance of so many American feminists—extremely defeating to solidarity among women as well as depressing to the most optimistic spirit. Our Mother had traveled and had every reason to understand that women's freedom was an idea whose time had come, and that it was an idea sweeping the world.

The women of China "hold up half the sky." They, who once had feet the size of pickles. The women of Cuba, fighting the combined oppression of African and Spanish macho, know that their revolution will be "shit" if they are the ones to do the laundry, dishes, and floors after working all day, side by side in factory and field with their men, "making the revolution." The women of Angola, Mozambique, and Eritrea have picked up the gun, and, propped against it, demand their right to fight the enemy within as well as the enemy without. The enemy within is the patriarchal system that has kept women virtual slaves throughout memory.

Our Mother understood that in America, white women who are truly feminist—for whom racism is inherently an impossibility, as long as some Black people can also be conceived of as women—are largely outnumbered by *average* American white women for whom racism, inasmuch as it assures white privilege, is an accepted way of life. Naturally, many of these women, to be trendy, will leap to the feminist banner because it is now the place to be seen. What was required of women of color, many of whom have, over the centuries, and with the best of reasons, become racialists if not racists themselves, was to learn to distinguish between who was the real feminist and who was not, and to exert energy in feminist collaborations only when there is little risk of wasting it. The rigors of this discernment will invariably keep throwing women of color back upon themselves, where there is, indeed, so much work, of a feminist nature, to be done. From the stamping out of clitoridectomy and "female circumcision" in large parts of Arabia and Africa to the heating of freezing urban tenements, in which poor mothers

and children are trapped alone, to freeze to death. From the encourage-
ment of women artists in Latin America to the founding of feminist
publications for women of color in North America. From the stopping of
pornography, child slavery and forced prostitution, and molestation of
minors in the home and in Times Square, to the defense of women beaten
and raped each Saturday night the world over, by their husbands.
To the extent that Black women dissociate themselves from the
women's movement, they abandon their responsibilities to women
throughout the world. This is a serious abdication from and misuse of
radical Black herstorical tradition: Harriet Tubman, Sojourner Truth,
Ida B. Wells, and Fannie Lou Hamer would not have liked it. Nor do I.

---

¹In the prologue to her book, The Female Imagination *(Knopf),
Patricia Meyer Spacks attempts to explain why her book deals solely with
women in the "Anglo-American literary tradition." She means, of course,*
white *women in the Anglo-American literary tradition. Speaking of the
books she has chosen to study, she writes: "Almost all delineate the lives
of white middle-class women. Phyllis Chesler has remarked, 'I have no
theory to offer of Third World female psychology in America.... As a
white woman, I'm reluctant and unable to construct theories about
experiences I haven't had.' So am I: the books I talk about* describe
familiar experience, belong to a familiar cultural setting; *their particular
immediacy depends partly on these facts. My bibliography* balances
works everyone knows (Jane Eyre, Middlemarch) *with works that should
be better known* (The Story of Mary MacLane). *Still, the question
remains: Why only these?"
Why only these? Because they are white, and middle class, and
because to Spacks, female imagination is only that. A limitation that even
white women must find restrictive. Perhaps, however, this is the white
female imagination, one that is "reluctant and unable to construct
theories about experiences I haven't had." Yet Spacks never lived in
nineteenth-century Yorkshire, so why theorize about the Brontës?
It took viewing "The Dinner Party," a feminist statement in art by
Judy Chicago, to illuminate—as art always will—the problem. In 1975
when her book,* Through the Flower *(Anchor), was published, I was
astonished, after reading it, to realize she knew nothing of Black women
painters. Not even that they exist. I was gratified therefore to learn that in
"The Dinner Party" there was a place "set," as it were, for Black women.
The illumination came when I stood in front of it.
All the other plates are creatively imagined vaginas (even the one that
looks like a piano and the one that bears a striking resemblance to a head*

of lettuce: and of course the museum guide flutters about talking of "Butterflies"!). The Sojourner Truth plate is the only one in the collection that shows—instead of a vagina—a face. In fact, three faces. One, weeping (a truly cliché tear), which "personifies" the Black woman's "oppression," and an other, screaming (a no less cliché scream) with little ugly pointed teeth, "her heroism," and a third, in gimcracky "African" dēsign, smiling; as if the African woman, pre-American slavery, or even today, had no woes. (There is of course a case to be made for being "personified" by a face rather than by a vagina, but that is not what this show is about.)

It occurred to me that perhaps white women feminists, no less than white women generally, cannot imagine Black women have vaginas. Or, if they can, where imagination leads them is too far to go.

However, to think of Black women as women is impossible if you cannot imagine them with vaginas. Sojourner Truth certainly had a vagina, as note her lament about her children, born of her body, but sold into slavery. Note her comment (straightforward, not bathetic) that when she cried out with a mother's grief, none but Jesus heard her. Surely a vagina has to be acknowledged when one reads these words. (A vagina the color of raspberries and blackberries—or scuppernongs and muscadines—and of that strong, silvery sweetness, with as well a sharp flavor of salt.)

And through that vagina, children.

Perhaps it is the Black woman's children, whom the white woman—having more to offer her own children, and certainly not having to offer them slavery or a slave heritage or poverty or hatred, generally speaking: segregated schools, slum neighborhoods, the worst of everything—resents. For they must always make her feel guilty. She fears knowing that Black women want the best for their children just as she does. But she also knows Black children are to have less in this world so that her children, white children, will have more (in some countries, all).

Better then to deny that the Black woman has a vagina. Is capable of motherhood. Is a woman.

[2]I am indebted to the brilliant African writer Ama Ata Aidoo for my sense of the usefulness of the phrase "Our Mother," after reading sections of her novel, then in progress, Our Sister Killjoy, or Reflections from a Black-Eyed Squint.

[3]In the Preface to Ellen Moers's book Literary Women: The Great Writers (Anchor), she writes: "Just as we are now trying to make sense of women's literature in the great feminist decade of the 1790s, when Mary Wollstonecraft blazed and died, and when, also, Mme. de Staël came to England and Jane Austen came of age, so the historians of the future will

try to order women's literature of the 1960s and 1970s. They will have to consider Sylvia Plath as a woman writer and as a poet; but what will they make of her contemporary compatriot, the playwright Lorraine Hansberry? Born two years before Plath, and dead two years after her in her early thirties, Hansberry was not a suicide but a victim of cancer; she eloquently affirmed life, as Plath brilliantly wooed death. Historians of the future will undoubtedly be satisfied with the title of Lorraine Hansberry's posthumous volume *(named not by Hansberry, but by her former husband who became executor of her estate),* To Be Young, Gifted and Black; *and they will talk of her admiration for Thomas Wolfe; but of Sylvia Plath they will have to say 'young, gifted* and a woman.' " *Emphasis, mine.*

It is, apparently, inconvenient, if not downright mind straining, for white women scholars to think of Black women as women, *perhaps because "woman" (like "man" among white males) is a name they are claiming for themselves, and themselves alone. Racism decrees that if* they *are now women (years ago they were ladies, but fashions change) then Black women must, perforce, be something else. (While they were "ladies," Black women could be "women," and so on.)*

In any case, Moers expects "historians of the future" to be as dense as those in the past, and at least as white. It doesn't occur *to her that they might be white women with a revolutionary rather than a reactionary or liberal approach to Literature, let alone* Black *women. Yet many are bound to be. Those future historians, working-class Black and white women, should have no difficulty comprehending: "Lorraine Hansberry—Young, Gifted, Black, Activist Woman, Eloquent Affirmer of Life"; and "Sylvia Plath—Young, Gifted, White, Nonactivist Woman (in fact, fatally self-centered), Brilliant Wooer of Death."*

5

Racism—A White Issue

ELLEN PENCE

I've written and rewritten this article only to find that because I am still only in the early stages of seriously examining my own racism and the racism in the battered women's movement, I am unable to articulate much of what I think needs to be said. I grew up in a home where my father believed and preached the natural superiority of whites. Because his racism was so blatant, it was easy for me to reject his ideas during the civil rights movement of the 1960s. Marching with Father Groppi for open housing in Milwaukee, sending my babysitting money to Martin Luther King, and making sure that I always went to confession to the Black priest in our lily-white parish were all signs to me that I had rejected the racist philosophy my father taught and had joined with the Third World people in their struggle for liberation.

As I began to get involved in neighborhood organizing and especially in the battered women's program, I watched Blacks and Indians accuse white feminist women of racism. Certainly, they didn't mean me—I had marched in Milwaukee. I too was oppressed by the white male. So when I heard women of color speaking of white privileges, I mentally inserted the word "male": "white male privileges."

I viewed the anger of women of color toward my white sisters as a cop out. We are the most vulnerable to this anger, we listened and tried to adjust. It seemed to me that because it is much easier for them to confront us than the racist system or the men in their communities who give no support to their participation in women's issues, we are the most aggressively confronted.

I also defended the decision-making process we used in developing grassroots organizations as totally open to all women. In response to complaints of exclusionary practices, special care is always taken to notify minority organizations and women of color of conferences, planning meetings, job openings, and workshops. Gradually, I began to realize the tremendous gap between my rhetoric about solidarity with Third World women and my gut feelings.

I began talking to a Black friend of mine, Ella Gross, about how sick I was getting of the whole issue. Ella, in her normal blunt, direct way, told me that I was sick of it because I didn't want to go past adjusting my behavior to recognizing my racism. In the many, many hours I spent talking to Ella, I began to see how white women ignored the need to reexamine the traditional white rigid methods of decision making, priority setting, and implementing decisions. Our idea of including women of color was to send out notices. We never came to the business table as equals. Women of color joined us on our terms.

I started seeing the similarities with how men have excluded the participation of women in their work through Roberts Rules of Order, encouraging us to set up subcommittees to discuss *our* problems but never seeing sexism as their problem. It became clear that in many ways I act the same way toward women of color, supporting them in dealing with *their* issues. As with liberal men's recognition of the oppression of women, I recognized the oppression of Third World people but never understood that I personally had anything to gain by the elimination of racism. While I fully understand how sexism dehumanizes men, it never crossed my mind that my racism must somehow dehumanize me.

As white women, we continually expect women of color to bring us to an understanding of our racism. White women rarely meet to examine collectively our attitudes, our actions, and, most importantly, our resistance to change. The oppression of men toward women is in so many ways parallel to the oppression of white women toward women of color. Asking a Black, Indian, or Chicana woman to define racism for us or to lay the historical background of Third World people's experience in this country is what allows us to continue our resistance to change. The history of racism in this country is white history, we know it, it is the story of our parents, grandparents, and ourselves. Why do we call upon those who have suffered the injustice of that history to explain it to us?

Knowing that we grew up in a society permeated with the belief that white values, culture, and lifestyle are superior, we can assume that regardless of our rejection of the concept we still act out of that socialization. The same anger and frustration that we have as women in dealing with men whose sexism is subtle, not blatant, are the frustration and anger women of color must feel toward us. The same helpless feelings we have in trying to expose that subtle sexism must be the feelings of women of color in working with us. I have sat through hundreds of meetings with men, constantly raising issues about women's involvement or the effects of decisions on women, and felt totally frustrated knowing that to them I'm being petty, my issues are relatively unimportant to the business at hand, my comments resented. I always end up feeling either crazy or absolutely enraged at the thought that they are deliberately acting dumb. I'm now beginning to realize that in many cases men do not understand because they have never committed themselves to understanding and by understanding, choosing to share their power. The lessons we've learned so well as women must be the basis for our understanding of ourselves as oppressive to the Third World women we work with.

We must acknowledge what we think we have to lose by this understanding and find what we have to gain by eliminating our racism. We must believe that racism causes us to be less human and work toward humanizing ourselves.

It seems that much of our resistance to change comes from being angry at women of color. There are many times that white women are put in a real bind so that no matter what we do we are accused of being racists. There are times when racism is inappropriately used as an issue when the disagreements are clearly philosophical. But those, often very legitimate, resentments we have cannot become a justification for perpetuating our racism. The confusion we feel about when and how this movement is racist will not be cleared up until we understand racism as our issue and our responsibility and begin addressing it among ourselves rather than depending totally on Third World women to raise and clarify the issue for us.

6

Racism and Women's Studies

BARBARA SMITH

Although my proposed topic is Black women's studies, I've decided to focus my remarks in a different way. Given that this is a gathering of predominantly white women, and given what has occurred during this Convention, it makes much more sense to discuss the issue of racism: racism in women's studies and racism in the women's movement generally.

"Oh no," I can hear some of you groaning inwardly. "Not that again. That's all we've talked about since we got here." This, of course, is not true. If it had been all we had all talked about since we got here, we might be at a point of radical transformation on the last day of this Convention that we clearly are not. For those of you who are tired of hearing about racism, imagine how much more tired *we* are of constantly experiencing it, second by literal second, how much more exhausted we are to see it constantly in your eyes. The degree to which it is hard or uncomfortable for you to have the issue raised is the degree to which you know inside of yourself that you aren't dealing with the issue, the degree to which you are hiding from the oppression that undermines Third World women's lives. I want to say right here that this is not a "guilt trip." It's a fact trip. The assessment of what's actually going on.

Why is racism being viewed and taken up as a pressing feminist issue at this time, and why is it being talked about in the context of women's studies? As usual, the impetus comes from the grassroots, activist women's movement. In my six years of being an avowed Black feminist, I have seen much change in how white women take responsibility for their racism, particularly within the last year. The formation of consciousness-raising groups to deal solely with this issue, study groups, and community meetings and workshops; the appearance of articles in our publications and letters in newspapers; and the beginning of real and equal coalitions between Third World and white women are all phenomena that have really begun to happen, and I feel confident that there will be no turning back.

The reason racism is a feminist issue is easily explained by the inherent definition of feminism. Feminism is the political theory and practice that struggles to free *all* women: women of color, working-class women, poor women, disabled women, lesbians, old women—as well as white, economically privileged, heterosexual women. Anything less than this vision of total freedom is not feminism, but merely female self-aggrandizement.

Let me make quite clear at this point, before going any further, something you must understand. White women don't work on racism to do a favor for someone else, solely to benefit Third World women. You have to comprehend how racism distorts and lessens your own lives as white women—that racism affects your chances for survival, too, and that it is very definitely your issue. Until you understand this, no fundamental change will come about.

Racism is being talked about in the context of women's studies because of its being raised in the women's movement generally, but also because women's studies is a context in which white and Third World women actually come together, a context that should be about studying and learning about all of our lives. I feel at this point that it is not only about getting Third World women's materials into the curriculum, although this must be done. This has been happening, and it is clear that racism still thrives, just as the inclusion of women's materials in a college curriculum does not prevent sexism from thriving. The stage we are at now is having to decide to change fundamental attitudes and behavior—the way people treat each other. In other words, we are at a stage of having to take some frightening risks.

I am sure that many women here are telling themselves they aren't racists because they are capable of being civil to Black women, having been raised by their parents to be anything but. It's not about merely being polite: "I'm not racist because I do not snarl and snap at Black people." It's much more subtle than that. It's not white women's fault that they have been raised, for the most part, not knowing how to talk to Black women, not knowing how to look us in the eye and laugh *with* us. Racism and racist behavior are our white patriarchal legacy. What is your fault is making no serious effort to change old patterns of contempt—to look at how you still believe yourselves to be superior to Third World women and how you communicate these attitudes in blatant and subtle ways.

A major roadblock for women involved in women's studies to changing their individual racism and challenging it institutionally is the pernicious ideology of professionalism. That word "professionalism" covers such a multitude of sins. I always cringe when I hear *anyone* describe herself as "professional," because what usually follows is an excuse for inaction, an excuse for ethical irresponsibility. It's a word and concept we don't need, because it is ultimately a way of dividing ourselves from others and escaping from reality. I think the way to be "successful" is to do work with integrity and work that is good. Not to play cutthroat tricks and insist on being called "Doctor." When I got involved in women's studies six years ago, and particularly during my three and a half years as the first Third World woman on the Modern Language Association Commission on the Status of Women, I began to recognize what I call women's studies or academic feminists: women who teach, research, and publish about women, but who are not involved in any way in making radical social and political change; women who are not involved in making the lives of living, breathing women more viable. The grassroots/community women's movement has given women's studies its life. How do we relate to it? How do we bring our gifts and our educational privilege back to it? Do we realize also how very much there is to learn in doing this essential work? Ask yourself what the women's movement is working on in your town or city. Are you a part of it? Ask yourself which women are living in the worst conditions in your town and how your work positively affects and directly touches their lives? If it doesn't, why not?

The question has been raised here whether this should be an activist association or an academic one. In many ways, this is an immoral question, an immoral and false dichotomy. The answer lies in the emphasis and the kinds of work that will lift oppression off of not only women, but all oppressed people: poor and working-class people, people of color in this country and in the colonized Third World. If lifting this oppression is not a priority to you, then it's problematic whether you are a part of the actual feminist movement.

There are two other roadblocks to our making feminism real which I'll mention briefly. First, there is Third World women's antifeminism, which I sometimes sense gets mixed up with opposition to white women's racism and is fueled by a history of justified distrust. To me, racist white women cannot be said to be actually feminist, at least not in the way I think and feel about the word. Feminism in and of itself would be fine. The problems arise with the mortals who practice it. As Third World women we must define a responsible and radical feminism for ourselves and not assume that bourgeois female self-aggrandizement is all that feminism is and therefore attack feminism wholesale.

The other roadblock is homophobia, that is, antilesbianism, an issue that both white and Third World women still have to deal with. Need I explicate in 1979 how enforced heterosexuality is the extreme manifestation of male domination and patriarchal rule and that women must not collude in the oppression of women who have chosen each other, that is, lesbians? I wish I had time here to speak also about the connections between the lesbian-feminist movement, being woman-identified, and the effective antiracist work that is being done by many, though not all, lesbians.

In conclusion, I'll say that I don't consider my talk today to be in any way conclusive or exhaustive. It has merely scratched the surface. I don't know exactly what's going on in your schools or in your lives. I can only talk about those qualities and skills that will help you to bring about change: integrity, awareness, courage, and redefining your own success.

I also feel that the women's movement will deal with racism in a way that it has not been dealt with before in any other movement: fundamentally, organically, and nonrhetorically. White women have a materially different relationship to the system of racism than white men. They get less out of it and often function as its pawns, whether they recognize this or not. It is something that living under white-male rule has imposed on us; and overthrowing racism is the inherent work of feminism and by extension feminist studies.

7

Face-to-Face, Day-to-Day—Racism CR

TIA CROSS, FREADA KLEIN, BARBARA SMITH, and BEVERLY SMITH

On April 4, 1979, four women met to discuss consciousness-raising guidelines for women's groups working on the issue of racism. All of us—Tia Cross, Freada Klein, Barbara Smith, and Beverly Smith—had had experiences as white and Black women thinking and talking about racism with white women's groups, or participating in ongoing racism groups ourselves. We taped our discussion, and the ideas and guidelines that follow are based upon it.

We feel that using consciousness-raising to explore our racism is particularly useful and appropriate. It is a feminist form based upon the ways women have always talked and listened to each other. The CR format encourages personal sharing, risk-taking, and involvement, which are essential for getting at how each of us is racist in a daily way; and it encourages the "personal" change that makes political transformation and action possible. The women's movement has begun to address racism in a way that no previous movement has, because we have a growing understanding that our racism often manifests itself in how we interact with other women. Doing CR acknowledges that how we feel can inhibit or lead to action, and that how we actually treat people does make a difference.

Theoretical and analytical comprehension of the political and historical causes of racism is essential, but this understanding on an intellectual level doesn't always help to make face-to-face meetings with women of color real, productive, or meaningful. We need both a political understanding of racism and a personal-political understanding of how it affects our daily lives. Many women start doing CR about racism because they are already confronting it in other areas of their lives and need a place to explore what is happening. CR about racism is not merely talk, talk, talk, and no action, but the essential talking that will make action possible. Doing CR is based upon the fact that as a person you simply cannot do political action without personal interaction. We also want to stress, however, that these guidelines are not instant solutions. You cannot spend fifteen minutes on each topic and assume that you're done. Racism is much too complex and brutal a system for that. The absence of language to explore our own racism contributes to the difficulty and is in itself part of the problem. Only one term, "racism," exists to describe the range of behavior from subtle, nonverbal daily experiences to murders by the Ku Klux Klan. "Racism" covers individual acts and institutional patterns. But this stumbling block of language presents another theme to explore, not a reason to give up. CR is just one step in the whole process of changing the legacy of oppression (based upon difference) that white-male rule has imposed on us.

Actions can grow out of the CR group directly. For example, the group can find out about and publicize the resources which exist in their area, such as other CR groups, study groups, Third World women's groups, and coalitions of Third World and white women. The group can compile reading lists about Black women, racism, and white women's antiracist activity. It can spread the word about the CR process through writing articles, and by giving workshops and talks. It can also compile its own CR guidelines. The legacy of racism in this country is long. It will take a great deal of time and ongoing commitment to bring about change, to alter the insidious and deep-rooted patiarchal attitudes we learn from the time we are children. It is important to show other women what is possible.

The following guidelines are divided into three sections: (1) Early Memories/Childhood Experiences, (2) Adolescence/Early Adulthood, and (3) Becoming a Feminist/Racism in the Women's Movement. The group should plan to spend a substantial amount of time sharing personal histories and feelings in order to build trust, especially at the beginning. It is good to pose questions constantly that make women backtrack and remember their own pasts. General questions which can be applied to any topic and which should be raised along the way are: "How do you experience yourself as a white person?" "What were your fears and what was your anger?" "What did you do with your fears and anger?"

We have included some guidelines that deal with anti-Semitism, but the primary focus of the guidelines is white racism against Black people. It is important for groups to discuss the ways in which anti-Semitism in

America is similar to and different from racism aimed against Black people. It is also important to connect racism aimed at Afro-Americans with the racism and oppression aimed at all people of color and with the discrimination aimed at white nationality groups who are not Anglo-Saxon Protestants. Insights about how class identity connects with racism should also provide an ongoing topic for discussion.

EARLY MEMORIES/CHILDHOOD EXPERIENCES

1. When were you first aware that there was such a thing as race and racial differences? How old were you? Recall an incident if you can. How did you feel?

2. What kind of contact did you have with people of different races? Were they adults, children, playmates?

3. How did you experience your own ethnic identity?

4. How did you first experience racism? From whom did you learn it? What did it mean to you? How did it function in your perception of yourself? How did it make you feel? How did it affect you in relation to other people?

5. When did you first notice yourself treating people of color in a different way?

6. When were you first aware that there was such a thing as anti-Semitism? How old were you? Recall an incident. How did you feel?

7. What did you learn at home about Black people and other people of color?

8. What did you learn about Jewish people?

9. How was what you learned about Black people and what you learned about Jewish people connected?

10. What terms did your parents use to refer to Black people and other people of color? If these terms were negative, how did hearing these terms make you feel—curious, uncomfortable, angry?

11. In the group say out loud and make a collective list of *all* the terms you were ever taught or heard about people of color. Also do the same activity with all the terms used for other ethnic and religious groups.

ADOLESCENCE/EARLY ADULTHOOD

1. What kinds of messages did you get about race as you entered adolescence? Did your group of friends change?

2. Discuss the connections between coming of age sexually and racial separation. (When the four of us discussed being a teenager, one woman pinpointed the sexual-racial dichotomy by saying, "It's about who you can't date!")

3. If you went to integrated schools, what messages did you get about Black people in general and about Black males specifically?

4. In what ways was race used by you or your friends as a subject of so-called teenage rebellion?

5. How did different groups of students get along in your school? Were you aware of divisions by race and class? How did it feel?

6. How were different groups of students treated by teachers and the school administration?

7. When you were growing up, what kind of information did you get about Black people through the media? How much of it was specifically about Black men?

8. If you had interactions with Black people through work during the 50s and 60s, through political groups, or socially, what proportion of these interactions were with Black men? With Black women?

9. What were your experiences as white women with Black men? What were the racial-sexual dynamics of these relationships? In what ways did these experiences help you to explore your own racism? In what ways did they fuel your own racism? How did they affect your developing feminism?

BECOMING A FEMINIST/RACISM IN THE WOMEN'S MOVEMENT

1. When did you begin to make the connection between your own experiences and the experiences of other women?

2. As you became a feminist, to what degree did you feel connected to women of all different backgrounds and lifestyles?

3. How do you see yourself as different from a Black woman? How do you see yourself as the same?

4. Think about your relationships with Black and white women who are co-workers, neighbors, and acquaintances. What are the differences resulting from race in these relationships? Have you ever had a really close woman friend who was Black? Can you imagine having such a friendship? Why or why not? Have you ever had a sexual relationship with a Black woman? Can you imagine having such a relationship? Why or why not?

5. How does your class background affect your racism and making connections with women different from yourself? What are the barriers you have to overcome to connect?

6. Everyone in the group fills in the blanks in the following statements. This exercise could be done out loud or by each person writing her response down first before hearing from the group. "Black women always _____. " "When I am with Black people I always feel or usually feel _____. " "I wouldn't want Black people to _____." "When I'm with Black people I'm afraid that_____." "I'm afraid I will _____." "I'm afraid they will _____."

7. Discuss different values you think white and Black women have about family, sexuality, childrearing, clothes, food, money, upward or downward mobility, and other issues.

8. How does racism affect your daily life as a white woman? The group could discuss Lillian Smith's statement (from *The Winner Names the Age*), "Back door treatment is humiliating to all who participate in it. Both leave stains on the soul."

9. Each week the group has the "homework assignment" of noticing racist situations—things each member sees, hears, or reads. Begin each session by sharing the things you have noticed.

10. Discuss what happens when you confront another white woman about her racism. What are your fears? How does it feel to do this?

11. In what way does being a lesbian connect to the whole issue of racism between white and Black women? What kinds of racism have you noticed in all-women's social situations, at bars and at cultural events? In what ways can shared lesbian oppression be used to build connections between white women and women of color?

12. Discuss the ways in which white women lower their standards for being feminist for Black and other Third World women. Do you find yourself "hiding" your feminism in a situation where there are Third World people? Are you afraid to confront Black women's antifeminism?

13. Discuss issues that the women's movement has worked on which might be considered racist because they did not address the experiences of women of color. Discuss feminist issues that cut across racial and class lines, touching the lives of all women. Which of all these issues have you worked on or considered a priority?

Women welders at the Landers, Frary, and Clark plant, New Britian, Connecticut, June 1943.

Section Three

Dispelling the Myths: Black Women and the Social Sciences

8

Studying Slavery: Some Literary and Pedagogical Considerations on the Black Female Slave

ERLENE STETSON

This essay is written out of a visceral need to make intelligible the experience of Black women in the slave community. Its major purpose is to describe teaching about that experience, and by implication to clarify the need to forge a theoretical and historical frame of reference for such teaching. Finding teaching materials written from the perspective of Black female slaves is a herculean task. The available materials held in various institutions are for the most part uncatalogued, unknown (to the general public at large), and restricted to limited access. Moreover, much of the slavery material pertaining to Black women is listed under the names of their owners. One easily finds abundant materials regarding the slaveholders' attitudes toward Black women; less often is the opposite true. The words and ideas of Black female slaves are nevertheless available (despite the paucity and hidden or submerged nature of the materials) in the form of narratives, letters, diaries, and unpublished documents, court transcripts, and sometimes bills of sale.

This state of affairs is partly explained by the society we live in, which neglects the in-depth study of women in general and has only begun to challenge stereotypic images and analyze the contradictions between those images and reality. Black women's history has been neglected in every epoch, but especially under slavery. Much material remains inaccessible unless one has the time to visit major collection holdings for primary resources. And, while the data on slavery are voluminous, it requires sifting and winnowing to find materials relating particularly to Black women.

Emphasis to date has been on the role of Black women in relation to Black men. Female slaves are discussed in the context of debate about Black family structure, with a focus that seldom extends beyond the limitations (never to the possibilities) of their role as mothers. Moreover, scholars treat the slavery experience as a Black male phenomenon, regarding Black women as biological functionaries whose destinies are rendered ephemeral—to lay their eggs and die. Thus, predictably, the tales of slave rebellions (not merely slave resistance) offer masculine images of active, dynamic personages—fighting men—excluding almost entirely women who actively resisted and rebelled (see Angela Davis, "Reflections on the Black Woman's Role in the Community of Slaves," *The Black Scholar*, December 1971), though not always by escaping. Tales of heroism center almost exclusively on those who left and almost never on those who by sheer force of effort (morally, physically, and otherwise) stayed because they would not/could not leave. Only the near-mythicized sagas of Harriet Tubman and Sojourner Truth have escaped obscurity. In a kind of multiple jeopardy, Black female slaves have been held hostages to a virtual industry.

To begin to restore an accurate history of the female experience and to create, so far as is possible, a language (both literary and historical) for talking about the female experience of slavery, I offered a course on the Black female slave experience as gleaned through primary and secondary sources. In this essay I want to share teaching strategies, methodologies, ideas, and curricular materials based on my teaching at Women's Studies College at the State University of New York at Buffalo. In addition, and in view of a perceived need to formulate a theoretical and historical framework for understanding the experiences of Black female slaves, I will describe a one-semester course intended to be of value not only to Afro-American and women's studies programs, but also to American studies, comparative literature, history, sociology, and all cross-cultural programs whether the emphasis is literary, historical, or social (especially the family as a social institution).

My class consisted of twenty-three women the first semester, and twenty-one the second. Their ages ranged from nineteen to thirty-five. Eighteen of the first-semester students were Black, and the number of white women (five) remained the same both semesters. The students' backgrounds were varied, though predominantly working-class. The white students were minoring in women's studies; the Black students were taking as many "Black-oriented" courses (this one was an elective) as were offered within the college, and were not minoring in women's studies because not enough "Black-oriented" courses were offered in that program. They were mostly English, history, or speech majors. All were generally wary of each other: women's studies at Buffalo was still beyond the pale, and students were thought "strange" for majoring, minoring, or having much to do with it. My approach was to begin with the inevitable problems posed by so controversial a subject as slavery. These included problems of definition, of perspective, and especially of sources: finding the authentic voices of Black women through primary sources (narrative writings, impressionistic accounts such as novels, slave autobiographies) and secondary sources ("told-to" accounts, travel journals of other women, and historical essays). Not only are such sources difficult to locate, but one has the further task of bringing together disparate works into a comprehensible whole.

From the very beginning it was obvious that Black female slave narratives would be our focus. Our syllabus included: Mattie Griffith (Browne), *The Autobiography of a Female Slave* (1858); Lydia Maria Child, *Incidents in the Life of a Slave Girl* (1861); Amanda Smith, *Amanda's Own Story* (1893); Zora Neale Hurston, *Their Eyes Were Watching God* (1937); Margaret Walker, *Jubilee* (1966); Frances Whipple Green, *Elleanor's Second Book* (1839); Annie L. Burton, *Memories of Childhood's Slavery Days* (1919); Harriet B. Stowe, *Uncle Tom's Cabin* (1852). Secondary sources included Frances A. Kemble, *Journal of a Resident on a Georgia Plantation in 1838-39;* Ray A. Billington, ed., *A Free Negro in the Slave Era: The Journal of Charlotte L. Forten* (1953); Harriet Martineau, *Society in America* (1832); Mary Ames, *A New England Woman's Diary in Dixie, 1865-66.*

Anticipating the more general problems of reading the slave narratives and allowing the students some time to finish their reading of the assigned narratives (some had to be shared), I began the semester with the intention of providing an historical overview of slavery and the varied positions taken by historians. The definition and perspective of the course were largely determined by the limitations of time, class size, class interests, and class resources. In the first class session, we discussed the scope, emphasis, and extent of the course. We decided that we would limit our study of American slavery to the continental United States, thereby forgoing comparative studies that might possibly have yielded a valuable cross-cultural perspective. Slavery in the Caribbean was the expressed interest of one of the students. Having defined our scope, we were then ready for the overview of existing historical materials and traditional interpretations.

We began with Ulrich Bonnell Phillips, *American Negro Slavery* (1918; reprinted, Baton Rouge: Louisiana State Univ. Press, 1966), who asserted to W. E. B. DuBois that slaves were innately inferior and that slavery was a blessing in disguise for them. DuBois, *Black Reconstruction in America, 1860–1880* (Cleveland: World Publishing Company, 1935), without the aid of sophisticated research methods, concluded long before Robert W. Fogel and Stanley L. Engerman, *Time on the Cross: The Economics of American Negro Slavery*, 2 vols. (Boston: Little, Brown, & Co., 1974), that "slavery of Negroes in the South was not a deliberately cruel system," that the slaves were "generally happy and well-fed," and "as well off and in some particulars better off" than the suffering freedman of Reconstruction, a wage peon, the victim of a deliberate and concentrated effort to deny basic rights by means of harsh Jim Crow laws and institutionalized racism. Extending DuBois's analysis of slavery as a "free labor system," Kenneth Stampp, *The Peculiar Institution: Slavery in the Ante-Bellum South* (New York: Knopf, 1956), described the slaveholding economy as one guided by the profit motive and a subversive, recalcitrant slave labor force. Coexisting with this interpretation was Stanley Elkins's opposing thesis in *Slavery: A Problem in American Institutional and Intellectual Life* (Chicago: Univ. of Chicago Press, 1959), that the "Sambo" personality—the inferior slave—was created, maintained, and even demanded by a master class of planters.

Our study of slave history and historians culminated with the revisionists of the sixties and seventies. They were more interesting, since they provided the class with more challenging research interpretations based on recognition of the slaves' autonomy as persons both within and outside the system of slavery. The admission that slaves were people of some complexity capable even of transcending external conditions was met by some students with a mixture of joy, anger, and ambivalence. Historians that we read included: Eugene D. Genovese, *The World the Slaveholders Made: Two Essays in Interpretation* (New York: Pantheon, 1969) and *Roll, Jordan, Roll: The World the Slaves Made* (New York: Pantheon, 1974); David Brion Davis, *The Problem of Slavery in Western Culture* (Ithaca: Cornell Univ. Press, 1966); John W. Blassingame, *The Slave Community: Plantation Life in the Antebellum South* (Baton Rouge: Louisiana State Univ. Press, 1972); Carol Stack, *All Our Kin* (New York: Harper & Row, 1974); Anne Firor Scott, *The Southern Lady* (Chicago: Univ. of Chicago Press, 1970); and Gerda Lerner *(Black Women in White America*, 1973). The best source on Black female slaves to date is Herbert Gutman's *The Black Family in Slavery and Freedom, 1750–1925* (New York: Pantheon, 1976). It provides a central focus and perspectives on Black female slaves lacking in previous studies. We found in Mina Caulfield's essay, "Imperialism, the Family and Culture of Resistance" *(Socialist Revolution*, #20, 1974), an especially timely socialist-feminist perspective. Herbert Aptheker's *American Negro Slave*

Revolts (1943; New York: International Publishers, 1963), and "Slave Guerilla Warfare," in *To Be Free: Studies in American Negro History* (New York, 1948), are very useful studies of slave rebellions and resistance. Fogel and Engerman (*Time on the Cross*, 1974) were easily our most controversial historians, because of their provocative research method—one that relies primarily on quantifiable data for research interpretation.

Despite the despair of students, it is worthwhile to take note of historians of varying persuasions, especially those with a traditional bent since they are often the shapers of social policy, to say nothing of public opinions (the "Moynihan Report" on the Black family being a case in point). I recommend a serious study of these historians also in order that an emerging generation of women scholars and historians may learn about the tactics of "acceptable" research techniques (manipulation?). Helping female students to absorb and make sense of the mass of material is difficult, but crucial.

Overwhelmingly, the historical overview forced us to focus on developing tools of criticism: how do we best deal with the opinions and positions of these historians? For instance, we are told that slaves played important supportive roles for their masters (*Roll, Jordan, Roll*); that slave society was considerably more "efficient" than had been previously believed (*Time on the Cross*); that slavery was an institution based on class rather than race (*The World the Slaveholders Made*); and that, in reality, slavery was not altogether different in the United States from what it was elsewhere (*The Problem of Slavery in Western Culture*). These statements suggest (we quickly determined) that research tended to interpret the nature of slavery pragmatically, along the lines of functions and roles, rather than from the perspective of the group studied. Moreover, we noted the tendency of these historians to reach a consensus that laid down the ground rules for further study. Overwhelmingly—and most importantly for our purpose—the research failed to consider women; and there were few attempts (except Gutman's) to interpret Black female slaves as complex entities with complex behavior and motivations. Predictably, we were encouraged to concur in the cynical notion that the lake one decides to fish in predetermines the kind of fish one will catch: that is, if one raises no questions about Black female slaves, one will get no answers about them. Clearly the research did not consider women's lives important.

To be sure, the problems posed by the historical material were not solely those of interpretation or of grasping research methods. The biggest obstacle was the inability of the class to deal critically with the statistical compilations of these researchers, whose data often appeared as incontrovertible "truth." Although we had been drilled in basic statistics, we could hardly struggle enough, even collectively, to master in so short a time what we hadn't expected to know in a lifetime. Like many of the female students, I, too, felt hostile to many of the historical studies: we were all ready to suspect each historian of malicious intent (especially with regard to seemingly unwarranted conclusions and the glaring manipulation of data), including those historians whom we trusted in our hearts even if we didn't say so. "Contemporary slaves," someone called us at one point.

Often, our discussions were heated and we felt little respect even for those who had made valuable contributions to research on Black life and history. Moreover, we found ourselves questioning with a vengeance even those historians who had been most liberal in challenging the public policy of neglect, distortion, and misinformation—those who *had* raised provocative questions about slave research methods. In a word, we felt betrayed by historians whose liberal views allowed them to envision the reality of male slaves (to a degree) but not that of female slaves. We had a sense of fighting the world. I suspect that those feelings of rage and anger preceding vigorous scientific inquiry must not be rationalized away but must be dealt with in order to face the real tasks of analysis and the rewriting of history. I am, however, deeply aware of the danger of allowing emotion to replace purposeful criticism and focus. It not only can happen, it almost did.

Our first three weeks proceeding in this fashion were never so orderly and sequential as might be suggested in the act of writing it down. In fact, logic and sequence were difficult to attain in our handling of the concept of slavery. Our eventual conclusions were not contained in the answers that we desperately wanted to grasp so much as in the questions we compulsively raised. Early on, the class became aware that a definition of slavery defied encapsulation: slavery by its very protean nature escaped easy codification. In attempting to define slavery we found it easier to talk about what it was not than about what it was. It was easier also to translate its surface import rather than its essence. This is part of the problem: the debate on slavery is an old one and it becomes intensified every decade or so with a spate of new books. Slavery research, to be sure, is quite important. However, the mere accumulation of data cannot be separated from the codification and interpretation of those data. The question of whose primary interests are served by a proliferation of publications at the hands of mostly white male historians accumulating yet more data on Black behavior is far from academic.

As Black and white women in a contemporary society, we asked ourselves whether the data told us anything about the lives of Black female slaves. The female slave narratives were our best beginning. We realized not only that research on slavery posed more questions than it answered but that the research did not ask the questions that we wanted to ask. We began to formulate questions around the central one: what would we like to know most about the lives of Black female slaves? Some of our questions were:

1. What were Black female slaves' attitudes toward housework and cooking, toward sexuality; to what extent would maintenance of a nuclear household elicit a threefold servitude—as wife, mother, and slave?

2. What was the status of slave women in an extended family?

3. What kinds of slave families were created by the material conditions of a slaveholding society?

4. What were the relations between Black slave women and white women?

5. Was it possible for Black women to maintain their identities, their sexuality, separate from the family?

6. Were Black slave women exploited and alienated by class or racial differences between owners and owned?

7. How has the status of Black women changed or not changed since slavery? Are the conditions for Black women under slavery comparable to those for Black women under the welfare state? Do Black women have the same problems today that they had when they were first brought to this country? How does this relate to work conditions, education, survival, economics, etc.?

8. What does it mean for slavery data to obscure the fact that the slave child—an owned surplus product of the Black woman's body that is owned—labored like men and women for the sustenance of a male-dominated class society? Why do historians (e.g., E. Franklin Frazier), rather than recognize this reality, hide behind an abstraction in saying that the slaveholding economy fostered more egalitarian roles among men, women, and children?

9. Since Black women held it in their power to reproduce the labor force, does this not make them central to an understanding of slave history?

10. How has Black women's intimate contact with white people made them interpreters and intermediaries of white culture in the Black home and, at the same time, partners in struggle with Black men to keep the Black family together and to help the Black community to survive?[1]

11. How do we analyze the position of Black slave women in a slaveholding society?

12. What are the Black woman's life and status in contemporary capitalist society?

13. What are the universal or general areas which define Black female oppression? The family, psychology of racism, capitalism, the concept of roles—femininity and sexuality: are any of these structures crucial?

14. However nonegalitarian their lives at work and at home, within the development of their psyches and their ideological and sociological roles as mothers and workers (outside the home), do Black women find that oppression is theirs and theirs alone?

15. What was the Black family like under slavery? What were the implications of monogamy for Black women—assuming that monogamy means that an individual lives with another as a unit for whatever purposes, including child-rearing? Were monogamous relationships possible between women, between white and Black women, or only between women and men?

16. Which family structures (nuclear/extended) advance/retard processes of revolution?

17. What was child care like under slavery? Was it different from today's child care? Whose responsibility was the child? Her/his own? The master's? The parents'? A parent's? The community's? A community person's?

18. What was Black women slaves' health like—considering the fact that both DuBois and later Fogel and Engerman have maintained that slaves were well fed? Presumably medical technology had no provisions for hypertension and heart disease.

19. What does it mean to say that Black women under slavery were never unemployed?

The above questions, provoked by our reading of historians, provided a very good approach to our reading of the female slave narratives. But it became obvious that these questions were not enough—that Black women's slave narratives contained some problems unique to themselves. For one thing, there is the question of genre: what are the most useful ways to study female slave narratives? Is there a generic way of describing them as literary-historical documents? Should slave narratives be studied as fiction (literary document), as history (antislavery documents), as autobiography (the slaves' own story)? Clearly the Black female slave narratives were the most exciting, perhaps because they seemed closer to literature than to history. It was to this literary emphasis that the class now turned.

An introductory lecture on women's autobiographies began with the premise that voices of the oppressed seldom speak but that women as a class have had spokespersons throughout the ages. *The Book of Margery Kempe* (1432) was cited as a paradigm of the genre. As one of the earliest autobiographical narratives, it reveals the problem facing the would-be female autobiographer in a patriarchal culture: the taboo against expressing anger and the necessity of resorting to the pretense of submission (hidden rebellion), and such conscious duplicities as submersion (hidden hostility) and inversion (the saying of one thing while revealing another); the lack of an artistic form appropriate to express the unique perspective of women's lives. The Kempe material prepared the class for the necessary reliance on historical intermediaries who have written down and published women's testimony. Kempe relied on a reluctant scribe. Similarly, slave women's narratives have been written down by men (clergy, physicians); by white women (Child, the Griffith narrative, Elleanor's books by Greene); and only sometimes by themselves (Burton, Smith).

Aphra Behn's *Oroonoko, or the Royal Slave* (1688) was a paradigm of the slave narrative written by a woman in the spirit of an oxymoronic blend of romance and realism that would sprout full grown in Child's narrative, the difference being that Child would give her readers a female "royal slave" (mulatto woman) and shape her adventures appropriate to nineteenth-century women's lives through certain motifs that embodied patterns of bondage, seclusion, multiple marriages, freedom, female rage, and submersion.

The class decided that it would be a distortion to approach the female slave narratives as solely this (autobiography or literature) or solely that (history or antislavery document), inasmuch as they were combinations of these genres. One way of beginning was to pose a general question that would allow us to deal with the multifunctional nature of the female slave narratives. The class decided that one question would suffice: what was life like for both Black slave women and white women within a patriarchal slaveholding society? This question, which formed the unifying thread for the entire course, proved to be especially valuable inasmuch as many of the students were frankly worried that the Black female narratives written by white women might constitute usurpation of Black female slaves' voices, a betrayal. A related but more vexing question concerned them as well: since our goal is to answer certain questions about the lives of Black female slaves, how do we decide when a narrative account is not "real" or not the authentic voice of the Black slave woman? Stated simply, when are Black slave women's narratives merely the adopted masks of white women? There were about eight students in the class who were familiar with at least three male slave narratives. This helped provide an implicit comparison between Black male slave narratives and Black female slave narratives, the latter being extensively "edited" by white women.

It was in an atmosphere of uneasiness that we proceeded to discuss impressionistic accounts: *Uncle Tom's Cabin, Their Eyes Were Watching God,* and *Jubilee.* The Black female slaves in *Uncle Tom's Cabin* were Cassy and Eliza (both mulattos). It was obvious that the book's focus was on the male slave. The fascination, however, was with Cassy, Stowe's alter ego who no doubt symbolized her very real fears of "spectral visitations." Masking and disguise were implicitly linked with Cassy, the Black female character who chose to prolong her escape for a gratuitous act of masking, bringing her master down to his knees. One of our primary questions from this reading was whether Cassy and Eliza revealed anything about the lives of women in general. *Jubilee,* a Black slave woman's account written by a Black woman writer, dealt with female exiles, one white and one Black, with undeniable emphasis on female friendship and female community. Zora Neale Hurston's novel, *Their Eyes Were Watching God* (1937), was easily the most provocative. The most important passages that provoked vigorous discussion were these:

> Well you know what dey say 'Uh white man and uh nigger woman is de freest thing on earth. Dey do as dey please.'[2]

> It was de cool of de evenin' when Mistis come walkin' in mah door. She throwed de door wide open and stood there lookin' at me outa her eyes and her face.... She come stood over me in de bed. 'Nanny Ah come to see that baby uh yourn.... Look like you don't know who is Mistis on dis plantation, Madam.... Nigger, what's you' baby doin' wid yaller hair?' She begin tuh slap mah jaws ever which a'way.[3]

Both passages reflect, reveal, and to some extent distort the experiences of Black women. In fact, we read the novel as a parallactic account of Black women's experiences of sexuality both within and outside the confines of marriage. The first passage is uttered by a Black man revealing his sexual grudge against Black women. Interestingly, he sees the Black woman as his oppressor; more damning, she is seen as if she were in collusion with white men. Janie, as a forerunner of modern women, has fled the domestic slavery symbolized in her two conventional marriages. Hence, the harshness of her male critic. The second passage reflects ex-slave Nanny's account of herself as a victim, a scapegoat of domestic politics. Unwittingly, it is also the "Mistis'" account of victimization as well. Both passages were especially important as reminders of the close connection between domestic slavery of women in general and the slavery of Black women in particular. These passages were also important as a reminder that patriarchy created similar conditions governing the lives of Black slave women and white women alike; while the positions that they held within the slaveholding society were very different—and the slave narratives we read reflected this difference—there were nevertheless amazing similarities, differences only by degree.

It seems to me that Black female slave narratives provide a theoretical frame of reference for working out the close analogy between the oppression of Black women and that of white women. We focused on characterization and the effectiveness of the mask of the female slave. It seems that Black female slave narratives written ("edited") by white women are expressions of white women's covert protest against their subordination, and of their hostility toward men as well as toward the Victorian home. Their value lies precisely in the fact that they allow us to see more clearly how white women were not inherently antagonistic toward Black women but rather joined voices with them to find in Black female slave narratives a uniquely appropriate form in which to express their hidden rebellions against the limitations of domesticity, slavery to household routines, the prison of sexual restraint, and the sexual exploitation of women by tyrannical fathers and husbands.

The Black female slave narratives written by Black women are interestingly more complex as literature and history. They range from narratives of conversion experiences (the only place where women are allowed the usually "male" experiences of authority and movement) to romantic and realistic fiction. They are important for the study of autobiography, because for the most part they challenge the male-defined genre and the "established" criteria of autobiography. As we had done before, we began with historical materials, mostly essays. In our attempts to reconstruct the period we looked at both the laws and the history of women in America. We relied mostly on essays that dealt with Black or white women and/or the relations between them.

The first groups of Africans and white women came to the American Colonies in the same year, 1619. The Africans came not as slaves but as indentured servants:

> Faced with the problem of [needing cheap and steady] labor, [the colonizers] attempted the use of Indian and white indentured servants. They soon found that the Indians did not make satisfactory slaves because the Indian men had left that work to the women, while they concentrated on hunting and warfare.... So that slavery developed only gradually, and as a substitute, as they

learned that the black slaves, who had been accustomed to farming in Africa, made more useful workers around farms and plantations.[4]

By the 1640s, several Africans within the colonies were serving life terms as indentured servants. The first recorded civil case establishing a Black person as a slave for life dates back to the mid-1650s, in the colony of Virginia. By 1661, there were provisions in the statutes concerning "Negroes" (no longer called Africans) which led to the establishment of Black slavery within Virginia. The first of these statutes declared that if any white indentured servant ran away with any Negro, the white servant must not only serve more time as punishment, but must serve the life term of the Black person, too.

By 1662, the Virginia colony had passed nine laws determining the status of newborn children. That is, all children born within the colony of Virginia would follow the condition of the mother. This law was significant in two ways. It was a change from English common law, which declared that a child's status was determined by the father's condition. It implicitly condoned sexual intercourse between white men and Black slave women, in effect allowing white men more legal, social, and psychological freedom by not holding them responsible for any offspring resulting from sexual relations with female slaves.

By 1667, a law was passed stating that a person could be a Christian and continue to be enslaved. In 1670, another law was passed stating that any non-Christian servant traveling by ship into Virginia was to be held a slave for life. It goes without saying that Africans were the only non-Christian servants entering Virginia by ship. The law was not to be outdone; it provided that non-Christian servants traveling to Virginia by land, if children, were required to serve until age thirty; if adults, for no longer than twelve years. By 1705, the General Assembly of Virginia was no longer oblique. It stated that:

> .... All Negro, mulatto and Indian slaves shall be held, taken, and adjudged to be real estate, in the same category as livestock and household furniture, wagons, and goods.[5]

By 1750, Black slavery had become a fact of life in Virginia, Maryland, Georgia, North Carolina, and South Carolina. A proliferation of slave codes pertaining to education, religion, marriage, etc., completed the subordination and submission of slave (as property) to master.

The economic basis of slavery, sanctioned by law, was buttressed by other systems that "explained" the placement of Blacks into the nonhuman category. After 1776, given the agitations for "human" rights, the ideology of the then popular Great Chain of Being was enlisted as a moral and religious justification. The Great Chain of Being established a hierarchy of life forms within the universe. God was believed to occupy the highest position of the Chain, which proceeded downward to the weakest, most unintelligent, and inferior form of life known to humanity. Regarding Black slaves, one contemporary writer notes:

> If the order of nature was divinely appointed, any attempt to subvert that order must run counter to the providential order explicit in the nature of things. Thus any attempt to alter the present condition of the Negro which was ordained by providence would destroy the very fabric of the universe. If the Negro was, as strongly suspected, a form of being mediate between the higher animals and man, his enslavement was justified and the social order of the South was the only social order in which was shown the will of the Divine Creator.[6]

Turning more specifically to the Black female slave, philosophers, scientists, lawmakers, scholars, physicians, and laymen all subscribed to the notion that the Black's position as somewhere between man and the higher animals (i.e., apes) was especially borne out in the Black woman. They agreed that orangutans showed a special attraction to the Black woman; that at some unspecified point in history the Black woman and the orangutan had mated. This notion, which was used to explain the creation of the Black race, was popularly expressed by Thomas Jefferson, who, in citing "the preference of the orangootan for the Black woman over those of his own species," justified this coupling of animal intelligence and human form as desirable eugenics:

> The circumstance of superior beauty is thought worthy attention in the propagation of our horses, dogs, and other domestic animals, why not in that of man?[7]

Female slaves, referred to as "female animals," described in terms of sexuality, were believed to have excessively "large nipples" and "an extraordinary ease of child bearing." Winthrop Jordan (*White Over Black*, 1968) stated that:

> Least surprising, perhaps, was the common assumption that Negro women were especially passionate, an idea which found at least literate expression especially in the *South Carolina Gazette* and in West Indian books. The Negro woman was the sunkissed embodiment of ardency:

> Next comes a warmer race, from sable sprung,
> To love each thought, to lust each nerve is strung;
> The Samboe dark, and the Mullattoe brown,
> The Mestize fair, the well-limb'd Quaderoon,
> And jetty Afric, from no spurious sire,
> Warm as her soil, and as her sun—on fire.
> These sooty dames, well vers'd in Venus' school,
> Make love an art, and boast they kiss by rule.[8]

One advertisement for the sale of a Black female slave boasts: "She is very prolific in her generating qualities, and affords a rare opportunity to any person who wishes to raise a family of healthy servants for their own use."[9] The slave woman's position as a "breeder" led an ex-slave "Antie" to say:

> Lawdy, Lawdy, them was tribbolashuns! Wunner dese her' womens was my Antie en she say dat she skacely call to min' he e'r whopping her, 'case she was er breeder woman en' brought in Chillum ev'y twelve mont's jes lak a cow bringin' a calf.... He orders she can't be put to no strain 'casen uv dat.[10]

Sarah Grimke summed up the position of the female slave as "breeder" mistress when she wrote:

> ...the virtue of female slaves is wholly at the mercy of irresponsible tyrants, and women are bought and sold in our slave markets, to gratify the brutal lust of those who bear the name of Christians. In our slave states, if amid all her degradation and ignorance, a woman desires to preserve her virtue unsullied, she is either bribed or whipped into compliance, or if she dare to resist her seducer, her life by the laws of some of the slave states may be and has actually been sacrificed to the fury of disappointed passion.[11]

Similarly, Linda Brent (*Incidents in the Life of a Slave Girl*) pleads:

> But, O, ye happy women, whose purity has been sheltered from childhood, who have been free to choose the objects of your affection, whose homes are protected by law, do not judge the poor desolate slave girl too severely! If slavery had been abolished, I, also, could have married the man of my choice, I could have had a home shielded by the laws.... but all my prospects have been

blighted by slavery.... I tried hard to preserve my self-respect."[12]

Female slaves were responsible for household tasks, including child care (Black and white), i.e., nursing, washing, feeding, dressing, grooming, and cleaning. As cooks, laundresses, seamstresses, and midwives, female slaves were expected to "serve." Their own household tasks came last. As guinea pigs they were sacrificed in the interests of an emerging science of gynecology. As field hands, they worked long, hard hours, even during pregnancy. A former slave said of her mother:

> She was as quick as a flash of lightning, and whatever she did could not be done better. She cooked, washed, ironed, spun, nursed and labored in the field. She made as good a field hand as she did a cook. I have heard Master Jenning say to his wife, 'Fannie has her faults but she can outwork any nigger in the country. I'd bet my life on that.'[13]

In examining the lives of white women in the Antebellum South one finds that during colonial times, because of the shortage of people and the need for workers, white women were allowed much freedom in their choices of lifestyles. In general, the work of white women centered around the home, but in many colonies they were allowed to purchase and own land, as well as to become professionals in areas of work which later came to be considered "men's work." Any work they performed was considered as valuable, as important, and as useful as the work men performed. During the colonial period, white women possessed much more autonomy and decision-making power than at any other point in history. Unmarried white women, although never totally accepted, were more accepted within colonial society than in later years, notably after 1776.

As the colonies became more populous, the real and apparent autonomy of women began to be checked. For one thing, the same laws that stated that children must follow the condition of the mother, and that slaves could not own property, made it implicitly obvious that the only way the white man could secure inheritance rights of private property was through his free children. Thus white women became "marriage material." Gradually, the white woman was forced into the "woman's sphere" of marriage, motherhood, and the family. English law, on which the laws of the newly formed states were based, stated that:

> By marriage, the husband and wife are one person in law; that is, the very being, or legal existence of the woman is suspended during the marriage, or at least is incorpor-

> ated and consolidated into that of the husband under
> whose mind, protection and cover she performs every-
> thing.... A woman's personal property by marriage
> becomes absolutely her husband's which, at his death, he
> may leave entirely away from her.... By the marriage,
> the husband is absolutely master of the profits of the
> wife's lands during the coverture....[14]

Another of the laws stated that:

> The husband, by the old law, might give his wife
> moderate correction, as he is to answer for her mis-
> behavior. The law thought it reasonable to entrust him
> with this power of restraining her by domestic chastise-
> ment. The courts of law will still permit a husband to
> restrain a wife of her liberty in case of any gross
> misbehavior.[15]

White women were assigned a position inferior to that of white men on
the Chain, with the white man asserting his intellectual superiority.

During slavery, some white women drew parallels between their
position in society and that of the slaves. Mary Chesnut wrote that "There
is no slave, after all, like a wife.... Poor women, poor slaves.... All
married women, all children and girls who live in their fathers' houses
are slaves."[16] White women, holding a higher position within patriarchal
society as "marriage material," could enter into marriage as their "proper
sphere," whereas Black female slaves were not legally allowed to marry.
This was a major difference between them. While Black slave women
were being implicated with orangutans, white women were undergoing
salpingectomy. Hence, it was through marriage, motherhood, and the
family that white women derived their status. Anne Firor Scott notes that
"proximity, a thoughtful consideration of land and family connections,
or the painful fear of being an old maid were often the basis for
marriage."[17] Sarah Grimké concurred that white women were "taught to
regard marriage as the one thing needful, the only avenue of distinction."[18] Religion aided in placing the white woman on a pedestal.
Congregationalist Horace Bushnell[19] puts it thus:

> Let us have a place of quiet, and some quiet minds which
> the din of our public war never embroils. Let a little of
> the sweetness and purity, and, if we can have it, of simple
> religion of life remain. God made the woman to be a help
> for man, not to be a wrestler with him.[20]

The lives of white women were adversely affected by being assigned and restricted. They tried to conform to the "proper sphere," as Scott notes:

> Many women assumed that if they were unhappy or discontented in the "sphere to which God had appointed them" it must be their own fault and that by renewed effort they could do better.... Women whose families and friends thought them "spotless" were themselves convinced that their souls were in danger.... Such women were cast into deep depression when they gave way to a temper, slapped a child, or admonished a slave.[21]

More frequently, white women directed their anger at Black female slaves. It was often misdirected, as Chesnut notes:

> Under slavery we live surrounded by prostitutes, like patriarchs of old, our men lie in one house with their wives and concubines.... A magnate who runs a hideous Black harem with its consequences under the same roof with his lovely white wife, and his beautiful accomplished daughters...poses as the model of all human virtues to these poor women whom God and the laws have given him. From the height of his awful majesty, he scolds and thunders at them, as if he never did wrong in his life.[22]

Other evidence suggests that the wives of slaveholders felt intense relief when slavery ended. Two such wives are cited in the following example:

> "Free at last," cried one white woman when she heard of the Emancipation Proclamation. "If slavery were restored and every Negro on the American continent offered to me," wrote another, "I should spurn them. I should prefer poverty rather than assume again the cares and perplexities of ownership...."[23]

Another white woman later remarked, "Our burden of work and responsibility was simply staggering.... I was glad and thankful on my own account when slavery ended, and I ceased to belong body and soul to my negroes."[24]

Black and white women, it can be seen, had opposite oppressive positions. Their total dependence on white men was mutual. It is not surprising, then, that white women readily perceived that their confinement to a set of domestic roles lay at the heart of their subjection and that subtle rebellion and subversion appeared in Black female slave narratives "edited" by themselves, women of antislavery sentiment. The female slave narratives met the demands of a largely female audience: themselves fugitives and exiles in their "Common House of Bondage."

Authentic Black female slave narratives, such as Annie L. Burton's *Memories of Childhood's Slavery Days* and *Amanda Smith's Own Story*, are almost total in their identification with white women. They do not seem to confuse the covert or overt complicity and acquiescence of some white women with the often tyrannical and incestuous behavior of the master. The Black female slave narratives as written by Black and white women evidence the first workings out of the analogy between the oppression of Black women and the oppression of white women.

Travel accounts and journals written by such observers as Frances Kemble, Harriet Martineau, Mary Ames, and the Grimké sisters represented valiant efforts on the part of these women, often working in a hostile environment, to deal in print with the lives of Black slave women. They described female slaves' lives as workers both inside and outside the home, their lives as mothers and wives, and they did more than allude to their victimization at the hands of the planters. Their accounts were filled with the contradictions inherent in the nineteenth-century Cult of True Womanhood. Blinded by nineteenth-century nurturance ideology regarding motherhood, these women sometimes judged Black motherhood and childhood with much ambivalence. Inevitably, these women, despite their lofty ideas, often measured the Black family against current views of Christian morality and white ideals—not realities. Nevertheless, these women valiantly attempted to destroy the dominant myth that Black slave mothers were devoid of emotional attachments/bonds toward their children. In this area they succeeded immensely. This perspective proved invaluable for my classes. It has to be realized that the women we studied dealt with the contradictions of a society that held to a monogamous ideal, sanctity of the home, and "pure virtues" of womanhood that were being ruthlessly flaunted in the case of Black women. In a class like ours, it became very easy to criticize what we regarded as negative behavior (in these women seen as racism or more often cultural snobbery) and not so easy to deal with the positive (the fact that for a time, as the only individualized voices for Black women, these women were challenging the moral fabric of the society they lived in).

In her journal Fanny Kemble described the function of the Black family as "mere breeding, bearing, sucking and there an end." While it is true that the main task of the family in a slaveholding economy was reproducing the labor force, it is foolish to argue that the family served this purpose exclusively. Thus, it is no contradiction to say that the family functioned on several levels—biological, economic, social, and political. According to the Child narrative, the slave girl Linda noted that her grandmother bought her family's freedom by baking cookies at night. It appears that the slave family was an organized unit within the overall societal structure and was noticeably more ideologically divided after Reconstruction. At least production and the family were one under a slaveholding economy. The family seems to have been guided by an all-embracing singlemindedness of purpose (i.e., freedom), which Amanda Smith aptly notes. Work (for a purpose) did not heighten the fragmentation and alienation of families. For many slave families work was a means to achieving an end. A kind of individualism under slavery was nurtured by the slave family. Walker's *Jubilee* speaks to this, as does Nat Turner, who describes being encouraged by his family to develop his religious proclivities (to be a Moses). There was the sense that those slaves who were talented enough, ingenious enough, and versatile enough could work to buy their own and their families' freedom. Amanda Smith's conversion experience narrative records the concerted effort of Smith's mother and grandmother to "give" religion to their mistress so that she might begin to see the un-Christianity of slavery and free them—another testimony to the fact that slave families who developed their resources and their emotional support systems to work toward their freedom were intrinsically involved in transforming themselves and the world of the slaveholders.

Elizabeth Hyde Botume (*First Days Amongst the Contrabands*) documents the tremendous hardships endured by female slaves who had to combine fieldwork with childbearing. Critical reading of a variety of slavery documents supports this view: "Lots of times she's so tired she go to bed without eatin' nothin' herself." Still, she was being measured by "virtues" promulgated by the Cult of True Womanhood, as indicated by at least one adult daughter:

> We had been in the main very happy, she was a good mother to us, a woman of deep piety, anxious above all things to touch our hearts with a sense of religion.... Now, I was once more with my best friend on earth, and under her care.[25]

Mary Ames (*A New England Woman's Diary in Dixie in 1865*), a schoolteacher in South Carolina, writes of the hardworking reality of the freedwoman:

> ...we went into a cabin, where a woman was so busy at a cotton gin that she did not turn her head when she greeted us. We asked how much cotton she could gin a

day. 'Don' no, missis, no 'casion for to task myself now; Rabs gone.'[26]

And in another instance Ames, a white woman, implicitly recognizes her kinship with all women Black and white, in an oblique reference:

> Meeting after meeting was held to reconcile them [Blacks] to the changed and difficult conditions. On one occasion, when explanations only seemed to create greater antagonism, I ventured a remark, and was quickly told by Ishmael, their leader, that I had 'Better go into the house and attend to study,' thus showing early in his life as a freedman, that he had learned the proper sphere of woman.[27]

Angelina Grimké Weld's testimony on child rearing practices suggests the possibilities of communal childrearing:

> Persons who own plantations and yet live in cities often take children from their parents (slaves) as soon as they are weaned, and send them into the country; because they do not want the mother taken up by attendance upon her children, it being too valuable to the mistress. As a favor, she is in some cases, permitted to go to see them once a year.[28]

SUMMARY

The need to conceptualize a feminist perspective within which the female slaves can be studied is urgent. The story of slavery cannot be told without pursuing significant questions about slave women and their historical development.

NOTES

[1]Gerda Lerner, Preface to *Black Women in White America* (Scranton, Pa.: Hadden Craftsmen, Inc., 1972).

[2]Zora Neale Hurston, *Their Eyes Were Watching God* (Connecticut: Fawcett Publications, 1965), p. 18.

[3]Ibid., p. 156.

[4]J. H. Clarke and V. Harding, eds., *Slave Trade and Slavery* (New York: Holt, Rinehart and Winston, Inc., 1970), p. 34.

[5]Ibid., p. 37.

[6]Richard Erno, *Dominant Images of the Negro in the Antebellum South* (Ann Arbor: A Xerox Company, 1961), p. 62.

[7]W. D. Jordan, *White Over Black* (Chapel Hill: University of North Carolina Press, 1968), p. 458.

[8]Ibid., p. 150.

[9]William Goodell, *The American Slave Code* (New York: Negro University Press, 1968), p. 86.

[10]Gerda Lerner, ed., *Black Women in White America* (New York: Vintage Books, 1973), p. 86.

[11]Sarah Grimké, *Letters on the Equality of the Sexes and the Condition of Women* (1839; rpt. New York: Source Book Press, 1970), p. 17.

[12][Linda Brent], *Incidents in the Life of a Slave Girl*, ed. Lydia Maria Child (Boston: Published for the Author, 1861; Detroit: Negro History Press, 1969), p. 54.

[13]Gerda Lerner, *Black Women in White America*, pp. 34-35.

[14]Grimké, *Letters*, pp. 75, 79, 80.

[15]Ibid., p. 78.

[16]Anne Firor Scott, *The Southern Lady* (Chicago: University of Chicago Press, 1970), pp. 50-51.

[17]Ibid., p. 24.

[18]Ibid., p. 62.

[19]Horace Bushnell (1802-76) was a minister at North Church, Hartford, Connecticut (1833-59), whose works helped shape modern religious thought.

[20]Ronald Hogeland, "'The Female Appendage': Feminine Life Styles in America, 1820-1860," in *Our American Sisters*, ed. J. E. Friedman and W. G. Shade (Boston: Allyn and Bacon, 1976), p. 138.

[21]Scott, *The Southern Lady*, p. 11-13.

[22]Ibid., pp. 52-53.

[23]Hogeland, "The Female Appendage," in *Our American Sisters*, p. 157.

[24]Scott, *The Southern Lady*, p. 49.

[25]Elizabeth Hyde Botume, *First Days Amongst the Contrabands* (New York: Arno Press, 1968).

[26]Mary Ames, *A New England Woman's Diary in Dixie in 1865* (Norwood, Mass.: Plimpton Press, Springfield, 1906), pp. 120-21.

[27]Ibid., p. 121.

[28]Testimony of Angelina Grimké Weld, in Theodore D. Weld, *American Slavery As It Is: Testimony of a Thousand Witnesses* (New York: American Anti-Slavery Society, 1839).

BIBLIOGRAPHY OF FEMALE SLAVE NARRATIVES

Slave narratives are a badly neglected genre. The primary materials are scattered and, for the most part, undervalued. The best resource to date is Marion Wilson Starling's unpublished doctoral dissertation "The Black Slave Narrative: Its Place in American Literary History" (1946), on microfilm at New York University. She cited a figure of 6,006 records of narratives collected, whether filed or unfiled. What follows is a selective list of female narratives.

Aunt Sally; or, The Cross The Way to Freedom. Narrative of the Slave Life and Purchase of the Mother of Reverend Isaac Williams of Detroit, Michigan. Cincinnati: Western Tract and Book Society, 1859. At Schomburg. This narrative was used as a Sunday School text; is labeled "bogus"; records the Uncle Tom–type suffering, saintly slave; is full of self-deprecating and pious sentiments.

Blake, Jane. *Memoirs of Margaret Jane Blake.* Related to Sarah R. Levering, Baltimore, whose father had owned Jane Blake. Philadelphia: Innes and Son, 1897. At Library of Congress.

Brown, Jane. *Narrative of the Life of Jane Brown and Her Two Children.* Related to the Reverend G. W. Offley. Hartford: Published for G. W. Offley, 1880. At Schomburg.

Burton, Annie L. *Memories of Childhood's Slavery Days.* Boston, 1919. At Schomburg. Retrospective, very ambivalent; focus on the "great sunny days of the South"; simultaneously on the suffering.

Dinah. *The Story of Dinah, as Related to John Hawkins Simpson, after Her Escape from the Horrors of the Virginia Slave Trade, to London.* London: A. W. Bennett, 1863. At Library of Congress.

Dormigold, Kate. *A Slave Girl's Story, The Autobiography of Kate Dormigold.* Brooklyn, New York, 1898. At Library of Congress.

Dubois, Silvia (Now 116 Years Old). *A Biography of the Slave Who Whipped Her Mistress and Gained Her Freedom.* New Jersey: Published by C. W. Larison, M. D. Ringoes, 1883.

Eldridge, Elleanor. *Elleanor's Second Book.* Edited by Frances Whipple Green. Providence, 1839. At Library of Congress. There are five books; except for the first one (which tells Elleanor's story), the rest are small volumes of short stories written to make money for Eldridge.

————. *Memoirs of Elleanor Eldridge.* Providence, 1843. At Spingarn-Moorland Collection.

————. *Memoirs.* Providence, 1846. At Boston Public Library.

Elizabeth, A Colored Minister of the Gospel, Born in Slavery. Philadelphia, 1889.

Griffiths (Brown), Mattie. *Autobiography of a Female Slave.* New York, 1857. Reads much like *Uncle Tom's Cabin;* the woman is a mulatto female; the little Eva figure is a young master; heavily sentimental. Also labeled "bogus" by many. Like Child's narrative, this is a reprint issued by Negro History Press. Its authenticity is vouched for by a J. S. Redfield, Clerk of the Southern District Court of New York.

Jacobs, Harriet (Linda Brent). *Incidents in the Life of a Slave Girl, Written by Herself.* Edited by L. Maria Child. Boston, 1861; rpt. Detroit: Negro History Press, 1969; New York: Harcourt Brace Jovanovich, 1973. At Schomburg. Interesting for its romantic-realistic elements; considered by many to be a "bogus" narrative.

Jones, Jane *Narrative.* Related to the Reverend G. W. Offley. Published for G. W. Offley. At Schomburg.

Kleckley, Elizabeth. *Behind the Scenes; or, Thirty Years a Slave and Four Years in the White House as Mrs. Lincoln's Maid.* New York: G. W. Carleton and Company, 1868. At Schomburg.

Lee, Jarena. *Religious Experience and Journal of Mrs. Jarena Lee, Giving an Account of Her Call to Preach the Gospel.* Philadelphia, 1849.

Parker, Janie. *Janie Parker, The Fugitive.* Related to Mrs. Emily Pierson, N.p., 1851. At New York Public Library.

Louisa Picquet, The Octoroon: A Tale of Southern Life. Published by Rev. H. Mattison. New York, 1861.

Prince, Nancy. *A Narrative of the Life and Travels of Mrs. Nancy Prince.* 2d ed. Boston, 1853.

Smith, Amanda. *An Autobiography of Mrs. Amanda Smith, the Colored Evangelist.* Chicago: Meyer and Bros., 1893. At Boston Public Library. A conversion experience narrative. Also published as *Amanda Smith's Own Story* (1893); previously published by a Rev. M. W. Taylor, D.D., *The Life and Mission of a Slave Girl,* copy extant.

———. *Amanda Smith's Own Story.* Boston, 1903. At Boston Public Library.

Spear, Chloe. *Narrative of Chloe Spear.* By a "Lady of Boston." Boston: American Anti-Slavery Society, 1832. At New York Historical Society.

Taylor, Susie King. *Reminiscences of My Life in Camp with the 33rd United States Colored Troops, Late 1st S.C. Volunteers.* Boston, 1902.

Tomlinson, Jane. "The First Fugitive Slave Case of Record in Ohio."

Truth, Sojourner. *Narrative of Sojourner Truth, a Northern Slave, Emancipated from Bodily Servitude by the State of New York, in 1828.* Narrated to Olive Gilbert, including Sojourner Truth's *Book of Life,* and a dialogue. Boston, 1850. At Library of Congress.

————. Boston: Published for Sojourner Truth, 1853. At Schomburg.

————. With introduction by Harriet B. Stowe. Boston, 1855. At Library of Congress.

————. *Narrative of Sojourner Truth, a Bondswoman of Olden Time, Emancipated by the New York Legislature in the Early Part of the Present Century.* Edited by Mrs. Francis W. Titus. Battle Creek: *Review and Herald* Office, 1884. At Massachusetts State Library.

Tubman, Harriet. *Scenes in the Life of Harriet Tubman.* As told by Sarah Bradford. New York and Auburn, 1869. At Schomburg.

Wheatley, Phillis. *Letters of Phillis Wheatley, the Negro Slave Poet of Boston.* Boston: Printed by John Wilson and Son, 1864. At Schomburg. Also printed in the *Proceedings of the Colonial Society of Massachusetts,* for 1864; and in Woodson, Carter, *Mind of the Negro Prior to 1860,* in the Introduction.

Useful Accounts

Billington, Ray Allen, ed. *A Free Negro in the Slave Era: The Journal of Charlotte L. Forten.* New York: Collier Books, 1953.

Botume, Elizabeth Hyde. *First Days Amongst the Contrabands.* New York: Arno Press, 1968.

Kemble, Frances Ann. *Journal of a Resident on a Georgia Plantation in 1838-1839.* London: Longmans, 1863. Contains seven narrative sketches. Currently a paperback reissue.

Martineau, Harriet. *Society in America.* 2 vols. London, 1832. Contains eleven narrative sketches.

Mott, Abigail Field. *Biographical Sketches and Interesting Anecdotes of Persons of Color.* New York: Printed by M. Day, 1825. Contains forty narrative sketches.

Stowe, Harriet B. *Key to Uncle Tom's Cabin....* Boston: John P. Jewett, 1853. Contains twenty narratives sketches.

9

Debunking Sapphire: Toward a Non-Racist and Non-Sexist Social Science

PATRICIA BELL SCOTT

INTRODUCTION

The term "Sapphire" is frequently used to describe an age-old image of Black women. The caricature of the dominating, emasculating Black woman is one which historically has saturated both the popular and scholarly literature. The purpose of this paper is to debunk the "Sapphire" caricature as it has been projected in American social science. By exposing the racist and sexist underpinnings of this stereotype, one hopes that more students and scholars might be sensitized and encouraged to contribute to the development of a nonracist and nonsexist social science.

The novice to the subject of Black women's studies generally encounters feelings of frustration...as she or he begins to explore the literature in quest of more knowledge relevant to the experience of being Black and female in America. One is almost overwhelmed with the depth and extent of the intellectual void that exists among social science scholars concerning the life experiences of Black women. Those persons who somehow manage to endure the frustrations involved in unearthing "bits and pieces" of data about Black women are further exacerbated by the following observations:

1. Despite the fact that Black women have always played important roles in American society, they have been almost totally ignored by students of American society and human behavior. From reading the literature, one might easily develop the impression that Black women

have never played any role in this society, and that they represent only a minute percentage of the total American population.
2. The experiences of Black women in both a historical and a contemporary sense have been discussed from a very narrow perspective. Their lives have been examined from a "problems" framework. As a result of this approach, the student begins to see the experiences of Black women as being limited in nature, and certainly in no way comparable to the "life and times of great white men."
3. The themes, hypotheses, and images used to explicate the experiences of Black women have not been significantly altered in the past forty years. As a result of the stagnant nature of the literature in this area, the beginning student might hastily yet erroneously conclude that the story of Black women in America is one which is uninteresting and outworn. Therefore, there is no point in delving for more insight into the dynamics of this situation.

These observations reflect a pervasive racist and sexist bias in social science scholarship. The more one begins to investigate the theoretical frameworks, concepts, methodologies, and jargon of American social science, the more glaring and ungrounded the racist and sexist assumptions become.

TRENDS IN THE INVESTIGATION
OF THE BLACK AND FEMALE EXPERIENCES

Until recently, most of the research related to Black women that has received any attention has been done by white male sociologists, psychologists, and historians who have been interested in race relations theory or the social structure of the Black family. From the literature several trends can be identified—the most popular trend being the emergence of an abundance of literature related to the role of Black women as matriarchs. The Black matriarchy thesis or perspective is representative of a "social problems" approach to the Black experience which became popular in the 1960s in the work of Moynihan (1965), though the notion of Black matriarchy has its origins in the early works of DuBois (1908) and Frazier (1939).

According to contemporary Black matriarchy theorists, Black women have had, and continue to have, an unnatural dominant role in Black families, and this role has had deleterious effects upon Black society (Bernard, 1966; Moynihan, 1965; Rainwater, 1970). For example, one social psychologist has attributed the occurrence of juvenile delinquency, self-hatred, low intelligence quotient scores, cultural deprivation, crimes against persons, and schizophrenia among Blacks to the alleged existence of a matriarchal family structure (Pettigrew, 1964).

Within the last several years, the Black matriarchy theorists have become subject to a barrage of criticisms. Numerous scholars have cited the gross problems in the statistical data, inferences, social concepts, instruments, and methodologies used in support of the Black matriarchy theory (Billingsley, 1969; Herzog, 1970; Hill, 1971; Staples, 1970). Though several of the critics of the Black matriarchy theory have indicted its proponents as blatant racists, few scholars have given attention to the fact that the Black matriarchy theorists have also been blatantly sexist!

At numerous conferences on the Black family and Black women, I have heard the statement made (usually by Black men) that "the Black matriarchy theorists are merely trying to victimize and ostracize the Black man by saying that he can't take care of his family." Given the predominantly white, middle-class orientation of most Black matriarchy theorists, it is not difficult to agree with this statement. However, at the same time that these theorists ostracize the Black man and label him as deviant, effeminate, and passive, Black women are also ostracized and labeled as doubly deviant, masculine, and unnaturally superior. These attitudes reflect heterosexist, as well as sexist, assumptions.

Another approach to the study of Black women which has emerged in recent times is the investigation of the "life and times" of prominent Black women (Boanes, 1975). Proponents of this approach have concentrated almost exclusively upon the public lives of nationally known Black women such as Mary Church Terrell, Mary McLeod Bethune, Ida Wells Barnett, Harriet Tubman, and Sojourner Truth. Implicit in this "life and times" approach is a class bias. Though it is often argued that more papers and data concerning prominent Black women are available for research, the prevailing or resulting impression is that Black working-class or low-income women are inconsequential to the American experience. Therefore, racist, sexist, and class biases are perpetuated in American historiography. All this is not to say that the lives of prominent Black women are not important; however, their lives represent only a few of the least generalizable circumstances that Black women have experienced. Most Black women have not been able to rise to prominence.

Another perspective which has been and remains popular among sociologists is the study of Black women in relationship to their familial roles. Studies representative of this perspective have dealt with the economic, political, and psychological experiences of Black women in the roles of mother, wife, and daughter (Rainwater, 1970). Thus, research which has grown out of this perspective has focused upon the economic difficulties of the female-headed household, and the political powerlessness and psychological problems of the married and unmarried Black woman. This approach completely disavows the existence of nonfamilial roles and role-related conflict among Black women; e.g., Black women as activists, politicians, religious leaders, athletes, and artists have remained unexplored.

SPECIFIC INDICATORS OF RACISM AND SEXISM IN THE SOCIAL SCIENCES

Several indicators or by-products of racism and sexism in social science scholarship can be identified. These indicators include:

1. *An emphasis upon the Black mother-son relationship and the impact of this dyadic relationship on the developing Black male personality.* Virtually no attention has been given to the Black father-daughter dyad. Implicit in the neglect of this relationship by researchers is the assumption that the sex role and personality development of Black females is unimportant. Also, in order to broaden our understanding of the female personality, it would be logical for social scientists to look more closely at mother-daughter relationships.

2. *The use of an overtly sexist social science lingo.* Rossi (1965) has pointed out the double standard which exists in the way social situations or phenomena involving men and women are differentially described. For example, when the mother-child dyad is dissolved or impaired in some way, the term "maternal deprivation" is used to describe the situation; however, when the father-child dyad is dissolved or impaired in some manner, the term "father absence" is generally used instead of "paternal deprivation." "Father absence" sounds less harmful than "maternal deprivation." Numerous researchers have cited other ways in which social concepts have been defined in terms favorable to the masculine tradition; e.g., the definitions of power, aggressiveness, and independence have a strong bias in favor of the male.

3. *The use of instruments biased against the culturally different, women, and working-class or low-income people.* Instruments such as the Minnesota Multi-phasic Personality Inventory (MMPI) and the Stanford-Binet and Wechsler IQ tests, and various Masculinity-Femininity (M-F) Scales, have been used to measure the psychosocial components of several "out-groups," and generally these instruments yield data which describe Blacks and women as deviant in some manner. Again, the real problems with these instruments are related to the conceptual frameworks upon which they are based—these frameworks being biased in terms of race, sex, and class in many instances (Pleck, 1975).

4. *The tendency to use male subjects in studies of a nonfamilial nature.* Much of the literature in the sociology of work and occupations, and achievement motivation, has been done on male subjects (Hochschild, 1971). Implicit in this tendency is the acceptance of the adage that "a woman's place is in the home"; therefore, there is no reason to investigate the experiences of women who are not in the family setting. Women who are in "a man's world," or the labor force, are generally considered to be abnormal or atypical, and thus unworthy of scholarly attention. Until recently most studies of Blacks in business and professions (excluding education) were concerned primarily with men.

5. *A preponderance of social science literature being written by men.* Prior to the 1950s, Black men were the primary writers in the area of Black family studies; however, since the late 1950s and early 1960s, white men have been most prolific in this area. It should be noted that the emergence of the white male scholar in this area is directly correlated with the popularity of the Black matriarchy myth. Fortunately, since the late 1960s and early 1970s, several aware and sensitive scholars have appeared on the horizon (Ryan, 1971; Ladner, 1972; Jackson, 1973; Staples, 1973). Such persons have refused to accept without question common notions about the experiences of Blacks and women in American society.

RESEARCH PRIORITIES AND ACTION-ORIENTED STRATEGIES FOR CENTURY III

Given the state of the social literature, there is a wealth of unexplored areas which must be investigated during the next century. There must be more examinations of the Black and female experience that are sensitive to the ways in which racism and sexism bear upon Black women. This would entail the development of theoretical frameworks that are not based upon patriarchal sentiments that view both Blacks and women as deviants or outsiders to the American experience. We can no longer allow the use of what Jackson refers to as a "Mother-God psychoanalytical paradigm" which attempts to explain how sick Black women really are.[1]

There must be more examination of Black women who are participants in nonfamilial roles. Such data would help to fill the gap in the literature on the sociology of work, occupations, and achievement motivation. Also, by exploring the roles of Black women in other societal institutions, we can learn more about the workings of racism and sexism at all levels of the American system.

There must be more exploration of the mental and physical health problems of Black women in all phases of the life cycle. Because Black women represent more than 50 percent of the total Black population, some knowledge of the social, psychological, and economic problems of this segment of the population would be helpful to public policymakers in designing health care and social services for the Black community.

There must be more exploration of Black father-daughter dyads and Black mother-daughter dyads, as well as other female-to-female relationships, both within and without the family group. It is only when we can understand the dynamics of these relationships that we can speak more precisely about female socialization in the Black community.

There must be more study of Black women in all strata of American society. We must know what the experiences of the masses are, in order to speak about the history of Black women. This will also entail a redefinition of several social concepts, such as power, weakness, and aggressiveness.

There must be more careful consideration of the implications of demographic trends of the Black community. For example, the imbalance in the sex ratio is one factor that will definitely influence the psychosocial experiences of Black women. Given the fact that there will not be an opportunity for each Black woman to enter into a permanent interpersonal relationship with a Black man, psychologists and other professionals must help to develop alternative support systems.

There must be more empirical and cross-cultural investigations of the life experiences of women. In other words, we cannot speak of a psychology or sociology or anthropology of women, if the frameworks of these perspectives are applicable to white. middle-class, or professional women only. Thus, those persons engaged in sex-role research or the teaching of courses on women or Blacks must make certain that they address the situation and experiences of nonwhite and ethnic women. Scholars and students in the humanities should also address the treatment of women in literature, art, and music, as well as the impact of women upon society as artists, musicians, and writers.

These research priorities must be coupled with some very practical, action-oriented strategies. These strategies should involve the sensitizing of members of this society to the "roots" and workings of overt, covert, and institutional racism and sexism. Black men must be made aware of the fact that sexism is not only a white problem, and white feminists must also be made aware of the fact that racism and class bias are not peculiar to white men only.

More Blacks and women should be encouraged to become scholars in Black women's studies, in order that a different perspective might be heard in academic circles. That is not to say that whites or men are to be discouraged from participation in this area; however, all persons engaged in the investigation of the Black and/or female experience in America should be encouraged to raise questions about the nature of many commonly held assumptions.

The movement of more Blacks and women into traditionally male-dominated areas, most notably academia, should result in some changes in the goals of professional social science organizations, and in the literature which is published in journals. Racism and sexism pervade American scholarship and are reflected in the preponderance of men in positions of power and authority in professional organizations and on editorial boards. This merely reflects the racist and sexist fabric of American society.

Organizations of parents and other interested groups should be encouraged to engage in discussions related to the media images of Black women. Discussions of this nature should heighten our awareness of the sexist and racist overtones in various television series and commercial advertisements.

In summary, as we examine the past two centuries of the American experience, there is no way in which the mark of the dual oppression of racism and sexism can be ignored. These "isms" can be likened to a cancer which has grown virtually uninhibited in a fertile host. As we begin Century III, we must work toward the dissolution of race, sex, and class bias in American institutions. It is only through the eradication of these "isms" that we can move toward a more humanistic and yet realistic philosophy of social science, a social science which will itself help to transform society. I challenge you to assist me in debunking Sapphire!

NOTE

[1]In the article "Black Women in a Racist Society" (listed in the references), Jacquelyne Jackson contends that most of the research and investigation into the lives of Black women have been based upon a conceptual framework that is biased against women. When this kind of framework is used, behavior which is feminine or female-oriented is judged abnormal. When Black families have been studied, social problems are always traced to the existence of so-called negative, female/motherly, and/or immoral influences.

REFERENCES

Bernard, J. *Marriage and Family Among Negroes.* Englewood Cliffs, N.J.: Prentice-Hall, 1966.

Billingsley, A. *Black Families in White America*. Englewood Cliffs, N.J.: Prentice-Hall, 1969.

Boanes, P. "Some Notes Toward Black Women's Historiography." Paper presented at the sixtieth annual meeting of the Association for the Study of Afro-American Life and History, Atlanta, October 1975.

DuBois, W. E. B. *The Negro American Family*. Atlanta: Atlanta University Press, 1908.

Frazier, E. *The Negro Family in the United States*. Chicago: University of Chicago Press, 1939.

Herzog, E. "Social Stereotypes and Social Research." *Journal of Social Issues* 26 (1970):109–25.

Hochschild, A. "A Review of Sex Role Research." *American Journal of Sociology* 78 (1971):1011–23.

Jackson, J. "Black Women in a Racist Society." In *Racism and Mental Health*. Edited by C. Willie, B. Kramer, and B. Brown. Pittsburgh: University of Pittsburgh Press, 1972.

Ladner, J. *Tomorrow's Tomorrow*. Garden City, N.Y.: Anchor Books, 1972.

Moynihan, D. *The Negro Family: A Case for National Action*. Washington, D.C.: Government Printing Office, 1965.

Pettigrew, T. *A Profile of the Negro American*. Princeton, N.J.: D. Van Nostrand, 1964.

Pleck, J. "Masculinity-Femininity: Current and Alternative Paradigms." *Sex Roles* 1 (1975):161–78.

Rainwater, L. *Behind Ghetto Walls*. Chicago: Aldine, 1970.

Rossi, A. "Equality Between the Sexes: An Immodest Proposal." In *The Woman in America*. Edited by R. Lifton. Westport, Conn.: Greenwood Press, 1977.

Ryan, W. *Blaming the Victim*. New York: Vintage Books, 1971.

Staples, R. "The Myth of the Black Matriarchy." *The Black Scholar* 1 (1970):8–16.

Staples, R. *The Black Woman in America: Sex, Marriage and the Family*. Chicago: Nelson-Hall, 1973.

Two Representative Issues in Contemporary Sociological Work on Black Women

ELIZABETH HIGGINBOTHAM

The past decade has seen a growing number of sociological works on Black women, including considerable work in social psychology. Two current trends can be identified in this contemporary body of sociological literature which foster a more realistic investigation of Black women's experiences than was previously the case: refuting the Black matriarchy myth, and redefining Black female identity.

BATTLING THE MYTHS

Articles clarifying the situation of Black women provide additional insights into past studies and often present demographic data exposing previous distortions.[1] One of the best of these articles is "Black Women in a Racist Society," by Jacquelyne Jackson, which provides a good review of previous literature and reveals the negative ways in which Black women have been viewed.[2] Jackson focuses particularly on questioning the validity of the matriarchy theory. Researchers, according to Jackson, have taken a "social-disorganizational approach" to Black people in general (i.e., focusing on the problems as evidence of the weaknesses of the group). Occasionally, researchers do recognize socioeconomic factors in their analysis of Black men, but they fail to do so with Black women. Jackson does mention in a positive manner articles by Frances Beale and by Jean Carey Bond and Pat Peery which call attention to the fact that both racism and sexism influence the status of Black women, and argues, as they do, in favor of putting the matriarchy theory to rest and focusing on the double victimization of Black women.[3]

The power of Jackson's article lies in her presentation and analysis of demographic data. Taking issue with past researchers, many of whom overreacted to or misinterpreted the same data, Jackson assesses the importance of the data by placing the figures in a social context. She puts great emphasis, for example, on the sex ratio (the number of Black males per 100 females), which in 1970 was 90.8, that is, about 91 Black males for every 100 Black females. This situation has important implications for social relationships between the sexes, marital status, and the shape of the family. Taking this type of demographic data into account, Jackson defines the female-headed family as an adaptation to larger social structural forces.

Furthermore, Jackson avoids the controversy that attempts to argue about which sex has suffered more. Instead, she believes that it is crucial to focus on the systematic mistreatment of both sexes. It is essential to address the *sources* of the problem rather than remain focused on the additional ways in which Black men and women hurt each other because they cannot attack the larger system. Jackson concludes:

> Black women, the most disadvantaged group in the United States, as evidenced by their unenviable occupational, educational, employment, income, and male-availability levels, have been "messed over" by distorters of reality. . . . This distortion successfully continues the oppression of Black women, and indirectly Black men, thereby masking the real racist and sexist culprits (with the latter being joined by some Black men as well).

Robert Staples's book, *Black Women in America*, summarizes much of the literature in the field and attempts to present Black women in a more positive light.[4] The book is disappointing because it fails to present new material and to provide a good theoretical framework. Staples's work also tends to focus on Black women's family roles and sexual life and gives little attention to their economic situation.

Other works clarifying the situation of Black women are often not successful. Occasionally, researchers are involved in arguing the issues within the framework already defined by dominant-culture social scientists. It is important to be able to abandon a defensive posture and introduce additional issues or a wider context into the debate. There is also a need to put more energy into empirical work, rather than into more summary articles.

"AND AIN'T I A WOMAN?"

A narrow definition of womanhood has never reflected the lives of Black or other racial minority women, or those of many white working-class women in the United States. Instead, these women, who often fail to conform to "appropriate" sex roles, have been pictured as, and made to feel, inadequate—even though, as women, they possess traits recognized as positive when held by men in the wider society. Such women are stigmatized because their lack of adherence to expected gender roles is seen as a threat to the value system.[5] As Angela Davis noted in an analysis of Black women in slavery: "In order to function as slave, the Black woman had to be annulled as woman, that is, as woman in her historical stance of wardship under the entire male hierarchy. The sheer force of things rendered her equal to her man."[6] Just as successful businesswomen have been defined out of the sex, Black women who have taken on economic and social roles to aid in the survival of their families are viewed as having given up some of their womanhood. Black women have not been praised by dominant-culture sociologists for their strong role in aiding family stability; on the contrary, they have been strongly criticized.[7]

Currently, dominant-culture families and women's roles are undergoing significant changes. The experiences of Black, working-class, and other nondominant-culture women can play an important part in their reformulation. Yet, before this can actually take place, it is essential to overcome the legacy of misunderstanding Black women (perceiving them either as inadequate or as superwomen) which has been fostered by biased research.[8]

Often researchers who seek to correct stereotypes of Black women are primarily involved in addressing issues which relate to the nature of Black womanhood. Once one abandons the deviant perspective used by most dominant-culture sociologists, where does one seek an alternative framework? Joyce Ladner, in *Tomorrow's Tomorrow*, explores the world of Black adolescent women and finds that they do not totally accept the values of the dominant society.[9] Their models for womanhood and patterns of behavior are shaped by their specific environment (in this case, a low-income housing project in St. Louis) and the historical experience of Black woman passed on from generation to generation, as well as the dominant-culture norms and values to which they are exposed. Even though Ladner's analysis does not fully explore the interaction of all these factors, she is successful in revealing the women's reactions to institutional racism:

I have endeavored to analyze their present lives as they emerge out of these historical forces (i.e., particular historical moment), for they have been involved in a strong reciprocal relationship in that they have been shaped by the forces of oppression but have also exerted their influence so as to alter certain of these patterns.[10]

Approaching the subject with a wider perspective than narrow cultural definitions afford, Ladner is able to present the ways in which Black women adapt to their environment. Such an approach presents their strengths rather than focusing on their weaknesses. Black women are not merely passive persons being acted upon by oppressive forces. Nevertheless, the zealousness with which Ladner demonstrates the women's adaptability to their harsh reality does not give enough attention to the sheer pain of living lives with few options.

In our eagerness to counteract the negative stereotypes, we must not create a different one, which also fails to reflect accurately the varied lives of Black women. Even though many Black women are able to overcome difficult situations, Black women are not "superwomen" devoid of needs and emotions. *All Our Kin*, by Carol Stack, indicates clearly that although Black families have developed survival strategies, which do satisfy certain needs, other needs are left unmet.[11] Good empirical studies, then, must reflect the diversity of Black women's experiences.

Bonnie Dill, in "The Dialectics of Black Womanhood," discusses the need for a well-documented historical framework and the need for an analytical framework which would focus on the complex relations Black women have in different spheres of society.[12] It is not useful for a researcher to proceed as if Black women existed only within Black culture. It is much more productive to do thoughtful empirical work which closely observes Black women's participation in both the dominant culture and Black subgroups. This type of empirical work is part of the groundwork essential for developing a theoretical perspective (or set of perspectives) addressing the roles of Black women in the family, in peer groups, in the wider Black community, and in the larger society. Dill, for example, examines the multiple roles of Black women when she investigates their participation in the labor force.

Lena Wright Meyers does not theorize about the self-esteem of Black women but investigates it. In "Black Women and Self-Esteem," she demonstrates that a high proportion of Black women regard Black women that they know (40 percent) or Black women in general (54.4 percent) as their reference group.[13] She notes: "Self-esteem is a... process in which Black women form their own reference group." In her work

Meyers provides us with insights into one way the subgroup exists within the larger scheme of values. Research depicting Black women as resourceful in the face of difficulties and proud of themselves is to be appreciated. Yet the current state of the field calls for more empirical work and the development of a perspective which seeks to reveal the complex lives of Black women. Any framework which attempts to do this must be equipped to handle positive and negative findings. The reality presented in the demographic data on employment, educational attainment, and income levels must be explored to explain how Black women cope with their situation. One does not have to return to the old social problems approach. Nevertheless, focusing on resourcefulness and adaptability cannot overshadow the fact that most Black women have difficult environments to contend with— with resultant stresses. High rates of hypertension, poor health records, and increasing rates of suicide have to be discussed within the context of poverty, racism, sexism, and other barriers.[14] Only through addressing the varied lives of Black women can we approach a view of womanhood which is inclusive. Furthermore, we can pinpoint the areas where change is needed.

NOTES

[1]Examples of such articles are Mae C. King, "The Politics of Sexual Stereotypes," in *Black Scholar* 4 (March–April 1973): 12–23, and Charmeynne D. Nelson, "Myths about Black Women Workers in Modern America," in *Black Scholar* 6 (March 1975): 11–15.

[2]Jacquelyne Jackson, "Black Women in a Racist Society," in *Racism and Mental Health*, ed. Charles Willie, Bernard Kramer, and Bentram Brown (Pittsburgh: University of Pittsburgh Press, 1972), pp. 185–268.

[3]See Frances Beale, "Double Jeopardy: To Be Black and Female," in *The Black Woman*, ed. Toni Cade (New York: New American Library, 1970), pp. 90–100; Jean Carey Bond and Pat Peery, "Is the Black Male Castrated?" in Cade, pp. 115–18.

[4]Robert Staples, *The Black Woman in America: Sex, Marriage and the Family* (Chicago: Nelson-Hall Publishers, 1973).

[5]Lucille Duberman, *Gender and Sex in Society* (New York: Praeger, 1975), p. 20.

[6]Angela Davis, "Reflections on the Black Woman's Role in the Community of Slaves," in *Black Scholar* 3 (December 1971):2–15.

[7]See Jackson, pp. 185–203, for documentation.

[8]Sources which hint of the "superwoman" bias include Cynthia Epstein, "The Positive Effects of the Multiple Negative: Explaining the Success of Black Professional Women," in *Changing Women in a Changing Society*, ed. Joan Huber (Chicago: University of Chicago Press, 1973), pp. 150–73, and Inez Smith Reid, *"Together" Black Women* (New York: Emerson Hall, 1971).

[9]Joyce Ladner, *Tomorrow's Tomorrow* (New York: Anchor, 1972).

[10]Ibid., p. 265.

[11]Carol Stack, *All Our Kin* (New York: Harper Colophon, 1970).

[12]Bonnie Dill, "The Dialectics of Black Womanhood," *Signs: Journal of Women in Culture and Society* 4, no. 3 (Spring 1979):343–55.

[13]Lena Wright Meyers, "Black Women and Self-Esteem, in *Another Voice*, ed. Marcia Millman and Rosabeth Kanter (New York: Anchor, 1975), pp. 240–50 (quote on p. 247).

[14]Black Women's Community Development Foundation, *Mental and Physical Health Problems of Black Women* (Washington, D.C.: 1975).

Group at Tuskegee Institute, 1906.

Section Four

Creative Survival: Preserving Body, Mind, and Spirit

Black Women's Health:
Notes for a Course

BEVERLY SMITH

The health of Black women is a subject of major importance for those of us who are committed to learning, teaching, and writing about our sisters. Exploring this topic is a way of discovering how we are broken physically and mentally in this oppressive society and also of finding out how we have struggled and survived.

The ideas and resources in this syllabus have been developed during the past four years as part of my involvement in the feminist movement and the women's health movement. My participation has included leading workshops on Black and Third World women's health issues at a number of conferences and working in the Combahee River Collective, a Black feminist organization, and in the Boston Committee to End Sterilization Abuse. My experiences teaching courses on Women and Health and on Black Americans and the Health Care System have also contributed to the syllabus. The inclusion of imaginative literature results from the success and pleasure I have had in using such materials in my courses. I have found that Black women writers, in their efforts to tell the truth about our lives, necessarily deal with health. Their works are extraordinarily valuable, much more so than most articles in medical journals, because they are vivid, whole, and accessible to all types of students.

A course similar to the one designed here would be valuable for a variety of students. Those who are preparing to become health workers or who are already working in health care might find it especially useful. I think the students for whom it would be most meaningful would be

Black and other Third World women. I have found that one of the most exciting aspects of teaching courses on women's health has been experiencing how we, as women, can interact with and augment the material being studied. Black women would be able to bring the richness of their lives to such a course. The course focuses almost entirely on Black women because this is the subject with which I am most familiar. I have found that other Third World women also see such material as very relevant to their own experiences and needs. I think the adding of other resources on Third World women in the United States and abroad to this course would greatly increase its appeal and usefulness. White women also seem to enjoy and benefit from discussion of these issues.

The course might be offered as an alternative to the more standard (and usually much more white) women's health courses given by women's studies programs or by other college departments. It should also fit comfortably in Black studies departments. Another possibility would be to take such a course out of the usual academic setting and into the various communities to which it relates. Shelters for battered women, drug and alcoholism treatment programs that serve Third World women, women's centers, and community centers in Black neighborhoods are all potential locations. There are many exciting possibilities. I can envision a version of this course being offered at a neighborhood health center with both workers and consumers participating.

Readings are often listed under more than one heading, for several reasons. One is to provide ideas about the different ways in which they may be used and combined. Another is that the distinctions among topics are not rigid. There is a good deal of overlap and, in approaching these materials, one should be open to the connections that can be made among them. This interrelationship may be indicative of the holistic way in which feminists view health and all of life. For example, the strict distinction made in Western, male medicine between mind and body is a distortion of reality. "It Happened on My Birthday," written by a young Black woman who was sterilized, though it is listed under "Reproductive Health," could just as appropriately be included in the resources on mental health. Similarly, in discussing violence against Black women, the devastating emotional effects must be considered along with the physical.

The greatest shortcoming in the following materials is the frequent absence of awareness that Black women's health is affected by sexism, racism, and class position. In many cases, instead of insights into this complexity we have the bare bones of facts or the frustrating hints and guesses of a partial analysis—for example, one that comprehends racism but not sexism, heterosexism, or class oppression. There is not a single article which provides a comprehensive analysis of all these factors as they relate to health. I see the following, though it is in the form of a syllabus, as an initial attempt at gathering the concepts which would be necessary for such an analysis.

THE POLITICS OF BLACK WOMEN'S HEALTH

The poor health of Black women can be documented in a number of ways. We die sooner than white women; our deaths from pregnancy and childbirth are several times higher; and our death rates from a number of diseases are also higher. These facts clearly indicate that our political position as Black women affects our health. The effects of racism, sexism, and class oppression make us less healthy and also deprive us of decent health care. Several of the articles describe how, as Black women, we are often singled out for especially brutal "treatment" —e.g., forced sterilization and experimentation—while others deal with unavailability of care of any kind. A careful consideration of the issues raised by these readings is essential background for the rest of the course.

Alexander, Daryl. "A Montgomery Tragedy: The Relf Family Refused to Be the Nameless Victims of Involuntary Sterilization." *Essence* (September 1973):42ff.

"Crimes in the Clinic: A Report on Boston City Hospital." *The Second Wave* 2:3 (1973):17-20.
This short article provides many examples of the abuse of Black, Latina, and white women in a large public hospital. It is one of the best articles available on the subject. *The Second Wave's* address is 20 Sacramento Street, Cambridge, MA 02138.

Poor Black Women, including "Birth Control Pills and Black Children," a statement by the Black Unity Party (Peekskill, N.Y.); "The Sisters Reply," by Patricia Haden et al.; and "Poor Black Women," by Patricia Robinson. Boston: New England Free Press, n.d. "The Sisters Reply" is also reprinted as "Statement on Birth Control," by the Black Women's Liberation Group, Mount Vernon, New York, in *Sisterhood Is Powerful: An Anthology of Writings from the Women's Liberation Movement*, ed. Robin Morgan. New York: Vintage Books, 1970.
This pamphlet may be ordered from the New England Free Press, 60 Union Square, Somerville, MA 02143, for $.15 a copy. Orders of five or more are given a 12½% (1/8) discount. Orders for which payment is made in advance do not have to be accompanied by postage; however, the payment of postage is greatly appreciated.

Reedy, Juanita. "Diary of a Prison Birth." *Majority Report* (May 31, 1975):1, 3.

Shakur, Assata (Joanne Chesimard). "Birth Journal," unpublished, n.d. (Typewritten.)

These two grimly similar articles detail the tortures endured by Black women who gave birth in prison. Their descriptions of their resistance to what was happening to them are inspiring.

"Sterilization: Relevance for Black Women." Black Women's Community Development Foundation, *Mental and Physical Health Problems of Black Women*. Washington, D.C., 1975, pp. 19-26.

This article is from the only book of which I am aware that focuses exclusively on the health of Black women. It is a report on a conference sponsored by the Foundation in March 1974. Topics covered are hypertension, cancers and fibroids, sterilization, and suicide and depression. Obviously, it is far from comprehensive, but its most serious flaw is that it is neither feminist nor socialist in its analysis; therefore, even though it is antiracist, it is unsatisfactory. Nevertheless, it is an extremely valuable resource, and many of its articles are included in this syllabus. It may be ordered from the Foundation, 1028 Connecticut Avenue, N.W., Suite 1010, Washington, DC 20036. The price of $9.95 includes postage.

Walker, Alice. "Strong Horse Tea." In *In Love and Trouble: Stories of Black Women*. New York: Harcourt Brace Jovanovich, 1973, pp. 88-98.

A poor, Black woman wants a "real doctor" for her gravely ill baby. This is a devastating story about how racism and poverty maim and destroy human life.

Wright, Sarah E. *This Child's Gonna Live*. New York: Dell, 1969. Set on the Maryland Eastern shore, this beautifully poetic novel tells the harrowing and haunting story of Mariah Upshur and her family, whose fundamental struggles include poverty, sickness, and lack of health care.

REPRODUCTIVE HEALTH

Black women, like all women, have always attempted to control their own reproduction. These attempts have been made against terrible odds—forced breeding during slavery; the selling away of the children of slaves; experimentation on Black women, which began during slavery and continues today; forced sterilization; the unavailability of safe, legal abortions to most Black women until recently, and the continued threat to this right by those who oppose abortion. One aspect of this struggle for control has been the development of traditional healing. Excellent resource people for this topic are rural Black midwives. Articles which provide a more clinical treatment on prenatal and maternal health might also be assigned.

Bradley, Valerie Jo. "It Happened on My Birthday." Black Women's Community Development Foundation, *Mental and Physical Health Problems of Black Women*. Washington, D.C., 1975, pp. 103-10.

The Chicago Maternity Center Story. Kartemquin/Haymarket Films, P.O. Box 1665, Evanston, IL; (312) 869-0602. Purchase: $400; rental: $75 to hospitals and universities, $60 to high schools and churches, $40 to community groups. 60 minutes, black/white.

This film documents the fight of Black, Latina, and white women to save the Center's home birth service.

Lerner, Gerda, ed. *Black Women in White America: A Documentary History:* "A Mother Is Sold Away from Her Children," pp. 10-12, and "A Woman's Fate," pp. 45-53. New York: Vintage Books, 1972.

Poor Black Women. Boston: New England Free Press, n.d.

Reedy, Juanita. "Diary of a Prison Birth," *Majority Report* (May 31, 1975):1, 3.

Sanders, Marion K. "The Right Not To Be Born." *Harper's Magazine* (April 1970):92-99.

The first part of this article describes the experience of a Black woman who was denied an abortion after being exposed to German measles and who consequently gave birth to a severely retarded daughter. It is a very moving and enraging article.

Shakur, Assata (Joanne Chesimard). "Birth Journal," unpublished, n.d. (Typewritten.)

"Sterilization: Relevance for Black Women." Black Women's Community Development Foundation, *Mental and Physical Health Problems of Black Women*. Washington, D.C., 1975, pp. 19-26.

Swartz, Donald P. "The Harlem Hospital Center Experience." In *The Abortion Experience: Psychological and Medical Impact*. Edited by Howard J. Osofsky and Joy D. Osofsky. Hagerstown, Md.: Harper and Row, 1973, pp. 94-121.

DISEASES OF BLACK WOMEN

While there are probably no diseases which are exclusive to Black women, there are some conditions which we are more likely to develop in comparison to other groups. These diseases include high blood pressure, uterine fibroids, and lupus. It is essential to consider the implications of such conditions for contraception, pregnancy, and childbearing. It is important, too, to note the different impact of diseases on Black women. For example, while fewer Black women get breast cancer, more die from it. It is probable that this higher death rate results from later detection and the lower quality of care we receive. Additional clinical information can be found by checking recent medical journals.

Lang, Frances. "The Sickle Cell and the Pill," unpublished, n.d. (Typewritten.) Copies are available from Women's Community Health Center, Inc., 639 Massachusetts Avenue, Cambridge, MA 02139. A donation of $.50 plus the cost of postage should be sent with requests for the article.

Loebl, Suzanne. "'SLE': Another Black Disease." *Essence* (September 1973):50-51.

This article describes a support group for women who have systemic lupus erythematosus, a chronic disease which has a higher incidence among Black women than among any other group.

"Cancers and Fibroids: Relevance for Black Women." Black Women's Community Development Foundation, *Mental and Physical Health Problems of Black Women.* Washington, D.C., 1975, pp. 11-17.

"Hypertension: Relevance for Black Women." Black Women's Community Development Foundation, *Mental and Physical Health Problems of Black Women.* Washington, D.C., 1975, pp. 1-9.

MENTAL HEALTH

The minds of Black women have been battered along with our bodies. One of the great, mostly untold, stories about Black women and men is how the centuries of oppression we have endured in this country have damaged our psyches. One theme that recurs in several of the following readings is the extreme narrowness of Black women's lives. Our possibilities are constricted by the system's severely limited notions of what we should be. We are officially defined by others and not by ourselves. Yet self-definition is the source of our strength.

Cox, Ida. "Wild Women Blues." In *The World Split Open: Four Centuries of Women Poets in England and America, 1552-1950.* Edited by Louise Bernikow. New York: Vintage Books, 1974, pp. 278-79.

Hughes, Langston. "The Gun." In *Something in Common and Other Stories.* New York: Hill and Wang, 1963, pp. 154-61.

This story describes some of the tragic ways in which racism and sexism intersect in the life of an isolated domestic worker.

Morrison, Toni. *The Bluest Eye.* New York: Holt, Rinehart and Winston, 1970.

A major focus of this superlative novel is the destructive effect of white beauty standards on the psyches of Black women.

Slater, Jack. "Suicide: A Growing Menace to Black Women." *Ebony* (September 1973):152ff.

"Suicide and Depression: Relevance for Black Women." Black Women's Community Development Foundation, *Mental and Physical Health Problems of Black Women.* Washington, D.C., 1975, pp. 27-35.

Toupin, Elizabeth Ann, and Luria, Zella. "Some Cultural Differences in Response to Co-ed Housing: A Case Report." Black Women's Community Development Foundation, *Mental and Physical Health Problems of Black Women.* Washington, D.C., 1975, pp. 126-35.

A Black male student declares in this article, "I have nothing against girls, now; I just don't want to live next door to them." This is a fascinating and discouraging article both for what it reveals about Black women's position in society and because the authors are oblivious to the sexism inherent in the limited options of Black women.

Walker, Alice. "Her Sweet Jerome." In *In Love and Trouble: Stories of Black Women.* New York: Harcourt Brace Jovanovich, 1973, pp. 24-34.

Walker, Alice. "Really, *Doesn't* Crime Pay?" In *In Love and Trouble: Stories of Black Women.* New York: Harcourt Brace Jovanovich, 1973, pp. 10-23.

These stories about a hairdresser and a middle-class "housewife" who wants to be a writer both treat the damaging psychological effect conventional marriage can have on Black women.

BLACK WOMEN HEALTH WORKERS

The Black women health workers who comprise a large part of the health labor force can be valuable resources for exploring this topic. Guest speakers who work at different levels in the health hierarchy, e.g., a nurse's aide, a dietary worker, a laboratory technician, a nurse, or a doctor, can be invited to talk with the class. Members of the class might also be able to share their experiences working in health care.

Brown, Carol A. "Women Workers in the Health Service Industry." *International Journal of Health Services* 5:2 (1975):173-84.

This article provides a good overview of the topic and includes some interesting observations on the implications of racism as well as sexism for union organizing.

Ferris, Louanne. *I'm Done Crying*. Edited by Beth Day. New York: New American Library, 1970.

In this autobiographical work, the author describes her experiences working in a large city hospital. She is first hired as a dietary worker and eventually becomes a nurse. The book is valuable for its treatment of hospital working conditions and for the information it provides on the inferior health care available to poor, Black people.

I Am Somebody. Contemporary/McGraw Hill, Princeton Road, Hightstown, NJ 08520 (609-448-1700), or 1714 Stockton Street, San Francisco, CA 94133 (415-362-3115). 28 minutes, color, 1970.

This film records the organizing of an 1199 local in a Southern city. Most of the hospital workers are Black women.

Women Health Workers. Women's Health Collective of Philadelphia. This slide presentation is available from the Slide Tape Collective, 36 Lee Street, Cambridge, MA 02139 (617-492-2949). Purchase: $100; rental: $40, regular price; $12, women's, worker, and community groups. 180 slides in carousels, script, and tape.

The slides focus on the Chicago Maternity Center.

SEXUALITY

The pervasiveness of racism and sexism in Black women's lives is revealed in the following readings on sexuality. Included in this section are articles which focus on sexual identity and on the emotional and social aspects of intimate relationships. The fact that our position as Black women affects something so seemingly private and individual as the ways in which we express our sexual feelings is a striking illustration of the basic feminist belief that the personal is political. In too many cases we have been deprived of the right to act in ways which are sexually authentic for us, in part because once again we have been defined by others. For example, white men for centuries have justified their sexual abuse of Black women by claiming that we are licentious, always "ready" for any sexual encounter. A desperate reaction to this slanderous myth is the attempt some of us have made to conform to the strictest versions of patriarchal "morality." Those of us who are lesbians have had to face the profound homophobia (hatred and fear of lesbians and homosexuals) of both Blacks and whites. Implicit in our communities' attitudes toward Black lesbians is the notion that they have transgressed both sexual *and* racial norms. Despite all of the forces with which we must contend, Black women have a strong tradition of sexual self-determination. The blues lyrics written and sung by Black women are examples of this tradition, as are many of the works listed below.

Bambara, Toni Cade. "My Man, Bovanne." In *Gorilla, My Love*. New York: Pocket Books, 1973, pp. 13–20.

An older woman asserts her right to pursue a relationship with a man over her children's objections.

Hurston, Zora Neale. *Their Eyes Were Watching God*. Urbana, Ill.: Univ. of Illinois Press, 1978.

This novel, first published in 1937, provides a rare description of an egalitarian relationship between Janie and her lover Tea Cake.

Lorde, Audre. "Scratching the Surface: Some Notes on Barriers to Women and Loving." *The Black Scholar* (April 1978):31–35.

Lorde analyzes attitudes toward Black lesbians in the Black community and provides a stunning description of woman-identified women in Africa.

"The Myth of the 'Bad' Black Woman." In *Black Women in White America: A Documentary History*. Edited by Gerda Lerner. New York: Vintage Books, 1972, pp. 163–71.

"Sharon." In *Our Bodies, Ourselves*. Edited by the Boston Women's Health Book Collective. 2d ed. New York: Simon and Schuster, 1976, pp. 84–85.

Thoughts on what it means to be a Black woman and a lesbian.

Suncircle, Pat. "A Day's Growth." *Christopher Street* (February 1977):23–27.

This short story describes a day in the life of a Black lesbian teenager. It is especially effective because the characters and events are rooted in familiar Afro-American cultural experiences.

Toupin, Elizabeth Ann, and Luria, Zella. "Some Cultural Differences in Response to Co-ed Housing: A Case Report." Black Women's Community Development Foundation, *Mental and Physical Health Problems of Black Women*. Washington, D.C., 1975, pp. 126–35.

Tyson, Joanne and Richard. "Sex and the Black Woman: They Are Now Seeking Advice." *Ebony* (August 1977):103ff.

Although this article contains some useful observations, the efforts of Black heterosexual women to create less oppressive relationships with men are not acknowledged and the existence of Black lesbians is totally ignored.

Walker, Alice. "The Child Who Favored Daughter." In *In Love and Trouble: Stories of Black Women*. New York: Harcourt Brace Jovanovich, 1973, pp. 35–46.

A young woman, "a black-eyed Susan...a slight, pretty flower...
[who] pledge[s] no allegiance to banners of any man" is destroyed
because her loving defies the bounds dictated by her race and class.

VIOLENCE AGAINST BLACK WOMEN

Violence against Black people has been synonymous with our
experience in this country. The very fact that we are here is the result of
the abduction of our ancestors from their homes in Africa. After the
nightmarish Middle Passage, our kin found themselves enslaved in one of
the most physically and psychologically brutal systems ever devised.

Black women have never been exempted from racist violence because
we are women. The physical abuse of Black women is unique, however,
because of its sexual and racial dimensions. The tradition of rape of Black
women by white men and forced sterilization points up two ways in
which we are terrorized simultaneously as women and as Black people.
For us to comprehend violence against Black women, we must realize that
all violence against all women is related to our position under patriarchy.
It is also essential to acknowledge, in approaching this topic, that Black
men as well as white men violate and attack us.

I would like to comment here on the importance of Alice Walker's
works in this syllabus. She is a writer dedicated to illuminating the
complexities of our lives. Her unflinching portrayals of violence against
Black women illustrate this commitment.

The readings that follow are grouped into several subcategories:

Battering

Hurston, Zora Neale. "Sweat." In *I Love Myself When I Am Laugh-
ing...And Then Again When I Am Looking Mean and Impressive:
A Zora Neale Hurston Reader*. Edited by Alice Walker. Old
Westbury, N.Y.: The Feminist Press, 1979, pp. 197-207.
In this short story, first published in 1926, Hurston creates a classic
character, a "traditional" Black woman who finally stands up to her
emotionally and physically battering husband.
Petry, Ann. "Like a Winding Sheet." In *Miss Muriel and Other Stories*.
Boston: Houghton Mifflin, 1971, pp. 198-210.
A Black man who is powerless in his miserable, menial job strikes at
the only target available to him, his wife. This story and the
following work by Walker provide insights into how racism and
capitalism foster violence by Black men against Black women.

Walker, Alice. *The Third Life of Grange Copeland*. New York: Harcourt Brace Jovanovich, 1970, pp. 43-123.
  Walker chronicles a man's incredibly cruel and systematic destruction of his wife.

Rape

Davis, Angela. "The Dialectics of Rape." *Ms.* (June 1975):74ff.
  The author relates the case of JoAnne Little to the history of rape and racism in the United States.
Friedman, Deb. "Rape, Racism—and Reality." *FAAR and NCN Newsletter* (July/August 1978):17-26.
  In this well-written article, Friedman includes an historical summary of the issues and discusses Black women's critiques of Susan Brownmiller's *Against Our Will*. The publication in which this article appeared has changed its name to *Aegis: Magazine on Ending Violence Against Women* (c/o FAAR, P.O. Box 21033, Washington, DC 20009).
"The Rape of Black Women as a Weapon of Terror." In *Black Women in White America: A Documentary History*. Edited by Gerda Lerner. New York: Vintage Books, 1972, pp. 172-93.

Violence Against Children

Angelou, Maya. *I Know Why the Caged Bird Sings*. New York: Bantam Books, 1969, pp. 58-74.
  This autobiographical work includes an extremely moving account of the sexual violation of a child. It is especially valuable because it is told from the child's perspective.
Hosken, Fran P. "Female Circumcision and Fertility in Africa." *Women and Health: Issues in Women's Health Care* (November/December 1976):3-11.
Morrison, Toni. *The Bluest Eye*. New York: Holt, Rinehart and Winston, 1970.
shange, ntozake. "is not so gd to be born a girl (1)." *The Black Scholar* (May/June 1979):28.
  Shange writes in stark, simple language about the varieties of violence against children. This poem was also published in *Sojourner: The New England Journal of News, Opinions, and the Arts* in February 1979.

Walker, Alice. "The Child Who Favored Daughter." In *In Love and Trouble: Stories of Black Women*. New York: Harcourt Brace Jovanovich, 1973, pp. 35-46.

GENERAL ANALYSIS AND DESCRIPTION

Combahee River Collective. "Eleven Black Women—Why Did They Die?" (Pamphlet, [1979].)
This Black feminist analysis of violence against Black women was written in response to the murders which occurred in Boston during the winter and spring of 1979. Copies can be obtained by writing to the Combahee River Collective, c/o AASC, P.O. Box 1, Cambridge, MA 02139. An earlier version, "Six Black Women—Why Did They Die?," was published in the May/June 1979 issue of *Aegis: Magazine on Ending Violence Against Women*.

shange, ntozake. "with no immediate cause." In *nappy edges*. New York: St. Martin's Press, 1978, pp. 114-17.

Three's a Crowd:
The Dilemma of the Black Woman
in Higher Education

CONSTANCE M. CARROLL

Four years ago, if anyone had said to me that the Black woman in higher education faces greater risks and problems now than in the past, I doubt I would have taken the remark seriously. I would have marveled at the rhetoric and pointed to federal legislation enacted on the crest of the civil rights movement of the 1950s and 1960s, and nodded proudly at the few Blacks in token ("you've got to begin somewhere") positions in major institutions. I would have pointed to such outstanding Black women as Mary McLeod Bethune, Mary Church Terrell, Coretta King, and Shirley Chisholm. "A great deal still needs to be done," I would have said, "but Blacks, including Black women, have come a long way."

In 1972, after four years of teaching and working in a university administration, I would nod my head in ready agreement if the same remark were made. My mind was changed not by startling new studies or surveys on the subject—indeed there are none—but by personal experience and by listening to accounts of Black women educators and administrators across the country. Black women in higher education are isolated, underutilized, and often demoralized. They note the efforts made to provide equal opportunities for Black men and white women in higher education, while they somehow are left behind in the wake of both the Black and feminist movements. The intent of this chapter is to assess the

Author's Note: I am grateful for the useful discussion and criticism of Dr. Konnilyn Feig and Dr. Rebecca Carroll.

situation of Black women in higher education—undergraduates, faculty, and administrators.

CIVIL RIGHTS AND THE BLACK WOMAN

In the past two decades, a wealth of material has appeared on the subject of Blacks in higher education; but most of these studies concern only Black men. This is understandable since the great majority of Blacks who have received advanced degrees in higher education are men. In a 1968 survey of doctoral and professional degrees conferred by Black institutions, it was found that 91 percent were awarded to Black men, only 9 percent to Black women. Such data militate against the general assumption that Black women have been included, on an equal basis with men, in the movement toward equal rights and increased educational and employment opportunities.

The few Black women in academe today feel isolated because they *are* isolated. Jacquelyne Johnson Jackson summarizes the situation well:

> Even if the facts were narrowed to higher education only, it is still true that Black females have been severely disadvantaged. In 1940, a slightly *larger* number of Black males (25 years and older) were more likely to complete four or more years of college than their female counterparts. Twenty years later, the pattern had reversed, when a very small percentage of Black females in that same age group had completed higher school grades than had Black males. By 1970, though, a larger percentage of Black males (21 years and older) had completed four or more years of college.[1]

Even though Black women enter college in roughly the same or often larger proportions than do Black men, Black men are more likely to receive an advanced degree beyond the Master's degree and thereby gain access to positions in colleges and universities. One has only to glance at the faculty or staff of any university or college to note the absence of Black women. My own institution, the University of Pittsburgh, represents a microcosm of this nationwide situation. Eight percent of the professional staff are Black, and a slightly larger proportion of the white staff members than of the minority staff members are women (17 percent compared to 14 percent). The most significant contrast is the difference in rank distribution—white men and Black men markedly exceed white women and Black women at the upper ranks. White men constitute 50 percent of the associate or full professor ranks, Black men 31 percent, white women 19 percent, and Black women 3 percent. Clearly, sex is more of a handicap than race in the upper ranks of the teaching staff at the University of Pittsburgh, and the disproportion between the sexes is far greater for Blacks than for whites. Among whites, men are about two and a half times more likely than women to be in the upper ranks, but among Blacks, men are ten times more likely than women to enjoy higher status.

Consistent with this profile is the tendency for women of both races to be disproportionately represented in such nontenured or "marginal" academic statuses as research associate or professional librarian. Much the same picture holds in the instance of administrative posts. These positions are far more likely to go to Black men than Black women—a difference also found among white academics. Jackson is right in saying,

> One must...understand that Black males have had greater access to the more prestigious institutions of higher learning. This means that the occupational opportunities of Black females have been limited.[2]

This situation is not unique to institutions of higher learning. The Black woman's status in higher education mirrors her impact on the national scene. One can leaf through the now famous 1971 *Ebony* roster of America's 100 leading Blacks and find the names of only *nine* women. The problem is clear. New surveys and data are not necessary to document what is painfully manifest: Mary Church Terrell, Jeanne Noble, and Shirley Chisholm notwithstanding, the Black woman has been excluded from institutions of higher education as she has been excluded from all other opportunities.

For the most part, Black women college graduates have moved into areas that traditionally have been "open" to them, e.g., elementary and secondary education, social work, and nursing. The United States Bureau of the Census survey of population employment in 1960 showed that among employed Black women, 5 percent were public school teachers; 19 percent were nurses; 5 percent were in social work; and 3.2 percent were health technicians. In comparison, 1.1 percent were employed by colleges as presidents (notably Bennett, a Black women's college), professors, and instructors; 0.1 percent were lawyers or judges; 0.3 percent were physicians and surgeons (U.S. Bureau of the Census, 1964). I see the same trends among Black women students whom I counsel, either because they were guided into these areas or because they believe that these are the only areas open to them.

Even in those areas where their numbers are large, Black women rarely receive the same promotional advancements as Black men. In public school systems few become principals and even fewer are promoted to upper administrative posts. The same is true in social and government agencies. This is not the case for Black men, who are usually given positions in which they can be highly visible in an agency's or institution's "crusade" for equal employment or affirmative action. For some uncanny reason, a Black woman at a board meeting is not thought to have the same "visibility" as a Black male. It would be easy to say that white men who control these agencies and institutions can identify more easily with Black men and thereby practice an "unconscious" sexism within their affirmative action programs. We are all familiar with the shock value of the joke:

—I saw God last night.

—Really? What's he like?

—Well, *he's* a *woman* and she's *Black!*

When one ponders this testimony to what the white male really feels to be his most polar opposite, one wonders how far we have come and how far we can really expect to go. The strongest antagonism in the joke is the *God: woman* equation; that is, the tension between sexual "opposites" (male language) appears to be greater and more difficult to transcend than the antagonism between the races.

There is no more isolated subgroup in academe than Black women. They have neither race nor sex in common with white males who dominate the decision-making stratum of academe; Black males in academe at least share with white males their predominance over women. Even in Black educational agencies and institutions, there is a disproportionately greater number of Black males than Black females in important positions. At the University of Pittsburgh, for example, there are only three women among the seventeen faculty members of the Black Studies Department. No calculator is necessary to count the number of Black women holding responsible appointments in the NAACP, the Urban League, Black colleges, Black studies departments, and minority programs in white institutions. Where they *are* found, women tend to be at lower salaries and to wait longer for promotion through the *cursus honorum.*

> When occupational comparisons are made, it becomes quite clear that Black women have *usually had the greatest access to the worst jobs at the lowest earnings.* Black females have consistently been in the minority among Black physicians, college presidents, attorneys, architects and other high level positions.[3]

It is clear that when translated into actual opportunities for employment really meant rights for Black men, just as, historically, the rights of men have referred to the rights of white men.

In this framework, Black women feel their academic opportunities are limited, that there are barriers to their futures in higher education and a built-in isolation in an academic career. Unlike white and Black men who more frequently are selected for apprenticeships or assistantships to make "people developers," Black women have had very few models or champions to encourage and assist them in their development. Black women have had to develop themselves on their own, with no help from whites or Black men, in order to "make it" in academic institutions. This has taken its toll on Black women in all areas of life and work.

UNDERGRADUATE WOMEN

In talking with Black women undergraduates, I have noticed an almost fierce single-mindedness in their preparation for careers. More than half express a desire to pursue careers in "traditional" areas, e.g., education, social work. With very few exceptions, they insist that they are fully prepared to pursue these careers despite plans for marriage. These findings are consistent with those found by Ladner (1971), Noble (1956), and others.[4] Black women undergraduates feel the pressures of both racial and sexual discrimination, and choose education and the hard struggle of career mobility as the "way out." Yet they have few role models with whom to identify in developing healthy self-concepts. The great majority of their professors are white men, or, if they take Black studies courses, Black men. Rarely do they see Black women in responsible academic or administrative positions; and so students must look to each other for support and role models. As a result, they often form peer groups similar to extended family structures.

In their survey of Black students at predominantly white universities and colleges Willie and Levy (1972) found that the greatest degree of social mobility and "freedom" among Black students exists in large institutions, particularly those in which the Black student population is sizable.

On campuses where Black populations are relatively small and the social lives of their members are limited to interaction with other Black students, the Black-student groups take on the character of extended families; when this occurs, all relationships, including those that might otherwise be secondary, become intensely personal. The Black students who make unlimited claims upon each other find such relationships sometimes supportive, but they also find them sometimes stultifying and confining.[5]

Willie and Levy also demonstrate that even on large campuses, the situation is far from ideal. Black men have more freedom than Black women to date both Black and white students.

> While nearly all Blacks on white campuses often feel isolated and confined, it is the Black women who feel it most heavily...our data indicate that the dating situation may be a function of the absence of opportunities.[6]

The Black women undergraduates with whom I have spoken confirm these assertions. They feel locked-in socially, are not awarded leadership roles in Black student groups, do not see impressive role models with whom to identify, and, as a result, they turn to their studies in the hope of escaping their dilemma some time in the future. In this respect, they are not unlike the small groups of Black students on small campuses.

BLACK WOMEN PROFESSORS AND ADMINISTRATORS

The sheer paucity of Black women among the faculty and administration in colleges and universities tends to force Black women into a small, isolated community. My own appointment is in the College of Arts and Sciences, which puts me in touch with most academic departments of the university. Nevertheless, with the exception of Black studies and minority programs I never come in contact with another Black woman professor or administrator in my day-to-day activities. This seems to be typical for most of the Black women in similar positions. There is no one with whom to share experiences and gain support, no one with whom to identify, no one on whom a Black woman can model herself. It takes a great deal of psychological strength "just to get through a day," the endless lunches, and meetings in which one is always "different." The feeling is much like the exhaustion a foreigner speaking an alien tongue feels at the end of the day.

In the wake of the HEW investigations of several hundred universities for noncompliance with the federal guidelines concerning equal treatment of minorities and women, Black women have raised their level of expectations and aspirations, just as Black men and white women have done. Affirmative action programs and recruitment programs have sprung up across the country, spotlighting the inequities and proposing solutions to them. Colleges and universities have stepped up their hiring of Black women in the same way they have gradually increased the roster of Black men. They have been recruited to fill secretarial positions, to staff Black studies and minority programs and, in rare cases, junior administrative posts. Overall, however, significant change has not yet occurred. In 1971, the total number of minority women faculty at the University of Pittsburgh was 57 (including part-time faculty), representing 1.8 percent of the total faculty of 3,043; the number of minority males in 1971 was 180, or 5.9 percent of the total faculty. There has been an increase of Blacks of both sexes since 1970, but the rate of increase has been far greater for men than for women. Viewing these developments, Black women feel a sense of frustration and hopelessness. It seems that just as civil rights in the 1950s and 1960s for the most part benefited Black men, so affirmative action programs in the 1970s may largely benefit Black men and white women.

When Black women question this disparity in representation, responses range from "we can't find them" to what may be called the "two-steps-behind" syndrome. No Black has ever accepted the "we can't find them" response. Black men, when seriously sought, have been found, encouraged, and promoted. In some cases, they have multiplied so rapidly, one begins to think twice about denouncing spontaneous generation. Everyone now knows that when an institution is seriously recruiting in a framework of (budgetary) reward and punishment, its minority deficiencies can easily be repaired. Obviously, no serious efforts have been made until very recently and on a very limited scale to recruit or promote Black women to important staff, faculty, or administrative positions in institutions of higher learning. If these institutions are to pursue an equitable policy that will not result in the demoralization of any of their constituency, *they must recruit and promote Black women at the same rate and in the same proportions as Black men in all areas of the academic structure.*

Another objection often raised that is even more disturbing is the "two-steps-behind" philosophy, which mitigates against equal benefits for Black women on the fallacious assumption that discrimination has had far more serious repercussions for Black men than for Black women: Black women must now take a back seat to the Black man as he "catches up." I have received such remarks and they seem to be fairly common even now. One writer rebuts it candidly:

> It must be pointed out at this time, that Black women are
> not resentful of the rise to power of Black men. We
> welcome it. We see in it the eventual liberation of all

Black people from this oppressive system of capitalism. Nevertheless, this does not mean that you have to negate one for the other. This kind of thinking is a product of miseducation; that it's either X or it's Y. It is a fallacious reasoning that in order for the Black man to be strong, the Black woman has to be weak. Those who are exerting their "manhood" by telling Black women to step back into a submissive role are assuming a counterrevolutionary position. Black women likewise have been abused by the system and we must begin talking about the elimination of all kinds of oppression.[7]

Black women have grown sensitive to this discrimination within discrimination, but their protests have not yet been translated into affirmative action on their own behalf. The Black woman is told that the Black man has fared far worse from racial discrimination than she has; that when Black men could find no work at all, she could always be a maid for "Miss Ann" or find some employment with "Mr. Charlie." Recent studies show that such arguments are based on false assumptions and incorrect data.[8] One would be hard pressed to say which is the more demoralizing circumstance: unemployment or servitude. The Black woman will never rediscover *her* pride and *her* identity by learning to be second-class a second time. Universities, Black and white, must take these issues into serious consideration if the ultimate goals of *human* freedom and equal opportunities are to be reached.

BLACK WOMEN'S LIBERATION AND HIGHER EDUCATION

The rise of women's liberation and the protests of Third World women in the late 1960s and early 1970s provided another framework in which Black women could evaluate their relationship to Black men and white women. From the outset, the women's liberation movement, at least philosophically, has sought to embrace and speak to the concerns of all women. This in itself is an impossible task because of the infinite complexity and variety of women in this country. As a goal, it represents the true cross-cultural and cross-racial orientation which was and is the basic unifying force in the movement. The danger in such an ideal arises when individuals or groups attempt to put it into practice without first dealing with its implicit assumptions. With regard to Black women, for example, the women's movement has attempted to transcend rather than confront the racial tensions and the complexities resulting from the Black woman's involvement in the movement. I have sat through meeting after meeting in which after a Black woman raises objections to certain of the movement's directions and orientations, the inevitable "reverential silence" sets in and then the discussion simply proceeds as before. Promises are often made to study the situation of the Black woman and she is reassured that the movement has her interests at heart because "she is a woman." *But Black women are different from white women.* Their situation is more than a parenthetical remark in a chapter which supposedly includes them.

Black women understandably have mixed feelings about women's liberation. At first glance, the women's movement casts an all-too-familiar picture. The Black woman finds herself in a special category in yet another white-dominated group—a division that in many ways mirrors society as a whole and toward which she has some deep-seated hostility. Many Black women feel that the life experiences and life styles of white women in the movement are dramatically different from theirs.

> Another major differentiation is that the white women's movement is basically middle-class. Very few of these women suffer the extreme economic exploitation that most Black women are subjected to day by day. It is not an intellectual persecution alone; it is not an intellectual outburst for us; it is quite real.[9]

Statistics bear out this point: 50 percent of all Black women work, in contrast to 42 percent of all white women, and Black women work in lower-status jobs and at lower pay than white women. These facts account in part for Black women's view of work as more of a necessity than an "opportunity," and that in turn may contribute to the misunderstandings and disagreements between Black and white women.

The Black woman sees that her numbers are few among the general membership of the women's movement, and nonexistent among its national leadership. She often is told that many of the problems she raises are problems of all Blacks and, as such, are not the special concern of the women's movement. Why, for example, should a new women's studies center with limited funds finance course offerings on Black women when there is already a Black studies center or department? Can academic issues affecting the Black woman even legitimately be separated from those affecting her race? These important questions and their implications have gone unanswered for the most part or have been relegated to Black women to work out themselves.

A Black woman's view of teaching methods and scholarship will also be different from that of her white counterpart. My own academic training has been in Classics and I have found, for example, that Black women students, much more than white women students, understand and can identify with the situation of Medea. When the chorus agree that the plight of *all* women is dismal, Medea makes some distinctions that are intrinsic to grasping one of the central issues of the play.

Surely of all creatures that have life and will, we
Women are the most wretched.
Still more, a foreign woman, coming among new laws,
New customs, needs the skill of magic, to find out what
Her home could not teach her...
    But the same arguments do not apply to you and me.
You have this city, your father's home, the enjoyment of
Your life, and your friend's company. I am alone, I
Have no city; now my husband insults me. I was taken as
Plunder from a land at the earth's edge. I have no
Mother, brother, nor any of my own blood to turn to in
This extremity.[10]

The Black woman in higher education is not unlike Medea. She is inexperienced in the system, just as most of her peers and family have traditionally been excluded from it. Black even more than white women need "magic," that is, superior ability, in order to receive equal opportunities.

Prior to my experience with the Chancellor's Advisory Council on Women's Opportunities at the University of Pittsburgh and my experience and involvement with the women's movement, I had unquestioningly accepted what I conceived to be the Black woman's role. I functioned by the tacit formulae followed by all Black women who wish to succeed in a man's (both Black and white) world:

You must be *better qualified* than the men.
You must be *more articulate.*
You must be *more aggressive.*
You must have *more stamina* to face inevitable setbacks.
You must have *more patience,* since you will advance *more slowly.*
Above all, you must remain *feminine* and *not appear threatening.*

I have found that Black women share these dicta with white women. However, Black women have an extra step in the syllogism which white women do not have, that is, *they must also be better than white women.* It is this seldom discussed fact which has generated bitterness toward white women in general. In a power ladder, the white woman is seen to be two steps removed from the power, but the Black woman is three steps removed. The Black woman cannot help being cautious in allying herself with a "privileged competitor."

With recognition of these similarities and differences, the Black woman's experience could add richness and depth to many areas of higher education. In a women's studies curriculum, for example, the Black woman's experience should be depicted and studied in contrast to the white woman's experience, for the benefit and growth of both Black and white students. This approach would also increase the involvement of Black women faculty in such programs. Iris Murdoch's book *The Time of the Angels* is an example of a starting point for such a venture. Pattie O'Driscoll symbolizes the experience of many young Black women who, surrounded by white women and men in academe, find themselves in a unique and dehumanizing situation. Her situation is poignantly summarized: "As a child she had not distinguished between the affliction of being colored and the affliction of being Pattie...whiteness seemed to join all the white people together in a cozy union, but blackness divided the Black, each into the loneliness of his own special hue."[11]

Among the faculty and administrative ranks, Black women face even more complex problems. Institutions have responded initially to the women's movement with twice the "deliberate speed" with which they responded to the Black movement, for white women are far more numerous in faculty and administrative positions than are either minority men or women. Institutions often have met the double threat of the Black and the women's movements by pitting the two groups against each other. Everyone who has worked in compliance and affirmative action programs knows that this is a favorite institutional ploy. Blacks and women often are lumped together in the competition for the same famous "slice of the pie," the same positions, and the same benefits. This ploy, in a period of financial crisis heightened by the pronouncements and activities of HEW, has caused new tensions and rivalries to arise. I do not know how many times I have gone to meetings on women's opportunities and institutional change where I have heard avuncular remarks to the effect that women would have to be patient since so much money had to be spent on providing more opportunities for minority candidates. I then hear the same administrators admonishing Black groups to be patient since the women were using up so much money. The ploy evidently works, for I know of no institution where the women's groups and Black groups have publicly allied to put an end to such divisive tactics; and I know of no institution where *significant* gains have been made for both white women and minority women and men. A bridge between these two groups is sorely needed for the benefit of both.

Caught between the claims of the women's movement and the Black movement the Black woman is being sorely pressed to define her political allegiances. While she has learned that involvement in the Black movement has not led to a significant advancement of Black women, strategically her association with the women's movement places her in an extremely awkward position and often damages her credibility among her Black friends and colleagues. I have often been criticized for "deserting" the Black cause and lessening the chances for Black advancement in working for the cause of women. Yet, once in the women's movement, I find that many of my concerns and different needs are ignored, overlooked, or rarely discussed due to the powerful myth of an all-embracing sisterhood.

Some Black women who have struggled with these conflicts have decided that the only solution is secession from both movements in favor of a third group exclusively devoted to the concerns of Black women. This route seems to ensure "purity," pride, identity, clarity in issues, and solidarity; but strategically it is the one most fraught with peril. By its aloof stance, a third movement is, in effect, disavowing both the women's movement and the Black movement. Unwittingly, it turns these other movements into unnatural enemies. Black women in this isolated position have forced themselves into a whole system of moves and countermoves which cannot fail to damage the other movements; at the same time, they invite institutional attempts to "slice the pie" yet a third way. My objection to this alternative is not ideological, nor am I suggesting malintent on the part of these women. I share their frustration and their impatience. But I have seen the resentment and fear engendered within and by these women faced with a dilemma, constantly at cross-purposes with themselves and others, as they stand alone to fight for what no one else will fight for quite hard enough.

Just as in some African myths of creation, the Black woman has been called upon to create herself without model or precedent. She has had enough experience to know that, unless it changes, she can never comfortably or confidently fit into the white-oriented women's movement. At the same time, she has been held back, overlooked, and chided enough to know that all of her problems cannot be answered in the male-oriented Black movement. She has had enough experience with institutional behavior and strategy to know that a third interest group (at least at this time) is lethal to the movements which, to a certain extent, have her concerns at heart.

There seems to be only one feasible course, one productive but difficult and lonely road if the Black woman is to achieve concrete benefits at the end of her struggle. She must be the gadfly who stings both movements into achieving their goals—prodding the women's movement into confronting its racism and working doubly hard for the concerns of

Black women; and prodding the less volatile Black movement into confronting its inherent sexism and righting the injustice it has done to Black women. The Black woman must work doubly hard in both movements; she must become the sorely needed bridge between them if their goals are to be translated into reality. The two movements must become "company" in affirmative action in order for the goal of human rights in higher education to become a reality.

NOTES

[1] Jacquelyne J. Jackson, "Where Are the Black Men?" *Ebony* 27 (1972): 99-106.

[2] Idem.

[3] Idem.

[4] See Joyce Ladner, *Tomorrow's Tomorrow—The Black Woman* (Garden City, N.Y.: Doubleday & Co., Inc., 1971), and Jeanne Noble, *The Negro Woman's College Education* (New York: Columbia University Press, 1956).

[5] Charles Willie and Joan Levy, "Black Is Lonely," *Psychology Today* 5:10 (1972):50-80.

[6] Ibid. p. 76.

[7] Frances M. Beal, "Double Jeopardy: To Be Black and Female," in *Sisterhood Is Powerful,* ed. Robin Morgan (New York: Vintage Books, 1970), pp. 343-44.

[8] Doris Wright, "On Black Womanhood," *The Second Wave* 1:4 (1972):13- 15.

[9] Beal, "Double Jeopardy," pp. 350-51.

[10] Euripides, *Medea* (New York: Penguin Books, 1964), pp. 24-25.

[11] Iris Murdoch, *The Time of the Angels* (New York: Bard Books, 1971), pp. 22-23.

BIBLIOGRAPHY

Drake, St. Clair. "The Black University in the American Social Order." *Daedalus* 100:3 (1971):833-97.

DuBois, W. E. B., ed. *The Negro American Family.* New York: New American Library, 1969.

Feig, Konnilyn. Myths of Female Liberation. University of Pittsburgh. Mimeographed, 1972.

Ferris, A. *Indicators of Trends in the Status of American Women.* New York: Russell Sage Foundation, 1971.

Miller, Albert H. "The Problems of the Minority Student on the Campus." *Liberal Education* 55 (1971):18-23.

Slaughter, Diane T. "Becoming an Afro-American Woman." *School Review* 80:2 (1972):299-317.

13

Slave Codes
and Liner Notes

MICHELE RUSSELL

...it was either live with music or die with noise, and we chose rather desperately to live.

—Ralph Ellison

What are we studying when we look at Black women's experience, once inside the United States?

Documents, for sure. Bills of Sale for cargo received. Agricultural production figures for tobacco, cotton, cane sugar, and rice in ten-million-pound units. The diaries of white women on the subject of concubinage and household management. The plantation ledgers of their husbands, calculating the dollar discrepancy paid for mulatto vs. full-blooded African children, both bred for comparative advantage on the domestic market.

This range of material yields important insights, primarily having to do with the peculiarly barbaric variable of slavery United States settler-culture fostered. Sometimes, in genteel circles, it goes by the name of "breeding." It meant wholesale rape for profit.

There are other dimensions to the story. Other documents: the vivid descriptions Black men have left of us escaping bondage, inciting rebellion among field workers, killing overseers, wrecking property, and protecting family. These are legion. Their perspectives are those of husbands, brothers, sons, coworkers, poets, and the collectors of lore. They demonstrate that we did not take rape lying down.

There are the ways others reacted to our being and doing. The stereotypes of the dominant culture which created Aunt Jemima,

Sapphire, Topsy, Pinky, Farina, and Sweet Thing. The biological metaphors which told us, in no uncertain terms, what kind of animal Anglo-Americans thought us to be. The consequences of those ideas in action: the spits and crossties where we were roasted after the hunt. Our mutilated body parts smoked and sold as trophies.

And again, in rebuttal, there are the works of art, skill, and craft created by us in bondage that give the lie to myths of our primitive savagery and sloth.

But above everything else tower Black women's own voices, raised in resistance to death and slavery—of the body and spirit. They cut a record, in continuous performance, expressing the restless movement of a captive people, for whom home is far away and heaven is out of sight. It is an old song with many verses, but just one refrain: freedom.

It starts with the humming which kept alive African rhythms in spite of the lock-step ankle-chains demanded, and the rocking of the slaveship's hold. It continues in the work shouts which coded our pain. It rose on Sundays and in the nighttime wilderness from which Harriet Tubman signaled us to steal away cause we were so tired o' this mess. And, closer to our own time, it is carried in the music of five women over the last fifty years: Bessie Smith, Bessie Jackson, Billie Holiday, Nina Simone, and Esther Phillips.

In helping Black women own their past, present, and future, these figures are primary. The content of their message, combined with the form of their delivery, make them so.

Blues, first and last, are a familiar, available idiom for Black women, even a staple of life. In the poorest city homes, records or a radio are the second purchase, after a hot plate. Sometimes, before. For the rural and the homeless, songs are always present.

We all know something about blues. Being about us, life is the only training we need to measure their truth. They talk to us, in our own language. They are the expression of a particular social process by which poor Black women have commented on all the major theoretical, practical, and political questions facing us and have created a mass audience who listens to what we say, in that form.

Bessie Smith, Bessie Jackson (Lucille Bogan), Billie Holiday, Nina Simone, and Esther Phillips recall the worst aspects of our collective situation and teach how to wring from that the best transformation consciousness can achieve at precise moments in history. They are the bearers of the self-determination tradition in Black women's blues. Unsentimental. Historical. Materialist. They are not afraid to name a job a slave, a marriage a meal ticket, and loving a grind. They all recreate our past differently. But each, in her own way and for her own day, travels the road from rape to revolution. Their rendering of that process is high art. The beat they step to goes like this.

BESSIE SMITH

Bessie Smith grasped daily survival rhythms when times were really hard. She comes to us, dressed as a Liberty Belle, uncracked after World War I. Her note was a clear peal, sounding the simple reminder that we were still alive, despite all. While Ma Rainey established that Black women were on the loose, traveling, Bessie Smith said we were here to stay.

She began by recognizing the constant chaos of our lives as an uprooted people, at the mercy of forces we couldn't control. And she made a stand.

Backwater blues done tole me to pack my things and go
Cause my house fell down, can't live there no more.
Umm-mm, but I can't move no more.
There ain't no place for a poor old girl to go.

Floods, famine, natural and unnatural disasters are chronicled in songs like "Backwater Blues." Since coming to the Black Belt, we have been through them all. But, yet and still (as a later Simple said), we had not died before our time. We were refusing to be swept away. We were staying put.

Bessie went further. Since the Apocalypse was a condition of everyday life, our resurrection had to be, too. She took our revival rituals out of the church and into the street, enlarged their performance from one day to seven and all night, too. She preached a spiritual lesson, but she took it from the Blues Book, Chapter Nine: "Women must learn how to take their time."

Bessie Smith redefined our time. In a deliberate inversion of the Puritanism of the Protestant ethic, she articulated, as clearly as anyone before or since, how fundamental sexuality was to survival. Where work was often the death of us, sex brought us back to life. It was better than food, and sometimes a necessary substitute.

With her, Black women in American culture could no longer just be regarded as sexual objects. She made us sexual subjects, the first step in taking control. She transformed our collective shame at being rape victims, treated like dogs or, worse, the meat dogs eat, by emphasizing the value of our allure. In so doing, she humanized sexuality for Black women. The importance of this is often lost. During a period when *The*

Birth of a Nation was projecting all of us as animalistic, and white "Citizens' Councils" gathered strength all over the country, Bessie Smith's ability to communicate human emotion in public and make whites and Blacks *hear* the humanity was a victory.

Beyond this, Bessie Smith gives us the first post-Emancipation musical portrayals of Black women working. In "Washwoman's Blues" (1928), for example, she delineates the difference between washwomen and scullions. This song is a classical lament, in the rhythm of the work being done. She sings:

> All day long I'm slavin', all day long I'm bustin' suds.
> Gee, my hands are tired, washin' out these dirty duds.

Proceeding to describe the volume of the workload she is expected to handle and its effects, she says:

> Lord, I do more work than forty-eleven Gold Dust twins
> Got myself a-achin' from my head down to my shins.

Most striking, however, is her image of deliverance:

> Rather be a scullion, cookin' in some white folks' yard.
> I could eat up plenty, wouldn't have to work so hard.

With these words, she reminds us that the old plantation division of labor between domestic workers and house servants persists and that being a house servant is still a privilege.

Most of her comments on domestic economy, however, center on the struggle to construct a relationship of equality in her own house with Black men. The battle between the sexes is waged in no uncertain terms in "Yes, Indeed He Do" and "I Used to Be Your Sweet Mama." And, in a whole group of songs, including "The Devil's Gonna Get You" and "Pinchbacks, Take 'Em Away," dating from the early twenties, her advice to women is: "Get a working man when you marry. Cause it takes money to run a business." The most extended treatment of her attitude is to be found in "Get It, Bring It, and Put It Right Here." It speaks for itself:

> I've had a man for fifteen years
> Give him his room and his board.
> Once he was like a Cadillac
> Now he's like an old worn-out Ford.
>
> He never brought me a lousy dime
> And put it in my hand.
> Oh, there'll be some changes from now on
> According to my plan.

He's got to get it, bring it, and put it right here
Or else he's gonna keep it out there.
If he must steal it, beg it, or borrow it somewhere
Long as he gets it, I don't care.

I'm tired of buying pork chops to grease his fat lips
And he'll have to find another place to park his ole hips
He's got to get it, bring it, and put it right here
Or else he's gonna keep it out there.

The bee gets the honey and brings it to the comb
Else he's kicked out of his home-sweet-home
To show you that they brings it watch the dog and the
    cat
Everything even brings it, from a mule to a gnat.

The rooster gets the worm and brings it to the hen
That ought to be a tip to all of you no-good men.
The groundhog even brings it, and puts it in his hole
So my man has got to bring it, doggone his soul.

He's got to get it, bring it, and put it right here
Or else he's gonna keep it out there.
He can steal it, beg it, or borrow it somewhere
Long as he gets it, chile, I don't care.

I'm gonna tell him like the chinaman when you don't
    bring-um check
You don't get-um laundry if you wring-um damn neck.
You got to get it, bring it, and put it right here
Or else you're gonna keep it out there.

Our ability to maintain that level of control was short-lived. Crop failures in the South and the stock market crash in the North drove us and our men out of house and home. Dispersed in cities, becoming marginal in both mechanized agriculture and manufacturing, barred from the skilled trades, once again our bodies and souls were all we could sell to live. In blues idiom, the reality was expressed like this:

Merchant got half the cotton
Boll Weevil got the rest.
Didn't leave the poor farmer's wife
But one old cotton dress
And it's full of holes; yes, it's full of holes.

The service jobs city living brought were humiliating beyond imagination. A familiar figure from this period is Richard Wright's friend who, as an elevator operator, let himself be kicked by white patrons for tips. With Bessie Jackson, however, the bottom line on Black women's self-esteem is drawn.

BESSIE JACKSON

Bessie Jackson goes with us into the marketplace of the Depression and says, "No more auction block for me." In her songs, we are shown refusing to prostitute ourselves, no matter how we were forced to work. Negotiating turf and hours. Sitting down. Battling over the conditions of our labor. In "Tricks Ain't Walkin' No More," she makes her position clear.

> Sometimes I'm up, sometimes I'm down
> I can't make my living around this town
> 'Cause Tricks ain't walkin', Tricks ain't walkin' no more.
> I got to make my livin', don't care where I go.

> I need some shoes on my feet, clothes on my back
> Got tired of walkin' these streets all dressed in black
> But Tricks ain't walkin', Tricks ain't walkin' no more.
> And I see four or five good tricks standin' in front of my
>   door.

> I got a store on the corner, sellin' stuff cheap
> I got a market 'cross the street where I sell my meat
> But Tricks ain't walkin', Tricks ain't walkin' no more.
> And if you think I'm lyin', follow me to my door.

Understanding as she did the market relations of capitalism, Bessie Jackson pictures how we bought as well as sold. Her songs dramatize the situations in which we became traders in the black market, watching the stock in the skin trade rise and fall (as in "Baking Powder Blues"), letting our chances for raising dough ride on a steady roll. She records how, even when powerless, one can transform physically debilitating circumstances into a means of material sustenance, like food. She follows us, as with much effort we worked ourselves *up* to the position of Bar-B-Que Bess, who takes pride in saying:

> When you come to my house, come down behind the
>   jail

I got a sign on my door, Bar-B-Que for Sale
I'm talkin' bout my Bar-B-Que
The only thing I sell
And if you want my meat, you can come to my house at
    twelve.

With total candor, she voices what Prof. Howard Stretch Johnson has characterized as "the pursuit of alternative entrepreneurial modalities by folk barred from mainstream society."

BILLIE HOLIDAY

Billie Holiday broke this pattern. With her, we began to consciously appropriate the best in white popular culture as a means of elaborating our style. She then went on to mainline the blend.

First, she made urban blues urbane. All-wise. In Cole Porter's "Love for Sale," she let us know she was Bessie Jackson's sister, subject to the same reality; but distinctions between them were developing. We had become fruit instead of meat. A delicacy, to sample. A Black woman, yes; and a lady.

From back alley stairs to (Small's) Paradise, we had made the climb. Appetizing, young, fresh and still unspoiled, only slightly soiled, she was prepared to sing about it all. And did. She said: "Let the poets pipe of love, in their childish way./I know every type of love, better far than they." Now, the dehumanizing context of our wisdom could be embellished, riffed, cultivated, and perfumed. It could be sung to strings. In so doing, she represented a Black woman who could conquer white men and their music, "Tenderly."

In her most sardonic mood, Billie Holiday enlarged on white fantasies of being a "kep' woman" and the self-mutilation that arrangement required, all the while telling us "I was only dreaming." When awake, she knew as well as the rest of us that "God Blessed the Child That's Got His Own."

She coded our pain by lacing it with sweetness, mixing "Fine and Mellow" with "Strange Fruit." On balance, however, she stirred a bitter brew. The silk and satin were only a covering. For her, as for her Black audience, depression and war blended together. She sang "I Got a Right To Sing the Blues" and enlarged her personal misery to embrace our collective situation.

By 1941, with the war in Europe in full swing and Black soldiers dying to make the world safe for democracy, she let everyone know that

Georgia was on her mind. In the stranglings of the period at home, the bulging eyes and twisted mouths, the victim's blood was ours. Unafraid, she voiced the genocidal results: "Black bodies swinging in the Southern breeze;/strange fruit, hanging from the poplar trees." Even the scent of magnolias, sweet and fresh, couldn't hide the smell of burning flesh. The smoke and the stink thickened over the next twenty years. Billie Holiday was one of many American casualties. Korea, Viet Nam, Sharpeville, rape, lynchings, and Jim Crow law all added fuel to the fire. In spite of the official freeze on information (called the Cold War), we heard of how other border skirmishes multiplied, saw the cracks in the walls, and attributed the disturbances, correctly, to volcanic eruptions in the Third World. The conscious musical voice making the bridge for us was Nina Simone.

NINA SIMONE

In the 1960s, Nina Simone used her music to revive our roots, to internationalize the terms of our self-determination, and to develop the cultural dimension of armed struggle. More than any of her predecessors, she was able to fuse ideology and art. Her perspective was that the whole world was being Africanized and for us to take our place on the stage of history, our awareness had to encompass the world. So, she opened old trade routes and plotted new explorers' maps whose only boundaries were determined by the "geography of our shed blood."

In "Four Women," she told the tale of violations marking our lives in the United States. With just that one song, she took us all the way back to "Washwoman's Blues," through Tricks, and watered the bitter crop Billie Holiday knew had been sown. In songs like "Seeline Woman," "Sinnerman," "Zungo," "I Put a Spell on You," and "One More Sunday in Savannah," she cultivated our folk memory. She invoked all the weapons we had used in the past to protect ourselves when organization failed: incantation, congregation, conjure, slave religion, dissembling, the appropriation of European and Anglo-American culture. But she put them to use in a situation and at a time when organization was developing and we were contending for power. The historical moment was such that, through her voice, even songs like "I Shall Be Released" took on a meaning relevant to our political struggle. Her most personal melodies (e.g., "When I Was in My Prime" and "Wild Is the Wind") always contained undertones of suppressed rebellion. When she began her crescendo, no one could ignore the dominant theme.

Nina Simone was not the first to be so direct. In the 1930s Bessie Smith could say to the rich:

> While you're living in your mansion
> You don't know what hard times mean
> A workingman's wife is starvin'
> Your wife is livin' like a queen.

The difference was that Bessie Smith concluded this song by pleading with the rich to have mercy on her plight and appealing to their conscience by asking: "If it wasn't for the poor man,/Mr. Rich man, what would you do?" By the 1960s, Nina Simone was taking the offensive. She performed "Old Jim Crow" and "Backlash Blues" to white audiences who knew they were under attack, and to Black audiences who were seizing the time. She wrote "show tunes" like "Mississippi, Goddam" and introduced them by saying "the show hadn't been written for them yet." Her voice rang with social judgment and there were no rebuttals when she told white America:

> Don't tell me, I'll tell you
> Me and my people just about due
> I've been there, so I know
> Keep on sayin', "Go slow."

> Yes, you lied to me all these years
> You told me to wash and clean my ears
> And talk real fine just like a lady
> And you'd stop calling me Sister Sadie.

> Oh, this whole country's full of lies
> Y'all gonna die and die like flies
> I don't trust you anymore
> When you keep sayin', "Go slow."

> But that's just the trouble—too slow
> Desegregation, mass participation, unification—too slow
> Do things gradually and bring more tragedy.

> You don't have to live next to me
> Just leave me my equality.
> Cause everybody knows about Mississippi, Goddam.

When that message was taken up by the poorest among us, and all the major cities in the United States were being shaken by Black rebellion, most white folk were either striking back or asking, "Why?" Nina Simone was answering by performing "Pirate Jenny." She had chosen carefully. She took a song originating in English light opera, adapted by German socialists Bertolt Brecht and Kurt Weill to comment on life in pre-Fascist Germany, and transformed it to apply to the anti-colonial revolutionary spirit growing in the American South, the Caribbean, South Africa, and situations south of every border. This was the coming storm that her prevailing Southerly blew. And, in the midst of it, still smiling, "looking nice with a ribbon in her hair,/but counting the heads as she's making the beds," was Aunt Sarah, Sister Sadie, Pirate Jenny—giving no quarter at the revolutionary moment. The cleaning woman's final task was stripping down the house and everything in it: to fumigate. All the covers were off now. The last had arisen and was demanding to be first. In 1969, the song that Nina Simone wrote to say it was "Revolution"—the last verse went as follows:

> Singin' about a Revolution, because we're talkin' about
>   a change.
> It's more than just air pollution
> Well, you know, you got to clean your brain.
> The only way that we can stand in fact
> Is when you get your foot off our back.
> Get. Off. Our Back.

The only issue was, how to do it. For that, we needed more than prophetic vision and exhortation.

If the last among us were truly to take command, all the weaknesses that our condition enforced had to be rooted out. The revolutionary process necessitated that people transform themselves as well as the social, economic, and political structures that governed our development. To reach the "new world" toward which Nina Simone directed our gaze, protracted struggles and long marches began. And there was nothing mystical about the trip. One such earthly pilgrim was Esther Phillips.

ESTHER PHILLIPS

After the high tide of Black rebellion, we all suffered in some measure from the system's retaliation. At a personal level, Esther Phillips experienced all the adulteration, dissipated direction, enforced isolation, and confusion that had been injected into the Black liberation movement in general. By the 1970s, she, and we, were trying to regroup. Her journey toward independence, though particularly lonely, had mass dimensions. Her fight was to overcome all the forms of personal decadence this society markets to prolong our slavery. Following Nina Simone's advice to

"Break Down and Let It All Out," her route led through penetration, not transcendence. And she did it alone. As her own deep-sea diver, she plumbed the depths of our degradation before surfacing with a synthesis. When on land, she said, "If it takes me all night long, I gotta keep walkin' til my back ain't got no bone."

Nothing was inevitable about the destination. She was always aware that one road would lead her home, and the other would lead far into the night. In songs like "That's All Right With Me," "Home Is Where the Hatred Is," and "Scarred Knees," she records all the ways we have voluntarily made slaves of ourselves. She deals directly with the three worst addictions capitalist social relations have encouraged in us: surrender to men, religion, and hard drugs. And she tells of their effects with the authority her own life provides.

In her middle passage, she rediscovers something of value in herself. "I'm Getting Long Alright," "CC Rider," "Cherry Red," "In the Evenin'," and "Bye-Bye Blackbird" are from this period. She begins to favor traveling music and straightens up off her knees. Musically, her choice of songs reasserts Bessie Smith's demand for domestic equality and Bessie Jackson's fight to establish market value with everyone she meets on the road toward home. In the '70s, the strenuous nature of those battles burned many people out. In political circles, varieties of separatism flourished. Esther Phillips's expression of this mood was "Too Many Roads Between Us" and "Hurtin' House."

Esther Phillips's triumph, however, is contained in "I've Only Known a Stranger," "Justified," "You Could Have Had Me," "Black-Eyed Blues," and "Turn Around, Look at Me." In this group of songs, she reviews her experiences with men and announces she is fed up with the terms of those relationships as they exist in this society. Speaking directly in "You Could Have Had Me," she says: "You could have had me, baby, in 1973./Now I'm older and wiser and you don't look so good to me.../It's too late, cause I've lost my appetite." Not a bit apologetic, in "Justified" she says: "My stock of patience done wore too thin/and I don't think that I could go through another funny scene again." She's leaving cause she got "less than she wanted and more than she should." She concludes: "Now, I'm just gonna be me. I've got no ill feelings, cause I know I'm justified."

She can face being alone and will only do what's functional. The only community she seeks are the roots of the "Black-Eyed Blues." In this return, the voice that shines through, loud and clear, blends feminism with nationalism in a strong statement of independence. She has gotten all the loads off her back, as Nina Simone counseled, and has taken a stand, where she can.

The only remaining task, for her and us, is to accomplish collectively what Bessie Smith, Bessie Jackson, Billie Holiday, and Nina Simone achieved personally. Maybe the music will help. Listen to it.

There is no conclusion to this paper. Only the reminder that the beat goes on.

14

Black Women and the Church

JACQUELYN GRANT

It is often said that women are the "backbone" of the church. On the surface, this may appear to be a compliment, considering the function of the backbone in the human anatomy. Theressa Hoover prefers to use the word "glue" to describe the function of women in the Black church. In any case, the telling portion of the word "backbone" is "back." It has become apparent to me that most of the ministers who use this term are referring to location rather than function. What they really mean is that women are in the "background" and should be kept there: they are merely support workers. This is borne out by my observation that in many churches women are consistently given responsibilities in the kitchen, while men are elected or appointed to the important boards and leadership positions. While decisions and policies may be discussed in the kitchen, they are certainly not made there.

A study I conducted recently in one conference of the African Methodist Episcopal Church indicated that women are accorded greater participation on the decision-making boards of smaller rather than larger churches.[1] This political maneuver helps to keep women "in their place" in the denomination as well as in the local congregations. The conspiracy to keep women relegated to the background is also aided by the continuous psychological and political strategizing that keeps women from realizing their own potential power in the church. Not only are they rewarded for performance in "backbone" or supportive positions, but they are penalized for trying to move from the backbone to the head position—the leadership of the church. It is by considering the distinction between prescribed support positions and policymaking leadership positions that the oppression of Black women in the Black church can be seen most clearly.

For the most part, men have monopolized the ministry as a profession. The ministry of women as fully ordained clergypersons has always been controversial. The Black church fathers were unable to see the injustices of their own practices, even when they paralleled the injustices of the white church against which they rebelled.

In the early nineteenth century, Rev. Richard Allen perceived that it was unjust for Blacks, whether free or slaves, to be relegated to the balcony and restricted to a special time to pray and kneel at the communion table. Yet because of his acceptance of the patriarchal system, Allen was unable to see the injustice in relegating women to one area of the church—the pews—by withholding ordination from women as he did in the case of Mrs. Jarena Lee.[2] Lee recorded Allen's response when she informed him of her call to "go preach the Gospel":

> He replied by asking in what sphere I wished to move ?
> I said, among the Methodists. He then replied, that a
> Mrs. Cook, a Methodist lady, had also some time before
> requested the same privilege; who, it was believed, had
> done much good in the way of *exhortation*, and *holding
> prayer meetings;* and who had been permitted to do so by
> the *verbal license* of the preacher in charge at the time.
> But as to women preaching, he said that our Discipline
> knew nothing at all about it—that *it did not call* for
> women preachers.[3]

Because of this response, Jarena Lee's preaching ministry was delayed for eight years. She was not unaware of the sexist injustice in Allen's response:

> Oh how careful ought we be, lest through our by-laws of
> church government and discipline, we bring into dis-
> repute even the word of life. For as unseemly as it may
> appear nowadays for a woman to preach, it should be
> remembered that nothing is impossible with God. And
> why should it be thought impossible, heterodox, or
> improper for a woman to preach, seeing the Savior died
> for the woman as well as the man?[4]

Another "colored minister of the gospel," "Elizabeth," was greatly troubled over her call to preach, or, more accurately, over the response of men to her call to preach. She said:

I often felt that I was unfit to assemble with the congregation with whom I had gathered....I felt that I was
despised on account of this gracious calling, and was
looked upon as a speckled bird by the ministers to whom
I looked for instruction...some [of the ministers] would
cry out, "You are an enthusiast," and others said, "The
Discipline did not allow of any such division of the
work."[5]

When questioned some time later about her authority to preach against
slavery and about her ordination status, she responded that she preached
"not by the commission of men's hands: if the Lord had ordained me, I
needed nothing better."[6] With this commitment to God rather than to a
male-dominated church structure, she led a fruitful ministry.

Mrs. Amanda Berry Smith, like Mrs. Jarena Lee, had to conduct her
ministry outside the structure of the A.M.E. Church. Smith described
herself as a "plain Christian woman" with "no money" and "no
prominence."[7] But she was intrigued with the idea of attending the
General Conference of 1872 in Nashville, Tennessee. Her inquiry into the
cost of going to Nashville brought the following comments from some of
the A.M.E. brethren:

"I tell you, Sister, it will cost money to go down there;
and if you ain't got plenty of it, it's no use to go";...
another said: "What does she want to go for?" "Woman
preacher; they want to be ordained," was the reply. "I
mean to fight that thing," said the other. "Yes, indeed, so
will I," said another.[8]

The oppression of women in the ministry took many forms. In
addition to their not being granted ordination, the authenticity of "the
call" of women was frequently put to the test. Lee, Elizabeth, and Smith
spoke of the many souls they had brought to Christ through their
preaching and singing in local Black congregations, as well as in white
and mixed congregations. It was not until Rev. Allen, now Bishop
Richard Allen, heard Jarena Lee preach that he was convinced that she
was of the Spirit. He still refused, however, to ordain her. The
"brethren," including some bishops of the 1872 General Conference of
the A.M.E. Church, were convinced that Amanda Berry Smith was blessed
with the spirit of God after hearing her sing at a session held at Fisk
University. Smith tells us that "...the Spirit of the Lord seemed to fall on
all the people. The preachers got happy...." This experience brought
invitations for her to preach at several churches, but it did not bring an

appointment as pastor to a local congregation, nor the right of ordination. She summed up the experience in this way: "...After that many of my brethren believed in me, especially as the question of ordination of women never was mooted in the Conference."[9]

Several Black denominations have since begun to ordain women.[10] But this matter of women preachers having the extra burden of proving their call to an extent not required of men still prevails in the Black church today. A study in which I participated at Union Theological Seminary in New York City bears this out. Interviews with Black ministers of different denominations revealed that their prejudices against women, and especially women in the ministry, resulted in unfair expectations and unjust treatment of women ministers whom they encountered.[11]

It is the unfair expectations placed upon women and blatant discrimination that keep them "in the pew" and "out of the pulpit"—sometimes to ridiculous extremes. At the 1971 Annual Convocation of the National Committee of Black Churchmen,[12] held at the Liberty Baptist Church in Chicago, I was slightly amused when, as I approached the pulpit to place my cassette tape recorder near the speaker, Walter Fauntroy, as several brothers had already done, I was stopped by a man who informed me that I could not enter the pulpit area. When I asked why not, he directed me to the pastor, who told me that women were not permitted in the pulpit, but that he would have a man place the recorder there for me. Although I could not believe that explanation a serious one, I agreed to have a man place it on the pulpit for me and returned to my seat in the sanctuary for the continuation of the convocation. The seriousness of the pastor's statement became clear to me later at that meeting when Mary Jane Patterson, a Presbyterian Church executive, was refused the right to speak from the pulpit.[13]

As far as the issue of women is concerned, it is obvious that the Black church described by C. Eric Lincoln has not fared much better than the Negro church of E. Franklin Frazier.[14] The failure of the Black church and Black theology to proclaim explicitly the liberation of Black women indicates that they cannot claim to be agents of divine liberation. If the theology, like the church, has no word for Black women, its conception of liberation is inauthentic.

THE BLACK EXPERIENCE
AND THE BLACK WOMAN

For the most part, Black church*men* have not dealt with the oppression of Black women in either the Black church or the Black community. Frederick Douglass was one notable exception in the nineteenth century. His active advocacy of women's rights was a demonstration against the contradiction between preaching "justice for all" and practicing the continued oppression of women. "He, therefore, dared not claim a right [for himself] which he would not concede to women."[15] These words describe the convictions of a man who was active both in the church and in the larger Black community. This is significant because there is usually a direct relationship between what goes on in the Black church and in the Black secular community.

The status of Black women in the community parallels that of Black women in the church. Black theology considers the Black experience to be the context out of which its questions about God and human existence are formulated. This is assumed to be the context in which God's revelation is received and interpreted. Only from the perspective of the poor and the oppressed can an adequate theology be created. Arising out of the Black Power Movement of the 1960s, Black theology purports to take seriously the experience of the larger community's struggle for liberation. But if this is indeed the case, Black theology must function in the secular community in the same way it should function in the church community. It must serve as a "self-test" to see whether the rhetoric or proclamation of the Black community's struggle for liberation is consistent with its practices.

How does the "self-test" principle operate among the poor and the oppressed? Certainly Black theology has spoken to some of the forms of oppression which exist within the community of the oppressed. Many of the injustices it has attacked are the same as those which gave rise to the prophets of the Old Testament. But the fact that Black theology does not include sexism specifically as one of those injustices is all too evident. It suggests that the theologians do not understand sexism to be one of the oppressive realities of the Black community. Silence on this specific issue can only mean conformity to the status quo. The most prominent Black theologian, James Cone, has recently broken this silence:

> The Black church, like all other churches, is a male-dominated church. The difficulty that Black male ministers have in supporting the equality of women in the church and society stems partly from the lack of a clear liberation-criterion rooted in the gospel and in the present struggles of oppressed peoples....It is truly amazing that many Black male ministers, young and old, can hear the message of liberation in the gospel when related to racism but remain deaf to a similar message in the context of sexism....[16]

It is difficult to understand how Black men manage to exclude the liberation of Black women from their interpretation of the liberating gospel. Any correct analysis of the poor and oppressed would reveal some interesting and inescapable facts about the situation of women within oppressed groups. Without succumbing to the long and fruitless debate of "who is more oppressed than whom," I want to make some pointed suggestions to Black male theologians.

It would not be very difficult to argue that since Black women are the poorest of the poor, the most oppressed of the oppressed, their experience provides a most fruitful context for doing Black theology. The research of Jacquelyne Jackson attests to the extreme deprivation of Black women. Jackson supports her claim with statistical data showing that "in comparison with Black males and white males and females, Black women yet constitute the most disadvantaged group in the United States, as evidenced especially by their largely unenviable educational, occupational, employment, and income levels, and availability of marital partners."[17] In other words, in spite of the "quite insignificant" educational advantage that Black women have over Black men, they have "had the greatest access to the worst jobs at the lowest earnings."[18] It is important to emphasize this fact in order to elevate to its rightful level of concern the condition of Black women, not only in the world at large, but in the Black community and the Black church. It is my contention that if Black theology speaks of the Black community as if the special problems of Black women do not exist, it is no different from the white theology it claims to reject precisely because of its inability to take account of the existence of Black people.

It is instructive to note that the experience of Black women working in the Black Power Movement further accentuated the problem of the oppression of women in the Black community. Because of their invisibility among the leadership of the movement, they, like women of the church, provided "support": they filled the streets when numbers were needed for demonstrations; they stuffed envelopes in the offices and performed other menial tasks. Kathleen Cleaver, in a *Black Scholar* interview, revealed some of the problems in the movement which caused her to become involved in women's liberation issues. While underscoring the crucial role played by women as Black Power activists, Kathleen Cleaver, nonetheless, acknowledged the presence of sex discrimination:

> I viewed myself as assisting everything that was done. . . .
> The form of assistance that women give in political movements to men is just as crucial as the leadership that men give to those movements. And this is something that

is never recognized and never dealt with. *Because women are always relegated to assistance,* and this is where I became interested in the liberation of women. Conflicts, constant conflicts came up, conflicts that would rise as a result of the fact that I was married to a member of the Central Committee and I was also an officer in the Party. Things that I would have suggested myself would be implemented. But if I suggested them the suggestion might be rejected. If they were suggested by a man the suggestion would be implemented.

It seemed throughout the history of my working with the Party, I always had to struggle with this. The suggestion itself was never viewed objectively. *The fact that the suggestion came from a woman gave it some lesser value.* And it seemed that it had something to do with the egos of the men involved. I know that the first demonstration that we had at the courthouse for Huey Newton, which I was very instrumental in organizing, the first time we went out on the soundtrucks, I was on the soundtrucks; the first leaflet we put out, I wrote; the first demonstration, I made up the pamphlets. And the members of that demonstration for the most part were women. I've noticed that throughout my dealings in the Black movement in the United States, that *the most anxious, the most eager, the most active, the most quick to understand the problem and quick to move are women.*[19]

Cleaver exposed the fact that even when women had leadership roles, sexism lurked in the wings. As Executive Secretary of the Student Nonviolent Coordinating Committee (SNCC), Ruby Doris Robinson was described as the "heartbeat of SNCC." Yet there were "the constant conflicts, the constant struggles that she was subjected to because she was a woman."[20]

Notwithstanding all the evidence to the contrary, some may want to argue that the central problem of Black women is related to their race and not their sex. Such an argument then presumes that the problem cannot be resolved apart from the Black struggle. I contend that as long as the Black struggle refuses to recognize and deal with its sexism, the idea that women will receive justice from that struggle alone will never work. It will not work because Black women will no longer allow Black men to ignore their unique problems and needs in the name of some distorted view of the "liberation of the total community." Consider the words of President Sekou Toure on the role of African women in the revolution: "If African women cannot possibly conduct their struggle in isolation from the struggle that our people wage for African liberation, African freedom, conversely, is not effective unless it brings about the liberation of African women."[21] Black men who have an investment in the patriarchal structure of White America and who intend to do Christian theology have yet to realize that if Jesus is liberator of the oppressed, all of the oppressed must be liberated. Perhaps the proponents of the argument that the cause of Black women must be subsumed under a larger cause should look to South African theologians Sabelo Ntwasa and Basil Moore. They affirm that "Black theology, as it struggles to formulate a theology of liberation relevant to South Africa, cannot afford to perpetuate any form of domination, not even male domination. If its liberation is not human enough to include the liberation of women, it will not be liberation."[22]

A CHALLENGE TO BLACK THEOLOGY

My central argument is this: Black theology cannot continue to treat Black women as if they were invisible creatures who are on the outside looking into the Black experience, the Black church, and the Black theological enterprise. It will have to deal with women as integral parts of the whole community. Black theology, therefore, must speak to the bishops who hide behind the statement, "Women don't want women pastors." It must speak to the pastors who say, "My church isn't ready for women preachers yet." It must teach the seminarians who feel that "Women have no place in seminary." It must address the women in the church and in the community who are content and complacent with their oppression. It must challenge the educators who would reeducate the people on every issue except the dignity and equality of women.

Black women represent more than 50 percent of the Black community and more than 70 percent of the Black church. How, then, can an authentic theology of liberation arise out of these communities without specifically addressing the liberation of women? Does the fact that certain questions are raised by Black women make them any less Black concerns? If, as I contend, the liberation of Black men and women is inseparable, then a radical split cannot be made between racism and sexism. Black women are oppressed by racism *and* sexism. It is therefore necessary that Black men and women be actively involved in combatting both evils.

Only as Black women in greater numbers make their way from the background to the forefront will the true strength of the Black community be fully realized. There is already a heritage of strong Black women and men upon which a stronger nation can be built. There is a tradition which declares that God is at work in the experience of the Black woman. This tradition, in the context of the total Black experience, can provide data for the development of a holistic Black theology. Such a theology will repudiate the God of classical theology who is presented as an absolute Patriarch, a deserting father who created Black men and women and then "walked out" in the face of responsibility. Such a theology will look at the meaning of the total Jesus Christ Event; it will consider how God through Jesus Christ is related not only to oppressed men, but to women as well. Such a theology will "allow" God through the Holy Spirit to work through persons without regard to race, sex, or class. This theology will exercise its prophetic function and serve as a "self-test" in a church characterized by the sins of racism, sexism, and other forms of oppression.

Until Black women theologians are fully participating in the theological enterprise, it is important to make Black male theologians and Black leaders aware of the fact that Black women are needed not only as Christian educators, but as theologians and church leaders. It is only when Black women and men share jointly the leadership in theology and in the church and community that the Black nation will become strong and liberated. Only then will there be the possibility that Black theology can become a theology of divine liberation.

One final word for those who argue that the issues of racism and sexism are too complicated and should not be confused. I agree that the issues should not be "confused." But the elimination of both racism and sexism is so crucial for the liberation of Black persons that we cannot shrink from facing them together. Sojourner Truth told us why in 1867, when she spoke out on the issue of suffrage, and what she said at that time is still relevant to us as we deal with the liberation of Black women today:

> I feel that if I had to answer for the deeds done in my body just as much as a man, I have a right to have just as much as a man. There is a great stir about colored men getting their rights, but not a word about the colored women; and if colored men get their rights, and not colored women theirs, you see the colored men will be masters over the women, and it will be just as bad as it was before. So I am for keeping the thing going while things are stirring: because if we wait til it is still, it will take a great while to get it going again....[23]

Black women have to keep the issue of sexism "going" in the Black community, in the Black church, and in Black theology until it has been eliminated. To do otherwise means that they will be pushed aside until eternity. Therefore, with Sojourner Truth, I am arguing for "keeping the thing going while things are stirring...."

NOTES

[1]Study of the Philadelphia Conference of the African Methodist Episcopal Church, May 1976. (The study also included sporadic samplings of churches in other conferences in the First Episcopal District.) For example, a church of 1660 members (500 men and 1160 women) had a trustee board of 8 men and 1 woman and a steward board of 13 men and 6 women. A church of 100 members (35 men and 65 women) had a trustee board of 5 men and 4 women and a steward board of 5 men and 4 women.

[2]Jarena Lee, *The Life and Religious Experience of Jarena Lee: A Colored Lady Giving an Account of Her Call to Preach the Gospel* (Philadelphia, 1836), printed in Dorothy Porter, ed., *Early Negro Writing, 1760-1837* (Boston: Beacon Press, 1971), 494-514.

[3]Ibid., p. 503 (italics mine). Carol George, in *Segregated Sabbaths* (New York: Oxford Univ. Press, 1973), presents a very positive picture of the relationship between Jarena Lee and Bishop Richard Allen. She feels that by the time Lee approached Allen, he had "modified his views on woman's rights" (129). She contends that since Allen was free from the Methodist Church he was able to "determine his own policy" with respect to women under the auspices of the A.M.E. Church. It should be noted that Bishop Allen accepted Rev. Lee as a woman preacher and not as an ordained preacher with full rights and privileges thereof. Even Carol George admitted that Lee traveled with Bishop Allen only "as an unofficial member of their delegation to conference sessions in New York and Baltimore"—"to attend," not to participate in them. I agree that this does represent progress in Bishop Allen's view from the time of Lee's first approach; on the second approach, he was at least encouraging. Then, he began "to promote her interests" (129)—but he did not ordain her.

[4]Ibid.

[5]"Elizabeth: A Colored Minister of the Gospel," reprinted in Bert James Loewenberg and Ruth Bogin, eds., *Black Women in Nineteenth-Century American Life* (University Park, Pa.: The Pennsylvania State Univ. Press, 1976), 132. The denomination of Elizabeth is not known to this writer. Her parents were Methodists, but she was separated from her

parents at the age of eleven. However, the master from whom she gained her freedom was Presbyterian. Her autobiography was published by the Philadelphia Quakers.

[6]Ibid. p. 133.

[7]Amanda Berry Smith, *An Autobiography: The Story of the Lord's Dealings with Mrs. Amanda Berry Smith, the Colored Evangelist* (Chicago, 1893), reprinted in Loewenberg and Bogin, *op.cit.*, p. 157.

[8]Ibid.

[9]Ibid., p. 159.

[10]The African Methodist Episcopal Church started ordaining women in 1948, according to the Rev. William P. Foley of Bridgestreet A.M.E. Church in Brooklyn, New York. The first ordained woman was Martha J. Keys.

The African Methodist Episcopal Zion Church ordained women as early as 1884, when Mrs. Julia A. Foote was ordained Deacon in the New York Annual Conference. In 1894, Mrs. Mary J. Small was ordained Deacon, and in 1898, she was ordained Elder. See David Henry Bradley, Sr., *A History of the A.M.E. Zion Church*, Vol. II: 1872–1968 (Nashville: The Parthenon Press, 1970), pp. 384 and 393.

The Christian Methodist Episcopal Church enacted legislation to ordain women in the 1970 General Conference. Since then approximately 75 women have been ordained. See the Rev. N. Charles Thomas, General Secretary of the C.M.E. Church and Director of the Department of Ministry, Memphis, Tennessee.

Many Baptists churches still do not ordain women. Some churches in the Pentecostal tradition do not ordain women. However, in some other Pentecostal churches, women are founders, pastors, elders, and bishops.

In the case of the A.M.E. Zion Church where women were ordained as early as 1884, the important question would be: What happened to the women who were ordained? In addition, all of these churches (except for those which do give leadership to women) should answer the following questions: Have women been assigned to pastor "class A" churches? Have women been appointed as presiding elders? (There is currently one woman presiding elder in the A.M.E. Church.) Have women been elected to serve as bishops of any of these churches? Have women served as presidents of Conventions?

[11]Yolande Herron, Jacquelyn Grant, Gwendolyn Johnson, and Samuel Roberts, "Black Women and the Field Education Experience at Union Theological Seminary: Problems and Prospects" (New York: Union Theological Seminary, May 1978).

[12]This organization continues to call itself the National Committee of Black Churchmen despite the protests of women members.

[13]NCBC has since decided to examine the policies of its host institutions (churches) to avoid the recurrence of such incidents.

[14]E. Franklin Frazier, *The Negro Church in America;* C. Eric Lincoln, *The Black Church Since Frazier* (New York: Schocken Books, 1974), passim.

[15]Philip S. Foner, ed., *Frederick Douglass on Women's Rights* (Westport, Conn.: Greenwood Press), p. 51.

[16]James Cone, "Black Ecumenism and the Liberation Struggle," delivered at Yale University, February 16-17, 1978, and Quinn Chapel A.M.E. Church, May 22, 1978. In two other recent papers Cone has voiced concern on women's issues, relating them to the larger question of liberation. These papers are: "New Roles in the Ministry: A Theological Appraisal" and "Black Theology and the Black Church: Where Do We Go from Here?"

[17]Jacquelyne Jackson, "But Where Are the Men?" *The Black Scholar, op.cit.* p. 30.

[18]Ibid., p. 32.

[19]Kathleen Cleaver was interviewed by Sister Julia Herve. Ibid., pp. 55-56.

[20]Ibid., p. 55.

[21]Sekou Toure, "The Role of Women in the Revolution," *The Black Scholar* 6:6 (March 1975):32.

[22]Sabelo Ntwasa and Basil Moore, "The Concept of God in Black Theology," in *The Challenge of Black Theology in South Africa,* ed. Basil Moore (Atlanta, Ga.: John Knox Press, 1974), pp. 25-26.

[23]Sojourner Truth, "Keeping the Things Going Whilst Things Are Stirring," reprinted in Miriam Schneir, ed., *Feminism: The Essential Historical Writings* (New York: Random House, 1972), pp. 129-30.

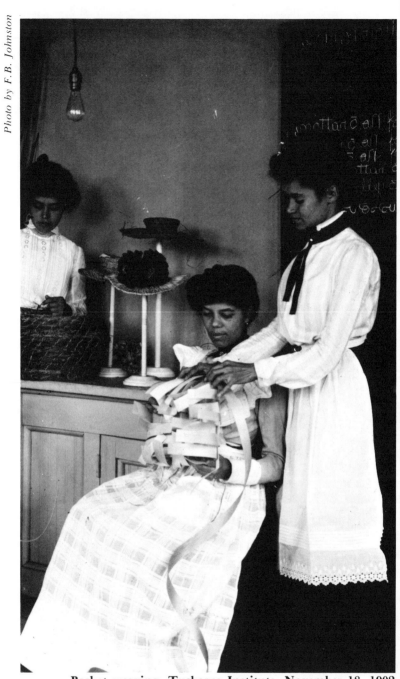

Basket weaving, Tuskegee Institute, November 18, 1902.

Section Five

"Necessary Bread": Black Women's Literature

15

Toward a Black Feminist Criticism

BARBARA SMITH

For all my sisters, especially Beverly and Demita

I do not know where to begin. Long before I tried to write this I realized that I was attempting something unprecedented, something dangerous merely by writing about Black women writers from a feminist perspective and about Black lesbian writers from any perspective at all. These things have not been done. Not by white male critics, expectedly. Not by Black male critics. Not by white women critics who think of themselves as feminists. And most crucially not by Black women critics who, although they pay the most attention to Black women writers as a group, seldom use a consistent feminist analysis or write about Black lesbian literature. All segments of the literary world—whether establishment, progressive, Black, female, or lesbian—do not know, or at least act as if they do not know, that Black women writers and Black lesbian writers exist.

For whites, this specialized lack of knowledge is inextricably connected to their not knowing in any concrete or politically transforming way that Black women of any description dwell in this place. Black women's existence, experience, and culture and the brutally complex systems of oppression which shape these are in the "real world" of white and/or male consciousness beneath consideration, invisible, unknown.

This invisibility, which goes beyond anything that either Black men or white women experience and tell about in their writing, is one reason it is so difficult for me to know where to start. It seems overwhelming to break such a massive silence. Even more numbing, however, is the realization that so many of the women who will read this have not yet noticed us missing either from their reading matter, their politics, or their lives. It is galling that ostensible feminists and acknowledged lesbians have been so blinded to the implications of any womanhood that is not white womanhood and that they have yet to struggle with the deep racism in themselves that is at the source of this blindness.

I think of the thousands and thousands of books, magazines, and articles which have been devoted, by this time, to the subject of women's writing and I am filled with rage at the fraction of those pages that mention Black and other Third World women. I finally do not know how to begin because in 1977 I want to be writing this for a Black feminist publication, for Black women who know and love these writers as I do and who, if they do not yet know their names, have at least profoundly felt the pain of their absence.

The conditions that coalesce into the impossibilities of this essay have as much to do with politics as with the practice of literature. Any discussion of Afro-American writers can rightfully begin with the fact that for most of the time we have been in this country we have been categorically denied not only literacy, but the most minimal possibility of a decent human life. In her landmark essay, "In Search of Our Mothers' Gardens," Alice Walker discloses how the political, economic, and social restrictions of slavery and racism have historically stunted the creative lives of Black women.[1]

At the present time I feel that the politics of feminism have a direct relationship to the state of Black women's literature. A viable, autonomous Black feminist movement in this country would open up the space needed for the exploration of Black women's lives and the creation of consciously Black woman-identified art. At the same time a redefinition of the goals and strategies of the white feminist movement would lead to much needed change in the focus and content of what is now generally accepted as women's culture.

I want to make in this essay some connections between the politics of Black women's lives, what we write about, and our situation as artists. In order to do this I will look at how Black women have been viewed critically by outsiders, demonstrate the necessity for Black feminist criticism, and try to understand what the existence or nonexistence of Black lesbian writing reveals about the state of Black women's culture and the intensity of *all* Black women's oppression.

The role that criticism plays in making a body of literature recognizable and real hardly needs to be explained here. The necessity for nonhostile and perceptive analysis of works written by persons outside the "mainstream" of white/male cultural rule has been proven by the Black cultural resurgence of the 1960s and '70s and by the even more recent growth of feminist literary scholarship. For books to be real and remembered they have to be talked about. For books to be understood they must be examined in such a way that the basic intentions of the writers are at least considered. Because of racism Black literature has usually been viewed as a discrete subcategory of American literature and there have been Black critics of Black literature who did much to keep it alive long before it caught the attention of whites. Before the advent of specifically feminist criticism in this decade, books by white women, on the other hand, were not clearly perceived as the cultural manifestation of an oppressed people. It took the surfacing of the second wave of the North American feminist movement to expose the fact that these works contain a stunningly accurate record of the impact of patriarchal values and practice upon the lives of women and more significantly that literature by women provides essential insights into female experience.

In speaking about the current situation of Black women writers, it is important to remember that the existence of a feminist movement was an essential precondition to the growth of feminist literature, criticism, and women's studies, which focused at the beginning almost entirely upon investigations of literature. The fact that a parallel Black feminist movement has been much slower in evolving cannot help but have impact upon the situation of Black women writers and artists and explains in part why during this very same period we have been so ignored.

There is no political movement to give power or support to those who want to examine Black women's experience through studying our history, literature, and culture. There is no political presence that demands a minimal level of consciousness and respect from those who write or talk about our lives. Finally, there is not a developed body of Black feminist political theory whose assumptions could be used in the study of Black women's art. When Black women's books are dealt with at all, it is usually in the context of Black literature which largely ignores the implications of sexual politics. When white women look at Black women's works they are of course ill-equipped to deal with the subtleties of racial politics. A Black feminist approach to literature that embodies the realization that the politics of sex as well as the politics of race and class are crucially interlocking factors in the works of Black women writers is an absolute necessity. Until a Black feminist criticism exists we will not even know what these writers mean. The citations from a variety of critics which follow prove that without a Black feminist critical perspective not only are books by Black women misunderstood, they are destroyed in the process. Jerry H.

Bryant, the *Nation's* white male reviewer of Alice Walker's *In Love & Trouble: Stories of Black Women,* wrote in 1973:

> The subtitle of the collection, "Stories of Black Women," is probably an attempt by the publisher to exploit not only black subjects but feminine ones. There is nothing feminist about these stories, however.[2]

Blackness and feminism are to his mind mutually exclusive and peripheral to the act of writing fiction. Bryant of course does not consider that Walker might have titled the work herself, nor did he apparently read the book which unequivocally reveals the author's feminist consciousness.

In *The Negro Novel in America,* a book that Black critics recognize as one of the worst examples of white racist pseudoscholarship, Robert Bone cavalierly dismisses Ann Petry's classic, *The Street.* He perceives it to be "...a superficial social analysis" of how slums victimize their Black inhabitants.[3] He further objects that:

> It is an attempt to interpret slum life in terms of *Negro* experience, when a larger frame of reference is required. As Alain Locke has observed, *"Knock on Any Door* is superior to *The Street* because it designates class and environment, rather than mere race and environment, as its antagonist."[4]

Neither Robert Bone nor Alain Locke, the Black male critic he cites, can recognize that *The Street* is one of the best delineations in literature of how sex, race, *and* class interact to oppress Black women.

In her review of Toni Morrison's *Sula* for *The New York Times Book Review* in 1973, putative feminist Sara Blackburn makes similarly racist comments. She writes:

> ...Toni Morrison is far too talented to remain only a marvelous recorder of the black side of provincial American life. If she is to maintain the large and serious audience she deserves, she is going to have to address a riskier contemporary reality than this beautiful but nevertheless distanced novel. *And if she does this, it seems to me that she might easily transcend that early and unintentionally limiting classification "black wom-*

*an writer" and take her place among the most serious,
important and talented American novelists now working.*[5] [Italics mine.]

Recognizing Morrison's exquisite gift, Blackburn unashamedly asserts
that Morrison is "too talented" to deal with mere Black folk, particularly
those double nonentities, Black women. In order to be accepted as
"serious," "important," "talented," and "American," she must obviously
focus her efforts upon chronicling the doings of white men.

The mishandling of Black women writers by whites is paralleled
more often by their not being handled at all, particularly in feminist
criticism. Although Elaine Showalter in her review essay on literary
criticism for *Signs* states that: "The best work being produced today [in
feminist criticism] is exacting and cosmopolitan," her essay is neither.[6] If
it were, she would not have failed to mention a single Black or Third
World woman writer, whether "major" or "minor," to cite her
questionable categories. That she also does not even hint that lesbian
writers of any color exist renders her purported overview virtually
meaningless. Showalter obviously thinks that the identities of being
Black and female are mutually exclusive, as this statement illustrates:

> Furthermore, there are other literary subcultures (black
> American novelists, for example) whose history offers a
> precedent for feminist scholarship to use.[7]

The idea of critics like Showalter *using* Black literature is chilling, a case
of barely disguised cultural imperialism. The final insult is that she
footnotes the preceding remark by pointing readers to works on Black
literature by white males Robert Bone and Roger Rosenblatt!

Two recent works by white women, Ellen Moers's *Literary Women:
The Great Writers* and Patricia Meyer Spacks's *The Female Imagination*,
evidence the same racist flaw.[8] Moers includes the names of four Black
and one Puertorriqueña writer in her seventy pages of bibliographical
notes and does not deal at all with Third World women in the body of her
book. Spacks refers to a comparison between Negroes (sic) and women in
Mary Ellmann's *Thinking About Women* under the index entry, "blacks,
women and." "*Black Boy* (Wright)" is the preceding entry. Nothing
follows. Again there is absolutely no recognition that Black and female
identity ever coexist, specifically in a group of Black women writers.
Perhaps one can assume that these women do not know who Black
women writers are, that they have little opportunity like most Americans
to learn about them. Perhaps. Their ignorance seems suspiciously
selective, however, particularly in the light of the dozens of truly obscure

white women writers they are able to unearth. Spacks was herself employed at Wellesley College at the same time that Alice Walker was there teaching one of the first courses on Black women writers in the country.

I am not trying to encourage racist criticism of Black women writers like that of Sara Blackburn, to cite only one example. As a beginning I would at least like to see in print white women's acknowledgment of the contradictions of who and what are being left out of their research and writing.[9]

Black male critics can also *act* as if they do not know that Black women writers exist and are, of course, hampered by an inability to comprehend Black women's experience in sexual as well as racial terms. Unfortunately there are also those who are as virulently sexist in their treatment of Black women writers as their white male counterparts. Darwin Turner's discussion of Zora Neale Hurston in his *In a Minor Chord: Three Afro-American Writers and Their Search for Identity* is a frightening example of the near assassination of a great Black woman writer.[10] His descriptions of her and her work as "artful," "coy," "irrational," "superficial," and "shallow" bear no relationship to the actual quality of her achievements. Turner is completely insensitive to the sexual political dynamics of Hurston's life and writing.

In a recent interview the notoriously misogynist writer, Ishmael Reed, comments in this way upon the low sales of his newest novel:

> ...but the book only sold 8000 copies. I don't mind giving out the figure: 8000. Maybe if I was one of those young *female* Afro-American writers that are so hot now, I'd sell more. You know, fill my books with ghetto women who can *do no wrong*....But come on, I think I could have sold 8000 copies by myself.[11]

The politics of the situation of Black women are glaringly illuminated by this statement. Neither Reed nor his white male interviewer has the slightest compunction about attacking Black women in print. They need not fear widespread public denunciation since Reed's statement is in perfect agreement with the values of a society that hates Black people, women, and Black women. Finally the two of them feel free to base their actions on the premise that Black women are powerless to alter either their political or cultural oppression.

In her introduction to "A Bibliography of Works Written by American Black Women" Ora Williams quotes some of the reactions of her colleagues toward her efforts to do research on Black women. She writes:

Others have reacted negatively with such statements as, "I really don't think you are going to find very much written," "Have 'they' written anything that is any good?" and, "I wouldn't go overboard with this woman's lib thing." When discussions touched on the possibility of teaching a course in which emphasis would be on the literature by Black women, one response was, "Ha, ha. That will certainly be the most nothing course ever offered!"[12]

A remark by Alice Walker capsulizes what all the preceding examples indicate about the position of Black women writers and the reasons for the damaging criticism about them. She responds to her interviewer's question, "Why do you think that the black woman writer has been so ignored in America? Does she have even more difficulty than the black male writer, who perhaps has just begun to gain recognition?" Walker replies:

> There are two reasons why the black woman writer is not taken as seriously as the black male writer. One is that she's a woman. Critics seem unusually ill-equipped to intelligently discuss and analyze the works of black women. Generally, they do not even make the attempt; they prefer, rather, to talk about the lives of black women writers, not about what they write. And, since black women writers are not—it would seem—very likable—until recently they were the least willing worshippers of male supremacy—comments about them tend to be cruel.[13]

A convincing case for Black feminist criticism can obviously be built solely upon the basis of the negativity of what already exists. It is far more gratifying, however, to demonstrate its necessity by showing how it can serve to reveal for the first time the profound subtleties of this particular body of literature.

Before suggesting how a Black feminist approach might be used to examine a specific work I will outline some of the principles that I think a Black feminist critic could use. Beginning with a primary commitment to exploring how both sexual and racial politics and Black and female identity are inextricable elements in Black women's writings, she would also work from the assumption that Black women writers constitute an identifiable literary tradition. The breadth of her familiarity with these writers would have shown her that not only is theirs a verifiable historical tradition that parallels in time the tradition of Black men and white women writing in this country, but that thematically, stylistically, aesthetically, and conceptually Black women writers manifest common approaches to the act of creating literature as a direct result of the specific political, social, and economic experience they have been obliged to share. The way, for example, that Zora Neale Hurston, Margaret Walker, Toni Morrison, and Alice Walker incorporate the traditional Black female activities of rootworking, herbal medicine, conjure, and midwifery into the fabric of their stories is not mere coincidence, nor is their use of specifically Black female language to express their own and their characters' thoughts accidental. The use of Black women's language and cultural experience in books *by* Black women *about* Black women results in a miraculously rich coalescing of form and content and also takes their writing far beyond the confines of white/male literary structures. The Black feminist critic would find innumerable commonalities in works by Black women.

Another principle which grows out of the concept of a tradition and which would also help to strengthen this tradition would be for the critic to look first for precedents and insights in interpretation within the works of other Black women. In other words she would think and write out of her own identity and not try to graft the ideas or methodology of white/male literary thought upon the precious materials of Black women's art. Black feminist criticism would by definition be highly innovative, embodying the daring spirit of the works themselves. The Black feminist critic would be constantly aware of the political implications of her work and would assert the connections between it and the political situation of all Black women. Logically developed, Black feminist criticism would owe its existence to a Black feminist movement while at the same time contributing ideas that women in the movement could use.

Black feminist criticism applied to a particular work can overturn previous assumptions about it and expose for the first time its actual dimensions. At the "Lesbians and Literature" discussion at the 1976 Modern Language Association convention Bertha Harris suggested that if in a woman writer's work a sentence refuses to do what it is supposed to do, if there are strong images of women and if there is a refusal to be linear, the result is innately lesbian literature. As usual, I wanted to see if these ideas might be applied to the Black women writers that I know and quickly realized that many of their works were, in Harris's sense, lesbian. Not because women are "lovers," but because they are the central figures, are positively portrayed and have pivotal relationships with one another. The form and language of these works are also nothing like what white patriarchal culture requires or expects.

I was particularly struck by the way in which Toni Morrison's novels *The Bluest Eye* and *Sula* could be explored from this new perspective.[14] In both works the relationships between girls and women are essential, yet at the same time physical sexuality is overtly expressed only between men and women. Despite the apparent heterosexuality of the female characters I discovered in re-reading *Sula* that it works as a lesbian novel not only because of the passionate friendship between Sula and Nel, but because of Morrison's consistently critical stance toward the heterosexual institutions of male/female relationships, marriage, and the family. Consciously or not, Morrison's work poses both lesbian and feminist questions about Black women's autonomy and their impact upon each other's lives.

Sula and Nel find each other in 1922 when each of them is twelve, on the brink of puberty and the discovery of boys. Even as awakening sexuality "clotted their dreams," each girl desires "a someone" obviously female with whom to share her feelings. Morrison writes:

> ...for it was in dreams that the two girls had met. Long before Edna Finch's Mellow House opened, even before they marched through the chocolate halls of Garfield Primary School...they had already made each other's acquaintance in the delirium of their noon dreams. They were solitary little girls whose loneliness was so profound it intoxicated them and sent them stumbling into Technicolored visions that always included a presence, a someone who, quite like the dreamer, shared the delight of the dream. When Nel, an only child, sat on the steps of her back porch surrounded by the high silence of her mother's incredibly orderly house, feeling the neatness pointing at her back, she studied the poplars and fell easily into a picture of herself lying on a flower bed, tangled in her own hair, waiting for some fiery prince. He approached but never quite arrived. But always, watching the dream along with her, were some smiling sympathetic eyes. Someone as interested as she herself in the flow of her imagined hair, the thickness of the mattress of flowers, the voile sleeves that closed below her elbows in gold-threaded cuffs.
>
> Similarly, Sula, also an only child, but wedged into a household of throbbing disorder constantly awry with things, people, voices and the slamming of doors, spent hours in the attic behind a roll of linoleum galloping through her own mind on a gray-and-white horse tasting

> sugar and smelling roses in full view of someone who shared both the taste and the speed.
>
> So when they met, first in those chocolate halls and next through the ropes of the swing, they felt the ease and comfort of old friends. Because each had discovered years before that they were neither white nor male, and that all freedom and triumph was forbidden to them, they had set about creating something else to be. Their meeting was fortunate, for it let them use each other to grow on. Daughters of distant mothers and incomprehensible fathers (Sula's because he was dead; Nel's because he wasn't), they found in each other's eyes the intimacy they were looking for. (51–52)

As this beautiful passage shows, their relationship, from the very beginning, is suffused with an erotic romanticism. The dreams in which they are initially drawn to each other are actually complementary aspects of the same sensuous fairytale. Nel imagines a "fiery prince" who never quite arrives while Sula gallops like a prince "on a gray-and-white horse."[15] The "real world" of patriarchy requires, however, that they channel this energy away from each other to the opposite sex. Lorraine Bethel explains this dynamic in her essay "Conversations With Ourselves: Black Female Relationships in Toni Cade Bambara's *Gorilla, My Love* and Toni Morrison's *Sula.*" She writes:

> I am not suggesting that Sula and Nel are being consciously sexual, or that their relationship has an overt lesbian nature. I am suggesting, however, that there is a certain sensuality in their interactions that is reinforced by the mirror-like nature of their relationship. Sexual exploration and coming of age is a natural part of adolescence. Sula and Nel discover men together, and though their flirtations with males are an important part of their sexual exploration, the sensuality that they experience in each other's company is equally important.[16]

Sula and Nel must also struggle with the constrictions of racism upon their lives. The knowledge that "they were neither white nor male" is the inherent explanation of their need for each other. Morrison depicts in literature the necessary bonding that has always taken place between Black women for the sake of barest survival. Together the two girls can find the courage to create themselves.

Their relationship is severed only when Nel marries Jude, an unexceptional young man who thinks of her as "the hem—the tuck and fold that hid his raveling edges" (83). Sula's inventive wildness cannot overcome social pressure or the influence of Nel's parents who "had succeeded in rubbing down to a dull glow any sparkle or splutter she had" (83). Nel falls prey to convention while Sula escapes it. Yet at the wedding which ends the first phase of their relationship, Nel's final action is to look past her husband toward Sula:

> ...a slim figure in blue, gliding, with just a hint of a strut, down the path towards the road....Even from the rear Nel could tell that it was Sula and that she was smiling; that something deep down in that litheness was amused. (85)

When Sula returns ten years later, her rebelliousness full-blown, a major source of the town's suspicions stems from the fact that although she is almost thirty, she is still unmarried. Sula's grandmother, Eva, does not hesitate to bring up the matter as soon as she arrives. She asks:

> "When you gone to get married? You need to have some babies. It'll settle you....Ain't no woman got no business floatin' around without no man." (92)

Sula replies: "I don't want to make somebody else. I want to make myself" (92). Self-definition is a dangerous activity for any woman to engage in, especially a Black one, and it expectedly earns Sula pariah status in Medallion.

Morrison clearly points out that it is the fact that Sula has not been tamed or broken by the exigencies of heterosexual family life which most galls the others. She writes:

> Among the weighty evidence piling up was the fact that Sula did not look her age. She was near thirty and, unlike them, had lost no teeth, suffered no bruises, developed no ring of fat at the waist or pocket at the back of her neck. (115)

In other words she is not a domestic serf, a woman run down by obligatory childbearing or a victim of battering. Sula also sleeps with the husbands of the town once and then discards them, needing them even less than her own mother did, for sexual gratification and affection. The town reacts to her disavowal of patriarchal values by becoming fanatically serious about their own family obligations, as if in this way they might counteract Sula's radical criticism of their lives.

Sula's presence in her community functions much like the presence of lesbians everywhere to expose the contradictions of supposedly "normal" life. The opening paragraph of the essay "Woman Identified Woman" has amazing relevance as an explanation of Sula's position and character in the novel. It asks:

> What is a lesbian? A lesbian is the rage of all women condensed to the point of explosion. She is the woman who, often beginning at an extremely early age, acts in accordance with her inner compulsion to be a more complete and freer human being than her society— perhaps then, but certainly later—cares to allow her. These needs and actions, over a period of years, bring her into painful conflict with people, situations, the accepted ways of thinking, feeling and behaving, until she is in a state of continual war with everything around her, and usually with herself. She may not be fully conscious of the political implications of what for her began as personal necessity, but on some level she has not been able to accept the limitations and oppression laid on her by the most basic role of her society—the female role.[17]

The limitations of the *Black* female role are even greater in a racist and sexist society as is the amount of courage it takes to challenge them. It is no wonder that the townspeople see Sula's independence as imminently dangerous.

Morrison is also careful to show the reader that despite their years of separation and their opposing paths, Nel and Sula's relationship retains its primacy for each of them. Nell feels transformed when Sula returns and thinks:

> It was like getting the use of an eye back, having a cataract removed. Her old friend had come home. Sula. Who made her laugh, who made her see old things with new eyes, in whose presence she felt clever, gentle and a little raunchy. (95)

Laughing together in the familiar "rib-scraping" way, Nel feels "new, soft and new" (98). Morrison uses here the visual imagery which symbolizes the women's closeness throughout the novel.

Sula fractures this closeness, however, by sleeping with Nel's husband, an act of little import according to her system of values. Nel, of course, cannot understand. Sula thinks ruefully:

Nel was the one person who had wanted nothing from her, who had accepted all aspects of her. Now she wanted everything, and all because of *that*. Nel was the first person who had been real to her, whose name she knew, who had seen as she had the slant of life that made it possible to stretch it to its limits. Now Nel was one of *them*. (119-20)

Sula also thinks at the realization of losing Nel about how unsatisfactory her relationships with men have been and admits:

She had been looking all along for a friend, and it took her a while to discover that a lover was not a comrade and could never be—for a woman. (121)

The nearest that Sula comes to actually loving a man is in a brief affair with Ajax and what she values most about him is the intellectual companionship he provides, the brilliance he "allows" her to show. Sula's feelings about sex with men are also consistent with a lesbian interpretation of the novel. Morrison writes:

She went to bed with men as frequently as she could. It was the only place where she could find what she was looking for: *misery and the ability to feel deep sorrow* . . . . During the lovemaking she found and needed to find the cutting edge. When she left off cooperating with her body and began to assert herself in the act, particles of strength gathered in her like steel shavings drawn to a spacious magnetic center, forming a tight cluster that nothing, it seemed, could break. *And there was utmost irony and outrage in lying under someone, in a position of surrender, feeling her own abiding strength and limitless power* . . . . When her partner disengaged himself, she looked up at him in wonder trying to recall his name . . . . waiting impatiently for him to turn away . . . . *leaving her to the postcoital privateness in which she met herself, welcomed herself, and joined herself in matchless harmony.* (122-23) [Italics mine.]

Sula uses men for sex which results not in communion with them, but in her further delving into self.

Ultimately the deepest communion and communication in the novel occurs between two women who love each other. After their last painful meeting, which does not bring reconciliation, Sula thinks as Nel leaves her:

> "So she will walk on down that road, her back so straight
> in that old green coat...thinking how much I have cost
> her and never remember the days when we were two
> throats and one eye and we had no price." (147)

It is difficult to imagine a more evocative metaphor for what women can be to each other, the "pricelessness" they achieve in refusing to sell themselves for male approval, the total worth that they can only find in each other's eyes.

Decades later the novel concludes with Nel's final comprehension of the source of the grief that has plagued her from the time her husband walked out. Morrison writes:

> "All that time, all that time, I thought I was missing
> Jude." And the loss pressed down on her chest and came
> up into her throat. "We was girls together," she said as
> though explaining something. "O Lord, Sula," she
> cried, "girl, girl, girlgirlgirl."
>
> It was a fine cry—loud and long—but it had no
> bottom and it had no top, just circles and circles of
> sorrow. (174)

Again Morrison exquisitely conveys what women, Black women, mean to each other. This final passage verifies the depth of Sula and Nel's relationship and its centrality to an accurate interpretation of the work.

Sula is an exceedingly lesbian novel in the emotions expressed, in the definition of female character, and in the way that the politics of heterosexuality are portrayed. The very meaning of lesbianism is being expanded in literature, just as it is being redefined through politics. The confusion that many readers have felt about *Sula* may well have a lesbian explanation. If one sees Sula's inexplicable "evil" and nonconformity as the evil of not being male-identified, many elements in the novel become clear. The work might be clearer still if Morrison had approached her subject with the consciousness that a lesbian relationship was at least a possibility for her characters. Obviously Morrison did not *intend* the reader to perceive Sula and Nel's relationship as inherently lesbian. However, this lack of intention only shows the way in which heterosexist assumptions can veil what may logically be expected to occur in a work. What I have tried to do here is not to prove that Morrison wrote something that she did not, but to point out how a Black feminist critical perspective at least allows consideration of this level of the novel's meaning.

In her interview in *Conditions: One* Adrienne Rich talks about unconsummated relationships and the need to re-evaluate the meaning of intense yet supposedly non-erotic connections between women. She asserts:

> We need a lot more documentation about what actually happened: I think we can also imagine it, because we know it happened—we know it out of our own lives.[18]

Black women are still in the position of having to "imagine," discover, and verify Black lesbian literature because so little has been written from an avowedly lesbian perspective. The near non-existence of Black lesbian literature which other Black lesbians and I so deeply feel has everything to do with the politics of our lives, the total suppression of identity that all Black women, lesbian or not, must face. This literary silence is again intensified by the unavailability of an autonomous Black feminist movement through which we could fight our oppression and also begin to name ourselves.

In a speech, "The Autonomy of Black Lesbian Women," Wilmette Brown comments upon the connection between our political reality and the literature we must invent:

> Because the isolation of Black lesbian women, given that we are superfreaks, given that our lesbianism defies both the sexual identity that capital gives us and the racial identity that capital gives us, the isolation of Black lesbian women from heterosexual Black women is very profound. Very profound. I have searched throughout Black history, Black literature, whatever, looking for some women that I could see were somehow lesbian. Now I know that in a certain sense they were all lesbian. But that was a very painful search.[19]

Heterosexual privilege is usually the only privilege that Black women have. None of us have racial or sexual privilege, almost none of us have class privilege, maintaining "straightness" is our last resort. Being out, particularly out in print, is the final renunciation of any claim to the crumbs of "tolerance" that nonthreatening "ladylike" Black women are sometimes fed. I am convinced that it is our lack of privilege and power in every other sphere that allows so few Black women to make the leap that many white women, particularly writers, have been able to make in this decade, not merely because they are white or have economic leverage, but because they have had the strength and support of a movement behind them.

As Black lesbians we must be out not only in white society, but in the

Black community as well, which is at least as homophobic. That the sanctions against Black lesbians are extremely high is well illustrated in this comment by Black male writer Ishmael Reed. Speaking about the inroads that whites make into Black culture, he asserts:

> In Manhattan you find people actively trying to impede intellectual debate among Afro-Americans. The powerful "liberal/radical/existentialist" influences of the Manhattan literary and drama establishment speak through tokens, like for example that ancient notion of the *one* black ideologue (who's usually a Communist), the *one* black poetess (who's usually a feminist lesbian).[20]

To Reed, "feminist" and "lesbian" are the most pejorative terms he can hurl at a Black woman and totally invalidate anything she might say, regardless of her actual politics or sexual identity. Such accusations are quite effective for keeping Black women writers who are writing with integrity and strength from any conceivable perspective in line, but especially ones who are actually feminist and lesbian. Unfortunately Reed's reactionary attitude is all too typical. A community which has not confronted sexism, because a widespread Black feminist movement has not required it to, has likewise not been challenged to examine its heterosexism. Even at this moment I am not convinced that one can write explicitly as a Black lesbian and live to tell about it.

Yet there are a handful of Black women who have risked everything for truth. Audre Lorde, Pat Parker, and Ann Allen Shockley have at least broken ground in the vast wilderness of works that do not exist.[21] Black feminist criticism will again have an essential role not only in creating a climate in which Black lesbian writers can survive, but in undertaking the total reassessment of Black literature and literary history needed to reveal the Black woman-identified-women that Wilmette Brown and so many of us are looking for.

Although I have concentrated here upon what does not exist and what needs to be done, a few Black feminist critics have already begun this work. Gloria T. Hull at the University of Delaware has discovered in her research on Black women poets of the Harlem Renaissance that many of the women who are considered "minor" writers of the period were in constant contact with each other and provided both intellectual stimulation and psychological support for each other's work. At least one of these writers, Angelina Weld Grimké, wrote many unpublished love poems to women. Lorraine Bethel, a recent graduate of Yale College, has done substantial work on Black women writers, particularly in her senior essay, "This Infinity of Conscious Pain: Blues Lyricism and Hurston's

Black Female Folk Aesthetic and Cultural Sensibility in *Their Eyes Were Watching God*," in which she brilliantly defines and uses the principles of Black feminist criticism. Elaine Scott at the State University of New York at Old Westbury is also involved in highly creative and politically resonant research on Hurston and other writers. The fact that these critics are young and, except for Hull, unpublished merely indicates the impediments we face. Undoubtedly there are other women working and writing whom I do not even know, simply because there is no place to read them. As Michele Wallace states in her article, "A Black Feminist's Search for Sisterhood":

> We exist as women who are Black who are feminists, each stranded for the moment, working independently because there is not yet an environment in this society remotely congenial to our struggle—[or our thoughts].[22]

I only hope that this essay is one way of breaking our silence and our isolation, of helping us to know each other.

Just as I did not know where to start I am not sure how to end. I feel that I have tried to say too much and at the same time have left too much unsaid. What I want this essay to do is lead everyone who reads it to examine *everything* that they have ever thought and believed about feminist culture and to ask themselves how their thoughts connect to the reality of Black women's writing and lives. I want to encourage in white women, as a first step, a sane accountability to all the women who write and live on this soil. I want most of all for Black women and Black lesbians somehow not to be so alone. This last will require the most expansive of revolutions as well as many new words to tell us how to make this revolution real. I finally want to express how much easier both my waking and my sleeping hours would be if there were one book in existence that would tell me something specific about my life. One book based in Black feminist and Black lesbian experience, fiction or nonfiction. Just one work to reflect the reality that I and the Black women whom I love are trying to create. When such a book exists then each of us will not only know better how to live, but how to dream.

July, 1977

NOTES

[1]Alice Walker, "In Search of Our Mothers' Gardens," in *Ms.* (May 1974) and in *Southern Exposure* 4:4, *Generations: Women in the South* (Winter 1977):60-64.

²Jerry H. Bryant, "The Outskirts of a New City," in the *Nation* 12 (November 1973):502.

³Robert Bone, *The Negro Novel in America* (New Haven: Yale University Press, 1958), p. 180.

⁴Idem. *(Knock on Any Door* is a novel by Black writer Willard Motley.)

⁵Sara Blackburn, "You Still Can't Go Home Again," in *The New York Times Book Review*, 30 December 1973, p. 3.

⁶Elaine Showalter, "Review Essay: Literary Criticism," *Signs* 2 (Winter 1975):460.

⁷Ibid., p. 445.

⁸Ellen Moers, *Literary Women: The Great Writers* (Garden City, N.Y.: Anchor Books, 1977); Patricia Meyer Spacks, *The Female Imagination* (New York: Avon Books, 1976).

⁹An article by Nancy Hoffman, "White Women, Black Women: Inventing an Adequate Pedagogy," in the *Women's Studies Newsletter* 5:1 & 2 (Spring 1977):21–24, gives valuable insights into how white women can approach the writing of Black women.

¹⁰Darwin T. Turner, *In a Minor Chord: Three Afro-American Writers and Their Search for Identity* (Carbondale and Edwardsville: Southern Illinois University Press, 1971).

¹¹John Domini, "Roots and Racism: An Interview with Ishmael Reed," in *The Boston Phoenix*, 5 April 1977, p. 20.

¹²Ora Williams, "A Bibliography of Works Written by American Black Women," in *College Language Association Journal* 15:3 (March 1972):355. There is an expanded book-length version of this bibliography: *American Black Women in the Arts and Social Sciences: A Bibliographic Survey* (Metuchen, N.J.: The Scarecrow Press, 1973; rev. and expanded ed., 1978).

¹³John O'Brien, ed., *Interviews with Black Writers* (New York: Liveright, 1973), p. 201.

¹⁴Toni Morrison, *The Bluest Eye* (New York: Pocket Books, 1972, 1976, orig. 1970) and *Sula* (New York: Alfred A. Knopf, 1974). All subsequent references to this work will be designated in the text.

¹⁵My sister, Beverly Smith, pointed out this connection to me.

¹⁶Lorraine Bethel, "Conversations With Ourselves: Black Female Relationships in Toni Cade Bambara's *Gorilla, My Love* and Toni Morrison's *Sula*," unpublished paper written at Yale, 1976, 47 pp. (Bethel has worked from a premise similar to mine in a much more developed treatment of the novel.)

¹⁷New York Radicalesbians, "Woman Identified Woman," in *Lesbians Speak Out* (Oakland: Women's Press Collective, 1974), p. 87.

[18]Elly Bulkin, "An Interview With Adrienne Rich: Part I," in *Conditions: One,* Vol. 1, no. 1 (April 1977), p. 62.

[19]Wilmette Brown, "The Autonomy of Black Lesbian Women," ms. of speech delivered July 24, 1976, Toronto, Canada, p. 7.

[20]Domini, op. cit., p. 18.

[21]Audre Lorde, *New York Head Shop and Museum* (Detroit: Broadside, 1974); *Coal* (New York: W. W. Norton, 1976); *Between Our Selves* (Point Reyes, Calif.: Eidolon Editions, 1976); *The Black Unicorn* (New York: W. W. Norton, 1978).

Pat Parker, *Child of Myself* (Oakland: Women's Press Collective, 1972 and 1974); *Pit Stop* (Oakland: Women's Press Collective, 1973); *Womanslaughter* (Oakland: Diana Press, 1978); *Movement in Black* (Oakland: Diana Press, 1978).

Ann Allen Shockley, *Loving Her* (Indianapolis: Bobbs-Merrill, 1974).

There is at least one Black lesbian writers' collective, Jemima, in New York. They do public readings and have available a collection of their poems. They can be contacted c/o Boyce, 41-11 Parsons Blvd., Flushing, NY 11355.

[22]Michele Wallace, "A Black Feminist's Search for Sisterhood," in *The Village Voice,* 28 July 1975, p. 7; reprinted above, pp. 5-12.

16

"This Infinity of Conscious Pain": Zora Neale Hurston and the Black Female Literary Tradition

LORRAINE BETHEL

No writer is under obligation to "appear" in his own works. Yet the psychic history of some women artists should have significance for us all. And when a whole generation of some of the most articulate of American women seem to have chosen not to appear in their own works in a particular way, then something may be said of it.

Hortense Calisher[1]

The psychic history of Black women writers, particularly that of Zora Neale Hurston, has great significance for us all, because writers in the Black female literary tradition have consistently chosen to appear in their own works in a particular way. In discussing these appearances Mary Helen Washington observes that:

Since *Iola Leroy,* the first novel written by a Black woman, published in 1892, one of the main preoccupations of the Black woman writer has been the Black woman herself—her aspirations, her conflicts, her relationship to her men and her children [and to other Black women, we might add], her creativity. The Black woman writer has looked at the Black woman from an insider's point of view....That these writers have firsthand knowledge of their subject ought to be enough to command attention and respect.[2]

Black women writers have consistently rejected the falsification of their Black/female experience, thereby avoiding the negative stereotypes such falsification has often created in the white American female and Black male literary traditions.[3] Unlike many of their Black male and white female peers, Black women writers have usually refused to dispense with whatever was clearly Black and/or female in their sensibilities in an effort to achieve the mythical "neutral" voice of universal art. Zora Neale Hurston's work, particularly the novel *Their Eyes Were Watching God*, exemplifies the immense potential contained in the Black female literary tradition for the resolution of critical aesthetic and political problems common to both the Afro-American and the American female literary traditions. Foremost among these problems is the question of how Black/female writers can create a body of literature capable of capturing the political and cultural realities of their experience while using literary forms created by and for white, upper-class men.

Hurston was a novelist, folklorist, and anthropologist. She was born in the all-Black town of Eatonville, Florida, around the turn of the century (there are conflicting theories about her exact birthdate). Always a rebellious, inquisitive child, she left home at the age of fourteen, when her mother died, and became a maid. She eventually worked as a wardrobe maid for an actress—a major educational experience which gave Hurston the determination to attend school. She left the theatrical company to take evening classes in Maryland, and then went on to Morgan Academy in 1917.

Hurston did well in her courses and finished two years of work in one, graduating in 1918. She enrolled at Howard University and held part-time jobs as a manicurist, maid, and waitress to support herself until she graduated in 1920. She worked all the time but was always in debt—a situation that would continue until she died penniless in 1960. When she was at Howard, Hurston published her first literary work—a short story—and thus began a thirty-year career, publishing more fiction than any Black American woman before her.[4]

A large and important part of Hurston's career took place during the Harlem Renaissance, which began in the 1920s while she was attending Howard. Hurston's best work, especially her novel *Their Eyes*, is the product of a Black female folk aesthetic and cultural sensibility that emerged from the best revolutionary ideals of the period. It also anticipates the comparable renaissance in contemporary women's literature. Despite, or perhaps because of, these achievements, Hurston, like many Black women writers, has suffered "intellectual lynching" at the hands of white and Black men and white women.

Typical of such treatment is the Black male critic Darwin Turner's description of Hurston's work as "artful, coy, irrational, superficial and shallow."[5] As Barbara Smith observes, these remarks "bear no relationship to the actual quality of Hurston's achievements and result from the fact that Turner is completely insensitive to the sexual political dynamics of Hurston's life and writing."[6]

I have subtitled this essay "Zora Neale Hurston and the Black Female Literary Tradition" because as a Black feminist critic I believe that there is a separable and identifiable tradition of Black women writers, simultaneously existing within and independent of the American, Afro-American, and American female literary traditions. Hurston's work forms a major part of this tradition and illustrates its unique simultaneity. The sheer volume of her work would make Hurston a central figure in Black female literature: she published three folklore collections, an autobiography, four novels, and various pieces of short fiction and articles, aside from accumulating a large body of unpublished work that includes several plays.

In order to present fully the dimensions of Hurston's achievements and to place them in their proper context, I will attempt here to outline briefly the principles involved both in the concept of a Black female literary tradition and in the Black feminist critical perspective necessary to understand Hurston's life and work. Such a survey simplifies this tradition, but is adequate for our purpose.

Black feminist literary criticism offers a framework for identifying the common socio-aesthetic problems of authors who attempt to fashion a literature of cultural identity in the midst of racial/sexual oppression. It incorporates a political analysis that enables us to comprehend and appreciate the incredible achievements Black women like Zora Neale Hurston made in establishing artistic and literary traditions of any sort, and to understand their qualities and sensibilities. Such understanding requires a consciousness of the oppression these artists faced daily in a society full of institutionalized and violent hatred for both their Black skins and their female bodies. Developing and maintaining this consciousness is a basic tenet of Black feminism.

Black women embody by their sheer physical presence two of the most hated identities in this racist/sexist country. Whiteness and maleness in this culture have not only been seen as physical identities, but codified into states of being and world views. The codification of Blackness and femaleness by whites and males is contained in the terms "thinking like a woman" and "acting like a nigger," both based on the premise that there are typically negative Black and female ways of acting and thinking. Therefore, the most pejorative concept in the white/male world view would be thinking and acting like a "nigger woman." This is useful for understanding literary criticism of Hurston's works, which often attacks her personally for simply conducting herself as what she was: a Black woman.

Black people have always bonded together in order to establish and maintain positive definitions of Blackness. The most important and common form of this racial bonding has been Afro-American folk culture: the musical, oral, and visual artistic expressions of Black identity that have been handed down from generation to generation. The Harlem Renaissance, whose spirit Hurston's work reflects, was a manifestation of this bonding, although it had many false revolutionaries and failed in some respects to realize its radical potential.

Yet, to see Hurston as simply Black-identified is not enough. Hurston wrote as a Black woman about her own experiences and therefore, in some respects, spoke to the general Black female experience in America. She wrote as a Black woman-identified Black woman, valuing her experiences as a woman as well as a Black person in a society where these areas of experience are generally regarded as valueless, insignificant, and inferior to white/male culture.

Women in this country have defied the dominant sexist society by developing a type of folk culture and oral literature based on the use of gender solidarity and female bonding as self-affirming rituals. Black women have a long tradition of bonding together in a community that has been a source of survival information, and psychic and emotional support. We have a distinct Black woman-identified folk culture based on our experiences in this society: symbols, language, and modes of expression that specifically reflect the realities of our lives as Black females in a dominant white/male culture. Because Black women rarely gained access to literary expression, this Black woman-identified bonding and folk culture have often gone unrecorded except through our individual lives and memories.

In her essay "In Search of Our Mothers' Gardens," Alice Walker has spoken perceptively of the way in which the material, economic, and political conditions of Black women's lives in a racist/sexist society have restricted their artistic expression.[7] The classist politics of culture have been criticized by Paul Lauter:

> Often, working-class art does not, at least initially, take written form, for a variety of reasons ranging from the denial of literacy to working people to the problem of access to media. For these and other reasons it simply is not useful to approach working-class art only in terms of a set of discrete texts—still the dominant mode of literary

study today. Gaining a more coherent view of working-class culture requires, we think, an effort to break out of such restrictive categories and to unify the study of the variety of forms—written poetry, oral poetry, needlework, for example—discussed here.[8]

The holistic cultural analysis Lauter proposes is also necessary to achieve a meaningful examination of Black women's culture.

Hurston's novel *Their Eyes* offers an excellent source for demonstrating the value of an interdisciplinary approach to Black women's culture in general and the Black female literary tradition in particular. Hurston locates her fiction firmly in Black women's traditional culture as developed and displayed through music and song. In presenting Janie's story as a narrative related by herself to her best Black woman friend, Phoebe, Hurston is able to draw upon the rich oral legacy of Black female storytelling and mythmaking that has its roots in Afro-American culture. The reader who is conscious of this tradition will experience the novel as an overheard conversation as well as a literary text.

Janie's narrative in *Their Eyes* reflects the Black female blues aesthetic—the very direct use to which Black women put language and song, in order, as critic Joanne Braxton states, to "transcend the most brutal, painful and personal of disasters in daily life and go on fighting—strong and alive."[9] The blues, according to Ralph Ellison, "does not skirt the painful facts of human experience, but works through them to an artistic transcendence"; Gene Bluestein relates this to "the formula of Emerson's prescription for achieving the epiphanic moment—to work through the natural fact in order to express the spiritual truth that underlies it."[10] Similarly, Janie, in her epiphanic experience with a blossoming pear tree, works through the physical and natural phenomena surrounding her in order to understand and express their underlying spiritual truths. As soon as Janie is able to formulate a vision of lyric selfhood, she must confront the obstacles that would prevent her from achieving it.

These obstacles are conveyed in *Their Eyes* partially through Hurston's use of symbolic geography. Janie's lyric vision is conceived outdoors, in her grandmother's "garden field."[11] When Janie goes inside the house, she reaches "the narrow hallway" and remembers that her grandmother is "home with a sick headache" (p. 25). As soon as she is outside, Janie asks herself where the "singing bees" of her lyric vision are, and we are told that "nothing on the place nor in her grandma's house answered her. She searched as much of the world as she could from the top of the front steps and then went on down to the front gate and leaned over to gaze up and down the road. Looking, waiting, breathing short with impatience. Waiting for the world to be made" (p. 25). A sense of the confinement and limitations of Janie's life with her grandmother comes through clearly in this passage. The small part of the world that Janie is able to observe from her grandmother's house is juxtaposed against the vast possibilities presented by the open road. Hurston is striving here to create symbols, images, and metaphors that can express Black female culture and experience. The metaphor of the open road comes in the first of a series of episodes in which Janie moves from the confinement of inner spaces into the open and down the road in search of her vision. Janie's search for answers to the questions posed by her lyric vision leads her to kiss Johnny Taylor. Both she and her grandmother experience the incident in a dreamlike state, but Janie's is induced by the intoxicating spring, while Nanny's comes from her illness and old age.

Hurston's first description of Nanny in *Their Eyes* establishes her as a representative of the religious experience that stands at the center of the Afro-American folk tradition. She is described in terms suggestive of a Christ figure. Janie makes Nanny a wreath of "palma christi leaves" (p. 26), and the words "bore" and "pierce" used in this passage invoke images of the crucifixion. While Janie represents the Black female folk aesthetic contained in the blues, her grandmother symbolizes the Black religious folk tradition embodied by spirituals.

The symbolic functions of Janie and Nanny are further established by their confrontation concerning Johnny Taylor's kiss. Nanny insists that Janie must get married immediately. Although she recognizes the innocence in Janie's action, Nanny is also acutely aware of the painful realities that make such exploration a luxury Janie cannot afford. Males like Johnny Taylor will perceive her now as sexually mature and an appropriate target for their advances. Her womanhood is forced upon her while she is still a child of sixteen because she is a Black female. Janie fails to understand this, however, and when she stubbornly rejects Nanny's suggestion that she marry Logan Killicks, a middle-aged widower, her grandmother slaps her.

Nanny's violent reaction to Janie's impulse to individuality is a protective measure like those defined by Ellison as characteristic of the southern Black community. She is attempting to adjust Janie to the prevailing sexual and racial milieu, and her protectiveness emerges as violence directed against Janie. Nanny attempts to explain to Janie the historical and social forces that make her innocent actions so serious:

Honey, de white man is de ruler of everything as fur as Ah been able tuh find out. Maybe it's some place way off in de ocean where de black man is in power, but we don't know nothin' but what we see. So de white man throw down de load and tell de nigger man tuh pick it up. He pick it up because he have to, but he don't tote it. He hand it to his women-folks. *De nigger woman is de mule uh de world so fur as Ah can see.* Ah been prayin' fur it tuh be different wid you. Lawd, Lawd, Lawd!" (p. 29).

Throughout the remainder of the novel we observe Janie's struggle against conforming to this definition of the Black woman as "de mule uh de world." Its cruelty stands out starkly against the potential contained in Janie's youthful vision. The image of Janie and Nanny as victims of oppressive forces neither of them can alter is powerful and moving. We are led to think of countless Black females coming of age, and countless Black grandmothers and mothers confronting them with the harsh realities of Black women's lives in a racist, sexist society. In this sense Janie and her grandmother illustrate the tragic continuity of Black female oppression in white/male America.

Because this oppression has assumed different forms in their lives, Janie and Nanny have developed conflicting world views. Janie is experiencing a need to explore the answers to the life questions symbolized by her lyric encounter with the pear tree. She can only see marriage to Killicks as an obstacle to such explorations, yet she cannot communicate the reality of her lyric vision to her grandmother, whose sensibilities are restricted by her nearness to the slave experience. Nanny reveals her proximity to this experience when she tells her slave narrative while "rocking Janie like an infant..."(p. 32). Nanny's tale of sexual abuse and violence contrasts starkly with Janie's innocence, and makes the premature ending of her childhood seem all the more tragic.

Nanny relates that she was raped by her master, and that after he left for the war, she was subjected to physical abuse by his wife. While recovering from childbirth, she was forced to escape with her week-old child. Nanny's desires to do something in praise of Black women, frustrated by sexual exploitation and slavery, were transferred to her daughter, Leafy, whom she prepared for a career as a teacher. This dream was also destroyed by particularly cruel and ironic sexual violence when the schoolteacher raped Leafy in the woods where Nanny had hidden to escape to freedom.

By the time of Janie's coming of age, Nanny's aspirations have been modified by the violent realities of Black female life in American society.

Her horrible experiences have led her to see the domestic pedestal as the safest escape from the dangers of racial/sexual oppression. As Killicks's wife Janie will be assured that "no trashy nigger, no breath-and-britches, lak Johnny Taylor," will use her "body to wipe his foots on" (p. 27), and that no "menfolks white or black" will make "a spit cup outa" her (p. 37). As Smith states, "Hurston is fully aware of the fundamental oppressiveness of traditional marriage, yet she has a deep understanding of what the institution represents to women who were formerly enslaved."[12]

Janie complies with her grandmother's request. She replaces her search for identity, as symbolized by the pear tree, with a search for romantic love in marriage. The remainder of *Their Eyes* details the shattering of Janie's romantic illusions as she becomes conscious of the tyranny of the pedestal her grandmother chose for her. Only after this process is completed does it become possible for Janie to once again become a Black woman in search of herself.

Hurston satirizes the romantic ideals that Janie uses to make "a sort of comfort for herself" (p. 38) when she marries Killicks. When Janie goes inside Killicks's house "to wait for love to begin" (p. 39), she is both a tragic and a comic figure. Eventually she begins to suspect that love does not come automatically with marriage and confronts her grandmother with the discrepancy: "You told me Ah mus gointer love him, and Ah don't. Maybe if somebody was to tell me how, Ah could do it" (p. 41). Nanny's reaction reveals her familiarity with the unpleasant realities of married life for women. Her first thoughts are that Janie is pregnant, or that Logan has been abusing her: "Don't tell me you done got knocked up already, less see—dis Saturday it's two months and two weeks.... You and Logan been fussin'? Lawd, Ah know dat grass-gut liver-lipted nigger ain't done took and beat mah baby already" (p. 40). The "already" in both sentences indicates that Nanny views pregnancy and violence as inevitable companions of married life for women. Her familiarity with domestic and sexual violence is also revealed when she explains to Janie earlier her reason for remaining unmarried once slavery ended: "Ah wouldn't marry nobody, though Ah could have uh heap uh times, cause Ah didn't want nobody mistreating mah baby" (p. 36).

Janie is still unable to communicate to Nanny the substance of the ideals symbolized by the pear tree. Though she sympathizes with her granddaughter, Nanny remains convinced that marriage to Killicks is the best possible arrangement for Janie. Nanny's religious beliefs to some extent allow her to justify Janie's suffering with the principle that "folks is meant to cry 'bout somethin' or other" (p. 43). Her character also reflects the solemnity and dignity inherent in the Afro-American female folk religious tradition and sensibility:

> Nanny sent Janie along with a stern mien, but she dwindled all the rest of the day as she worked. And when she gained the privacy of her own little shack she stayed on her knees so long she forgot she was there herself. There is a basin in the mind where words float around on thought and thought on sound and sight. Then there is a depth of thought untouched by words, and deeper still a gulf of formless feelings untouched by thought. Nanny entered this infinity of conscious pain again on her old knees. Towards morning she muttered, "Lawd, you know mah heart. Ah done de best Ah could do. De rest is left to you." She scuffled up from her knees and fell heavily across the bed. A month later she was dead. (p. 43).

The "infinity of conscious pain" involved in the dynamics of Black womanhood in America was a permanent reality for Zora Neale Hurston. She not only had to deal with the racial/sexual politics of day-to-day life as a Black woman, but she chose to confront life as an independent, woman-identified Black female artist and social scientist, a stance requiring great courage and strength.

Black woman-identification, the basis of Black feminism and Black feminist literary criticism, is most simply the idea of Black women seeking their own identity and defining themselves through bonding on various levels—psychic, intellectual, and emotional, as well as physical—with other Black women. Choosing Black lesbianism, feminism, or woman-identification is the political process and struggle of choosing a hated identity: choosing to be a Black woman, not only in body, but in spirit as well. It is the process of identifying one's self and the selves of other Black women as inherently valuable, and it is perceived by the dominant white/male culture as most threatening because it challenges that culture's foundations. Black woman-identification is Black women not accepting male—including Black male—definitions of femaleness or Black womanhood, just as Black-identification consists of Blacks rejecting white definitions of Blackness and creating autonomous standards for evaluating Black culture.

I see Hurston's Black woman-identification not only in her words, but in her visual appearance as well. The pictures we have show her as a naturally handsome woman who confronted sexual/gender conventions even in the way she dressed—frequently in rakish hats and in pants—and acted on the street, smoking publicly at a time when it was not considered ladylike. I see her as refusing to mutilate or alter either her mind or her body to achieve someone else's standard of what she should be as a Black woman.

It is important to point out that Hurston's pain was increased by a section of the Black community that felt threatened by her innate woman-identification and feminism. One of the saddest and most painful episodes of Hurston's life was at the hands of Blacks, not whites, who cruelly sensationalized her case when she was charged in 1948 with having molested a child. The boy's mother was angry at Hurston for some remarks she had made concerning the child, and the case was obviously totally fabricated—Hurston was not even in the country at the time of the supposed attack. However, the Black media grabbed the opportunity to attempt to destroy her. Robert Hemenway provides valuable details on the case and the media coverage surrounding it in his biography of Hurston:

> The national edition of Baltimore's *Afro-American* headlined Zora's troubles in its October 23, 1948, edition.... The Hurston story itself was both inaccurate and sensational. The one boy had become three, while the charges were characterized as "particularly sordid." Most repulsive of all, the paper quoted Jim's plea to Arvay [in Hurston's *Seraph on the Sewanee*], "I'm just as hungry as a dog for a knowing and a doing love," and asked if Zora sought the same affection. A week later, after objections to such coverage, the *Afro-American* defended itself with haughty self-righteousness: "It is the *Afro's* belief that a hush-hush attitude about perversion has permitted this menace to increase."[13]

Clearly, the Black press reaction was related to more than the case itself. On the simplest level, it was a way of getting back at an uppity woman. Secondly, it illustrates that sexism creates an attitude in the Black community which considers it highly unnatural for Black women to love themselves. Finally, the tone and language of the *Afro's* smug justification—with its implied generalization about "perversion"—is a reminder that, for many people, fear of self-defined Black women is fear of lesbianism.

There is an inherent Black woman-identification in the Black female literary tradition because Black women have used writing as a way of capturing and exalting their experience. There is also a strong critique of the politics of heterosexuality in much male-identified Black women's literature, although it may be unrecognized or unacknowledged by the writers themselves. Conversely, lesbian, feminist, and woman-identified Black women writers have given moving portrayals of heterosexual loving (such as that of Janie and Teacake in *Their Eyes*). These women relationships with men: they are usually not in an oppressive sexual relationship with a man, and therefore have less bitterness and hostility toward men than do committed male-identified heterosexual women, who are often struggling for their lives in such relationships.

Hurston's sophisticated analysis of sexual politics and the politics of heterosexuality for Black women is an important part of her work that is characteristic of the Black woman-identified tradition in Black female writing. I think the essence of Black woman-identification is its possibility for making visible the emotionally intense, though not necessarily sexual, relationships between Black women—always an integral, but usually hidden, part of the Black community. Hurston renders an account of what may be a relationship of this type between herself and another woman, "Big Sweet," in her autobiography, *Dust Tracks on a Road.*

The book contains a detailed account of how Big Sweet—a strong Black woman with a reputation for physical courage and bold language—comes to Hurston's rescue when she is collecting folklore in a Southern mining town. Hurston incurs the wrath of a local woman who believes she is trying to take her boyfriend away from her because Hurston spends so much time talking with him and the other Black men of the town. The woman refuses to believe that Hurston is only conducting an anthropological investigation and attacks her in a bar. Big Sweet comes to her defense and helps Hurston escape.

We never learn what happened to Big Sweet, but one thing is certain: Hurston owed her life to that Black woman who did not have access to a public medium for the expression of her strong, creative spirit, and she repaid this debt by sharing her voice with her. All of Hurston's writings can be epitomized as her commitment to expressing the lives and thoughts of Black women who have been silenced too long.

In her foreword to Hemenway's *Zora Neale Hurston,* Alice Walker presents an inspiring vision of three Black women artists drawing sustenance from one another:

> In my mind, Zora Neale Hurston, Billie Holiday, and Bessie Smith form a sort of unholy trinity....Like Billie and Bessie she [Zora] followed her own road, believed in her own gods, pursued her own dream, and refused to separate herself from "common" people. It would have been nice if the three of them had one another to turn to in times of need.[14]

Hurston herself said that "it is one of the blessings of this world that few people see visions and dream dreams," because of the "cosmic loneliness" and the infinity of conscious pain created for the visionary.[15] It is one of the great blessings of our lives that she nevertheless saw and recorded Black female visions and dreams. Her life and work exemplify the magnificent visions and dreams that are possible for a Black woman-identified Black woman, and I imagine her with Bessie, Billie, Big Sweet, her mother, and all of our sisters, mothers, great-grandmothers, and aunts with an infinity of conscious Black female joy and peace.

In her autobiography, Hurston describes a series of prophetic visions she had as a child, including this account of her final dream:

> And last of all, I would come to a big house. Two women waited there for me. I could not see their faces, but I knew one to be young and one to be old. One of them was arranging some queer-shaped flowers such as I have never seen. When I had come to these women, then I would be at the end of my pilgrimage, but not the end of my life. Then I would know peace and love and what goes with those things, and not before.[16]

Hurston's vision is not only woman-identified, but also lesbian in that it acknowledges and asserts the validity of primary love relationships between women. Although she says that all of her visions came true, we never learn the form that this one took in Hurston's adult existence.

Hurston's final vision was one of her earliest contacts with a principle that was to become the guiding force behind her finest and most honest writing—the concept that when Black women come to each other as Black woman-identified women, we are at the end of our pilgrimage to know and be ourselves. Then, and not before, we know peace and love and what goes with these things. Hurston knew this Black woman-identified love in her life and work. When we make her Black woman-identified conscious joy a reality in the daily lives of Black women, we shall see flowers such as no one has ever seen before—the same flowers hidden all these years in all of our mothers' gardens.

NOTES

[1]Hortense Calisher, "No Important Woman Writer," in *Women's Liberation and Literature,* ed. Elaine Showalter (New York: Harcourt Brace Jovanovich, 1971), p. 52.

[2]*Black-Eyed Susans: Classic Stories by and about Black Women,* ed. Mary Helen Washington (Garden City, N.Y.: Doubleday, 1975), p. x.

[3]Richard Wright's *Native Son* is one example of how the falsification of the Black experience for the purpose of political protest can result in characters that reinforce racist stereotypes.

⁴This biographical material is taken from Robert Hemenway, *Zora Neale Hurston: A Literary Biography* (Champaign: University of Illinois Press, 1977).

⁵Quoted in Barbara Smith, "Sexual Politics and the Fiction of Zora Neale Hurston," *Radical Teacher* 8 (May 1978). Mary Helen Washington analyzes the traditional criticism of Hurston by Turner and others as an "intellectual lynching" in her introduction to *I Love Myself...A Zora Neale Hurston Reader,* ed. Alice Walker (Old Westbury, N.Y.: The Feminist Press, 1979), p. 7.

⁶Ibid.

⁷Alice Walker, "In Search of Our Mothers' Gardens," *Ms.* (May 1974):64–70.

⁸Paul Lauter, "Working-Class Culture," *Radical Teacher* (March 1977):1.

⁹Joanne Braxton, "Zora Hurston's Blues Book," unpublished paper.

¹⁰Gene Bluestein, *The Voice of the Folk* (Amherst, Mass.: University of Massachusetts Press, 1972), p. 123.

¹¹Zora Neale Hurston, *Their Eyes Were Watching God* (New York: Negro University Press, 1969), p. 9. All references are to this edition, hereafter cited in text.

¹²Smith.

¹³Hemenway, p. 320.

¹⁴Ibid., p. xvii.

¹⁵Zora Neale Hurston, *Dust Tracks on a Road* (Philadelphia: J. B. Lippincott, 1942; 1971), p. 60.

¹⁶Ibid., p. 58.

17

Researching Alice Dunbar-Nelson: A Personal and Literary Perspective

GLORIA T. HULL

Soon after I began teaching one of my first Black American literature courses a few years ago, a student in the class—a young Black woman— came up to me after a session on Paul Laurence Dunbar and told me that she knew a lady in the city who was his niece. While I was digesting that information, she ran on, saying something about Dunbar, his wife Alice, the niece, the niece's collection of materials about them, and ended by stressing that there was, as she put it, "a *lot* of stuff." From that unlikely, chance beginning has developed my single most significant research undertaking—one which has led me into the farthest reaches of Black feminist criticism, and resulted in new literary scholarship and exhilarating personal growth.

This essay is a description of that process of researching and writing about Alice Dunbar-Nelson. It is only my own, one Black woman's experience, but in a certain limited sense, it can also be regarded as something of a "case study" of Black feminist scholarship. We need to uncover and (re)write our own multi-storied history, and talk to one another as we are doing so. I emerged from (not to say survived) this particular experience with insights relevant to myself, to Dunbar-Nelson as woman and writer, and to the practice of Black women's literary criticism.

At the end of that first conversation, the student promised to introduce me to Ms. Pauline A. Young—Dunbar's niece by virtue of his marriage to her mother's sister—but somehow this never happened. A year or so passed, and I finally met Ms. Young after she happened to see me discussing her "Aunt Alice" on a local television program and called the producer. By this time, I had begun a serious study of early-twentieth-century Black women poets, including Alice Dunbar-Nelson, and was convinced that she was an important and fascinating figure who warranted more than the passing attention which she had heretofore received.

A good deal of this attention focused upon her as the wife of Paul Laurence Dunbar (1872–1906), America's first nationally-recognized Black poet. Nevertheless, on her own merits, Alice Dunbar-Nelson was an outstanding writer and public person. She was born in New Orleans in 1875, grew up in the city, taught school there, and was prominent in its Black society, especially in musical and literary circles. She moved North, finally settling in Wilmington, Delaware, in 1902, where she remained until shortly before her death in 1935. From this base, she achieved local and national renown as a platform speaker, clubwoman, and political activist. She associated with other leaders like W. E. B. DuBois, Mary Church Terrell, and Leslie Pinckney Hill. In addition, she was a writer all through her life. She poured out newspaper columns, published many stories and poems, the bulk of which appeared in two books and in magazines like *Crisis* and *Collier's*, and edited two additional works.

Knowing what I had already learned about Dunbar-Nelson, I was more than eager to become acquainted with Ms. Young and her materials. When I did, I was astounded. There in the small cottage where she lived was a trove of precious information—manuscript boxes of letters, diaries, and journals; scrapbooks on tables; two unpublished novels and drafts of published works in file folders; clippings and pictures under beds and bookshelves. I looked at it and thought—ruefully and ironically—of how, first, word-of-mouth (our enduring oral tradition) and, then, sheer happenstance accounted for my being there. I also thought of how this illustrated—once more—the distressing fact that much valuable, unique, irreplaceable material on women writers, and especially minority women writers, is not bibliographed and/or publicized, is not easily accessible, and is moldering away in unusual places.

In order to use this collection, I had to impose myself and become a bit of a nuisance. Being a Black woman certainly helped me here; but, even so, Ms. Young was understandably careful and protective of her documents. She never told me exactly everything she had (indeed, she may not have remembered it all herself) and allowed me to see it a little at a time until gradually I gained her confidence, got the run of the house, learned what was there, and began to use it. As I did so, my good fortune became even more apparent. This one source was the only place where some of these materials existed. They will probably be willed to the

Moorland-Spingarn Research Center at Howard University, and then scholars will have to wait some years before they are sorted, catalogued, and readied for public use. Ms. Young herself is a retired librarian and Delaware historian—which partly accounts for her consciousness of the worth of her holdings. Her years of trained habit also, no doubt, put many of the dates and sources on what would otherwise have been tantalizingly anonymous pictures and pieces of newsprint. In general, Ms. Young proved to be one of the biggest resources of all. With her memories and knowledge, she could share family history, identify people and references, and give invaluable information about their relationship to her aunt which no one else could provide. Once I puzzled for two days over the name of a companion in Alice's diaries only to learn finally from Ms. Young that it was the family dog.

Our personal relationship was even more charged and catalytic in ways which benefited us as individuals and further enhanced the work which we were doing. Interacting, we moved from cordiality to closeness. Several factors could have hindered or even stopped this development—the most elemental being Ms. Young's instinctive protectiveness of her aunt and family. Although her feelings probably included some ambivalence (and possibly more difficult unresolved emotions), these had been softened by time until her most powerful motivations were admiration and the desire to see her aunt get her due. Other complicating factors could have been the generational differences of perspective between us, and whatever undercurrent of feeling could have resulted from the fact that my writing on her aunt fulfilled a wish which unpropitious external circumstances had made it harder for Ms. Young herself to realize.

What tied us together was our common bond of radical Blackness and shared womanhood. We were two Black women joined together by and for a third Black woman/writer whose life and work we were committed to affirming. Our building of trust and rapport was crucial to this whole process. Despite some rough spots, it enabled us to relate to each other in a basically honest, usually up-front manner, and to devise means (both informal and legal) for apportioning the labor and the credit.

The episode which most challenged—but ultimately proved—our relationship was the question of how Dunbar-Nelson's sexuality should be handled. When I discovered while editing Dunbar-Nelson's diary that her woman-identification extended to romantic liaisons with at least two of her friends, I imparted this information to Ms. Young. Her genuinely surprised response was, "Oh, Aunt Alice," and then immediately, "Well, we don't have to leave this in!" The two of us talked and re-talked the issue, with me saying over and over again that these relationships did not besmirch Dunbar-Nelson's character or reputation, that they did not harm anyone else, that there is nothing wrong with love between women, that her attraction to women was only one part of her total identity and did not wipe out the other aspects of her other selves, and that, finally, showing her and the diary as they in fact were was simply the right thing to do. I knew that everything was fine when at last Ms. Young quipped, "Maybe it will sell a few more books," and we both laughed. Inwardly, I rejoiced that at least this one time, this one Black woman/writer would be presented without the lies and distortions which have marked far too many of us.

Studying Dunbar-Nelson brought many such surprises and insights. Their cumulative meaning can be stated in terms of her *marginality*, on the one hand, and her *power*, on the other—a dual concept which suggests a way of talking not only about her, but also about other Black women writers, singly or as a group. First of all, Dunbar-Nelson has usually been seen as the wife of America's first famous Black poet who incidentally "wrote a little" herself. This is a situation which those of us who research minority and/or women writers are familiar with—having to rescue these figures from some comfortable, circumscribed shadow and place them in their own light. Furthermore, Dunbar-Nelson's basic personal status in the world as a Black woman was precarious. On the economic level, for instance, she always had to struggle for survival and for psychic necessities. That this was so, graphically illustrates how the notion of her as "genteel, bourgeoise" needs revision. Black women generally occupy an ambiguous relationship with regard to class. Even those who are educated, "middle-class," and professional, and who manage to become writers, almost always derive from and/or have first-hand knowledge of working- or "lower"-class situations. Also, being Black, they have no entrenched and comfortable security in even their achieved class status (gained via breeding, education, culture, looks, etc., and not so much by money). And, being women, their position is rendered doubly tangential and complex. Dunbar-Nelson herself revealed these contradictions in the dichotomy between her outward aristocratic bearing, and the intimate realities of her straitened finances and private fun.

Her determination to work in society as a writer also made her vulnerable. Things were not set up for her, a *Black woman*, to be able to make her living in this way. This had to do with the avenues of publication which were open to her and the circles of prestige from which she was automatically excluded. When she needed one most, she was not able to get a job with even the *Crisis* or the NAACP, or a Black newspaper or press service—her excellent qualifications notwithstanding. She was compelled always to accept or to create low-paying employment for herself, and to work under the most trying conditions.

Only the power emanating from within herself and strengthened by certain external networks of support enabled Dunbar-Nelson to transcend these destructive forces. Her mother, sister, and nieces in their inseparable, female-centered household constituted a first line of resistance (sometimes in conjunction with her second husband). Then came other Black women of visible achievement, such as Edwina B. Kruse, Georgia Douglas Johnson, and Mary McLeod Bethune, with whom she associated. In varying ways, they assured each other of their sanity and worth, and collectively validated their individual efforts to make the possible real. Yet, in the end, Dunbar-Nelson had to rely on her own power—the power of her deep-seated and cosmic spirituality, and the power which came from the ultimately unshakable inner knowledge of her own value and talent.

Everything that I have been saying throughout this essay illustrates the Black feminist critical approach which I used in researching Dunbar-Nelson. Having said this much, I am tempted to let the statement stand without further elaboration since, for me at least, it is much easier to do this work than to talk about the methodological principles undergirding it. There is the danger of omitting some point which is so fundamental and/or so integrally a part of the process and oneself as to feel obvious. And, with so much feminist theory being published, there is the risk of sounding too simple or repetitive.

Very briefly, then, here are the fundamental tenets: (1) everything about the subject is important for a total understanding and analysis of her life and work; (2) the proper scholarly stance is engaged rather than "objective"; (3) the personal (both the subject's and the critic's) *is* political; (4) description must be accompanied by analysis; (5) consciously maintaining at all times the angle of vision of a person who is both Black and female is imperative, as is the necessity for a class-conscious, anticapitalist perspective; (6) being principled requires rigorous truthfulness and "telling it all"; (7) research/criticism is not an academic/intellectual game, but a pursuit with social meanings rooted in the "real world." I always proceed from the assumption that Dunbar-Nelson had much to say to us and, even more importantly, that dealing honestly with her could, in a more-than-metaphoric sense, "save" some Black woman's life—as being able to write in this manner about her had, in a very concrete way, "saved" my own.

It goes without saying that I approached her as an important writer and her work as genuine literature. Probably as an (over?)reaction to the condescending, witty but empty, British urbanity of tone which is the hallmark of traditional white male literary scholarship (and which I dislike intensely), I usually discuss Dunbar-Nelson with level high seriousness—and always with caring. Related to this are my slowly-evolving attempts at being so far unfettered by conventional style as to write creatively, even poetically, if that is the way the feeling flows. Here, the question of audience is key. Having painfully developed these convictions and a modicum of courage to buttress them, I now include/ visualize everybody (my department chair, the promotion and tenure committee, my mother and brother, my Black feminist sisters, the chair of Afro-American Studies, lovers, colleagues, friends) for each organic article, rather than write sneaky, schizophrenic essays from under two or three different hats.

In the final analysis, I sometimes feel that I am as ruthlessly unsparing of Dunbar-Nelson as I am of myself. And the process of personal examination is very much the same. For a Black woman, being face-to-face with another Black woman makes the most cruel and beautiful mirror. This is as true in scholarly research as it is on the everyday plane. Once I was dissecting an attitude of Dunbar-Nelson's of which I disapproved to a dear friend who has known me all of our adult lives. He gave me a bemused look and said, "You can't stand her because you're too much like her." I had never thought of it in quite those exact terms. Then, I rose to her/my/our defense.

However, it is true that Dunbar-Nelson and I are locked in uneasy sisterhood. On the one hand, I feel identity, our similarities, and closeness. On the other, there are differences, ambivalence, and critical distance. Superficially, one can see such commonalities as the facts that we were both born in Louisiana, lived in Delaware, wrote poetry, engaged in social-political activism, put a lot of energy into our jobs, appreciated our own accomplishments, did needlework, liked cats, and so on down a rather long list. External differences are equally obvious.

On a deeper level (as my friend perceptively pointed out), our relationship becomes most strenuous when I am forced to confront in Dunbar-Nelson those things about myself which I do not relish—a tendency toward egoistic stubbornness and toward letting oneself get sidetracked by the desire for comfortably assimilated acceptance, to divulge but two examples. Seeing my faults in her and, beyond that, seeing how they relate to us as Black women, fuels my efforts at self-improvement: her most enduring role-model effect is positive, inspirational. I think of her existence from its beginnings to the eventual scattering of her ashes over the Delaware River, and know that she was a magnificent woman.

Now that most of my work on her has been completed, she is no longer as strong a presence in my life, though she remains a constant. Hanging in my hall is a painting which she owned (a small watercolor given to her by a woman who was her friend-lover); and two of her copper mint-and-nut plates sit among the dishes on a pantry shelf. Alice herself has not deigned to trouble me—which I take as a sign that all is well between us.

18

Black-Eyed Blues Connections: Teaching Black Women

MICHELE RUSSELL

Political education for Black women in America begins with the memory of four hundred years of enslavement, diaspora, forced labor, beatings, bombings, lynchings, and rape. It takes on inspirational dimensions when we begin cataloguing the heroic individuals and organizations in our history who have battled against these atrocities, and triumphed over them. It becomes practical when we are confronted with the problems of how to organize food cooperatives for women on food-stamp budgets or how to prove one's fitness as a mother in court. It becomes radical when, as teachers, we develop a methodology that places daily life at the center of history and enables Black women to struggle for survival with the knowledge that they are making history.

One setting where such connections can be made is the classroom. In the absence of any land, or turf, which we actually control, the classroom serves as a temporary space where we can evoke and evaluate our collective memory of what is done to us, and what we do in turn.

In Detroit, I am at the Downtown YWCA. Rooms on the upper floors are used by Wayne County Community College as learning centers. It is 10 A.M. and I am convening an introductory Black studies class for women on Community and Identity. The twenty-two women who appear are all on their way from somewhere to something. This is a breather in their day. They range in age from nineteen to fifty-five. They all have been pregnant more than once and have made various decisions about abortion, adoption, monogamy, custody, and sterilization. Some are great-grandmothers. A few have their children along. They are a cross-section of hundreds of Black women I have known and learned from in the past fifteen years, inside the movement and outside of it. We have an hour together. The course is a survey. The first topic of conversation—among themselves and with me—is what they went through just to make it in the door, on time. That, in itself, becomes a lesson. We start where they are. We exchange stories of children's clothes ripped or lost, of having to go to school with sons and explain why Che is always late and how he got that funny name, anyway, to teachers who shouldn't have to ask and don't really care. They tell of waiting for men to come home from the night shift so they can get the money or car necessary to get downtown, or power failures in the neighborhood, or administrative red tape at the college, or compulsory overtime on their own jobs, or the length of food stamp lines, or just being tired and needing sleep. Some of the stories are funny, some sad; some elicit outrage and praise from the group. It's a familiar and comfortable ritual in Black culture. It's called testifying.

The role of the teacher? Making the process conscious, the content significant. Want to know, yourself, how the problems in the stories got resolved. Learn what daily survival wisdom these women have. Care. Don't let it stop at commiseration. Try to help them generalize from the specifics. Raise issues of who and what they continually have to bump up against on the life-road they've planned for themselves. Make lists on the board. Keep the scale human. Who are the people that get in the way? The social worker, the small-claims court officer, husbands, the teacher, cops, kids on the block. Ask: what forces do they represent? Get as much consensus as possible before moving on. Note that there is most argument and disagreement on "husbands" and "kids on the block." Define a task for the next meeting. To sharpen their thinking on husbands and kids, have them make three lists. All the positive and negative things they can think of about men, children, and families. Anticipate in advance that they probably won't have the time or will to write out full lists. But they will think about the question and be ready to respond in class.

Stop short of giving advice. Build confidence in their own ability to make it through whatever morass to be there at 10 A.M. the next day. Make showing up for class a triumph in itself. Because it is.

Try to make the class meeting a daily activity. Every day during the week. Like a language, new ways of seeing and thinking must be reinforced, even if only for half an hour. Otherwise the continuity is lost. The perpetual bombardment of other pressures upsets the rhythm of your movement together. No matter how much time you take with them or who they are, the following methodological principles are critical:

Take one subject at a time—but treat it with interdisciplinary depth and scope. In a variety of ways the women in class have been speeding. Literally, they may either be on medication, be suffering from chronic hypertension, or be skittish from some street encounter. Encourage them to slow down. This does not mean drift—they experience that too much already. Have at least three directions in mind for every class session, but let their mood and uppermost concerns determine your choice. They have come to you for help in getting pulled together. The loose ends of their experience jangle discordantly like bracelets from their arms. You must be able to do with subject matter what they want to do with their lives. Get it under control in ways which thrive on complication.

Encourage storytelling. The oldest form of building historical consciousness in community is storytelling. The transfer of knowledge, skill, and value from one generation to the next, the deliberate accumulation of a people's collective memory, has particular significance in diaspora culture. Robbed of all other continuities, prohibited free expression, denied a written history for centuries by white America, Black people have been driven to rely on oral recitation for our sense of the past. Today, however, that tradition is under severe attack. Urban migrations, apartment living, mass media dependency, and the break-up of generational units within the family have corroded our ability to renew community through oral forms. History becomes "what's in books." Authority depends on academic credentials after one's name or the dollar amount of one's paycheck: the distance one has traveled, rather than the roots one has sunk. Significant categories of time are defined by television's thirty-second spots or thirty-minute features.

Piecing together our identity and community under these circumstances requires developing each other's powers of memory and concentration. When, as a teacher, you first ask women in class, "Where did you come from?" you will get spontaneous answers ranging from "my mamma" and "12th Street" to "Texas," "Africa," and "Psych. 101." They are scattered and don't know what question you are asking in the first place. Still the responses say something about their associational framework. The most important thing about them is their truth. Build on that with the objective of expanding their reference points.

Formalize the process. Begin with blood lines. Share your own family history and have class members do the same. Curiosity will provoke diligence, and the abstractions of "identity" and "community" will give way before the faces of ancestry.

Historical narrative will be most difficult for the younger members of the class. Their knowledge of what it means to "take the A-train," for example, will in most cases be limited to hearsay or music. They relate to

TV. Minimally, you want to get them to a point where they will enjoy evaluating all their contemporaries on "Soul Train" or the three generations of Black women in "The Jeffersons" series in relation to all the family history of Black people over the last fifty years that they have been discovering with other class members. To start that process, convene the class (as a field trip) to watch "Soul Train" and "The Jeffersons." Then press for answers to the question they ask all the time, anyway, when watching each other: "Who does *that* one think SHE is?" In this setting, help history to prevail over personality.

Or begin with one photograph from a family album. Have each person bring in and tell a story just about that one picture. Go from there. One eventual outcome of such a project may be to encourage Black women to record these stories in writing, still an intimidating idea. Use a tape recorder to ease the transition.

To help increase their powers of observation and their capacity for identification, have each woman sit, in a location of her own choosing, for one hour and record what she sees. It can be anywhere: a shopping mall, a beauty shop, a bar, restaurant, park, window. Whatever they feel most natural with. Ride an unfamiliar bus to the end of the line and be alert to the community it attracts. Spend a week riding with domestic workers on suburban express lines. Record the conversations. Help women learn how to use the streets for investigation instead of exhibition. Have them go out in pairs and compare notes, bringing the results back to the group.

Give political value to daily life. Take aspects of what they already celebrate and enrich its meaning so that they see their spontaneous tastes in a larger way than before. This means they will see themselves with new significance. It also imposes the responsibility of selectivity on the teacher. Embrace that. Apply your own political acumen to the myriad survival mechanisms that colonization and domestication breed into subject peoples. Remind them of the choices they make all the time.

No life-area is too trivial for political analysis. Note that a number of Black women, myself included, have begun choosing long dresses for daily wear. In one class session, discussion begins with the remark that they're more "comfortable" in this mode. What does comfort consist of? For those who are heavy, it means anything not physically constricting. For working mothers, comfort means "easy to iron." For the budget-conscious, "easy to make." For some of the young women in class, comfort is attached to the added respect this mode of dress elicits from brothers they pass on the street. For a Muslim grandmother, cleanliness and modesty are signified. For her daughter, also in the Nation, Africa is being invoked. The general principle which emerges is that this particular form of cover allows us greater freedom of expression and movement. Don't stop here. Go from their bodies to their heads. A casual remark about wearing wigs can (and should) develop into a discussion of Frantz Fanon's essay "Algeria Unveiled," in which he analyzes the role of protective coverings, adornment, camouflage, as tactical survival modes for women in the self-defense stage of a movement. Help them to recall the stages of consciousness they've all experienced in relation to their own hair. When did they start to regard "straightening" or "doing" hair as "processing" it? When did they stop? Why? If some women in the class still change their hair texture, does that mean their *minds* are processed, too? Read Malcolm on the subject. How do they feel about Alelia Walker in this context: the first Black woman in America to become a millionaire—for producing and marketing hair straighteners and skin bleaches. Take them as far as memory and material allow. Normally, there will be at least three generations of social experience personally represented in community college classes. Try to work with it all.

Go beyond what is represented in class. Recall all the ways, historically, that Black women in America have used physical disguise for political purposes. Begin with Ellen Craft, escaping from a Georgia plantation to Boston in 1848, passing as a white man. Talk about the contradictory impact of miscegenation on their thinking and action. Then connect this to class members' public demeanor: the variations they choose and the purposes at work. What uniforms do they consciously adopt? Focus on motive as well as image; make intent as important as affect, a way to judge results.

Be able to speak in tongues. Idiom, the medium through which ideas are communicated and organic links of association established (i.e., community) must be in Black women's own tradition. When Black women "speak," "give a reading," or "sound" a situation, a whole history of using language as a weapon is invoked. Rooted in slave folk wisdom which says: "Don't say no more with your mouth than your back can stand," our vocalizing is directly linked to a willingness to meet hostilities head-on and persevere. Take the following description of a Black woman "specifying" by Zora Neale Hurston, for example:

> Big Sweet came to my notice within the first week that I arrived.... I heard somebody, a woman's voice 'specifying' up this line of houses from where I lived, and asked who it was.
> "Dat's Big Sweet," my landlady told me. "She got her foot up on somebody. Ain't she specifying?"
> She was really giving the particulars. She was giving

a reading, a word borrowed from the fortunetellers. She was giving her opponent lurid data and bringing him up to date on his ancestry, his looks, smell, gait, clothes, and his route through Hell in the hereafter. My landlady went outside where nearly everybody else of the four or five hundred people on the 'job' were to listen to the reading. Big Sweet broke the news to him, in one of her mildest bulletins, that his pa was a double humpted camel and his ma was a grass-gut cow, but even so, he tore her wide open in the act of getting born, and so on and so forth. He was a bitch's baby out of a buzzard egg. My landlady explained to me what was meant by 'putting your foot up' on a person. If you are sufficiently armed—enough to stand off a panzer division—and know what to do with your weapons after you get 'em, it is all right to go to the house of your enemy, put one foot up on his steps, rest one elbow on your knee and play in the family. That is another way of saying play the dozens, which also is a way of saying low-rate your enemy's ancestors and him, down to the present moment for reference, and then go into his future as far as your imagination leads you. But if you have no faith in your personal courage and confidence in your arsenal, don't try it. It is a risky pleasure. So then I had a measure of this Big Sweet.

"Hurt who?" Mrs. Bertha snorted at my fears. "Big Sweet? Humph! Tain't a man, woman nor child on this job going to tackle Big Sweet. If God send her a pistol she'll send him a man. She can handle a knife with anybody. She'll join hands and cut a duel. Dat Cracker Quarters Boss wears two pistols round his waist and goes for bad, but he won't break a breath with Big Sweet lessen he got his pistol in his hand. Cause if he start anything with her, he won't never get a chance to draw it. She ain't mean. She don't bother nobody. She just don't stand for no foolishness, dat's all."

Talking bad. Is it still going on? Some class members do it all the time. All know women who do. Some, with a concern for manners, find the activity embarrassing. One woman observes that it's getting harder and harder these days to find targets worthy of such invention. Another, bringing the prior comments together, says there's too little audience for the energy it takes. Whatever our particular attitudes, we all recognize in

Big Sweet a pistol-packin' mamma, conjure woman, voice of Judgment, and reservoir of ancestral memory—all of which are the bases of a fighting tradition also personified in Harriet Tubman, Marie Leveau, Sojourner Truth, and Ericka Huggins. Discover the continuities in their words and acts, and in the deeds done in their name. Emphasize how they transformed personal anger into political weapons, enlarged personal grudges to encompass a people's outrage. When words failed, remember how Aunt Jemima's most famous recipe, ground glass plantation pancakes, made the masters choke.

Take the blues. Study it as a coded language of resistance. In response to questions from class members about whether feminism has ever had anything to do with Black women, play Ma Rainey singing, "I won't be your dog no more." Remind them of our constant complaints about being treated as a "meal-ticket woman," our frustration at baking powder men losing their risables and of going hungry for days. Know the ways in which Peaches are Strange Fruit. Introduce them to a depression-era Bessie Jackson responding humorously, but resolutely, to our options for feeding ourselves when that period's diaspora forced us onto city streets....

Bring the idiomatic articulation of Black women's feminism up to date by sharing stories of the first time we all *heard* what Aretha was asking us to *think* about, instead of just dancing to it. Let Esther Phillips speak on how she's *justified* and find out if class members feel the same way.

Be able to translate ideological shorthand into terms organic to Black women's popular culture. Let the concept of internationalism be introduced. But approach it from the standpoint of a South African Miriam Makeba, an Alabama-born Big Mama Thornton, or a Caribbean Nina Simone all singing Bob Dylan's "I Shall Be Released." Concentrate the discussion on each woman's roots, her place of national origin. Reflect on the history behind the special emphasis each woman gives to phrases such as: "Every distance is not near," "I remember every face of every man who put me here," "Inside these walls." Ask: what kinds of jails are they in? And what happens when we start acting to effect our own release? Devote one class session to a debate over whether it is an antagonistic contradiction for Black women to use Bob Dylan's music as an expressive vehicle. Explore the limits of nationalism in this way.

The whole world is ours to appropriate, not just five states in the South, or one Dark Continent. Treat the meaning of this statement through Nina Simone's recreation of Pirate Jenny. Play the music. Know the history it comes out of and the changes rung: from *The Beggar's Opera*, through Brecht and Weill's *Threepenny Opera*, to the Caribbean and Southern situations everywhere that Simone takes as her reference point. Know the political history involved and the international community of the oppressed she exhorts to rise. Particularly notice the cleaning woman's role. Recall the rebellions of the 1960s, when Nina Simone was performing this song. We all lived through the rebellions, but how did we relate to them? At what point did class members begin associating Detroit with Algiers, Watts with Lesotho, the Mississippi with the Mekong Delta, Amerika with Germany? Share your own experience and growth.

Use everything. Especially, use the physical space of the classroom to illustrate the effects of environment on consciousness. The size and design of the desks, for example. They are wooden, with one-sided, stationary writing arms attached. The embodiment of a poor school. Small. Unyielding. Thirty years old. Most of the Black women are amplebodied. When the desks were new and built for twelve-year-old, seventh-grade bodies, some class members may have sat in them for the first time. Now, sitting there for one hour—not to mention trying to concentrate and work—is a contortionist's miracle, or a stoic's. It feels like getting left back.

With desks as a starting point for thinking about our youth in school, class members are prompted to recall the mental state such seats encouraged. They cite awkwardness, restlessness, and furtive embarrassment. When they took away our full-top desks with interior compartments, we remember how *exposed* we felt, unable to hide anything: not spitballs, notes, nor scarred knees, prominent between too-short, hand-me-down dresses and scuffed shoes. They remember the belligerence which was all the protection we were allowed.

We talked about all the unnecessary, but deliberate, ways the educational process is made uncomfortable for the poor. Most women in class hate to read aloud. So we relive how they were taught to read, the pain involved in individual, stand-up recitation. The foil one was for a teacher's scapegoating ridicule. The peer pressure to make mistakes. We look back on how good reading came to mean proper elocution to our teachers in school and in the church.

We remember that one reason many of us stopped going to school was that it became an invasion of privacy. Not like church, which was only once a week, an event you could get up for. School was every day, among strangers, whether you felt like it or not, even if you ran out of clean clothes for the ritual. Showing up was the hardest part. After that, it was just a series of games.

Then, of course, someone inevitably says, "But here we are, back again." Is that a joke on us? Is it still a game? What are we trying to do differently this time around? To answer those questions, have women devise their own criteria for evaluating the educational process they engage in with you.

Be concrete. In every way possible, take a materialistic approach to the issue of Black women's structural place in America. Focus attention on the building where we are learning our history. Notice who's still scrubbing the floors. In response to class members who pin their hopes for the future on "new careers," pose the following questions: How is a nurse's aide different from a maid? What physical spaces are the majority of us still locked into as Black women who must take jobs in the subsistence and state sectors of the economy? Do we ever get to do more than clean up other people's messes, whether we are executive secretaries, social workers, police officers, or wives? Within what confines do we live and work?

Reflect on the culture of the stoop; the storefront; the doorway; the housing project; the rooming-house bathroom; the bankteller's cage; the corner grocery store; the bus; hotels and motels; school, hospital, and corporate corridors; and waiting rooms everywhere. What constraints do they impose?

If we conclude that most of our lives are spent as social servants, and state dependents, what blend of sex, race, and class consciousness does that produce? To cut quickly to the core of unity in experience, read the words of Johnny Tillmon, founder of the National Welfare Rights Organization in Watts, 1965:

> I'm a woman. I'm a Black woman. I'm a poor woman. I'm a fat woman. I'm a middle-aged woman. And I'm on welfare.
>
> In this country, if you're any one of those things— poor, Black, fat, female, middle-aged, on welfare—you count less as a human being. If you're all of those things, you don't count at all. Except as a statistic.
>
> I am a statistic. I am forty-five years old. I have raised six children. I grew up in Arkansas and I worked there for fifteen years in a laundry, making about twenty or thirty dollars a week, picking cotton on the side for carfare. I moved to California in 1959 and worked in a laundry there for nearly four years. In 1963, I got too sick to work anymore. My husband and I had split up. Friends helped me to go on welfare.
>
> They didn't call it welfare. They called it AFDC— Aid to Families with Dependent Children. Each month I get $363 for my kids and me. I pay $128 a month rent; $30 for utilities, which include gas, electricity, and water;

$120 for food and nonedible household essentials; $50 for
school lunches for the three children in junior and senior
high school who are not eligible for reduced-cost meal
programs. This leaves $5 per person a month for
everything else—clothing, shoes, recreation, incidental
personal expenses, and transportation. This check allows
$1 a month for transportation for me but none for my
children. That's how we live.

Welfare is all about dependency. It is the most
prejudiced institution in this country, even more than
marriage, which it tries to imitate.

The truth is that AFDC is like a super-sexist
marriage. You trade in *a* man for *the* man. But you can't
divorce him if he treats you bad. He can divorce you, of
course, cut you off anytime he wants. But in that case, he
keeps the kids, not you.

The man runs everything. In ordinary marriage, sex
is supposed to be for your husband. On AFDC, you're
not supposed to have any sex at all. You give up control
of your own body. It's a condition of aid. You may even
have to agree to get your tubes tied so you can never have
more children, just to avoid being cut off welfare.

The man, the welfare system, controls your money.
He tells you what to buy, what not to buy, where to buy
it, and how much things cost. If things—rent, for instance—really cost more than he says they do, it's just too
bad for you. You've just got to make your money stretch.

The man can break into your home any time he
wants to and poke into your things. You've got no right
to protest. You've got no right to privacy. Like I said,
welfare's a super-sexist marriage.

Discuss what it means to live like that. What lines of force and power in
society does it imply? A significant percentage of Black women have had
direct experience with welfare, either as children or as mothers. In
discussing "how it happened to them," all become aware of how every
woman in class is just one step away from that bottom line. A separation,
a work injury, layoffs, a prolonged illness, a child's disability could put
them on those rolls. It is a sobering realization, breaking through some of
the superior attitudes even Black women have internalized about AFDC
recipients.

What other work do we do, and how does it shape our thinking?
Read Studs Terkel's *Working* and compare Maggie Holmes, domestic;
Alice Washington, shoe factory order-filler; Diane Wilson, process clerk.

Study what women just like those in class say about themselves. Although, as with everything, a whole course could be devoted just to analyzing the content, process, and consciousness of Black women's jobs, be satisfied in this survey to personify history so that it becomes recognizable and immediate; something they participate in.

Have a dream. The conclusion to be drawn from any study of our history in America is that the balance of power is not on our side, while the burden of justice is. This can be an overwhelming insight, particularly in times of economic stagnation, physical deterioration, and organizational confusion. Therefore, it is important to balance any discussion of the material circumstances of Black women's lives with some attention to the realm of their dreams.

In all other areas of life, we can talk about struggle, organization, sabotage, survival, even tactical and strategic victory. However, only in dreams are liberation and judgment at the center of vision. That is where we do all the things in imagination that our awareness demands but our situation does not yet permit. In dreams, we seek the place in the sun that society denies us. And here, as in everything, a continuum of consciousness will be represented.

At their most fetishistic, Black women's spiritual dreams are embodied in the culture of numbers, signs, and gambling. In every poor community, holy water, herb, astrology, and dream book shops are for women what poolrooms, pawnshops, and bars are for men. Places to hang on, hoping for a hit. As Etheridge Knight has observed in *Black Voices from Prison,* "It is as common to hear a mother say, 'I gotta get my number in today' with the same concern and sometimes in the same breath as she says, 'I gotta feed the baby.'... In some homes the dream book is as familiar and treated with as much reverence as the Bible." In many homes, dream books produce more tangible results.

The most progressive expression of our dreams, however, in which mass liberation takes precedence over individual relief, and planning replaces luck, is occasionally articulated in literature. Sarah Wright provides such an example in *This Child's Gonna Live.* In that story of a Black family desperately trying to hold on to its territorial birthright and each other in depression Maryland, the most fundamental religiosity of poor Black people is recreated, its naturalism released. The landscape is made to hold our suffering and signify our fate. Particularly in the person of Mariah Upshur, the faith of the oppressed which helps us to fight on long after a cause seems lost is complemented by a belief that righteousness can make you invincible. Colloquially speaking, all that's needed is for God to send the sufferers a pretty day. Then, children will be cured of worms, the land thieves will be driven from the community, the wind will be calm for the oystermen, the newly planted rye will hold, and a future will be possible in a land of "slowing-up roads" and death. That is, if we're deserving. What does "deserving" mean? Discuss Richard Wright's approach to this subject in "Bright and Morning Star."

Relate the fundamental hopes and values of Mariah Upshur's dream to other belief systems through which people have been able to attain freedom. The concrete experience of people "moving mountains" is communicated by the story of Tachai in the People's Republic of China. The triumph of vision, perseverance, and organization over brute force to regain land is demonstrated in Vietnam and Cuba. Spell out the commonalities in all liberation struggles in this age which vanquish the moneychangers. Find examples in our own history where beginnings have been made of this kind. Make the Word become Flesh, so the new day that's dawning belongs to you and me.

As teachers, we should be able to explore all these things and more without resorting to conventional ideological labels. This is the basic, introductory course. Once the experiential base of the class-in-itself is richly felt and understood, theoretical threads can be woven between W. E. B. DuBois, Zora Neale Hurston, and Frantz Fanon. Then bridges can be built connecting the lives of ghettoized women of every color and nationality. In the third series of courses, great individuals can be put in historical perspective; organized movements can be studied. In the fourth stage, movements, themselves, may arise. Political possibilities for action then flow from an understanding conditioned by life on the block, but not bound by it. And the beginnings of a class-for-itself may take shape. But the first step, and the most fundamental, should be the goal of the first course: recognizing ourselves in history.

19

Teaching *Black-Eyed Susans:* An Approach to the Study of Black Women Writers

MARY HELEN WASHINGTON

Although *Black-Eyed Susans* (Anchor Press/Doubleday, 1975) is a slim anthology—there are only ten stories included—it is designed for maximum contact with Black women writers of the twentieth century. Seven of the most outstanding contemporary American Black women writers have short stories in this collection: Jean Wheeler Smith, Toni Morrison, Toni Cade Bambara, Alice Walker, Louise Meriwether, Paule Marshall, and Gwendolyn Brooks. Following each story there is a bio-critical sketch of the author, which provides background for the writer's life and gives an overall perspective of the writer's works, concentrating on the major themes. And the book begins with the editor's twenty-page introduction which looks at the image of the Black woman as seen from the special angle of these Black women writers. Following all of the stories is an extensive bibliography which points the way to further study of each of the seven writers in the collection.

THE THEMATIC APPROACH

The introduction and the critiques suggest several methods of approach to the study of the Black woman writer. One, of course, is the tracing of themes that recur in the literature of these writers. The themes that occur in the writings of Black women are sometimes unique; at other times they overlap themes presented in the writings of Black men writers or white women writers. For example, the theme of double consciousness is found in most literature by Blacks, and the theme of the divided self, woman split in two (which is closely akin to double consciousness), is found in literature by women, white and Black. Perhaps one of the most illuminating themes in Black women's writings is that of the Black woman as suppressed artist, a theme occurring with such frequency in this literature that it surely provides great insight into the lives of Black women. One might begin the inquiry into this theme with a study of an essay by Alice Walker, "In Search of Our Mothers' Gardens: The Creativity of Black Women in the South" (*Ms.*, May 1974), which defines in personal, historical and literary terms the ways in which Black women have been denied artistic expression. It is Walker's contention that, for two centuries, Black women have been hidden artists—creative geniuses in some cases—whose creative impulses have been denied and thwarted in a society in which they have been valued only as a source of cheap labor. Walker asks:

> What did it mean for a Black woman to be an artist in our grandmothers' time...? How was the creativity of the Black woman kept alive, year after year and century after century, when for most of the years Black people have been in America, it was a punishable crime for a Black person to read or write? And the freedom to paint, to sculpt, to expand the mind with action, did not exist.
>
> ("Our Mothers' Gardens," p. 66)

This landmark essay by Alice Walker suggests a most overlooked aspect of the Black woman's life, and it also suggests a reassessment of the Black woman writer who, in various forms, has dealt with this theme. We find it most clearly in Toni Morrison's *The Bluest Eye* (1971) and *Sula* (1974). In the former there is a character named Pauline Williams who, as a young farm girl in Kentucky, is, without knowing it, an artist:

> She liked, most of all, to arrange things. To line things up in rows—jars on shelves at canning, peach pits on the step, sticks, stones, leaves—and the members of her family let these arrangements be.... Whatever portable plurality she found, she organized into neat lines, according to their size, shape, or gradations of color. Just as she would never align a pine needle with the leaf of a cottonwood tree, she would never put the jars of tomatoes next to the green beans.... She missed— without knowing what she missed—paints and crayons.[1]

This excerpt from *The Bluest Eye*, which appears as a short story in *Black-Eyed Susans*, is one of the best examples of the suppressed artist theme because it shows the Black woman artist in embryonic form, perhaps unrecognizable except to the eye of the Black woman writer; then, too, Morrison shows us the destruction of the artist. Walker says in "Our Mothers' Gardens" that those Black women artists and creators, who were stifled instead of cultivated, spent their lives in slow motion and, unaware of their own richness, they "stared out at the world, wildly, like lunatics—or quietly, like suicides" (p. 64). Both of Morrison's characters—Pauline and Sula—follow the pattern Walker indicates. Their artistic impulses are turned inward and become destructive forces in their lives. Pauline becomes the ideal servant, worshipping the luxury and artistry of white homes where she finds "beauty, order, cleanliness, and praise."[2] Sula, also, becomes destructive to fill the void in her life caused by the lack of artistic tools and an outlet for her artistic temperament. She becomes simply arbitrary—doing whatever she wants regardless of the consequences, acting out all of her unconventional behavior until she is feared and despised by the whole town of Medallion.

Thus, using Walker's essay as a guide, one can trace the theme of the Black woman as suppressed artist throughout the two novels of Morrison, in Walker's story "A Sudden Trip Home in the Spring,"[3] in Nella Larsen's *Quicksand* (1929), in male author Jean Toomer's *Cane* (1923), in Gayl Jones's *Corregidora* (1975), and in Alice Walker's "Really Doesn't Crime Pay?"[4]

A second recurrent theme in the literature of Black women writers is the intimidation of color. It has been given an entire section in *Black-Eyed Susans* because it is such a persistent and revealing theme in the lives and the literature of Black women. As the "Introduction" to *Black-Eyed Susans* states:

> The subject of the black woman's physical beauty occurs with such frequency in the writing of black women that it indicates they have been deeply affected by the discrimination against the shade of their skin and the texture of their hair. In almost every novel or autobiography written by a black woman, there is at least one incident in which the dark-skinned girl wishes to be either white or light-skinned with "good" hair. (p. xv)

In *Black-Eyed Susans* there are three examples of this theme: one is "The Coming of Maureen Peal" from Morrison's *The Bluest Eye;* another example, from childhood, is Paule Marshall's "Reena" in which the young Reena speaks of the dreams she had in which she woke up to find her "ugly" dark self replaced by a little girl with skin like milk, blonde curls, and blue eyes. Maud Martha in Gwendolyn Brooks's "If You're Light and Have Long Hair" tells the story of the intimidation of color from the side of the adult Black woman. For further study of this theme one could explore Maya Angelou's autobiography *I Know Why the Caged Bird Sings*, Gwendolyn Brooks's novel *Maud Martha* or her autobiographical statement *Report From Part One*, and Zora Hurston's *Their Eyes Were Watching God*.

A good way to develop discussion of the "light skin, straight hair" theme as it intimidates Black women is to consider Arthur P. Davis's article "The Black-and-Tan Motif in the Poetry of Gwendolyn Brooks,"[5] which deals with what Davis calls the "inside color line." Davis begins his essay by citing early examples of color prejudice, and he traces this theme of rejection of the dark girl or woman by the tan boy or man or woman throughout the poetry of Gwendolyn Brooks. Davis maintains that the problem of color prejudice is symbolic of the larger rejection of all Blacks by the American system.

Several other themes present valuable ways to study the works of Black women writers but these themes require an in-depth study of a particular writer rather than a broad look at many writers. The theme of the cyclic nature of oppression can be approached through a study of Jean Wheeler Smith's short stories. In the story "Frankie Mae," the young girl's father is a sharecropper and the timekeeper for Mr. White, Jr., a position which allows him to watch the other field hands and keep himself out of the sun. Even this small act of collusion with the white boss contributes to the sum total of oppression, and when his own daughter is victimized, the father hands in his timekeeper's watch as an act that symbolizes the first step in breaking the cycle. Smith has written three other stories dealing with this theme: "That She Would Dance No More," "The Machine," and "Something-to-Eat," all listed in the *Black-Eyed Susans* bibliography.

One theme that has become central to the works of Louise Meriwether, Toni Morrison, and Alice Walker is the collective and historical violation of Black women. Meriwether, for example, portrays all her women characters in roles that Black women have historically been forced to play: Francie's mother in Meriwether's *Daddy Was a Number Runner* has to leave the family to do domestic work and, in a final indignity, has to face the welfare worker to apply for relief. That same collective and historical sense pervades Meriwether's short story "That Girl From Creektown." When Lonnie Lyttle, the main character of that story, finishes high school, she is unable to find work except as a maid in the little Southern town where she lives. Her mother has preached long and hard for her to stay in school so she "won't have to wash out some white woman's drawers for twenty dollars a week." The same theme is operative in Zora Neale Hurston's novel *Their Eyes Were Watching God* (1937): Nanny tells her granddaughter Janie that she wants her child "to pick from a higher bush and a sweeter berry."

AN HISTORICAL APPROACH

This theme of the collective and historical violation of Black women not only offers one possibility for an in-depth study of Louise Meriwether, but it can also be used to point the way to an intensive historical study of the Black woman writer and the Black woman herself. In an interview I had with Alice Walker, she outlined a personal historical view of Black women: she sees the experiences of Black women as a series of movements from a woman totally victimized by society and by men to a growing, developing woman whose consciousness allows her to have some control over her life.

The Suspended Woman

The evolutionary process is both historical and psychological and consists of three interrelated cycles: suspension, assimilation, and emergence. In historical terms the women in the first cycle belong to the nineteenth century and the early decades of the twentieth century.[6] They are, in the words of Zora Neale Hurston, "the mules of the world," carrying the burdens heaped upon them by society and by family, victims of both racial and sexual oppression. The three women in Walker's first novel, *The Third Life of Grange Copeland,* are examples of women in this first cycle; and seven of the thirteen women in her short story collection *In Love & Trouble* are also part of the cycle in which the women are subjected to and often destroyed by oppression and violence. Pain, violence, and death form the essential content of these women's lives. Walker refers to them as "suspended" women because the pressures against them are so great they cannot move anywhere.[7] Suspended in time and place, they are women whose life choices are so severely limited that they either kill themselves, retreat into insanity, or are simply defeated one way or another by the external circumstances of their lives. Most of these women suffer severe physical abuse, sometimes at the hands of their men, sometimes because of poverty or child-bearing. One critic calls them Alice Walker's black-eyed susans—flowers of the blood-soaked American soil. As John Callahan has observed, "in love and trouble" is an apt description of these women since it expresses the same condition of Black women that is evident in the blues tradition which also developed in the early twentieth century.[8]

For examples of women in this "suspended" cycle we can go as far back as slavery and, in literature, as far back as the first novel written by a Black woman, *Iola Leroy* (1892) by Frances Harper. From Harper's early novel to the latest one by Gayl Jones, *Eva's Man*, there are suspended Black women stumbling, in Walker's words, "blindly through their lives...abused and mutilated in body," unaware of the richness of their gifts but nonetheless suffering as their gifts are denied.[9]

The Assimilated Woman

The women in the second cycle are also victims, not of physical violence, but of a kind of a psychic violence that alienates them from their roots and cuts them off from real contact with their own people and also from a part of themselves. What is typical of the women in this cycle is that they are more aware of their condition than those women in the first cycle, but, in spite of their greater potential for shaping their lives, they are still thwarted because they feel themselves coming to life before the necessary changes have been made in the political environment, before there is space for them to move into.

Historically the women of this second cycle belong to the decades of the forties and fifties, those decades when Black people (the Negroes) wanted to be part of the mainstream of American life even though assimilation required total denial of one's ethnicity. Again this idea is part of Walker's unique construction of the history of Black women:

> I have this theory that Black women in the Fifties, in the Forties—the late Forties and early Fifties—got away from their roots much more than they will probably ever do again, because that was the time of greatest striving to get into White Society and to erase all the backgrounds of poverty. It was a time when you could be the exception, could be The One, and my sister was The One. But I think she's not unique—so many, many Black families have a daughter or a sister who was the one who escaped because, you see, that was what was set up for her; she was going to be the one who escaped....

Thus, even though these women appear to have more options than sisters before them—they are educated, they are not subjected to extreme physical abuse, they have even managed to become acceptable to the

white world—the price they have to pay for their acceptance is the
negation of their racial identity and the separation from the sustenance
that such an identity could afford them.

The Emergent Woman

In an interview in 1973 Walker made one of the first statements about
the direction and development of her Black woman characters into a third
cycle:

> My women, in the future, will not burn themselves
> up—that's what I mean by coming to the end of a cycle,
> and understanding something to the end.... Now I am
> ready to look at women who have made the room larger
> for others to move in.... I think one reason I never stay
> away from the Southern Movement is because I realize
> how deeply political changes affect the choices and
> lifestyles of people. The movement of the Sixties, Black
> Power, the Muslims, the Panthers...have changed the
> options of Black people generally and of Black women in
> particular. So that my women characters won't all end
> the way they have been, because Black women now offer
> varied, live models of how it is possible to live. We have
> made a new place to move.

The women of this third cycle are, for the most part, women of the late
sixties, although there are some older women in Walker's fiction who
exhibit the qualities of the developing, emergent model. Greatly
influenced by the political events of the sixties and the changes resulting
from the freedom movement, they are women coming just to the edge of a
new awareness and making the first tentative steps into an uncharted
region. And, although they are more fully conscious of their political and
psychological oppression and more capable of creating new options for
themselves, they must undergo a harsh initiation before they are ready to
occupy and claim any new territory. Alice Walker, herself a real-life
prototype of the emergent Black woman, speaks of having been called to
life by the civil rights movement of the sixties as being called from the
shadows of a world in which Black people existed as statistics, problems,
beasts of burden, a life that resembled death; for one was not aware of the
possibilities within one's self or of the possibilities in the larger world
outside of the narrow restraints of the world Black people inhabited
before the struggles of the sixties.[10] When Walker and other civil rights

activists like Fannie Lou Hamer began the fight for their lives, they were beaten, jailed, and, in Fannie Lou Hamer's case, widowed and made homeless, but they never lost the energy and courage for revolt.[11] In the same way, Walker's own characters, through suffering and struggle, lay the groundwork for a new type of woman to emerge.

Besides political activism, a fundamental activity the women in the third cycle engage in is the search for meaning in their roots and traditions. As they struggle to reclaim their past and to re-examine their relationship to the Black community, there is a consequent reconciliation between themselves and their cultural heritage and between themselves and Black men.

The process of cyclical movement in the lives of Walker's Black women is first evident in her first novel, *The Third Life of Grange Copeland*. The girl Ruth is the daughter and granddaughter of two women whose lives are lived out under extreme forms of oppression. Raised in the sixties, Ruth becomes the natural inheritor of the changes in the new order, thus marking the transition of the women in her family from death to life. In Walker's second novel, *Meridian*, the cyclical process is clearly defined in the life of the main character, Meridian Hill, who evolves from a woman trapped by racial and sexual oppression to a revolutionary figure, effecting action and strategy to bring freedom to herself and other poor and disenfranchised Blacks in the South. Like other third cycle women who are depicted in the short story collection *In Love & Trouble*, the characters in the two novels follow certain patterns. They begin existence in a numb state, deadened, insensible to a life beyond poverty and degradation; they are awakened to life by a powerful political force; and in discovering and expanding their creativity, there is a consequent effort to reintegrate themselves into their culture in order to rediscover its value. Historically, the second novel, dealing with a woman who comes of age during the sixties, brings Walker's women characters into the first few years of the seventies.

It is possible to use Walker's personal construct of the history of Black women, to analyze Black women characters in the literature of Black women writers in order to see relevant changes in the depiction of the Black woman's image—as the following chart suggests.

Cycle 1: The Suspended Woman

Iola Leroy in Frances Harper's *Iola Leroy* (1892)
Nannie in Zora Neale Hurston's *Their Eyes Were Watching God* (1937)
Lutie in Ann Petry's *The Street* (1940)

Mem and Margaret in Alice Walker's *The Third Life of Grange Copeland*
(1971)
Pauline in Toni Morrison's *The Bluest Eye* (1971)
Roselily, Hannah Kemhuff, Myrna, Rannie Toomer in Alice Walker's *In
Love & Trouble* (1973)
Sula in Toni Morrison's *Sula* (1974)

Cycle 2: The Assimilated Woman

Helga Crane in Nella Larsen's *Quicksand* (1928)
Clare Kendry in Nella Larsen's *Passing* (1929)
Mrs. Turner in Zora Neale Hurston's *Their Eyes Were Watching God*
(1937)
Cleo in Dorothy West's *The Living Is Easy* (1948)
Geraldine in Toni Morrison's *The Bluest Eye* (1971)
Dee in Alice Walker's "Everyday Use" (1973) in *Black-Eyed Susans*

Cycle 3: The Emergent Woman

Janie in Zora Neale Hurston's *Their Eyes Were Watching God* (1937)
Beneatha in Lorraine Hansberry's *A Raisin in the Sun* (1959)
Selina Boyce in Paule Marshall's *Brown Girl, Brownstones* (1959)
Reena in Paule Marshall's "Reena" (1966) in *Black-Eyed Susans*
Vyry in Margaret Walker's *Jubilee* (1966)
Merle Kibona in Paule Marshall's *The Chosen Place, The Timeless
People* (1969)
Sarah Davis in Alice Walker's "A Sudden Trip Home in the Spring"
(1971) in *Black-Eyed Susans*
Meridian in Alice Walker's *Meridian* (1976)

The chart involves some oversimplification, and it by no means
contains a complete list of all the women characters created by Black
women writers. But the list serves several functions, the most important
being that it is a way of showing historical progression in the image of
the Black woman, a progression that can be noted only in the literature of
Black women writers. Most other writers seem to be able to see Black
women only in the role of servant or long-suffering wife and mother and
have forced the Black woman's image to become stereotyped. Looking at
the historical progression of Black women figures suggested by the
cyclical construct set up here, we are able to see in the image of Black
women—*as created by Black women writers*—complexity, diversity, and
depth. It is the function of *Black-Eyed Susans* to present a set of characters

that reflect those qualities, and thereby show the unique and competent way that Black women writers have handled their major preoccupation— the Black woman.

NOTES

[1]"SEEMOTHERMOTHERISVERYNICE," in *Black-Eyed Susans*, p. 94.

[2]Ibid., p. 109.

[3]In *Black-Eyed Susans.*

[4]In Walker's *In Love & Trouble: Stories of Black Women.*

[5]*CLA Journal* 6 (December 1962): 90-97.

[6]There is much overlapping in Walker's construct; there are, obviously, Black women who are, in the 1970s, still as victimized as the women of this first cycle; but, significantly, there are no women characters in early Black fiction who clearly are part of the third cycle, and though there were always Black women like the ones of the emergent developing model, it has only been since the post–civil rights era that they have had the chance to exist in numbers.

[7]The concept of the suspended woman, developed in a speech given by Alice Walker at a symposium on Black women held at Radcliffe College in May 1972, and based on Walker's personal sense of the history of Black women in America, will be expanded on in the body of this paper.

[8]"The Higher Ground of Alice Walker," *New Republic*, September 14, 1974, p. 21.

[9]This comment on Walker and those which follow are taken from interviews I elicited from her in June 1973.

[10]See "The Civil Rights Movement: What Good Was It," *American Scholar* 36 (1970-71):551.

[11]The identification of Hamer as a model for the emergent woman is developed in Walker's review of a biography of Hamer by June Jordan (*New York Times Book Review*, April 29, 1973).

Group at Tuskegee Institute, 1906.

Section Six

Bibliographies and Bibliographic Essays

20

Afro-American Women, 1800–1910: Excerpts from a Working Bibliography

JEAN FAGAN YELLIN

INTRODUCTION

Their presence is what is most important. If we are unaware of Black women in nineteenth-century America, it is not because they were not here; if we know nothing of their literature and culture, it is not because they left no records. It is because their lives and their work have been profoundly ignored. Both as the producers of culture and as the subjects of the cultural productions of others, however, their traces are everywhere.

For example, Ethel S. Bolton and Eva J. Coe list in *American*

*This is a series of excerpts from the working manuscript of a book-length reference tool, *Writings By and About Nineteenth-Century Afro-American Women,* planned for publication by G. K. Hall Company as part of the Yale Afro-American Reference Series under the general editorship of Charles T. Davis. I have based this listing on my own work, and earnestly invite comments, additions, and corrections. I wish to thank Ruth Bogin, William R. Ferris, Jr., Ernest Kaiser, and Joan R. Sherman for their valuable aid. It would have been impossible to move my project even this far along without Bruce Bergman, Assistant University Librarian, and the staff of the Pace University Library in New York City; without Jean Blackwell Hutson, Director, and the staff of the Schomburg Collection of the New York Public Library; and without Rose Ann Burstein, Librarian, and the staff of the Sarah Lawrence College Library. I am grateful for their patient help.

Samplers (1921)—the standard work on a folk art expressive of female education—the sampler of Phebe Cash. The identity of the young needlewoman, described as a "Negro child belonging to Mrs. Sarah (Kent) Atkins, widow of Dudley Atkins, Esq. of Newburgh," is recorded. Significantly, she is defined in terms of her enslavement to a woman who is herself defined by her marriage to a man; obviously even after death he retains an autonomy denied both living females.

A second nineteenth-century Afro-American sampler was worked by Rosena Disery at the New York African Free School. Her embroidery raises questions about the education of Afro-American females in New York in 1820. How many attended the school? Were boys and girls educated together? What did they study? Did they have Black teachers? Black women teachers?

Traces of the existence of young Black women can be found not only in their own embroideries, but in the needlework of others. Sally Johnson's sampler, finished the year before the nineteenth century opened, depicts a tropical setting in which a tiny Black girl follows an even tinier white girl. It is a matter of speculation whether this scene was a response to the Haitian revolt which ushered the era of Emancipation into the New World; but there is no question that it attests to one white Massachusetts girl's awareness of a Black female presence.

This awareness has been lost. Yet for us to view American culture steadily and whole, it must be restored. Rather than express surprise when we encounter Black women in the study of nineteenth-century America, we need to ask why they are missing when we do not. Then we need to search and find them.

The importance of restoring the historical presence of Black women cannot be overemphasized, given their absence from otherwise responsible materials in women's studies and in Black studies. This has not always been the case; Black women were often included in the early, pioneering works. In *The Afro-American Press and Its Editors,* published in 1891, I. Garland Penn included a sixty-page chapter entitled "Afro-American Women in Journalism." Similarly, when Elizabeth Cady Stanton and others of the first feminist generation began their *History of Woman Suffrage* (6 vols., 1881–1922), they recorded the activities of more than a dozen Black feminists.[1] But female journalists are omitted in a later standard study, Frederick G. Detweiler's *The Negro Press in the United States* (1922); and not a single Afro-American is included among the 1,500 biographical subjects treated by feminists Frances E. Willard and Mary A. Livermore in *American Women: A Comprehensive Encyclopedia of the Lives and Achievements of American Women during the Nineteenth Century,* 2 vols. (1897; reprinted in 1973).

So conspicuous is the absence of Black women from most standard works in Black studies and women's studies today that one wonders whether they were systematically excluded as these materials were professionalized and introduced into the universities. This would not be too surprising: Afro-Americans and women became subjects of serious academic consideration during a period of rupture between the movement for women's rights and the movement for the rights of Afro-Americans. (See Aileen Kraditor, *The Ideas of the Woman Suffrage Movement, 1890-1920* [1965], ch. 7; and see my own "DuBois' *Crisis* and Woman's Suffrage," *Massachusetts Review* 14 [Spring 1973]: 365-75.)

Black women are not, however, ignored in all standard reference works. The discussions that follow consistently refer the reader to two generally available resources on women which include Afro-Americans: Eleanor Flexner, *Century of Struggle: The Woman's Rights Movement in the United States* (1959; 1970); and Edward T. and Janet W. James, eds., *Notable American Women, 1607-1950: A Biographical Dictionary*, 3 vols. (1971). Because it is similarly available, a number of references are also made to the standard Afro-American bibliography, James M. McPherson, Laurence B. Holland, James M. Banner, Jr., Nancy C. Weiss, and Michael D. Bell, *Blacks in America: Bibliographical Essays* (1971); although its index lists only two items under "women," a large number of the works cited—particularly the older ones—include discussions of women. But a word of warning is in order. All too often these early studies present inaccurate details. With a few significant exceptions, it is only recently that writings by and about Black women have begun to be organized and presented systematically.

Teaching about nineteenth-century Afro-American women has become easier since the 1960s because of the publication of a handful of books. Five of these are anthologies, and two are historical and critical studies. Two of the anthologies focus on Afro-American women: the pioneering Gerda Lerner, ed., *Black Women in White America: A Documentary History* (1972); and Bert James Loewenberg and Ruth Bogin, eds., *Black Women in Nineteenth-Century American Life: Their Words, Their Thoughts, Their Feelings* (1976). The three other collections present Black writings before the twentieth century: these are Dorothy Porter's excellent *Early Negro Writing, 1760-1837* (1971), and two anthologies edited by William H. Robinson, *Early Black American Poets: Selections with Biographical Introductions* (1969) and *Early Black American Prose: Selections with Biographical Introductions* (1971)— companion volumes which, despite errors, are of value.

The book-length study by Joan R. Sherman, *Invisible Poets: Afro-Americans of the Nineteenth Century* (1974), presents a series of critical essays, meticulous notes, and suggestions for further work. *The Afro-American Woman: Struggles and Images* (1978), edited by Sharon Harley and Rosalyn Terborg-Penn, includes six essays in which scholars offer historical perspectives on such topics as employment, women's organizations, feminism, and the blues tradition; the editors then focus on three women, two of whom (Anna J. Cooper and Nannie Burroughs) worked within the period here considered. With the appearance of these volumes—and with the publication of paperback editions of some of the slave narratives, autobiographies, and journals of nineteenth-century women, including Charlotte Forten, Harriet Brent Jacobs, Harriet Tubman, Sojourner Truth, and Ida B. Wells—a series of primary readings for students can now be readily compiled.

As back-up sources, the reprinting of landmark books in Afro-American studies and women's studies since the late 1960s has made it possible for libraries and for individual scholars to acquire reference works that had long been out of print. Concurrently, a number of new bibliographical tools have been developed for the study of Black literature and culture which systematically present the multiple roles of women. These are discussed in appropriate sections below.

The topics presented here are Reference Tools; General Discussions; Arts, Fine and Folk; Education; Employment; Public Affairs: Women's Organizations; Religion; and Urban Life. To update these, see the sections on "Women's History" and "Black History" listed under "Social History" in *Writings in American History* (1962–), an annual; and see "Recent Articles" listed in each number of the *Journal of Christian History*.

REFERENCE TOOLS

The single most useful source of general information about Afro-American women in the nineteenth century is Mabel M. Smythe, ed., *The Black American Reference Book* (1976). This is a second edition of *The American Negro Reference Book* (1966); a preliminary note announces that this revision attempts to eliminate sexual bias. The volume includes Ernestine Walker's basic essay, "The Black Woman," followed by a "Selected List of Black Women of Achievement." Arna Bontemps's indispensable "Black Contribution to American Letters" again appears.

A half-dozen research tools on Afro-American women were developed in the 1970s. Gerda Lerner's bibliographical essay in *Black Women in White America: A Documentary History* (1972) is a major contribution. In conjunction with this, see Lenwood G. Davis's valuable *Black Woman in American Society: A Selected Annotated Bibliography* (1975).

The focus of Janet L. Sims's topically organized *Black Women: A Selected Bibliography* (1978) is on the twentieth century, as is that of Ora Williams, *American Black Women in the Arts and Social Sciences: A Bibliographic Survey* (1973). For women in nineteenth- and twentieth-century urban life, see a second listing by Davis, *Black Women in the Cities, 1870–1975: A Bibliography*, 2d ed. (1975). Johnetta B. Cole's innovative "Black Women in America: An Annotated Bibliography," *Black Scholar* 3:4 (December 1971):42–53, which uses a cross-cultural approach, cites a number of materials on the nineteenth century.

Most standard Afro-American reference tools list pertinent materials on nineteenth-century women. Although not identified as a topic in James M. McPherson et al., *Blacks in America: Bibliographical Essays* (1971), women are the subject of many of the discussions, as well as of many of the resources to which they refer. Similarly, although Dwight L. Smith, ed., *Afro-American History: A Bibliography* (1974), does not list women as a subject, this collection from *America: History and Life*, an abstracting journal which covers hundreds of professional periodicals, is valuable for materials on nineteenth-century women.

Additional Afro-American studies bibliographies useful for locating materials on nineteenth-century women include the excellent Emma N. Kaplan, comp., *Guide to Research in Afro-American History and Culture: A Selected and Annotated Bibliography of Materials in the Smith College Library*, 3 vols., mimeographed (1972; rev. 1975). Elizabeth W. Miller, *The Negro in America: A Bibliography*, 2d rev. ed., comp. Mary L. Fisher (1970), is strong on social and political concerns, though weak on literature. Dorothy Porter, comp., *The Negro in the United States: A Selected Bibliography* (1970), presents a wide range of materials, including sections on art, economics, education, folklore, music, and the press. A reference tool developed a generation ago, Edgar T. and Alma Thompson, *Race and Region: A Descriptive Bibliography Compiled with Special Reference to Relations between Whites and Negroes in the United States* (1949), discusses such topics as "The Negro in Domestic Service," "The Negro Family," and "Negro Educational Institutions."

For demographic information, see Reynolds Farley, *Growth of the Black Population: A Study of Demographic Trends* (1971); and United States, Bureau of the Census, *Negro Population, 1790–1915* (1918). Harry A. Polski and Ernest Kaiser, eds., *The Negro Almanac*, 2d ed. (1971), and 3d ed., ed. Harry A. Polski and Warren Mantt (1976), as well as Erwin A. Salk, *A Layman's Guide to Negro History* (1967), are good for quick reference. For a rich gathering of visual materials, see Middleton Harris, *The Black Book* (1974).

One traditional approach to Afro-American studies has been broadly cross-cultural. For an introduction to this method, popular among anthropologists, folklorists, and historians, see Inez Smith Reid, "Black Americans and Africa," in Mabel M. Smythe, ed., *The Black American Reference Book* (1976); and three classics: Carter G. Woodson, *The African Background Outlined: A Handbook for the Study of the Negro* (1936; reprinted in 1969); W. E. B. DuBois, *Black Folk Then and Now: An Essay in the History and Sociology of the Negro Race* (1939); and Melville J. Herskovitz, *The Myth of the Negro Past* (1941; reprinted 1969). A recent book, useful for this approach, is N. J. Hafkin and E. G. Bay, eds., *Women in Africa* (1976).

A number of recent reference tools designed for students of American culture use a multiethnic perspective. These include Priscilla S. Oaks, *Minority Studies: A Selected Annotated Bibliography* (1976); Philip Whitney, *America's Third World: A Guide to Bibliographic Resources in the Library of the University of California, Berkeley* (1970); Clara O. Jackson, *A Bibliography of Afro-American and Other American Minorities Represented in Library and Library-Related Listings* (1970; suppl. 1972); and Wayne C. Miller's monumental *Comprehensive Bibliography for the Study of American Minorities* (1976); his companion *Handbook of American Minorities* (1976) is composed of bibliographical essays.

Women's studies reference tools which discuss materials on nineteenth-century Afro-Americans include Cynthia E. Harrison, ed., *Women in American History: A Bibliography* (1979), which presents relevant abstracts that appeared in *America: History and Life* (1964– 1977); Esther Stineman, *Women's Studies: A Recommended Core Bibliography* (1979); Gerda Lerner, *A Bibliography in the History of American Women, 3d rev. ed.* (1978); The Common Woman Collective, *Women in U.S. History: An Annotated Bibliography* (1976); and Marie B. Rosenberg and Len V. Bergstrom, eds., *Women and Society: A Critical Review of the Literature, With a Selected Annotated Bibliography* (1975). A supplement to the last, ed. Jo Ann Een and Maria Rosenberg-Dishman, has recently appeared (1978). Also see Albert Krichmar et al., *The Women's Rights Movement in the United States, 1848-1970: A Bibliography and Sourcebook* (1972); and Kathleen Burke McKee, *Women's Studies: A Guide to Reference Sources* (1977). A basic women's studies tool designed for cross-cultural work is Sue-Ellen Jacobs's exhaustive listing *Women in Perspective: A Guide for Cross-Cultural Studies* (1974); geographically and topically organized, this list covers women in societies throughout the world, and includes Afro-American culture as well as a number of African cultures.

Biographical information on nineteenth-century Afro-American women is often hard to find; but recently published tools designed for work in Afro-American studies and women's studies are helpful. Theresa G. Rush et al., *Black American Writers Past and Present: A Biographical and Bibliographical Dictionary*, 2 vols. (1975), is, despite limitations, indispensable. James A. Page, *Selected Black American Authors: An Illustrated Bio-Bibliography* (1977), while derivative, is a handy volume; it includes ten nineteenth-century women. The standard biographical dictionary for women, Edward T. and Janet W. James, eds., *Notable American Women, 1607-1950: A Biographical Dictionary*, 3 vols. (1971), includes forty-one Afro-Americans; see 3:720. And James de T. Abajian, *Blacks in Selected Newspapers, Censuses and Other Sources: An Index to Names and Subjects* (1977), is extraordinarily useful. Wilhelmina S. Robinson, *Historical Negro Biographies* (1967), includes materials on fifty women. For more, see Barbara Bell, *Black Biographical Sources* (1970), an annotated bibliography of biographies.

Both obscure and eminent women are generally included in nineteenth-century collective biographies of Afro-Americans; see, for example, the early volume compiled by Abigail F. Mott, *Biographical Sketches and Interesting Anecdotes of Persons of Color* (1826 and 1837; rev. 1839 and 1850); and, at the turn of the century, Daniel Wallace Culp, ed., *Twentieth-Century Negro Literature* (1902), and John Edward Bruce, *Short Biographical Sketches of Eminent Negro Men and Women in Europe and the United States* (1910). Afro-Americans were, however, generally ignored in the collective biographies of American women published before 1910: Mary Peake and Charlotte Ray are the only Black women in Phebe Hannaford, *Daughters of America* (1882); Julia Ward Howe, ed., *Representative Women of New England* (1904), lists only Josephine St. Pierre Ruffin.

It was perhaps this latter exclusion which sparked the publication of a special group of collective biographies of Afro-American women, most of which appeared around 1900. Written in the tradition of the classic works by Martin R. Delaney, William C. Nell, and William Wells Brown, which had included biographical sketches of Afro-American women, these collective biographies represent a unique resource. The earliest I have identified—evidently written in response to William J. Simmons, *Men of Mark* (1887; 1968)—is Susan Elizabeth Frazier, "Some Afro-American Women of Mark," *A.M.E. Church Review* 8 (April 1892): 378-86. Two collective biographies by Black male authors appeared the following year: Lawson Andrew Scruggs, *Women of Distinction* (1893), presented nearly a hundred subjects, and Monroe Alphus Majors, *Noted Negro Women: Their Triumphs and Activities* (1893; 1971), tripled that number. Mrs. N. F. Mossell (Gertrude E. H. Bustill Mossell), *The Work of the Afro-American Woman* (1894; 1971), mentioned hundreds of women, then moved beyond collective biography to present a series of discussions of women's activities. (In "A Lofty Study," anticipating Virginia Woolf, she asserts that women who write should establish "a place to one's self.") Hallie Q. Brown, ed., *Homespun Heroines and*

Other Women of Distinction (1926), presented more than fifty subjects; Benjamin G. Brawley, in contrast, limited himself to five in *Women of Achievement* (1919); and, more recently, Sadie Iola Daniel, *Women Builders* (1931), focused on seven women who established social and educational institutions for Afro-American youth.

Although not a collective biography, Elizabeth Lindsay Davis, *Lifting As They Climb: The National Association of Colored Women* (1933), an assemblage of appreciations, reminiscences, records, and documents, expresses the adulatory spirit of these volumes. Mossell articulates, in her introductory remarks, what I take to be the purpose shared by the Afro-American men and women who wrote them. These collective biographies were intended to inspire an audience of young Black women. Thus, despite their frequent inclusion of uncritical, derivative, even erroneous materials, they testify to an historic effort. At a time when the dominant society not only devalued, but utterly denied, Afro-American women, these collective biographies by Black Americans celebrated them.

Some of the other collective biographies published after 1910 which include nineteenth-century Afro-American women among their subjects are: Mary White Ovington, *Portraits in Color* (1927); Henrietta Buckmaster, *Women Who Shaped History* (1938); Alma A. Polk, *Twelve Pioneer Women in the A.M.E. Church* (1947); Rebecca Chalmers Barton, *Witnesses for Freedom: Negro Americans in Autobiography* (1948; reprinted 1976); Samuel Sillen, *Women Against Slavery* (1955); Richard Bardolph, *The Negro Vanguard* (1959); Charlemae Hill Rollins, *They Showed the Way: Forty American Negro Leaders* (1964); Dorothy Sterling and Benjamin Quarles, *Lift Every Voice* (1965); Philip Sterling and Rayford Logan, *Four Took Freedom* (1967); and Dorothy Sterling, *Black Foremothers* (1979).

Handbooks and directories include *Negro Year Book: An Annual Encyclopedia of the Negro* (1912–1952; no editions for 1920–21, 1923–24, 1929–30); Florence Murray, ed., *The Negro Handbook* (1942–49); *Who's Who of the Colored Race: A General Biographical Dictionary of Men and Women of African Descent* (1915); *Who's Who in Colored America: A Biographical Dictionary of Notable Living Persons of Negro Descent in America* (1927–1938/40); and *Who's Who in Colored America: A Biographical Dictionary of Notable Living Persons...*, 7 vols. (1927–1950).

Research collections of materials on Afro-American women include the Afro-American Women's Collection, Thomas F. Holgate Library, Bennett College (Macon Street, Greensboro, NC 27420); the special collections at Atlanta, Fisk, and Howard Universities, and the Schomburg Collection, New York Public Library—all of which include women as a subject in their card catalogs; the Black Women's Employment Project, NAACP Legal Defense and Educational Fund, Inc. (10 Columbus Circle, New York, NY 10019; and the Black Women's Institute, National Council of Negro Women (1346 Connecticut Ave., N.W., Washington, DC 20036). For discussions of research collections of Afro-American materials, see E. J. Josey and Ann Allen Shockley, eds., *Handbook of Black Librarianship* (1977); Jessie Carney Smith, *Black Academic Libraries and Research Collections: An Historical Survey* (1977); and Walter Schatz's excellent *Directory of Afro-American Resources* (1970). Doctoral research is listed in Earl H. West, comp., *A Bibliography of Doctoral Research on the Negro, 1933–1966* (1969); the most recent update is University Microfilm International's *Black Women's Studies: A Dissertation Bibliography. A Bibliography of Doctoral Research on the Negro, 1967–1977*, is a Supplement to E. H. West.

The basic research tool for women's materials is now Andrea Harding, Ames Sheldon Bower, and Clark A. Chambers, eds., *Women's History Sources: A Guide to Archives and Manuscript Collections in the United States*, 2 vols. (1979); this includes "Afro-Americans" as a subject heading. It supersedes Andrea Hinding and Rosemary Richardson, *Archival and Manuscript Resources for the Study of Women's History: A Beginning* (1972).

Two excellent research collections of women's materials which include items on nineteenth-century Afro-Americans are the Arthur and Elizabeth Schlesinger Library on the History of Women in America, Radcliffe College (Cambridge, MA 02138) and the Sophia Smith Collection, Smith College (Northampton, MA 01060). Also see two pertinent articles in the *Quarterly Journal of the Library of Congress* 32 (October 1975): Anita Nolen, "The Feminine Presence: Women's Papers in the Manuscript Division," and Sylvia L. Render, "Afro-American Women: The Outstanding and the Obscure."

The *Index to Periodical Articles by and about Negroes* (1950–), previously entitled *Index to Selected Negro Periodicals* (and earlier, *Index to Selected Periodicals Received in the Hallie Q. Brown Library*), lists much of the periodical literature. There is a cumulative index covering the years 1960–70; supplements are dated 1971 and 1972. For periodical articles on women, see the indispensable *Women's Studies Abstracts* (1972–), a quarterly. And see the intermittent review articles in *Signs: A Journal of Women in Culture and Society* (1975–). Particularly useful is Patricia K. Ballou's "Bibliographies for Research on Women," *Signs* 3 (Winter 1977); 346–50; this has been expanded into *Women: A Bibliography of Bibliographies* (1980), which includes a section on Black women.

GENERAL DISCUSSIONS

Two landmark feminist studies which deal seriously with the subject of nineteenth-century Afro-American women are the pioneering Lydia Maria Child, *Brief History of the Condition of Women*, 2 vols. (1835), and the standard Eleanor Flexner, *A Century of Struggle* (1959; republished 1970). A more recent provocative discussion of issues of interest to students of feminism and of Afro-American culture is William H. Chafe, "Sex and Race: The Analogy of Social Control," *Massachusetts Review* 18 (1977):147–76.

The subject of Black women was repeatedly addressed by Black male leaders; see Philip S. Foner, ed., *Frederick Douglass on Women's Rights* (1976); Alexander Crummell, *The Black Woman of the South: Her Neglects and Her Needs* (1883); Kelly Miller, "Surplus Negro Women," *Southern Workman* 34:10 (October 1905):522–28, reprinted in his *Race Adjustment: Essays* (1908; republished 1968); and two essays by Booker T. Washington: "The New Negro Woman," *Lend a Hand* 15 (1895):254, and "Negro Women and Their Work," in *The Story of the Negro* (1909), vol. 2, ch. 12. W. E. B. DuBois repeatedly considered this topic; see, for example, *The Souls of Black Folk* (1903; republished 1970); *The Gift of Black Folk* (1924; republished 1970); *Some Efforts of American Negroes for Their Own Social Betterment* (1898); *Efforts for Social Betterment among Negro Americans* (1909); and writings in *The Crisis* beginning in 1910. For an historical essay on this topic, see Rosalyn Terborg-Penn, "Black Male Perspectives on the Nineteenth-Century Woman," in Sharon Harley and Rosalyn Terborg-Penn, eds., *The Afro-American Woman: Struggles and Images* (1978).

The Voice of the Negro ran a special issue on women in July 1904 (1:7) and published a number of general discussions on women. These include John H. Adams, Jr., "Rough Sketches: A Study of the Features of the New Negro Woman," 1:8 (August 1904):323–26; Addie Hunton, "Negro Womanhood Defended," 1:7 (July 1904):280–82; a two-part article by Anna H. Jones: "The Century's Progress by the American Colored Woman," 2:9 (September 1905):631–33, and "The American Colored Woman," 2:10 (October 1905):692–94; and Sylvanie Fancaz Williams, "The Social Status of the Negro Woman," 1:7 (July 1904):298–300.

Other items in periodicals include Mrs. L. H. Harris, "Negro Womanhood," *The Independent* 51 (June 1899):1687–89; Olive Ruth Jefferson, "The Southern Negro Woman," *The Chautauquan* 8 (1893): 91; Frances A. Kellor, "To Help Negro Women," *Boston Traveler* (May 31, 1905); and L. S. Orrick, "Advance of Negro Women in the South,"

National Monthly (Boston) 21 (1905):172. *The Outlook* carried Edith A. Abbott, "The Negro Woman and the South," 77 (May 21, 1904):165–68, and Eleanor Tayleur, "Negro Woman," 76 (January 30, 1904):266–71. Anna E. Murray's response to Tayleur is "The Negro Woman," *Southern Workman* 33 (April 1904):232–34.

Among the book-length discussions of Black women which appeared during—or immediately following—the period under consideration, a work of great importance is Gertrude Bustill Mossell, *The Work of the Afro-American Woman* (1894; republished 1971). Also see David Bryant Fulton, *A Plea for Social Justice for the Negro Woman* (1912); Lily H. Hammond, *Southern Women and Racial Adjustment*, Occasional Paper Number 19, The Slater Fund (1917); Elizabeth Christophers Kimball Hobson, *A Report Concerning the Colored Women of the South*, Occasional Paper Number 9, The Slater Fund (1896); and Frances Hoggan, *American Negro Women During Their First Fifty Years of Freedom* (1913).

Briefer general discussions to be found in works on Black Americans appearing before 1910 include John T. Haley, comp., "Opportunities and Responsibilities of Colored Women," in the *Afro-American Encyclopedia* (1895); H. F. Kletzing and W. G. Crogman, "The Colored Woman of Today," *Progress of a Race* (1897); G. F. Richings, "Prominent Colored Women," in *Evidences of Progress among Colored People* (1909); and Wilson A. Armistead, *A Tribute for the Negro* (1848).

General discussions by two leading Afro-American women are Mary Church Terrell, "What Role Is the Educated Negro Woman to Play in the Uplifting of Her Race?" in Daniel W. Culp, ed., *Twentieth-Century Negro Literature* (1902; republished 1969), and Mary McLeod Bethune, "A Century of Progress of Negro Women," a 1933 typescript excerpted in Gerda Lerner, ed., *Black Women in White America: A Documentary History* (1972).

Other twentieth-century comments on the nineteenth century include Herbert Aptheker, "The Negro Woman," *Masses and Mainstream* 2:2 (February 1949):10–17; Lerone Bennett, "The Negro Woman," *Ebony* 15:10 (August 1960):38–42, 44–46; segments of Benjamin Brawley, *Negro Builders and Heroes* (1937); materials in Middleton Harris, *The Black Book* (1974); Maude White Katz, "She Who Would Be Free: Resistance," *Freedomways* 2 (Winter 1962):60–70; May C. King, "The Politics of Sexual Stereotype," *Black Scholar* 4 (March-April 1973):12–23; Joyce Ladner, *Tomorrow's Tomorrow* (1971); Marjorie McKenzie, *Fifty Years of Progress for Negro Women* (1950); and Anne Firor Scott, ed., *The American Woman—Who Was She?* (1971). And see also two brief, important recent comments by Afro-American women: Ann Allen

Shockley, "The Negro Woman in Retrospect," *Negro History Bulletin* 29 (December 1963):55–56, 62, 70; and Alice Walker, "In Search of Our Mothers' Gardens: The Creativity of Black Women in the South," *Ms.* 2 (May 1974):64–70.

THE ARTS—FINE AND FOLK

A basic reference tool for the study of Afro-American art is Theresa D. Cederholm, *Afro-American Artists: A Bio-Bibliography* (1973). Also see Ralph L. Harley, Jr., "A Checklist of Afro-American Art and Artists," *Serif* 7:4 (1970):3–63. For a brief background, see Edmund B. Gaither, "Afro-American Art," in Mabel M. Smythe, *The Black American Reference Book* (1976). For additional background, see Margaret Just Butcher, *The Negro in American Culture* (1956); Benjamin Brawley, *The Negro Genius* (1937); and Alain Locke, ed., *The New Negro* (1925; 1968), which, despite its title, includes discussions of the nineteenth century. For a popular brief treatment, see Allan Morrison, "(Black) Women in the Arts," *Ebony* (August 1966):90–94, and Alpha Kappa Alpha, *Afro-American Women in Art* (1969). Also see Lindsay Patterson, comp., *The Negro in Music and Art*, 2d ed. (1968).

Recent book-length studies of Afro-American fine art discussing nineteenth-century women artists include Samella Lewis, *Art: African-American* (1977), which treats Edmonia Lewis, Meta Fuller, and Laura Wheeler Waring; New York (City) City College, *The Evolution of Afro-American Artists, 1800–1950*, Exhibition Catalog (1967), which includes Lewis and Fuller; and Elsa Honig Fine, *The Afro-American Artist: A Search for Identity* (1973). Also see David C. Driscoll's *Two Centuries of Black American Art*, Exhibition Catalog (1976). Standard book-length studies that include discussions of nineteenth-century women are Cedric Dover, *American Negro Art* (1960; 1967); and the classics: Alain Locke, *The Negro in Art* (1940; 1969), and James A. Porter, *Modern Negro Art* (1943; 1969). I have found especially useful the discussions of Edmonia Lewis and Annie E. Walker in Porter's *Ten Afro-American Artists of the Nineteenth Century*, Exhibition Catalog (1967).

Afro-Americans as the subjects of fine art are presented in Bowdoin College Museum of Art, *The Portrayal of the Negro in American Painting*, Exhibition Catalog (1964); in Sidney Kaplan, "The Negro in the Art of Homer and Eakins," in Sidney Kaplan and Jules Chametsky, eds., *Black and White in American Culture* (1969); and in Ellwood Perry, *The Image of the Indian and the Black Man in American Art, 1590–1900* (1974). (Despite the title of the latter, images of women are included.)

Sidney Kaplan, *The Black Presence in the Era of the American Revolution, 1770–1800* (1973), includes a rich gathering far beyond the restrictions its name suggests. For more, see the listings in James M. McPherson et al., eds., *Blacks in America: Bibliographical Essays* (1971), pp. 180–81.

Recent studies of women artists include Vassar College Art Gallery, *The White Marmorean Flock: Nineteenth-Century American Women Neoclassical Sculptors,* Exhibition Catalog (1972); Eleanor Tufts, *Our Hidden Heritage: Five Centuries of Women Artists* (1974), which presents a chapter-length discussion of Edmonia Lewis; Karen Peterson and J. J. Wilson, *Women Artists: Recognition and Reappraisal from the Middle Ages to the Twentieth Century* (1976); and Elsa Honig Fine, *Women and Art: A History of Women Painters and Sculptors from the Renaissance to The Twentieth Century* (1978).

Edmonia Lewis is the subject of a biographical entry in Edward T. and Janet W. James, eds., *Notable American Women* (1971).

For slides of works by nineteenth-century Afro-American women artists, see the Catalog of the Afro-American Slide Depository, available from the Department of Art, University of South Alabama (Mobile, AL 36608); and see Mary D. Garrard, comp., *Slides of Works by Women Artists: A Source Book* (1974).

African survivals in Afro-American folk arts and crafts are discussed in Robert Farris Thompson, "African Influence on the Art of the United States," in Armistead L. Robinson, Craig C. Foster, and Donald H. Olgilve, eds., *Black Studies in the University* (1969); in Judith Wragg Chase, *Afro-American Art and Craft* (1971); and in M. Vlatch, *The Afro-American Tradition in Decorative Arts* (1978). In the latter volume, the discussions of basketry, quilting, and weaving are especially interesting. For films and videotapes of traditional Afro-American crafts, a number of which present works by women, see Bill Ferris and Judy Piser, eds., *American Folklore Films and Videotapes: An Index (1976).*

EDUCATION

For a bibliographical discussion of the education of Afro-American women, see Gerda Lerner, ed., *Black Women in White America* (1972), pp. 621–23. An early presentation focusing on the education of Afro-American women and on Afro-American women as educators is William T. Alexander, "Women's Higher Education," in *History of the Colored Race in America* (1887).

Of particular interest are comments by women on the education of

Afro-American women that appeared in Afro-American publications before World War I. These include Josephine Silone-Yates, "Afro-American Women as Educators," and Josephine Turpin Washington, "Higher Education for Women," in Lawson A. Scruggs, ed., *Women of Distinction* (1893), pp. 309-19 and 365-72; Josephine D. Bruce, "What Has Education Done for Colored Women?" *The Voice of the Negro* 1:7 (July 1904):294-98; and Grace Bigelow House, "The Fiftieth Anniversary of the Penn School," *Southern Workman* 41:5 (May 1912): 317-20. And see Alice Dunbar-Nelson, "Is It Time for the Negro Colleges of the South to Be Put into the Hands of Negro Teachers?" in D. W. Culp, ed., *Twentieth-Century Negro Literature* (1902; republished 1969), pp. 139-41; and Mary Church Terrell, "History of the High Schools for Negroes in Washington," *Journal of Negro History* 2 (1917):252-66.

Three titles suggest varying approaches to the education of Black women in the early years of the twentieth century: Spelman College is the subject of M. Parsons, "Mount Holyoak of the South," *Home Mission Monthly* (1908); "Southern Training School for Colored Women," R. M. F. Berry's article in *Good Housekeeping* 53 (October 1911):562-63, describes preparing Black women for jobs as domestics; and Emma Soch, "Gardening for Girls," *Southern Workman* 36:12 (December 1907):661-64, suggests a third approach. For a sample of what Black children read in school, see Thomas G. Dyer, "An Early Black Textbook: *Floyd's Flowers on Duty and Beauty for Colored Children*," *Phylon* 37 (1976):359-61.

From the beginning, Afro-American women engaged in struggles against segregated education. For the involvement of a prominent schoolgirl, Frederick Douglass's daughter, see Herbert Aptheker, ed., *A Documentary History of the Negro People in the United States*, 3 vols. (1951; republished 1969), 1:274; in the same collection; see also Sarah Roberts's suit against segregated Boston schools, 1:297, and William Nell's 1855 discussion of the women's efforts, 1:376-78. Arthur O. White describes the involvement of women teachers and boycotting mothers in "Antebellum School Reform in Boston: Integrationists and Separatists," *Phylon* 34:2 (June 1973):203-17.

Historical studies of the higher education of Afro-American women in the nineteenth century include Lucy D. Slowe, "Higher Education for Negro Women," *Journal of Negro Education* 2 (July 1937):352-58; Marion V. Cuthbert, *Education and Marginality: A Study of the Negro Woman College Graduate* (1942); Jeanne L. Noble, "Negro Women Today and Their Education," *Journal of Negro Education* 26 (1957):15-21; and Noble's full-length study, *The Negro Woman's College Education* (1956). Also see Florence Read, *The Story of Spelman College* (1961).

Two nineteenth-century white women who attempted to establish schools for Afro-American women and girls have been the subject of several studies. Prudence Crandall's efforts are discussed in Edwin W. and Miriam R. Small, "Prudence Crandall: Champion of Negro Education," *New England Quarterly* 17 (December 1944):506–29; in Edmund Fuller, *Prudence Crandall: An Incident of Racism in Nineteenth-Century Connecticut* (1971); and, even more recently, in Lawrence J. Friedman, "Racism and Sexism in Ante-Bellum America: The Prudence Crandall Episode Reconsidered," *Societas* 4 (Summer 1974):211–27. For Crandall's letters, see A. B. Spingarn, "Letter Collection," *Journal of Negro History* 18 (1933):78–84.

Myrtilla Miner's work is discussed in G. Smith Wormley, "Myrtilla Miner," *Journal of Negro History* 5 (1920):448–57; in Sadie St. Clair, "Myrtilla Miner: Pioneer in the Teacher Education of Negroes," *Journal of Negro History* 34 (1949):30–45; and in Ellen O'Connor, *Myrtilla Miner, A Memoir, and the School for Colored Girls in Washington, D.C.* (1885; 1969).

Dorothy Porter, "The Organized Educational Activities of Negro Literary Societies, 1828–1846," *Journal of Negro Education* 5 (1936): 556–66, discusses pioneering self-education during the period when Maria Stewart, the first American woman public speaker, delivered her addresses. The book-length memoirs and journals of two Afro-American women, Charlotte L. Forten Grimké and Susie King Taylor, present important accounts of the education of the freedmen and freedwomen during and after the Civil War. See also Lewis C. Lockwood, *Mary S. Peake: The Colored Teacher at Fort Monroe* (1862). The autobiographies of Frances Jackson Coppin and Anna Julia Cooper, both born in slavery, make significant comments on crucial educational issues of the day.

For general discussions of Afro-American education before 1910, see a recent compilation, Vincent P. Franklin and James D. Anderson, eds., *New Perspectives on Black Educational History* (1978); and the classic studies by Horace Mann Bond, *The Education of the Negro in the American Social Order* (1934; republished 1966), and Carter G. Woodson, *The Education of the Negro Prior to 1861* (1919; republished 1968). Studies with a special focus include the pioneering W. E. B. DuBois and A. Dill, eds., *The College-Bred American Negro: Report of a Social Study Made by Atlanta University...* (1910); Dwight Oliver Wendell Holmes, *The Evolution of the Negro College* (1934; 1969); Henry A. Bullock, *A History of Negro Education in the South: From 1619 to the Present* (1967); Arthur D. Wright, *The Negro Rural School Fund, Inc. (Anna T. Jeanes Foundation):1907–1933* (1933): G. E. Jones, *The Jeanes Teacher in the U.S.* (1937); and Louis D. Rubin, Jr., *Teach the Freedmen: The Correspondence of R. B. Hayes and the Slater Fund for Negro Education,*

2 vols. (1959). For early freedmen's and freedwomen's education on the Sea Islands, see Willie Lee Rose's classic *Rehearsal for Reconstruction: The Port Royal Experiment* (1964). For additional information, consult James M. McPherson et al., *Blacks in America: Bibliographical Essays* (1971), especially pp. 119-21 and 162-64.

Women's education is briefly surveyed in Andrew Peiser, "The Education of Women: A Historical View," *Social Studies* 67 (March-April 1976):69-72, and in Eleanor Flexner, *Century of Struggle* (1959; republished 1970).

For more on Black women educators in the nineteenth century, see "Employment," below.

EMPLOYMENT

For a short bibliographical discussion of the employment of Black women, see Gerda Lerner, ed., *Black Women in White America* (1972), pp. 623-24. Brief bibliographical essays on Black farm workers after Emancipation and on Black workers and the labor movement before World War I can be found in James M. McPherson et al., *Blacks in America: Bibliographical Essays* (1971), pp. 166-70.

Data on the employment of Afro-American women before 1910 are included in United States, Bureau of the Census, *Special Reports, Occupations at the Twelfth Census* (1904); and in United States, Bureau of the Census, *Thirteenth Census of the United States Taken in the Year 1910*, Vol. IV: Population 1910, Occupation Statistics (1914). See also Women's Bureau, Department of Labor, *Negro Women in Industry*, Bulletin 20 (1922).

Discussions of the employment of Afro-American women include Lorenzo J. Greene and Carter G. Woodson, *The Negro Wage Earner* (1930; republished 1970); Charles H. Wesley, *Negro Labor in the United States, 1850-1925* (1927; republished 1967); and Alice Henry, "The Negro Woman," in *Woman in the Labor Movement* (1923), pp. 202-11. For women's employment in a study focused on a single city, see (despite its title) Mary White Ovington, *Half a Man: The Status of the Negro in New York* (1911; republished 1969); chapter six is "The Colored Woman as a Breadwinner." Also see George E. Haynes, *The Negro at Work in New York City: A Study in Economic Progress* (1912; republished 1968). Two interesting recent analyses are Claudia Golden, "Female Labor Force Participation: The Origin of Black and White Differences," *Journal of Economic History* 37 (March 1977):87-112; and Sharon Harley, "Northern Black Female Workers: Jacksonian Era," in Sharon Harley and

Rosalyn Terborg-Penn, eds., *The Afro-American Woman: Struggles and Images* (1978). For more information, see Eleanor Flexner, *Century of Struggle* (1959; republished 1970), pp. 52-61, 78-79, 131-42, and 240-47. During the period here considered, a great many female Black wage earners worked as domestics. Relevant discussions published before 1910 include Lucy Maynard Salmon, *Domestic Service* (1897); O. Langhorne, "Domestic Service in the South," *American Journal of Social Sciences* 39 (1901):169; and *A Special Report on Domestic Service By Isabel Eaton*, published with W. E. B. DuBois, *The Philadelphia Negro* (1899; 1967). Walter Lynwood Fleming, "The Servant Problem in a Black Belt Village," *Sewanee Review* 13 (January 1905):1-17, describes difficulties keeping servants in Alabama. S. H. Bishop, "Industrial Conditions of Negro Women in New York," *Southern Workman* 39:10 (September 1910):525-28, does not discuss the problems of women employed in industry, but the problem of the lack of industrial employment for Black women. And see W. E. B. DuBois, *Economic Cooperation among Negro Americans* (1907).

An early discussion of job opportunities by a Black woman is Katherine D. Tillman, "Paying Professions for Colored Girls," *The Voice of the Negro* 4:1 (January-February 1907):54-55. Eva D. Boweles, "Opportunities for the Educated Colored Woman," *Opportunity* 1:4 (March 1923):8-10, presents teaching, social work, nursing, medicine, business, and law as possible areas of employment, and names Black women successfully working in these fields.

Discussions of the two outstanding Black businesswomen of the period, Sarah Breedlove Walker (Mme. C. J. Walker), founder of a million-dollar beauty industry, and Maggie Lena Walker (no relation), insurance and banking executive, can be found in Sadie Iola Daniel, *Women Builders* (1931), and Benjamin Brawley, *Negro Builders and Heroes* (1937).

Even before 1910, Afro-American women had entered the traditional professions. They are discussed in Bettina Aptheker, "Quest for Dignity: Black Women in the Professions, 1865-1900," a paper presented at the Fourth Berkshire Conference on the History of Women, Mount Holyoke College, August 25, 1978; and in Marion Kilson, "Black Women in the Professions, 1890-1970," *Monthly Labor Review* 100 (May 1977):38-41. Important treatments of professional women written by Afro-Americans during the period include Gertrude Bustill Mossell, *The Work of the Afro-American Woman* (1894; republished 1971); Monroe A. Majors, *Noted Negro Women...* (1893); and, a few years later, Hallie Q. Brown, *Homespun Heroines...* (1926). For educators, examine Benjamin Brawley's appreciation, "Women Who Have Led in Education," *Negro*

Builders and Heroes (1937), pp. 273-88; Mary Anthony, "Dean of the School Marms," *Negro Digest* 9:7 (May 1951):31-32, a discussion of Charlotte Stevens; W. B. Hartgrove, "The Story of Mary Louise Moore and Fannie M. Richards," *Journal of Negro History* 1 (January 1916):23-33; and two articles on Catherine Ferguson: one by Allen Hartnick in *Negro History Bulletin* 35 (December 1977):176-77, and the other by Catherine Latimer in *Negro History Bulletin* 5 (November 1941):38-39. In addition, see Delores C. Leffall and Janet L. Sims, "Mary McLeod Bethune, the Educator: Also Including a Selected Annotated Bibliography," *Journal of Negro Education* 45 (Summer 1976):342. For lawyers, see Sadie T. M. Alexander, "Women as Practitioners of Law in the U.S.," *National Bar Journal* 1:1 (July 1941):56-64. For medicine, see Susan Maria Smith Steward, *Women in Medicine: A Paper Read before the National Association of Colored Women's Clubs at Wilberforce, Ohio, August 6, 1914* (1914); Sara W. Brown, "Colored Women Physicians," *Southern Workman* 52 (December 1923):580-93; and Adah B. Thoms, *Pathfinders: A History of the Progress of Colored Graduate Nurses* (1929).

Edward T. and Janet W. James, eds., *Notable American Women* (1971), includes biographies of Afro-American businesswomen Sarah Breedlove Walker and Maggie Lena Walker. Black educators discussed in these volumes are Maria Louisa Baldwin, Hallie Q. Brown, Mary Ann Shadd Cary, Fanny M. Jackson Coppin, Sarah Mapps Douglass Douglass, Sarah J. Smith Thompson Garnet, Charlotte Forten Grimké, Lucy Craft Laney, Lucy Ella Moten, Alice Dunbar-Nelson, and Maria W. Stewart. Lawyers listed are Mary Ann Shadd Cary and Charlotte E. Ray. Women in medicine included are Sarah Parker Remond, physician, and nurses Mary Eliza Mahoney and Adah B. Samuels Thoms.

PUBLIC AFFAIRS—WOMEN'S ORGANIZATIONS

A useful reference tool for materials on women's organizations after the Civil War is Lenwood G. Davis, *Black Women in the Cities, 1872-1975: A Bibliography of Published Works on the Life and Achievements of Black Women in Cities in the United States*, 2d ed. (1975).

For representative documents central to two early types of organizations, see Afric-American Female Intelligence Society of Boston, "Constitution," *Genius of Universal Emancipation* 2:10, 3d ser. (March 1832):162-63, reprinted in Gerda Lerner, ed., *Black Women in White America* (1972); and "Address to the Female Literary Association of Philadelphia, May, 1832," in Dorothy Porter, ed., *Early Negro Writing,*

1760-1837 (1971). A number of early women's organizations are listed among "Negro Societies in Philadelphia, 1831," in Herbert Aptheker, ed., *A Documentary History of the Negro People in the United States,* 3 vols. (1951; republished 1962), 1:113–14.

The history of the female anti-slavery societies, Black and/or white, has not been written; but see a recent article: Ira V. Brown, "Cradle of Feminism: The Philadelphia Female Anti-Slavery Society, 1833–1840," *Pennsylvania Magazine of History and Biography* 102 (April 1978):143–66. See also Eleanor Flexner, *Century of Struggle* (1959; 1970), pp. 42–52; two articles by Charles H. Wesley: "The Negro in the Organization of Abolition," in John H. Bracey, comp., *Blacks in the Abolitionist Movement* (1971), and "The Negroes of New York in the Emancipation Movement," *Journal of Negro History* 24 (1939):65–103; and Benjamin Quarles, *Black Abolitionists* (1969), especially pp. 26–30. Another item of interest is the "Address of the Ladies' Anti-Slavery Society of Delaware, Ohio, to The State Convention of Negro Men...1856," in Herbert Aptheker, ed., *A Documentary History of the Negro People in the United States,* 3 vols. (1951; republished 1962), 1:380–83.

Two articles on a prominent Afro-American female abolitionist are Dorothy Porter, "Sarah Parker Remond, Abolitionist and Physician," *Journal of Negro History* 20 (July 1935):287–93, and Ruth Bogin, "Sarah Parker Remond: Black Abolitionist from Salem," *Essex Institute Historical Collections* 110 (April 1974):120–50. For Frances Ellen Watkins Harper's anti-slavery work, see Samuel Sillen, *Women Against Slavery* (1955); and see selections in Herbert Aptheker, ed., *A Documentary History of the Negro People in the United States,* 3 vols. (1951; republished 1962), 1:390, 408, and 440. Though Black abolitionism is discussed in James M. McPherson et al., *Blacks in America: Bibliographic Essays* (1971), pp. 92–94, the work of women is not mentioned. McPherson's more recent *The Abolitionist Legacy* (1975), however, is a useful source of information. Additional references to the organized anti-slavery activities of Black women can be found in the biographies, memoirs, and letters of white male and female abolitionists, and of Black male abolitionists. Additional information can be gleaned from abolitionist periodicals, Black and white.

Also unwritten as yet is the comprehensive history of the role of Afro-American women in the struggle for Black suffrage and for women's suffrage. Three important contributions by Rosalyn Terborg-Penn are: "The Historical Treatment of the Afro-American Woman in the Woman's Suffrage Movement, 1900–1920: A Bibliographical Essay," *Current Bibliography on African Affairs* 7 (Summer 1974):245–59; "Nineteenth-Century Black Women and Woman Suffrage," *Potomac Review*

7:3 (Spring-Summer 1977):13-24; and "Discrimination against Afro-American Women in the Women's Movement," in Sharon Harley and Rosalyn Terborg-Penn, eds., *The Afro-American Woman: Struggles and Images* (1978). Several studies discuss Douglass's position on women's rights: see Benjamin Quarles, "Frederick Douglass and the Woman's Rights Movement," *Journal of Negro History* 25 (January 1940):35-44; S. Jay Walker, "Frederick Douglass and Woman Suffrage," *Black Scholar* 4 (March-April 1973):24-31; and Philip Foner, ed., *Frederick Douglass on Women's Rights* (1976). For comments written during the period, see Adella Hunt Logan, "Woman Suffrage," *Colored American Magazine* 9:3 (1905):487-89; and David Augustus Straker, *Citizenship, Its Rights and Duties—Woman Suffrage: A Lecture* (1874). In addition, specific Black women leaders are referred to in Elizabeth Cady Stanton et al., eds., *History of Woman Suffrage*, 6 vols. (1881-1922) (see NOTE, below). Racism within the woman suffrage movement is the topic of a chapter in Robert L. and Pamela P. Allen, *Reluctant Reformers* (1974), pp. 121-63; of Aileen Kraditor, "The 'Southern Question,'" in *The Ideas of the Woman Suffrage Movement, 1890-1920* (1965); and of my "DuBois' *Crisis* and Woman's Suffrage," *Massachusetts Review* (Spring 1973):365-75. Important Black women suffragists of the period include Ida B. Wells, Frances Ellen Watkins Harper, Josephine St. Pierre Ruffin, Mary Church Terrell, Sojourner Truth, and Harriet Tubman. All but Terrell are subjects of biographical sketches in Edward T. and Janet W. James, eds., *Notable American Women* (1971). For Terrell's speech on the fiftieth anniversary of the National American Woman Suffrage Association, see *"The Progress and Problems of Colored Women": An Address* (1898).

Brief discussions of the women's club movement can be found in Eleanor Flexner, *Century of Struggle* (1959; 1970), pp. 187-92; in August Meier, *Negro Thought in America, 1880-1915* (1966); and in Ruby M. Kendrick, "They Also Serve: The National Association of Colored Women, Inc., 1896-1964," *Negro History Bulletin* 17 (March 1954):171-75. Also see the introductory materials and documents in Gerda Lerner, ed., *Black Women in White America* (1972), pp. 435-58; and her "Early Community Work of Black Club Women," *Journal of Negro History* 59 (April 1974):158-67. An important new discussion is Cynthia Neverdon-Morton, "The Black Woman's Struggle for Equality in the South, 1895-1925," in Sharon Harley and Rosalyn Terborg-Penn, eds., *The Afro-American Woman: Struggles and Images* (1978). Central to the study of this topic are two books by Elizabeth L. Davis: *Story of the Illinois Federation of Colored Women's Clubs, 1900-1922* (1922), and *Lifting as They Climb: The National Association of Colored Women* (1933). Club leaders included in Edward T. and Janet W. James, eds., *Notable*

American Women (1971), are Ida B. Wells, Josephine St. Pierre Ruffin, and Fannie B. Williams.

Articles on the club movement published in *The Voice of the Negro* by Afro-American women during the period include Josephine Bruce, "The Afterglow of the Women's Convention," 1:11 (November 1904): 541-43; Addie Watts Hunton, "The Southern Federation of Colored Women," 2:12 (December 1905):850-54; and Josephine Silone Yates, "The National Association of Colored Women," 1:7 (July 1904):283-87. Mary Church Terrell's "Club Work of Colored Women" appeared in *Southern Workman* 30 (1901):435-38, and Mrs. Harris Barrett's "Negro Women's Clubs and the Community" in *Southern Workman* 39 (January 1910):33- 34. See also Susan M. Steward, "Women's Clubs," *Crisis* 3 (November 1911):33-35.

Pertinent articles by Fannie Barrier Williams include "The Club Movement among the Colored Women," *The Voice of the Negro* 1:3 (March 1904):99-102, which is reprinted in Gerda Lerner, ed., *Black Women in White America* (1972) under the title "The Ruffin Incident"; "Club Movement Among Negro Women," in John W. Gibson and William H. Crogman, eds., *The Colored American from Slavery to Honorable Citizenship* (1902), pp. 197-231; "The Clubs and Their Location in All the States of the National Association of Colored Women and Their Mission," in John E. MacBrady, ed., *A New Negro for a New Century* (1900), pp. 406-28; "An Extension of the Conference Spirit," *The Voice of the Negro* 1:7 (July 1904):300-303; "The Frederick Douglass Center," *Southern Workman* 35:6 (June 1906):334-36; "Social Bonds in the 'Black Belt' of Chicago," *Charities: The Negro in the Cities in the North* (October 7, 1905), republished as *The Survey, The Negro in the Cities of the North* (1905).

Three discussions of this subject by Margaret J. Murray Washington can be found in A. Johnston, "Mrs. Booker T. Washington's Club for Women," *Harper's Bazaar* 32 (March 1899):186; Margaret J. M. Washington, "Club Work among Negro Women," in [John W. Gibson, ed.,] *Progress of a Race* (1912; republished 1929), pp. 177-209, and "The Tuskegee Women's Club," *Southern Workman* 49 (August 1920):365. Also see Josephine St. Pierre Ruffin, "Address, First National Conference of Colored Women," *Woman's Era* 2 (September 1895):14, excerpted in Gerda Lerner, ed., *Black Women in White America* (1972); and see "Open Letter to the Education League of Georgia, 1899," in Alice Dunbar-Nelson, ed., *Masterpieces of Negro Eloquence* (1914).

For information on an Afro-American sorority, see Sallie C. Boyer, "Visit with Ethel Hedgeman Lyle: Founder of Alpha Kappa Alpha Sorority," *The Brown American* 4 (November-December 1941):18-19; and

Marjorie H. Parker, *Alpha Kappa Alpha Sorority: 1908-1958* (1958). An Afro-American association of professional women is the subject of *National Association of Colored Graduate Nurses: Four Decades of Service* (1948).

For material on organized efforts to aid Black women in the cities, see Frances A. Kellor, "Associations for Protection of Colored Women," *Colored American* 9 (December 1905):695-99; and the National League for the Protection of Colored Women, *Annual Report* (November 1910). The pioneering work of Janie Porter Barrett on behalf of young Black women who ran afoul of the law is described in Edward T. and Janet W. James, eds., *Notable American Women* (1971).

For a discussion of the struggles of the heroic Black woman who organized campaigns to end lynchings, see Bettina Aptheker, "The Suppression of Free Speech: Ida B. Wells and the Memphis Lynchings, 1892," *San Jose Studies* 3 (November 1977):34-40.

RELIGION

Standard works on Afro-American religion include Carter G. Woodson, *The History of the Negro Church*, 2d ed. (1945); E. Franklin Frazier, *The Negro Church in America* (1964); and W. E. B. DuBois, *The Negro Church*, Atlanta University Series, Number 8 (1903; 1968), and "Of the Faith of the Fathers," in *The Souls of Black Folk* (1903; republished repeatedly). Also see Benjamin Mays, *The Negro's God as Reflected in His Literature* (1938); Howard Thurman, *Deep River: Reflections on the Religious Insight of Certain Negro Spirituals* (1955), and *The Negro Spiritual Speaks of Life and Death* (1947). For more information, see James M. McPherson et al., eds., *Blacks in America: Bibliographic Essays* (1971), pp. 81-86, 153-57; and Ethel L. Williams, ed., *Afro-American Religious Studies: A Cumulative Bibliography* (1971-).

Some of the Black anti-slavery women were involved with the Quakers. For Sarah Mapps Douglass Douglass's protest against segregation in meeting, see her letter to William Basset, December 1837, in *Letters of Theodore Dwight Weld, Angelina Grimké Weld, and Sarah Grimké*, 2 vols. (1934), pp. 829-32, excerpted in Gerda Lerner, ed., *Black Women in White America* (1972), and in Dorothy Sterling, ed., *Speak Out in Thunder Tones: Letters and Other Writings By Black Northerners, 1787-1865* (1973).

Discussions of missionary work undertaken by, and among, Afro-American women in the nineteenth century which were written before 1910 include M. G. Burdette, "Woman and the American Negro:

Woman's Work for the Afro-American," in *Women in Missions: Papers and Addresses Presented at the Women's Congress of Missions, October 2-4, 1893...*(1894), pp. 125-44; Women's Baptist Home Mission Society, Chicago, *Twenty-Nine Years' Work Among Negroes* (1906); and Mary Helm, "Work of the Woman's Home Missionary Societies," in *From Darkness to Light: The Story of Negro Progress* (1909; republished 1969). See also "Women of the West in the Development of the A.M.E. Church," in Lawson A. Scruggs, *Women of Distinction* (1893). For a later discussion by an Afro-American woman, see Sara Jane Regulus McAfee, *History of the Woman's Missionary Society in the Colored Methodist Episcopal Church...*(1934). Women in the home missions and the missionary education movement are discussed in Lily Hammond, *In the Vanguard of a Race* (1922), which details the work of Nannie H. Burroughs, Janie Porter Barrett, Maggie L. Walker, and Martha Drummer. For a sample of Burroughs' writing on this topic, see her *Grow...A Handy Guide for Progressive Church Women* (n.d.).

Other Afro-American women who published books on religion before 1910 include Charlotte Gilbury Draper, *For the Presbyterian Female of Color's Enterprising Society in Baltimore...January 25, 1860* (1860); Viola Mae Young, *Little Helps for Pastors and Members* (1909); and Susan L. Shorter, *Heroines of African Methodism* (1891).

Significant religious leaders included in Edward T. and Janet W. James, eds., *Notable American Women* (1971) are Fanny M. Jackson Coppin, foreign missionary, and Amanda Barry Smith, evangelist and missionary.

SOCIOLOGY—URBAN LIFE

The basic bibliographical tool for materials on Afro-American women and urban life is Lenwood G. Davis, *Black Women in the Cities: 1872-1975: A Bibliography of Published Works on the Life and Achievements of Black Women in Cities in the U.S.*, 2d ed. (1975).

Standard references include W. E. B. DuBois, ed., *Social and Physical Conditions of Negroes in Cities* (1897); and Arna Bontemps and Jack Conroy, *They Seek a City* (1945), revised and reprinted under the title *Anyplace But Here* (1966). A special study is Richard C. Wade, *Slavery in the Cities: The South, 1820-60* (1964); see also Richard B. Sherman, *The Negro and the City* (1970).

Articles published before 1910 discussing the threat posed to Black women by the urban environment include V. C. Matthews, "Dangers Encountered by Southern Girls in Northern Cities," Hampton Negro

Conference, *Proceedings* (July 1898); and two pieces by Frances A. Kellor: "Opportunities for Southern Negro Women in Northern Cities," *The Voice of the Negro* 2:7 (July 1905):470–73, and "Southern Colored Girls in the North," *Charities* (March 18, 1905). For discussions of Black nineteenth-century women in specific cities, see works dealing with Afro-Americans in a specific geographical region, such as Olive W. Burt, *Negroes in the Early West* (1969), or in a particular state, such as Arthur L. Tolson, *The Black Oklahomans: A History, 1541–1972* (1976), or in a major city, such as W. E. B. DuBois's classic *The Philadelphia Negro* (1899).

NOTE

[1]Black women in the *History of Woman Suffrage* volumes include the following (volume and page numbers are cited because most of these women are omitted from the notoriously poor indices of these invaluable books): Linda Brent (Linda Brent Jacobs), 1:324; Mary Ann Shadd Cary, 3:61, 72–73, 151, 955; Coralee F. Cook, 4:395, 398–99; Grace Douglass, 1:325; Sarah Mapps Douglass, 1:325, 332, 337; Margaretta Forten, 1:325; Sarah L. Forten, 1:325; Betty Francis, 4:572; Margaret Garner, 1:324; Frances Ellen Watkins Harper, 2:171, 178, 391–92, 399, and 4:425; Jane Johnson, 1:329; Susan Paul, 1:337; Nancy Prince, 1:384; Harriet Purvis, 2:222; Caroline Remond Putnam, 3:268–69; Sarah Parker Remond, 1:668 and 2:182; Mary Church Terrell, 4:298, 358, 572, and 5:105; Sojourner Truth, 1:114–17, 220, 224, 567–69, 668, 824, and 2:183, 193–94, 222; Harriet Tubman, 1:276; Fannie Barrier Williams, 5:203; Sylvanie Williams, 5:60.

21

Afro-American Women Poets of the Nineteenth Century: A Guide to Research and Bio-Bibliographies of the Poets

JOAN R. SHERMAN

The search for Black women poets of the nineteenth century presents three problems: (1) identifying women who wrote poetry; (2) finding their published works; (3) locating accurate biographical documents. Although our concern here is with women, my remarks and suggestions on sources, based on three years of research for *Invisible Poets* (Urbana: University of Illinois Press, 1974), apply to nineteenth-century Black poets of both sexes.

In any area, research is simplified by knowing where *not* to look: no Black women poets will be found in nineteenth-century bibliographies of American literature or history, anthologies, literary histories, biographical dictionaries, collective biographies, or encyclopedias, nor in "white" magazines and newspapers. Similar nineteenth-century publications by and about Afro-Americans, with the exception of early Black periodicals (see below), as well as twentieth-century bibliographies of Black literature, Black collective biographies, dictionaries, literary histories, anthologies, and periodical articles on Black literature through 1975, may also be eliminated by current researchers, for I have thoroughly explored such resources.

The research tools described here are those I found most valuable for studying early Black poets; I exclude from this discussion materials pertinent to individual poets' biographies, as well as articles and books which were not especially useful. (For all works consulted, see my "Bibliographical Essay," notes, and sources in *Invisible Poets.*)

BIBLIOGRAPHIES AND FINDING AIDS

Arthur A. Schomburg, comp., *A Bibliographical Checklist of American Negro Poetry* (New York: Charles F. Heartman, 1916), although incomplete and inaccurate, offers a twenty-two-page listing of volumes and single poems and is the basis for most later compilations. A comprehensive summary of bibliographies, books, pamphlets, and articles on Black literature to 1928 is Monroe Work, *Bibliography of the Negro in Africa and America* (New York: H. W. Wilson, 1928). Vernon Loggins appends a detailed bibliography of Black writings to his study, *The Negro Author: His Development in America to 1900* (New York: Columbia Univ. Press, 1931). Dorothy B. Porter, *North American Negro Poets: A Bibliographical Checklist of Their Writings...1760–1944* (Hattiesburg, Miss.: Book Farm, 1945), furnishes exhaustive data on volumes, broadsides, and pamphlets, accurately notated and located. Her "Early American Negro Writing," *Bibliographical Society of American Papers* 39 (1945):192–268, is the most scholarly account of prose and poetry to 1835, and her introduction here is essential reading for researchers in early Black literature. Janheinz Jahn, *A Bibliography of Neo-African Literature* (New York: Praeger, 1965), lists volumes only by Black authors from the 1700s to date. John Lask, "The American Negro and American Literature," *Bulletin of Bibliography* 19 (Sept.-Dec. 1946):12– 15; 19 (Jan.-April 1947):33–36, offers excellent annotated guides to 572 items by and about Black writers.

Three recent bibliographies in the field of Black studies include some literature. Geraldine O. Matthews and AAMP Staff, *Black American Writers, 1773–1949: A Bibliography and Union List* (1975), includes 1600 authors of monographs only, very few of them nineteenth-century poets. Some books listed may provide useful background, and the index of authors' names might be checked when new poems have been located in periodicals. Theressa G. Rush et al., *Black American Writers Past and Present: A Biographical and Bibliographical Dictionary*, 2 vols. (1975), seems to collect all previous twentieth-century references without checking their accuracy or completeness, and no original data are offered for nineteenth-century poets. The Frances Harper entry, for example, contains many errors made by previous writers; and minor figures, like Gertrude Mossell, are not included. An ambitious and excellent new guide is James de T. Abajian, *Blacks and Their Contributions to the American West: A Bibliography and Union List of Library Holdings through 1970* (1974). Abajian's meticulous work includes literature but will probably be of greater value in locating secondary materials that can lead to the poets. He lists books, periodicals, and manuscripts by and about Blacks who lived or wrote in thirteen Western states; the materials are held in libraries throughout the United States.

Although not actually bibliographies, of first importance for determining the race and sex of poets whose work you have found, for identifying their other publications, and for locating primary and secondary materials are the *Dictionary Catalogs* of the Schomburg Collection; the Howard University Moorland and Spingarn Collections; and the Library of Congress *National Union Catalogue: Pre-1965 Imprints.*

Other published catalogues of this kind that should be consulted are *Afro-Americana, 1553-1906: Author Catalog of the Library Committee of Philadelphia and The Historical Society of Pennsylvania* (1973); and *Dictionary Catalogs* of Afro-American collections in Fisk and Atlanta University libraries.

BOOKS: BIOGRAPHY AND CRITICISM

There is virtually no reliable published biography or literary criticism on nineteenth-century Black poets. Existing accounts are secondhand, inaccurate, and heavily biased by racial attitudes. Writers perpetuate apocryphal and erroneous data derived from previous writers or from the poets' own prefaces, speeches, essays, letters, and poems; these primary sources are used without verification or acknowledgment of indebtedness. Therefore, all undocumented materials must be approached with great caution.

Among Black collective biographies and literary studies, only nine books, listed in order of their importance, can be recommended as major sources, and even these are not free from inaccuracy and bias. William J. Simmons, *Men of Mark: Eminent, Progressive, and Rising* (1887; rpt. New York: Arno, 1968), is a male bastion, but the husbands, fathers, or other male relatives of a few female poets are included. William Wells Brown, *The Black Man: His Antecedents, His Genius, and His Achievements* (New York, 1863), and Brown's largely repetitive sequel, **The Rising Son (Boston: A. G. Brown, 1874),** are valuable for firsthand descriptions of several poets. Sterling Brown, *Negro Poetry and Drama* (Washington, D.C.: Associates in Negro Folk Education, 1937), offers detailed criticism with additional general comments on nineteenth-century poetry. J. Saunders Redding, *To Make a Poet Black* (Chapel Hill: Univ. of North Carolina Press, 1939), contributes criticism; Vernon Loggins, *The Negro Author* (1931), remains the best all-around introduction to nineteenth-century Black writers. A companion work, Jean Wagner, *Black Poets of the United States* (Urbana: Univ. of Illinois Press, 1973), concentrates on Dunbar and other male poets of the Harlem

Renaissance, but it offers original and sensible criticism of many earlier poets and their literary backgrounds. Two dictionaries—*Who's Who of the Colored Race*, ed. Frank Mather (Chicago, 1915), and *Who's Who in Colored America*, ed. Joseph J. Boris (New York, 1927, 1929), and Thomas Yenser (New York, 1933)—contribute biographical data. Among anthologies, only Benjamin Brawley, *Early Negro American Writers* (1935), includes biographies with some evidence of original source material. Several recent guides to biographical research are valuable. Barbara Bell, *Black Biographical Sources* (New Haven, Conn.: Yale University Library, 1970), an annotated guide to collective biographies and reference tools, is a good starting point for locating biographical data. Russell Brignano, *Black Americans in Autobiography...Written Since the Civil War* (Durham, N.C.: Duke Univ. Press, 1974), is a fine scholarly work, helpfully indexed by occupations, geographical locations, and educational institutions. It will help readers to locate books written by Black women who may also have written poetry; in addition, its authors' first-hand accounts will provide useful background and biographical materials (e.g., the husbands of a few Black women poets wrote autobiographies).

Since published biography for Black poets was so scanty and unreliable, for my own study I verified and supplemented it by correspondence with historical societies, boards of health and education, chambers of commerce, probate courts, colleges, and church-affiliated and racial societies throughout the United States; and I personally examined the vertical files, scrapbooks, and "family papers" in Afro-American collections, principally at the Schomburg and Howard University libraries. Slavery records and birth certificates for the early writers were generally not available; but I obtained marriage and death certificates, academic records, city directory listings, and manuscripts of the poets' correspondence. In a few cases, I found surviving friends and relatives who could provide information. (See also "Periodicals.") Directories which facilitate research by correspondence include *Directory: Historical Societies and Agencies in the United States and Canada, College and University Archives in the United States and Canada*, and three HEW pamphlets, *Where to Write for Birth and Death...Marriage...Divorce Records* (USGPO, 1976).

PERIODICALS

The best sources of poetry and prose by Black women (and men), outside of their individually published volumes, were periodicals directed to Black readers and others supporting abolitionism. They were also important sources of biography and criticism. Among newspapers, the most valuable were: *Freedom's Journal* (1827-39), *Liberator* (1831-65), *National Anti-Slavery Standard* (1840-70), and *North Star* and *Frederick Douglass' Paper* (1847-60). The most useful magazines were: *Douglass' Monthly* (1858-Aug. 1863), *Anglo-African Magazine* (1859-60), *African Methodist Episcopal Church Review* (1883-1927), *Voice of the Negro* (1904-7), and *Alexander's Magazine* (1905-9). These are only a few of the literally hundreds of early Black periodicals: daily and weekly papers; magazines of political, religious, educational, and fraternal organizations; literary, family life, and women's publications. Some well-known publications are available in facsimile reprints or on microfilm; but the majority—obscure and short-lived periodicals—must be examined in local libraries and repositories of Afro-Americana, if they have been located, or searched out in still-unknown basements. (See "Finding Aids to Periodicals" and "Manuscripts.")

In addition to poems, I found information on the poets in periodical accounts of Black antislavery, civil rights, educational, and moral reform conventions; stories describing the dedication of Black churches and monuments, or the activities of missionaries and clubwomen; announcements of lecture tours, travels, marriages, and school graduations; annual reports of school boards; letters to the editor; book reviews; and obituaries. Only a handful of "general" articles mentioning several Black poets provided significant information: five of these, by Dunnigan, Mossell, Bentley, and Tillman, appear in the "Reference Key" below; others are Joseph T. Wilson, "Some Negro Poets," *AMECR* 4 (1888):236-45; Newman Ivy White, "Racial Feelings in Negro Poetry," *South Atlantic Quarterly* 21 (January 1922):14-29; Charles H. Good, "The First American Negro Literary Movement," *Opportunity* 10 (March 1932):76-79; and Richard Wright, "The Literature of the Negro in the United States," in *White Man, Listen!* (New York: Doubleday, 1957).

Other articles, by Black and white writers, found in twentieth-century periodicals and books, fall into four categories: (1) accounts of early Black literature which dismiss pre-Dunbar poetry as worthless trash; (2) articles with "Negro Poetry" in their titles which deal either with white poets' work on Black subjects or with only twentieth-century Black poets; (3) articles that summarize material from published anthologies; and (4) articles which do not mention early Black poets but give helpful data on Black literature and history, or on the problems of the Black author. Among the fourth group are two whole issues of *Annals of the American Academy of Political and Social Science* (September 1913, November 1928); the Harlem issue of *Survey Graphic* (March 1925); an issue of *Phylon* (December 1950); the Emancipation Centennial issue of *Ebony* (September 1963); and *Midcontinent American Studies* (Fall

1970). Also useful are James Weldon Johnson, "The Dilemma of the Negro Author," *American Mercury* (December 1928):477- 81; Edward Bland, "Racial Bias and Negro Poetry," *Poetry* 63 (March 1944):328-33; J. Saunders Redding, "American Negro Literature," *American Scholar* 18 (Spring 1949):137-48; discussions of the "Black aesthetic" in Black journals of the late 1960s and 1970s; and essays and symposia papers in some collections of 1925-60—noted in *Invisible Poets*.

AIDS FOR FINDING PERIODICALS AND PERIODICAL LITERATURE

Since Black magazines and newspapers (and manuscripts; see below) of the last century are without doubt the best resources for original research on Black women, identifying and locating periodicals is the imperative task today. A few early finding aids for newspapers which may still be useful are George W. Williams, *History of the Negro Race from 1619 to 1880* (New York: G. P. Putnam's, 1885); W. E. B. DuBois, "Efforts for Social Betterment among Negro Americans," Atlanta University Publication No. 14 (1909), which lists 261 newspapers, 1852-1909; and Monroe Work's *Bibliography* (1928), which also lists school, church, and organization periodicals. Data on many Black newspapers appear in *N. W. Ayer & Son's Directory of Newspapers and Periodicals* (1880-) and *Rowell's American Newspaper Directory* (1869-80, 1885, 1890, 1900). There are specialized bibliographies of abolitionist papers, and two valuable studies of Black journalism: I. Garland Penn, *The Afro-American Press and Its Editors* (Springfield, Mass.: Willey, 1891), and Frederick Detweiler, *The Negro Press in the United States* (Chicago: Univ. of Chicago Press, 1922).

More recent aids are Warren Brown, *Checklist of Negro Newspapers in the United States* (Jefferson City, Mo.: Lincoln Univ. School of Journalism, 1946), listing 467 papers published between 1827 and 1946, with their locations, if known; Armistead L. Pride, "A Register and History of Negro Newspapers in the United States" (Diss., Northwestern University, 1950), covering publications from 1827 to 1950, with locations and availability of microfilm copies (see also Pride's *Negro Newspapers on Microfilm* [1953]; and see *Guide. to Microforms in Print* [1971]). Recent studies of Black newspaper history and holdings in specific repositories are very promising: William M. Tuttle, Jr., and Surendra Bhana, "Black Newspapers in Kansas," *American Studies* (1972); A. Gilbert Belles, "The Black Press in Illinois," *J. Illinois State Historical Society* (1975); Susan Bryl and Erwin K. Welsch, *Black Periodicals and Newspapers: A Union List of Holdings...* in the libraries of the

University and State Historical Society of Wisconsin (1975); and James de T. Abajian's listings for papers of the American West (see above).

Newspapers named in the early bibliographies for which no location is given in later compilations probably have not survived; but in "no location" cases, the paper's city or town of publication is shown, and an energetic researcher in Palestine, Texas, or Augusta, Georgia, may be able to locate the paper's remains.

There is only one finding aid for early Black magazines: Penelope L. Bullock, *The Negro Periodical Press in the United States, 1838-1908* (Diss., University of Michigan, 1971; rpt. University Microfilms, 1972). Bullock offers annotated bibliographies of eighty-four magazines, with locations, as well as excellent appendices and a bibliography of sources (for magazines, see also Work, *Directory Catalogs*, Abajian, and Bryl, above). Indexes to the contents of nineteenth-century Black periodicals are not available; to find information on Black women's lives and poetry, periodicals must be scanned, page by page, microframe by microframe. Some articles from early-twentieth-century Black publications are "indexed" in literary bibliographies, as noted above (e.g., Work and Lash); and W. E. B. DuBois's monthly *Horizon* (1907-10) indexes several magazines. For later articles, there are *The Index to Selected [Negro] Periodicals* (1950-), and bibliographies in many modern Black journals, beginning with the *Journal of Negro Education* in 1931; in recent years, the *PMLA* annual bibliography has added Afro-American literature listings.

Largely untouched sources of information on early Black women are master's theses from such universities as Atlanta, Howard, Fisk, Hampton, and Tuskegee, which issue typescript or printed lists of the theses. I found the best work on Frances Harper for my study on such a list. There is also Earle H. West, *Bibliography of Doctoral Research on the Negro, 1933-66* (1969); none of these dissertations were relevant to Black women poets, but I note a new one that may be of interest: Patricia A. R. Williams, "Poets of Freedom: The English Romantics and Early Nineteenth-Century Black Poets" (*DAI* 35:7277A-78A, 1975).

ANTHOLOGIES

With very few exceptions, poetry and literature anthologies, early and modern, Black and white, are of no value to a study of early Black poets. As mentioned before, Blacks are excluded from all nineteenth-century American anthologies, even those supporting abolitionism. For example, in *The Liberty Bell* (Boston, 1839-58), essentially an antislavery anthology in periodical form, I found hundreds of poems by more than sixty white poets but none by Afro-Americans. Lydia Maria Child's *The Freedman's Book* (Boston: Ticknor and Fields, 1865) did yield twelve poems by Blacks, but Child's book is a potpourri, not an anthology. Among anthologies of "Negro Writing," the only nineteenth-century contribution is the "Thoughts, Doings and Sayings of the Race" section of the *Afro-American Encyclopedia*, comp. James T. Haley (Nashville, 1896), with over two dozen poems, mostly by minor Black poets. Twentieth-century collections from 1920 on usually include only Dunbar; a few also notice Horton and Harper. Those with a greater representation of poets have other flaws: Robert Kerlin, *Negro Poets and Their Poems*, (Washington, D.C.: Associated Publishers, 1923), highly overpraise the poetry; Newman I. White and Walter C. Jackson, *An Anthology of Verse by American Negroes* (Durham, N.C.: Trinity College, 1924), gives inaccurate biography and only strongly negative criticism; William H. Robinson, *Early Black American Poets* (Dubuque, Iowa: William C. Brown, 1969), is marred throughout by gross factual errors in bibliography, biography, and transcription of the poetry. On the other hand, a fine work in this category is James Weldon Johnson, *The Book of American Negro Poetry* (New York: Harcourt, Brace, 1922; rev. 1931, 1958), with many early poets and invaluable introductory essays. Sterling Brown, *Outline for the Study of the Poetry of American Negroes* (New York, 1931), is a useful study guide to the Johnson anthology. Benjamin Brawley, *Early Negro American Writers* (1935; rpt. New York: Books for Libraries Press, 1968), gives the best coverage of Black poets, combined with criticism that is more objective than most. None of the recent anthologies, enormous as they are, match Johnson's and Brawley's early efforts: Richard A. Long, *Afro-American Writing*, in two volumes (1972), and Richard Barksdale and Kenneth Kinnamon, *Black Writers of America: A* Comprehensive *Anthology* (my emphasis) include only the usual Black women, Harper in the first case, and Harper and Forten in the second.

Researchers would do well to avoid published anthologies altogether and instead seek out such unpublished "anthologies" as "Scrapbook 3" (MS 2200, Bruce Collection, Schomburg), which contains written and newsprint copies of seventy-three poems, many by nineteenth-century women.

MANUSCRIPTS

Along with periodicals, manuscript materials offer the greatest potential for discovering Black women poets' lives and works. There are many good articles, books, and "Calendars" which describe collections of

Afro-Americana, as do several more generalized guides to government, school, and library resources in national and state archives. The most comprehensive guide is the *Directory of Afro-American Resources*, ed. Walter Schatz (New York: Race Relations Information Center, 1970), with detailed descriptions of 5,365 collections at 2,108 institutions, and a bibliography of about 275 publications on Afro-American source material. If such published surveys clearly identify an item you need, it is possible (though expensive) to obtain a photocopy of it by mail; but ordinarily, the researcher must comb possibly relevant files of letters, clippings, family records, etc., at the repository.

Visibility of Black women has greatly increased in recent years: Frances E. Willard and Mary A. Livermore, *American Women: A Comprehensive Encyclopedia of the Lives and Achievements of American Women During the Nineteenth Century* (New York, 1897), contains 1500 biographies—but none of the women are Black. *Notable American Women, 1607–1950* (1971), however, includes forty-one Black women. A search for more nineteenth-century notables will probably not yield another Frances Harper; but it will surely reveal many "occasional" Black women poets whose verse, in turn, will enlarge our understanding of the minds and hearts of their contemporaries.

BIO-BIBLIOGRAPHIES

Among the bio-bibliographies that follow, those of Grimké, Harper, Plato, Ray, and Thompson are condensed from *Invisible Poets* (1974); here I include titles and dates only of the poets' first editions, and only a few easily accessible sources of biography and criticism. For bibliographical details, complete sources, and criticism of the poetry, see *Invisible Poets*.

GRIMKÉ, CHARLOTTE L. FORTEN (b. August 17, 1837; d. July 23, 1914), granddaughter of the eminent abolitionist and reformer James Forten, daughter of Robert Bridges and Mary Wood Forten, was born in Philadelphia. For many years as a child and later as an adult, Charlotte Forten lived at Byberry, a refuge for radical abolitionists, with her uncle, Robert Purvis, president of the American Anti-Slavery Society. From the age of sixteen, she resided in Salem, Massachusetts; there she was graduated from Higginson Grammar School (1855) and Salem Normal School (1856), after which she taught in the all-white Epes Grammar School (1856–58; 1860; 1861). At the home of Charles Lenox Remond, at antislavery fairs and abolitionist meetings, Forten won the friendship of William Wells Brown, William Lloyd Garrison, Lydia Maria Child, Charles Sumner, Lucretia Mott, Maria Chapman, Wendell Phillips, and, above all, John Greenleaf Whittier. She shared an affectionate friendship with Whittier for thirty-five years and recorded it in her "Personal Recollections of Whittier" (1893).

In her diary of the years 1854-64, Forten is revealed as a passionate champion of liberty and racial equality; a devoted scholar of languages, literature, music, and art; and a lonely, love-starved young woman, fragile in health, who wrote schoolgirlish poems: "To W. L. G. on Reading His 'Chosen Queen'" (1855); "A Parting Hymn," "[Graduation] Poem" (1856); "Two Voices" (1858); "The Wind Among the Poplars," "The Slave Girl's Prayer" (1859); "In the Country" (1860). The best of her early verses is the dreamlike and sensitive "The Angel's Visit" (c. 1860), lavishly praised by William Wells Brown. An early essay, "Glimpses of New England" (1858), shows Forten's finely descriptive prose style.

Forten lived for a few years in Philadelphia and in the Cambridge-Boston area where she worked for the Freedmen's Aid Society. Dating from these years are another poem, "Charles Sumner" (1874); a long essay on the 1876 Centennial Exposition in Philadelphia; and a translation of Emile Erkmann and Alexandre Chatrian's *Madame Thérèse; or, The Volunteers of '92* (1869). On December 19, 1878, after moving to Washington, D.C., Forten married Francis James Grimké, a nephew of Sarah and Angelina Grimké. Their only child died in 1880 at the age of six months. Except for four years in Jacksonville, Florida (1885-89), the Grimkés lived in Washington, where their shared interests in race progress and the fine arts made their home a social and cultural center. In the late 1880s and 1890s, Mrs. Grimké wrote some poems: "A June Song" (1885); "At Newport" (c. 1888); "The Grand Army of the Republic" (1890); "In Florida" (1893); and, her most successful poems, in blank verse, "Wordsworth" (n.d.) and "Charlotte Corday" (n.d.). The prose of her mature years is especially fine: fiery letters to newspapers on racial issues; strong, succinct, and beautifully vivid essays, such as "Midsummer Days in the Capital: The Corcoran Art Gallery"; and her tributes to Whittier and Frederick Douglass.

After Mrs. Grimké's death, which came after many years of illness and invalidism, she was memorialized by a scholarship in her name at Lincoln University and by letters of tribute from many eminent Americans.

[Two excellent sources of biography are Forten's own diary, *The Journal of Charlotte L. Forten*, ed. Ray A. Billington (New York: Dryden, 1953); rpt. Collier, 1961); and the two-volume study by Anna Julia Cooper, *Life and Writings of the Grimké Family*, 2 vols. in 1 (N.p.: Author, 1951), which contains Grimké's letters, prose, and poetry in one convenient place. Her manuscript diaries and the papers of Francis J. Grimké are in the Howard University Library. See also William Wells

Brown, *The Black Man* (1863); and Billington's sketch in *Notable American Women* (1971).]

HARPER, FRANCES ELLEN WATKINS (b. 1824; d. February 20, 1911), was born in Baltimore, the only child of free parents. From the age of four, when her mother died, she was raised by an aunt and attended the school run by her uncle, the abolitionist William Watkins, until she was fourteen. While working as a housekeeper and seamstress in the home of a Baltimore bookstore owner from 1838 to 1849, Frances Watkins educated herself in his library. She then taught in a vocational school, Union Seminary, near Columbus, Ohio (1850-52), and for a year in Little York, Pennsylvania, where, moved by the plight of fugitive slaves, she pledged her life's service to the causes of abolitionism and racial justice.

In 1854, in Boston, Watkins published the first of nine books of poetry, *Poems on Miscellaneous Subjects;* and, after delivering her first lecture, "The Elevation and Education of Our People," she was hired as a lecturer by the Maine Anti-Slavery Society. For the next six years (1854-60), under the auspices of several antislavery societies, she toured eight states, speaking and reading her poetry. A charismatic orator, with piercing black eyes and a strong, musical voice, she drew large audiences and glowing press notices. During these years, as her letters to William Still and John Brown reveal, her passionate dedication to freedom grew even stronger.

On November 22, 1860, she left the lecture circuit to marry Fenton Harper and subsequently had a daughter, Mary. At her husband's death in 1864, Harper resumed traveling in the North until the end of the Civil War; then, until 1871, at her own expense, she lectured throughout thirteen Southern states, urging the freedmen to become educated, landowning, responsible Christian citizens. She derived her income from sales of her latest poetry—*Moses: A Story of the Nile* (1869), *Poems* (1871), *Sketches of Southern Life* (1872)—and from sales of reprints of her first volume, which reached a twentieth edition in 1871.

After making Philadelphia her permanent home in 1871, Harper devoted herself to writing and lecturing on social and moral issues of nationwide concern: temperance, women's and children's rights, and education. As a lecturer, writer, or officer, she served the National Association of Colored Women, the National Council of Women of the United States, the American Association of Educators of Colored Youth and Author's Association, the African Methodist Episcopal Church (although she was a Unitarian), the Universal Peace Union, and, above all, the National Women's Christian Temperance Union (1875-96). Harper's name was entered on the Red Letter Calendar of the World WCTU in 1922.

During these busy years, she wrote articles on many subjects: for example, "The Democratic Return to Power" (1884); "The WCTU and the Colored Woman" (1888); "True and False Politeness" (1898). She was the first Black woman to publish a novel, *Iola Leroy; or Shadows Uplifted* (1893), as she had been the first to publish a short story, "The Two Offers," in 1859. In addition, new poetry and reissues of old poems under new titles continued to appear: *The Sparrow's Fall and Other Poems* (1890?); *The Martyr of Alabama and Other Poems* (1894); *Atlanta Offering* (1895); *Poems* (1896); and *Light Beyond the Darkness* (n.d.). Harper's frankly propagandist verses in traditional nineteenth-century forms, language, and techniques served her causes—religion, race, and social reform—with little variation over fifty years. Her fervid pleas for Christian values, retributive justice, and race advancement, and her sentimental laments for the weak and oppressed—slaves, women, and children of alcoholics—are only occasionally enlivened by personal passion and particularity. Although extremely effective when recited, most of her generic verses have only historical value today. However, with *Moses*, a forty-page narrative in blank verse, and the witty, ironic Aunt Chloe series in *Sketches*, which introduced colloquial language to Black poetry, Harper achieves notable artistic success.

Harper's celebrity as a poet, lecturer, and reformer was virtually unsurpassed in her day. She died of heart disease and was buried on February 24, 1911, from the Unitarian Church, in Eden Cemetery, Philadelphia.

[From the 1880s to date, comments on Harper are derived from one another, and originally from William Still, *Still's Underground Rail Road Records* (1872; rev. ed., Philadelphia: William Still, 1886), which includes Harper's letters; only Theodora Williams Daniel, "The Poems of Frances E. W. Harper" (M.A. diss., Howard Univ., 1937), provides original biographical and bibliographical data; Vernon Loggins, *The Negro Author* (1931), appraises the poetry, as does J. Saunders Redding, *To Make a Poet Black* (1939). Some early comments may be found in S. Elizabeth Frazier, "Some Afro-American Women of Mark," *AMECR* 8 (April 1892):378–81; George F. Bragg, Jr., *Men of Maryland* (Baltimore: Church Advocate Press, 1925); and Hallie Q. Brown, *Homespun Heroines and Other Women of Distinction* (Xenia, Ohio: Aldine, 1926). See also Benjamin Quarles, *Black Abolitionists* (New York: Oxford Univ. Press, 1969), and a good summary by Louis Filler in *Notable American Women* (1971).]

HEARD, JOSEPHINE DELPHINE (HENDERSON) (b. October 11, 1861) was born in Salisbury, North Carolina, to Lafayette and Anna M. Henderson, slaves who hired their time in Charlotte. An "Historical Sketch" in *Morning Glories* (Philadelphia: Author, 1890) claims that

Josephine Henderson taught school in North and South Carolina and Tennessee. On January 22, 1882, she married William Henry Heard, who became Minister to Liberia (1895-99) and a Bishop of the AME Church (1908). The Heards traveled widely through the United States and Europe; they lived in six states at various times and in Africa for eight years (1909-17). They had no children. The twelve dozen verses in two editions of *Morning Glories* preach Christian morality and faith, eulogize famous persons, or throb with the anguish of lost love; they are uniformly banal and poetically weak.

[The "Historical Sketch" by her husband recounts her early life, and Heard's autobiography, *From Slavery to the Bishopric in the A.M.E. Church* (Philadelphia: A.M.E. Book Concern, 1924), covers the years 1882-1924; reviews of *Morning Glories* are in *AMECR* (July and October 1890).]

PLATO, ANN, lived in Hartford, Connecticut, where she published *Essays: Including Biographies and Miscellaneous Pieces, in Prose and Poetry* (1841). Her twenty poems are the pious, moralistic effusions of a teenaged girl.

[James W. C. Pennington, "To the Reader," in *Essays*, is the only source; see also Vernon Loggins, *The Negro Author* (1931).]

RAY, HENRIETTA CORDELIA (c.1852-1916), was born in New York City, one of seven children of the Reverend Charles Bennett Ray, a leading abolitionist, reformer, and editor of the *Colored American*, and his second wife, Charlotte Augusta Burrough of Savannah, Georgia. Henrietta and her sister Florence, neither of whom married, were lifetime companions. Both earned Master of Pedagogy degrees from the University of the City of New York and became grammar school teachers in New York City. Their sister, Charlotte E. Ray, was the first Black woman admitted to the bar in Washington, D.C.

Henrietta Ray's ode, "Lincoln" (published in 1893), was read at the unveiling of the Freedmen's Monument in Washington in 1876. She published many poems in periodicals during the last two decades of the nineteenth century and, with Florence, produced a memorial volume, *Sketch of the Life of Rev. Charles B. Ray* (New York: J. J. Little, 1887). In Ray's 146 poems in two collections, *Sonnets* (New York: J. J. Little, 1893) and *Poems* (New York: Grafton, 1910), language, thought, and sentiments are impoverished by her respect for scholarship, decoration, and socially respectable attitudes. Her poetic subjects are nature, Christian morality and idealism, love, literature, and the struggle for freedom. Although the verse is generally tedious, Ray's technical skills are innovative and unusually rich.

In the early 1900s, retired on a city pension, the Rays lived in

Woodside, Long Island. Henrietta tutored privately in music, mathematics, and languages, and she taught literature to teachers. [Hallie Q. Brown, *Homespun Heroines* (1926), and the Rays' *Sketch* give biography.]

THOMPSON, ELOISE BIBB (b. June 29, 1878; d. 1927), was born Eloise Alberta Veronica Bibb in New Orleans, daughter of Charles H. and Catherine Adele Bibb. At age seventeen, she published *Poems* (Boston, 1895); a majority of the twenty-six verses are romantic narratives of star-crossed lovers and agonized heroes, while others more successfully treat historical and biblical subjects. Bibb attended Oberlin Academy (1899–1901), taught school, and after graduating from Teacher's College of Howard University in 1908, she became head resident of the Colored Social Settlement in Washington, D.C., until 1911. On August 4, 1911, in Chicago, Bibb married Noah D. Thompson and moved to Los Angeles, California; they had one child, Noah Murphy. Eloise Thompson wrote special feature articles for newspapers and published poetry and articles in Catholic magazines in the Los Angeles area. [Biography is found in Beasley (1919) and *Who's Who of the Colored Race*, ed. Frank L. Mather (1915).]

The following poets were mentioned in the appendices to *Invisible Poets*. I include some supplemental data here, but for publication details on Ada, Fordham, Lambert, Lee, and Mossell, see *Invisible Poets*.

ADA. Ada contributed twelve poems to the *Liberator* in 1831–37.

FORDHAM, MARY WESTON (b. c.1862). Poetry: *Magnolia Leaves* (1897), with "Introductory" by Booker T. Washington. The sixty-six verses, on the subjects of nature, religion, and death, are conventionally superficial. Memorial verses here suggest that her great-grandmother was Mary Furman Weston Byrd, a woman of Moroccan-French ancestry; a "grandparent" was Mrs. Jennette Boneau; the poet's parents were the Reverend Samuel and Louise B. Weston. The volume is favorably reviewed by William S. Braithwaite, *Colored American 3* (November 1901):73–74.

LAMBERT, MARY ELIZA (PERINE) TUCKER (b. 1838), was editor of *St. Matthew's Lyceum Journal*. Poetry: *Lowe's Bridge, A Broadway Idyl* (1867); *Poems* (1867); *AMECR* (1885, 1886). Prose: *Life of Mark M. Pomeroy* (1868). Sources: *AMECR* (1885–94, *passim*); Mossell 1885 and *Work*; *National Union Catalogue*. *NUC* gives name as Tucker; others as Mrs. J. H. or M. E. Lambert.

LEE, MARY EFFIE ASHE (Mrs. Benjamin Franklin). Poetry and Prose: *AMECR* (1892, 1895, 1901, 1916–22), *passim*; Mossell 1885. Sources: Bentley; Mossell *Work*; Tillman 1895 and 1898; Obituary: "Bishop B. F. Lee," *AMECR* (1926).

MOSSELL, GERTRUDE S. (Mrs. Nathan F.) (b. 1855, Philadelphia), was a journalist and author. Poetry: Several dozen poems, Mossell *Work; AMECR* (1888, 1889). Prose: Mossell *Work*, 1894, 1898, 1908 eds.; *AMECR* (1885-1901), *passim; Colored American* (August 1901). Two volumes are attributed to a "Gertrude E. H. Bustill Mossell" in Matthews, *Black American Writers* (see "Bibliographies," above). Sources: *Crisis* (December 1916); Dunningan; *Voice of the Negro* (February 1906).

CHANCELLOR, A. E. Poetry: *Weekly Anglo-African* (December 17, 1859); Loggins, *The Negro Author* (1931).

CHAPMAN, KATIE DAVIS (b. 1870, Mound City, Illinois), was a journalist. Sources: Dunningan; Penn, as DAVIS, KATIE CHAPMAN.

FOX, MAMIE ELOISE. Poetry: *AMECR* (1899). Sources: Penn; Tillman 1898.

GARNET, ESTA. Poetry: Mossell 1895.

LUCKIE, IDA EVANS. Poetry: *AMECR* (1898).

MAPPS, GRACE. Poetry: *Anglo-African Magazine* (1859). Source: Mossell *Work*.

MASON, LENA DOOLIN (Mrs. George) (b. 1864, Quincy, Illinois), was an Evangelist. Poetry and Source: D. W. Culp, ed., *Twentieth-Century Negro Literature* (1902; rpt. New York: Arno, 1969).

SIMPSON, IDA V. Poetry: *AMECR* (1889).

THOMPSON, LILLIAN V. Poetry: *AMECR* (1891).

TILLMAN, KATHERINE D. Poetry: *AMECR* (1892); Prose: Tillman 1895, 1898; Drama: two plays.

WASHINGTON, JOSEPHINE TURPIN (b. Virginia), was a journalist. Poetry: *AMECR* (1890). Source: Dunningan.

WEIR, NANCY M. Poetry: *Liberator* (June 27, 1862).

WHITSETT, VIRGIE. Poetry: *AMECR* (1899). Sources: Penn; Tillman 1898.

Poetry by F. E. H. Wassom, C. M. Thompson, Nannie A. Barber, Edith M. Thomas, Jessie E. Beard, Linnie H. Drake, and Margaret E. Langster appears in the *Afro-American Encyclopedia*, comp. James T. Haley (1896). Priscilla Stewart, Cecelia Williams, and Eva Carter Buckner are quoted and discussed in Beasley. Lucy Hughes Brown and Ida F. Johnson are quoted and discussed in Mossell *Work*.

REFERENCE KEY

AMECR   *African Methodist Episcopal Church Review*
Beasley   Delilah L. Beasley, *The Negro Trail Blazers of California* (Los Angeles, 1919).

Bentley   Fannie C. L. Bentley, "The Women of Our Race Worthy
                   of Imitation," *AMECR* 6 (1890):473-77.
Dunningan   Alice E. Dunningan, "Early History of Negro Women in
                   Journalism," *Negro History Bulletin* 28 (Summer 1965):
                   178-79, 193, 197.
Mossell 1885   Mrs. N. F. Mossell, "The Colored Woman in Verse,"
                   AMECR 2 (1885):60-67.
Mossell *Work*   Mrs. N. F. Mossell, *The Work of the Afro-American
                   Woman*, 2d ed. (Philadelphia, 1908).
Penn   I. Garland Penn, "Rise and Progress of Afro-American
                   Literature," in Henry Northrup et al., eds., *The College of
                   Life* (Chicago, 1895).
Tillman 1895   Katherine D. Tillman, "Afro-American Women and
                   Their Work," *AMECR* 11 (1895):477-99.
Tillman 1898   Katherine D. Tillman, "Afro-American Poets and Their
                   Verse," *AMECR* 14 (1898):421-28.

22

On the Novels Written by Selected Black American Women: A Bibliographical Essay

RITA B. DANDRIDGE

Novels written by Black American women have been woefully neglected by scholars, Black and white. They have been mentioned in footnotes, cited in cross-references, tucked away in bibliographies, and glossed over in reviews and surveys. Few are mentioned in the *Encyclopedia Americana*. No comprehensive study of the novels by Black American women exists. To date, no individual Black American female novelist and her novels have been dealt with in a book-length published study. Doctoral dissertations on Black American female novelists are only just beginning to emerge, and contributions to scholarly journals on their novels are few and far between. In view of the neglect of these novels, this essay has been written as a guide for teachers and students.

GUIDE TO THE NOVELS

Bibliographies

Several bibliographies, including a listing of novels by Black American women, are available. Robert A. Corrigan, former director of the Institute for Afro-American Culture, University of Iowa, published a "Bibliography of Afro-American Fiction: 1853–1970" in the Summer 1970 issue of *Studies in Black Literature*, pp. 51–86. Though Corrigan lists a considerable number of novels by Black American women, gives the prices of the novels, and indicates which novels can be obtained in paperback, his bibliography has two serious drawbacks: secondary works written by Blacks are not distinguished from those written by whites, and most novels are not distinguished from short story collections. A slightly better bibliography, published the same year, is Darwin T. Turner's *Afro-American Writers* (New York: Appleton-Century-Crofts, 1970). With emphasis on the major works published by Afro-American writers in the twentieth century, Turner lists eighteen Black American female novelists and their works. Special features of the Turner bibliography include such annotations as an asterisk following an entry to indicate novels of special importance and a dagger sign to indicate the availability of the work in paperback. Turner also cites the criticism available on the novels. An extensive listing of novels written by Black American women is that of Ora Williams in *American Black Women in the Arts and Social Sciences*, revised and expanded ed. (Metuchen, New Jersey: The Scarecrow Press, Inc., 1978).

Supplement to Bibliographies

Novels published before 1973 but not included in the current bibliographies are Dorothy Lee Dickens's *Black on the Rainbow* (New York: Pageant Press, 1952); Pauline Hopkins's *Contending Forces* (Boston: Colored Cooperative Publishing Co., 1900); Audrey Lee's *The Workers* (New York: McGraw-Hill, 1969); Cleo Overstreet's *The Boar Hog Woman* (Garden City, N.Y.: Doubleday, 1972); Carlene Hatcher Polite's *The Flagellants* (New York: Farrar, Straus and Giroux, 1967), also published in France under the title of *Les Flagellants* in 1966; and Zara Wright's *Kenneth,* published under the same cover with her *Black and White Tangled Threads* (Chicago: Barnard and Miller, 1920). Most of the foregoing out-of-print older novels and difficult-to-purchase newer ones can be ordered from several reputable distribution points: (1) AMS Press, Inc., 56 East 13th Street, New York, New York 10003; (2) McBlain Books, Box 971, Des Moines, Iowa 50304; and (3) University Place Book Store, 840 Broadway, New York, New York, 10003.

LITERARY AND PERSONAL BACKGROUND SOURCES

Sources of information about the literary backgrounds and personal lives of Black American woman novelists are scarce and generally unpublished. Information relating to the unpublished sources of novels by Black American women still living can be obtained either by writing to the authors listed in Ann Allen Shockley and Sue P. Chandler's biographical directory entitled *Living Black American Authors* (New York: R. R. Bowker, 1973) or by writing to the authors not listed in the directory in care of their publishers.

Autobiographies

The two published autobiographies by Black American women novelists are Gwendolyn Brooks's *Report from Part One: The Autobiography of Gwendolyn Brooks* (Detroit: Broadside Press, 1972) and Zora Neale Hurston's *Dust Tracks on a Road* (Philadelphia: J. B. Lippincott Company, 1942).

Gwendolyn Brooks, author of one novel, *Maud Martha* (1953), and the first Black to win the Pulitzer Prize, gives an account of her life and career in her autobiography. Born in Topeka, Kansas, on June 7, 1917, she grew up and has spent most of her life in Chicago, the city from which she draws most of her character types for her poems and novels. In reviewing her life as mother, wife, teacher, and writer, Brooks divides her autobiography into six sections. In addition to the interviews, the Appendix is important for comments on her novel, for in it, Brooks gives a point-by-point explanation of what is autobiographical in *Maud Martha*.

Author of a large number of works, including four novels, Zora Neale Hurston gives an easy-to-follow account of her life in *Dust Tracks on a Road*. She was born in 1901 in Eatonville, Florida, the all-Negro town which figures prominently in two of her novels, *Jonah's Gourd Vine* (1934) and *Their Eyes Were Watching God* (1937). After her mother's death, she was passed around from one relative to another; eventually traveling North, she worked at a succession of odd jobs and attended school at Morgan College, Howard, and then Barnard College and Columbia University, where she studied folklore, which would later be important to her fiction. In her autobiography Hurston explains the circumstances involved in the writing of her novels and also provides information about her relationships with family members and with whites that enables us better to understand her works.

Letters and Personal Papers

To my knowledge, no letters of a single Black American female novelist have been published. Zora Neale Hurston's letters and papers, however, can be found in the University of Florida library at Gainesville, and in the James Weldon Johnson Collection at Yale University. Ann Petry's letters and papers can be found at Boston University. Another important source of background material about an individual author's work is Margaret Walker's paper, *How I Wrote Jubilee*, published in pamphlet form by Third World Press in 1972. In this thirty-six-page pamphlet, Margaret Walker explains the genesis of *Jubilee* (1966), the laborious research that was required to document historical facts presented in the novel, and the setbacks and problems she encountered in the more than thirty years it took to complete the work. Appended to this essay are an afterword, a list of valuable questions for discussion and further research, and a selected list of books to which Margaret Walker has referred in the essay.

Articles

There are several articles in which Black American female novelists offer insights into their writing. Zora Neale Hurston, in "Characteristics of Negro Expression," *Negro: An Anthology*, ed. Nancy Cunard (New York: Frederick Ungar Publishing Company, [reprint] 1970), describes the primary characteristics of Negro expression and names the Negro's three major contributions to the language: the use of metaphor and simile, the use of the double descriptive, and the use of the verbal noun. These observations help us to understand Hurston's novels, in which she makes extensive use of Black expressions. Margaret Walker, in "Willing to Pay the Price," *Many Shades of Black*, ed. Stanton L. Wormley and Lewis H. Fenderson (New York: William Morrow and Company, Inc., 1969), discusses the difficulty of becoming a good creative writer and mentions pointers given to her by other writers. She also mentions letters in her possession from such famous writers as Stephen Vincent Benét, Richard Wright, and Langston Hughes. "The Task of the Negro Writer as Artist," *Negro Digest* 14 (April 1965): 54-74, includes notes by Gwendolyn Brooks and Kristin Hunter on what a good Black writer should be. In "Black Writers' Views on Literary Lions and Values," *Negro Digest* 17 (January 1968): 10-47, Gwendolyn Brooks, Alice Childress, Kristin Hunter, Alice Walker, and Margaret Walker examine the values and literary characteristics of Black writers. In "The Negro Woman in American Literature," *Freedomways* 6 (Winter 1966): 8-25, Sarah E. Wright, Alice Childress, and Paule Marshall discuss and criticize the negative image of Black women portrayed in American literature and also point out the few good images of Black women in literature. They rightly conclude that most of the good images of Black women are provided by Black women writers themselves. An important article in the Books News Section of *The Buffalo Evening News*, Saturday, November 15, 1975, contained relevant statements by and about Charlene Hatcher Polite that shed light on her background as a writer. Born in Detroit, she became fascinated with words when she received her first library card and began checking books out of the library. Having then ventured into dance, she says, "Dance taught me some very important things about writing. I learned the rhythm, the pulse, and the discipline. It taught me how to straddle a typewriter." Years later, while working as a bunny in the Playboy Club in Detroit, Polite saved enough money to travel to Paris, where she eventually settled for some time and wrote her first novel, *The Flagellants*, in nine months. While in Paris, Polite says she "lived on fellowships and book royalties." *The Flagellants*, published in several languages, received a Pulitzer Prize nomination. It was followed by her seldom-mentioned fictional autobiography, *Apology to a Rabbit*—based primarily on Polite's experiences as a Playboy bunny—and by the novel *Sister X and the Victims of Foul Play*. Among several important points Polite makes about her works, she says, "Even though my characters are Black, non-Black readers know the same situations. Language and race don't separate us from sharing the joy of living, the pain of survival, love, sadness, the wish to refine one's existence."

Interviews

Two relevant interviews with Gwendolyn Brooks have been published— first separately in journals, and later together in her autobiography, *Report from Part One*. In her interview with Ida Lewis, first published in *Essence* 2 (April 1971): 27-31, Gwendolyn Brooks discusses her views on the Black revolution of the 1960s. In her comments on racial strife and color bias, she equates her insecure and inferior feelings as a dark-complexioned child with the feelings of a dark-hued girl in *Maud Martha* (1953) who is being rejected by a boy in favor of a light-complexioned girl. In her interview with George Stavros, which first appeared in *Contemporary Literature* 11 (1970):1-20, Gwendolyn Brooks, in addition to discussing her poetry, answers very specific questions about the portraits of character in *Maud Martha* and the purpose, form, and setting of the novel. She concludes her comments by stating that she has no intention of writing another novel.

Jerry Ward's "Legitimate Resources of the Soul: An Interview with

Arthenia Bates Millican," *Obsidian* 3 (Spring 1977):14-34, reveals Millican's views on Black humanism and the Black esthetic, and includes comments on her poetry, short stories, and novel. Millican explains that her novel, *The Deity Nodded*—chapter 51 of which was originally published as "A Ceremony of Innocence" in her short-story collection *Seeds Beneath the Snow* (New York: Greenwich Book Publishers, 1969)— was based upon her sister's conversion to the Muslim faith. She answers questions relating to her research on the Nation of Islam preparatory to writing the novel and addresses herself to problems of religion which she poses in the novel. An earlier interview between Millican and Hollie West appeared in the *Washington Post* June 11, 1970, p. 32.

In the December 1976 (7:8) issue of *Essence*, pp. 54, 56, 90-92, Jessica Harris interviews Toni Morrison, at the time author of two novels, and editor at Random House for nine years, as well as mother of two sons. In her role as editor, Morrison has edited Gayl Jones's two novels, *Corregidora* and *Eva's Man*, which have been criticized for their portrayal of Black men.

Not intending to become a writer, Morrison started writing what became her first novel, *The Bluest Eye*, years ago. She completed the novel some years later as a therapeutic means of dealing with loneliness when she lived in Syracuse. She says, "I realized in the process of *The Bluest Eye* that writing had become a compulsion so I became a writer....I will always be a writer." A meticulous writer, Morrison admits to rewriting extensively.

James Ivy, in his article-interview entitled "Ann Petry Talks about Her First Novel," *Crisis* 53 (February 1946):48-49 gives a physical description and his personal first impressions of Ann Petry. Then he records the novelist's aims in writing *The Street:* "to show how simply and easily the environment can change the course of a person's life..., to show why the Negro has a high crime rate, a high death rate, and little or no chance of keeping his family unit intact in large Northern cities..., to write a story that moves swiftly so that it would hold the attention of people who might ordinarily shy away from a so-called problem novel...and to show them [Negroes] as people with the same capacity for love and hate, for tears and laughter, and the same instincts for survival possessed by all men."

Ann Petry's interview with John O'Brien twenty-seven years later, in *Interviews with Black Writers* (New York: Liveright, 1973) pp. 153-63, shows the author more reticent than she was in the earlier interview. Author of three novels, Petry does not like talking about her work and considers it an imposition to have to explain anything in them. In the course of the interview, however, she reveals the genesis of her works and discusses the craft of writing. Interestingly, although Petry is aware that critics have labeled *The Street* (1946) as naturalistic writing, she does not consider herself as belonging to the naturalistic school.

In the same volume, O'Brien interviews Alice Walker, pp. 185–211. Having agreed on an interview by mail because circumstances would not allow otherwise, Walker provides essay-type answers to O'Brien's questions about her poetry, short stories, and novel, *The Third Life of Grange Copeland* (1970). In relation to her novel she discusses her preoccupation with the oppression and triumphs of Black women, her faith in the "spiritual survival" of Black people, and her belief in the personal and political change that can occur in a person and does occur in her major character, Grange Copeland. Walker also mentions a novel in progress, *Meridian* (1976).

Alice Walker's second novel, *Meridian*, is the focus of Jessica Harris's interview with her in *Essence* 7 (July 1976):33. When Harris asked of Alice Walker, who had been a voter registration worker, how closely her life paralleled that of the female protagonist, Meridian, Walker answered, "I suppose that it's not quite accurate to say that Meridian doesn't parallel my life, for in a way, what she does in her 'sane madness'—her psychological suffering—parallels some of my psychological suffering. But my life, on the surface, was not like hers, not as extreme. Of course, I knew and had experienced some of those things—the marching, the awareness of prayer limited as a social tool. I fit somewhere between Ann-Marion and Meridian." After revealing that the germ of *Meridian* was provided by the recently deceased Doris Robinson, a founder of SNCC, Walker concludes by pointing up the value of Meridian's nonconformity even while working in the civil rights movement. Walker's idea is that it is more important to love one's self and treat people as human beings, as Meridian does, than it is to mouth pompous statements in the manner of some of the other characters—a tendency which the civil rights struggle of the 1960s sometimes encouraged.

CRITICISM

General Criticism

Although no full-length study on the novels by Black American women has appeared, novels written by Black American women have received token notice in other book-length studies. The first full-length study of Black fiction in America, Nick Aaron Ford's *Contemporary Negro Novel* (Boston: Meador Co., 1936), includes some discussion of novels written by Black American women. Ford examines novels from 1914 to 1936 in order to illuminate the views of Black writers on issues of race. He concentrates on the way such issues as segregation, passing, prejudice, imitation, and social intermingling are reflected in the novels. As important as Ford's study is, he establishes limits which were generally accepted by later critics. While Ford analyzes the Black American novel from a social and racial point of view, he explicitly shows a bias toward male novelists by including in his study nine men and two women (Fauset and Larsen); he does not refer to any Black female novelists before Fauset, and he does not examine all the novels of the two Black women he has chosen to write on (e.g., he omits Fauset's *Comedy American Style* [1933], though it is relevant to his discussion).

Published twelve years after Ford's study was Hugh Gloster's *Negro Voices in American Fiction* (Chapel Hill: The University of North Carolina Press, 1948). Examining novels written by Black Americans from Reconstruction to the 1940s from a sociological perspective Gloster, like Ford, gives more attention to the novels of Fauset and Larsen than to novels by any other women. Though he does devote one or two pages each to such novels as Frances Harper's *Iola Leroy* (1892), Pauline Hopkins's *Contending Forces* (1900), Sarah Fleming's *Hope's Highway* (1918), and Zora Neale Hurston's *Jonah's Gourd Vine* (1934) and *Their Eyes Were Watching God* (1937), Gloster's discussion of these novels consists mainly of plot summaries.

A minor work of the 1950s is Carl Milton Hughes's *The Negro Novelist* (New York: Books for Libraries Press, 1953). Updating material already published on Black fiction, Hughes discusses American Black novelists from 1940 to 1950. He analyzes Ann Petry's *The Street* (1946) as a naturalistic novel and Zora Neale Hurston's *Seraph on the Suwanee* (1948) as a product of Freudian psychology.

A popular and often quoted study—despite its serious deficiencies—that emerged in the late 1950s is Robert Bone's *The Negro Novel in America* (New Haven: Yale University Press, 1958). Bone views the Black novel as following the historical development of the American novel but having "a life of its own which springs from the soil of a distinctive minority culture." Examining novels from William Wells Brown's *Clotel* (1853) to James Baldwin's *Another Country* (1962), he divides his study of the novel into four parts. In Part I, "The Novel of the Rising Middle Class: 1890-1920," Bone mentions the first Black American female novelist, Frances Harper, but devotes only one insignificant paragraph to her novel, *Iola Leroy* (1892). In Part II, "The Discovery of the Folk: 1920-1930," Bone barely reserves the last five pages to the two most popular Black American female novelists of the time, Fauset and Larsen.

Though Bone admits that Fauset wrote more novels than any other Black American from 1924 to 1933, he dismisses her four novels as being "sophomoric, trivial, and dull" and devotes one sentence to each of them. In the case of Nella Larsen, Bone cagily admits that the novel *Passing* (1929) is "probably the best treatment of the subject in Negro fiction" but devotes only half a paragraph to discussing it. His discussion of Larsen's *Quicksand* (1928) is lengthier, since, like most critics, he considers it the better novel, with a well-conceived metaphorical framework. In Part III, "The Search for a Tradition: 1930–1940," Bone comments at length on Zora Neale Hurston's *Their Eyes Were Watching God* (1937), mentions in passing *Jonah's Gourd Vine* (1934) and *Seraph on the Suwanee* (1948), and omits entirely *Moses, Man of the Mountain* (1939). In Part IV, "The Revolt against Protest: 1940–1952," Bone devotes two sentences to Ann Petry's *The Street* (1946), although it was a best seller, and two sentences to *Country Place* (1947), but does not mention *The Narrows* (1953). His comments about Dorothy West's *The Living Is Easy* (1948) focus on the "bitchery" of the Black female protagonist, Cleo Judson. A shortcoming of this study is that Bone, in attempting to classify all novels as being works of either protest, accommodation, or assimilation, fails to give full critical attention to the novels of Black American women, which may not fit into rigid male-defined categories.

Robert Bone's hit-or-miss discussions of novels by Black American women are typical of white male critics' treatment of those novels in the 1960s. David Littlejohn, who published *Black on White* (New York: Grossman Publishers, 1966), a myopic, chauvinistic, and Negrophobic study, views only Ann Petry as having "a place almost as prominent and promising as that of the bigger three [Wright, Baldwin, Ellison]." Roger Rosenblatt, in *Black Fiction* (Cambridge, Mass.: Harvard University Press, 1974), views the novels of only two Black American women, Zora Neale Hurston and Ann Petry, as fitting into his study. In *Black American Literature* (New Jersey: Littlefield, Adams and Company, 1974), Roger Whitlow, whose book is full of questionable points, examines Black literature from its inception to the 1970s. Typically, in his section on the 1960s, Whitlow omits many important novels by Black American women and includes only the novels of Kristin Hunter, Sarah Wright, and Paule Marshall.

In the 1970s several studies have included information about the novels of Black women: Nathan Huggins's *The Harlem Renaissance* (New York: Oxford University Press, 1971); Noel Schraufnagel's *The Black American Novel* (Deland, Florida: Everette/Edwards, Inc., 1973); Amritjit Singh's *The Novels of the Harlem Renaissance* (University Park: Pennsylvania State University Press, 1976); and James O. Young's *Black*

Writers of the Thirties (Baton Rouge: Louisiana State University Press, 1973). Of the four, the Schraufnagel and Singh works are the most important. Schraufnagel's book, examining novels by Black Americans from 1940 to 1970, introduces novels by Black American women that have been omitted in previous studies. From Schraufnagel, one learns, for the first time in a full-length study, the contents and critical assessments of such novels as Rosa Guy's *Bird at my Window* (1966), Charlene Polite's *The Flagellants* (1966), and Odella Wood's *High Ground* (1945). A shortcoming of this study, however, is that Schraufnagel, like Robert Bone, categorizes most Black American novels as works of protest, accommodation, or assimilation.

Amritjit Singh's *The Novels of the Harlem Renaissance* examines twenty-one novels published by Black writers between 1923 and 1933, six of which are by Fauset and Larsen. Singh focuses "on the intraracial issues of self-definition, class, caste, and color..., using an integrated approach that simultaneously evaluates aesthetic and sociocultural impulses." Though Singh's approach is not new, his treatment of Fauset and Larsen is refreshing. He views Larsen as a better writer, technically, than Fauset and considers Fauset's *Plum Bun* "her most successful novel." An important element of the Singh study is that he incorporates in his discussion the critical reception of the novels at the time of their publication.

From the Dark Tower (Washington, D. C.: Howard University Press, 1974), by Arthur P. Davis, is a valuable reference guide to the study of Black literature. Continuing where Vernon Loggins's *The Negro Author* (New York: Columbia University Press, 1931) left off, Davis surveys major works of Black literature from 1900 to 1965 and includes the novels of Jessie Fauset, Nella Larsen, Zora Neale Hurston, Margaret Walker, Gwendolyn Brooks, and Ann Petry. An important feature of this reference guide is the inclusion of extensive biographical information which leads to a better understanding and appreciation of the writers' novels.

Darwin Turner's *In a Minor Chord: Three Afro-American Writers and Their Search for Identity* (Carbondale: Southern Illinois Press, 1971) examines the writings of Jean Toomer, Countee Cullen, and Zora Neale Hurston, three writers who comprise a "melancholy minor chord" because of their inability to find satisfaction in their search for their heritage. In a chapter entitled "Zora Neale Hurston: The Wandering Minstrel," Turner presents Hurston as a rootless loner, full of insensitivities and contradictions. An analysis of Hurston's autobiography leads Turner to comment: "The Zora Neale Hurston who takes shape from her autobiography and from the accounts of those who knew her is an imaginative, somewhat shallow, quick-tempered woman, desperate for recognition and reassurance to assuage her feelings of inferiority; a blind follower of that social code which approves arrogance toward one's assumed peers and inferiors but requires total psychological commitment to a subservient posture before one's supposed superiors."

Though Turner uses this erroneous image of Hurston as the basis for examining her novels, he praises Hurston's symbols in *Jonah's Gourd Vine,* her characterizations in *Their Eyes Were Watching God,* her satire and dialect in *Moses, Man of the Mountain,* and her dramatic quality in *Seraph on the Suwanee,* and concludes that Hurston was "the most competent [though not necessarily the most successful] Black female novelist before 1950."

Individual Criticism

The following guide to individual criticism of Black American women novelists necessarily excludes book reviews and newspaper articles. Reviews of some of the novels can be traced through the *Book Review Digest* and the index to *The New York Times Book Review.* Reviews of other novels can be found by surveying the book review sections of such journals as *Black Creation, Black Scholar, CLA Journal, Crisis, Freedomways, Negro Digest/Black World, Obsidian,* and *Phylon.* Newspaper articles on the novels can be found in such newspapers as the *Amsterdam News,* the *Baltimore Sun,* the *Chicago Defender,* the *Norfolk Journal and Guide,* the *Pittsburgh Courier,* and the *Washington Post.* The *New York Herald Tribune* is also an occasional source for notes on novels by Black women. Only full-length scholarly articles are included here. Two good articles which do not fall into the individual author category are Sandra Towns's "Our Dark-Skinned Selves: Three Women Writers of the Harlem Renaissance," *Umoja* 1:2 (Old Series 1973):5–9, and Mary Helen Washington's "Black Women Image Makers," *Black World* 23 (August 1974):10–18.

Gwendolyn Brooks

Lauded as a world-renowned poet, Gwendolyn Brooks is barely noticed by critics as the author of the novel *Maud Martha.* Consequently, Annette Oliver Shands's article, "Gwendolyn Brooks as Novelist," *Black World* 22 (June 1973):22–30, is a rare find. This article explores the theme of humanness found in *Maud Martha* and points up Brooks's ideas and technique in the novel that are also evident in her poems.

Jessie Fauset

Jessie Fauset has received attention in several articles. In "The Novels of Jessie Fauset," *Opportunity* 12 (January 1934):24-28, William Stanley Braithwaite perceives Fauset as standing in the front rank of Negro novelists of her time because the theme and milieu of her novels were at variance with those of her Negro contemporaries. Braithwaite also places Fauset above such American women novelists as Willa Cather, Ellen Glasgow, Sarah Orne Jewett, and Mary E. Wilkins Freeman because none of them discovered "a new world of racial experience and character...buffeted, baffled, scorned, and rejected, by pressure of an encircling political, economic, social, and spiritual society...." After labeling Fauset the Jane Austen of Negro literature and chastising both white and Black critics for misreading Fauset's novels, Braithwaite claims that Fauset's four novels embody the Shakespearean conflict of will and passion. "In this Negro society which Miss Fauset has created imaginatively from the realities," comments Braithwaite, "there is the *will*, the confused but burning *will*, to master the *passion* of the organized body of lusty American prejudice."

Joseph J. Feeney's article, "Greek Tragic Patterns in a Black Novel: Jessie Fauset's *The Chinaberry Tree*," *CLA Journal* 18 (December 1974):211-15, examines several techniques of Greek tragedy in Fauset's *The Chinaberry Tree*, including the family curse, fate ruling events, a tragic inevitability, and recognition scenes. Feeney also finds images and phrases in the novel that contribute to the Greek tone. Though the novel succeeds on the plot level as a Greek tragedy, comments Feeney, it does not include the "religious beliefs and philosophical undercurrents of the Greeks." Because much of the novel focuses on the love story of Melissa Paul, basically it must be read, says Feeney, as a "domestic" novel.

Marion L. Starkey's article, "Jessie Fauset," *Southern Workman* 61 (1932):217-20, provides useful notes on Fauset as a writer. Fauset's literary career began when she read the white T. S. Stribling's novel on Blacks, who in real life, Fauset felt, did not act and react the way Stribling described them. Financially unable to give up her job as a French teacher at DeWitt Clinton High School in New York City, Fauset wrote her novels during her teaching career. The first eighty pages of *The Chinaberry Tree* were written one summer after her 8 o'clock French class. In her novels, Fauset writes what she considers a good story taken from real life; *The Chinaberry Tree,* for example, was based on a true story Fauset had heard when she was fifteen. Starkey says that all Fauset's plots were held in her memory for years; thus, when she wrote, she did so without revision. The fact that she did not revise may explain the tedium in her novels.

Zora Neale Hurston

More readable as a novelist than Brooks or Fauset is Zora Neale Hurston, about whose works and personality numerous articles have been written. Fannie Hurst, for whom Hurston worked as a secretary and later as a chauffeur gives her condescending view of Zora in "Zora Hurston: A Personality Sketch," *Yale University Library Gazette* 35 (1961):17-22. Though she views Hurston as irresponsible, gluttonous, carefree, and displaying little concern for her race, Hurst comments that "in spite of herself, her [Hurston's] rich heritage cropped out not only in her personality but more importantly in her writing." *Their Eyes Were Watching God,* for instance, is considered by Hurst to be as much a part of Negro Americana as fried chitterlings, which, she says, Hurston loved.

A more favorable portrait of Hurston and a more searching discussion of her novels are provided by Larry Neale in "Eatonville's Zora Neale Hurston: A Profile," *Black Review* (New York: William Morrow and Company, 1972). This article is superseded, however, by Alice Walker's profound and moving article, "In Search of Zora Neale Hurston, *Ms.* 3 (March 1975):74-79, 85-89, written after Walker traveled through the backwoods of Florida in search of Hurston's burial site and found only a weed-grown field and no grave marker to indicate where Hurston is buried. There are also several minor articles on Hurston, including James W. Byrd's "Zora Neale Hurston: A Novel Folklorist," *Tennessee Folklore Society Bulletin* 21 (1955):37-41; Evelyn Thomas Helmick's "Zora Neale Hurston," *Carrell* 11 (1970):1-19; and Blyden Jackson's "Some Negroes in the Land of Goshen," *Tennessee Folklore Society Bulletin* 19 (1953):103-7.

A concern with the survival of Zora Neale Hurston as an affirmative writer is the focus of two important articles published in *Black World.* June Jordan, "On Richard Wright and Zora Neale Hurston," *Black World* 23 (August 1974):4-8, questions why Richard Wright enjoyed literary fame while Zora Neale Hurston, who finally died a penniless ward of the State of Florida, endured critical neglect, despite the fact that both wrote at the same time and both "achieved unprecedented, powerful, and extremely important depths of Black vision and commitment in their life work." Pointing to the white mass media as the culprit, Jordan designates Richard Wright's *Native Son* as the prototype of a Black protest novel and Zora Neale Hurston's *Their Eyes Were Watching God* as the prototype of a novel of Black affirmation and convincingly argues that "the functions of protest and affirmation are not, ultimately, distinct: that...affirmation of Black values and lifestyles within the American context is, indeed, an act of protest." Regarding *Their Eyes Were Watching God* as the most convincing novel of Black love, Jordan sees no reason why Bigger Thomas, Wright's protagonist, should represent Blacks any more than Janie Starks, Hurston's protagonist.

In the same issue of *Black World*, in an article entitled "Zora Neale Hurston: The Novelist-Anthropologist's Life/Works," *Black World* 23 (August 1974):20–30, Ellease Southerland gives an overview of the life and works of Hurston. Using Hurston's often misunderstood comments on race which have engendered damaging comments from critics who view her as devoid of "serious race consciousness," Southerland examines each of Hurston's novels to show how they belie the false accusations of critics and demonstrate affirmatively Hurston's love, respect, and appreciation for Black life. According to Southerland, Hurston, seemingly a victim of criticism most of her life, fell into literary silence when, after the publication of her fourth novel, *Seraph on the Suwanee* (1948), "false charges of indecent behavior [were] brought against her, supposedly involving two demented minors and one adult."

Ann L. Rayson, in "The Novels of Zora Neale Hurston," *Studies in Black Literature* 5 (Winter 1974):1–10, claims that though Hurston's four novels have superficial differences, they follow similar patterns in the characters' use of the Southern folk idiom, their espousal of "a transcendent philosophy of harmony with one's own sexual role and the cosmos," and Hurston's use of a one-plot formula in which protagonists find their way to understanding and love.

Darwin Turner, "The Negro Novelist and the South," *Southern Humanities Review* 1 (1967):21–29, considers Zora Neale Hurston one of the five Negro novelists of the South (James Weldon Johnson, George Henderson, Richard Wright, and Frank Yerby are the other four) who have "failed to picture the Southern Negroes and their milieu fully and faithfully."

A much more convincing article is Mary Helen Washington's "The Black Woman's Search for Identity," *Black World* 21 (August 1972):68–75. Examining Hurston's *Their Eyes Were Watching God*, Washington praises Hurston for omitting the suffering, humiliation, and degradation of Black people, so often the subject matter of Black writers, and for including the laughter and loving that are a part of Black life. According to Washington, Hurston achieves "the Black frame of reference" in three ways: "the language is authentic dialect of Black rural life; the characters are firmly rooted in Black folk culture; and Janie's search for identity is an integral part of her search for Blackness." Washington satisfactorily proves her point by documenting her ideas with anecdotes and stories from folk history.

Another view of Hurston's *Their Eyes Were Watching God* is presented in S. Jay Walker's "Zora Neale Hurston's *Their Eyes Were Watching God:* Black Novel of Sexism," *Modern Fiction Studies* 20 (Winter 1974-75):519-27. Walker sees *Their Eyes Were Watching God* as "an interpretation of love that denies not sexuality but sex-role stereotypes." Following the protagonist, Janie Starks, through her first two marriages (Janie marries her second husband before divorcing the first), Walker points out that Janie's life was unfulfilled in both instances because her movements were dictated by her husbands' insistence on stereotyped sex roles. With her marriage to her third husband, Tea Cake, however, Janie maintains her autonomy as a woman because sex roles become nonexistent and the relationship is one "between acknowledged equals." The recently released, meticulously researched, book-length biography of Hurston, Robert Hemenway's *Zora Neale Hurston: A Literary Biography*, with a foreword by Alice Walker (Urbana: University of Illinois Press, 1977), will undoubtedly become the standard reference for information about Hurston's life and works.

Nella Larsen

Hortense E. Thornton, in "Sexism as Quagmire: Nella Larsen's *Quicksand*," *CLA Journal* 16 (March 1973):285-301, argues in a scholarly and forthright manner that Nella Larsen's *Quicksand* is a novel about sexism as well as racism because Helga Crane's tragedy stems more from her being a woman than her being a mulatto. Condemning critics for analyzing the novel as a race novel, Thornton writes: "To label Helga's plight as typical of the tragic mulatto motif. . . is to reduce Larsen's novel to a melodramatic fantasy intended to titillate readers still hanging on to certain myths about the myriad advantages of the caucasian blood strain." In analyzing Helga's plight, Thornton observes that Helga is a "pursued, courted, and adored object in her encounters with men." Seldom accepted as a "sensitive human being," Helga is "dependent upon these men for some aspect of her existence." Comparing the results of Helga's search for happiness in life to a downward spiral, Thornton sees Helga as entrapped by her femaleness. In the final episode of the novel, in which Helga is pregnant a fifth time by a husband she no longer loves, Thornton says, "Her [Helga's] womb entraps her so much that through childbearing she is left a tragic lifeless shell."

Nella Larsen's second novel is the subject of Mary Mabel Youman's "Nella Larsen's *Passing:* A Study in Irony," *CLA Journal* 18 (December 1974):235-41. Contrary to other critics who argue that *Passing* is a novel about a Black "passing for white," Youman contends that *Passing* is a novel which reveals that "Blacks can and do lose the spiritual values of Blackness though them remain in a Black world." Youman, then, views Irene Redfield, who has lost her heritage, as the protagonist and as the one who "passes." In an effort to maintain her secure life, Irene Redfield, according to Youman, "has passed into the conventionalized, mechanized, non-humane white world."

Paule Marshall

Two articles on the novels of Paule Marshall appeared in the September 1972 issue of *CLA Journal.* In "Domestic Themes and Technique in Paule Marshall's Fiction" (pp. 49-59), Leela Kapai examines four themes occurring in *Brown Girl, Brownstones* and *The Chosen Place, The Timeless People:* the identity crisis, the race problem, the importance of tradition for Black Americans, and the need to share in order to foster meaningful relationships. Using notes generously supplied by Marshall, Kapai also comments on Marshall's technique. Kapai states that Marshall's plots contain conflict and suspense; a mixture of "the old and the new in fictional tradition"; a blending of setting, action, and character; and excellent nonstereotypic character portrayals. The second article, by Winifred L. Stoelting, "Time Past and Time Present: The Search for Viable Links in *The Chosen Place, The Timeless People* by Paule Marshall" (pp. 60-71), maintains that tragedy ensues for those generations in *The Chosen Place, The Timeless People* who refuse "to forge a viable link between the traditions of the past and the needs of the future."

Two articles on Paule Marshall also appear together in the Fall 1975 issue of *Negro American Literature Forum.* In "Architectural Imagery and Unity in Paule Marshall's *Brown Girl, Brownstones*" (pp. 67-70), Kimberly Benston, judging the novel to be only superficially unified thematically, sees a more important unifying element in the novel's imagery and symbolism. Of the seven major images or image clusters (light and dark, water, blindness, silence, color, machinery, and architecture) constantly used in the novel, architectural images are the most important. This imagery, posits Benston, "affects the novel as a unifying force on at least five major imaginative levels: (1) organization of the plot; (2) delineation of character; (3) definition of overall environment; (4) construction of the novel's language; and (5) creation of an all-inclusive metaphor for the novel."

Marcia Keizs, in the second article, "Themes and Style in the Works of Paule Marshall" (pp. 67, 71–76), argues that Marshall's Black female protagonists, unlike those in many novels by other Blacks, are not narrow and one-sided, and that it is through their complexities that Marshall develops her themes. In *Brown Girl, Brownstones,* for instance, the protagonist, Selina, as she comes in contact with her family and friends, is an embodiment of numerous complexities, around which Marshall develops the strength-vs.-weakness theme. In *The Chosen Place, The Timeless People,* an allegory of Western civilization, the female character Merle Kibona embodies the reconciliation attempt of the warring East and West. No less important than Marshall's themes is her style, which Keizs views as crisp, lucid, graceful, and detailed.

Ann Petry

Several good articles have been written about Petry and her works. David Dempsey, in "Uncle Tom's Ghost and the Literary Abolitionists," *Antioch Review* 6 (September 1946):442–48, views Ann Petry as one of several literary abolitionists writing in 1946 who do not include a lynching scene in their novels. She is considered to be one of the "bellwethers of a new trend" because in her novel *The Street* she presents a heroine who represents an emerging class of professionals. Petry's protagonist, Lutie Johnson, however, does not achieve success like the protagonists of other novels examined by Dempsey. She commits a murder and flees in fright—a fate, says Dempsey, presented by Petry "to show how segregation ultimately defeats the best in people, just as surely as it brings out the worst."

Marjorie Green's "Ann Petry Planned to Write," *Opportunity* 24 (Spring 1946):78–79, points out the adjustments Ann Petry made in her life to become a writer. Satisfying an urge to write, Petry left her job as a pharmacist in Connecticut to become a newspaper reporter in New York City, where she further enhanced her understanding of people by pursuing courses in psychology and psychiatry. After successfully publishing several short stories and being asked by Houghton Mifflin if she was working on a novel, Petry started writing *The Street,* for which she won Houghton Mifflin's $2,400 literary fellowship in 1945.

Thelma J. Shinn, in "Women in the Novels of Ann Petry," *Critique: Studies in Modern Fiction* 16:1 (1974):110-20, argues that women in Petry's novels, whether white or Black, are forced to conform to society's female stereotype no matter how much they struggle against it. This conformity, argues Shinn, results from "the sordidness of realities, the inequities and false illusions of society, and the inadequacies of the possibilities for women [which] rob strong and weak alike of a chance for personal development and a sense of security."

Toni Morrison and Alice Walker

Two prolific contemporary writers, Toni Morrison and Alice Walker, have received much recent critical attention. Their books have been widely reviewed in Black and women's periodicals as well as in establishment publications. Morrison and Walker have been frequently interviewed, and a body of scholarly criticism of their works is also beginning to develop. For example, a very useful bibliography, "Echoes from Small Town Ohio: A Toni Morrison Bibliography," by Robert Fikes, Jr., is now available, in *Obsidian: Black Literature in Review* 5:1&2 (Spring/Summer 1979):142-48. Citations of these materials are easily found by checking the usual reference indexes.

Dissertations

Several doctoral dissertations exist which include discussion of novels by Black American women: Clifford Doyl Harper's "A Study of the Disunity Theme in the Afro-American Experience: An Examination of Five Representative Novels" (Diss., Saint Louis University, 1972); D. H. Melhem's "Gwendolyn Brooks: Prophecy and Poetic Process" (Diss., City University of New York, 1976); Marie Katella Mootry's "Studies in Black Pastoral: Five Afro-American Writers" (Diss., Northwestern University, 1974); Priscilla Barbara Ann Ramsey's "A Study of Black Identity in 'Passing' Novels of the Nineteenth and Early Twentieth Centuries" (Diss., The American University, 1975); Carolyn Wedin Sylvander's "Jessie Redmon Fauset, Black American Writer: Her Relationships, Biographical and Literary, with Black and White Writers, 1910-1935" (Diss., The University of Wisconsin-Madison, 1976); and Mary Mabel Youman's "The Other Side of Harlem: The Middle-Class Novel and the New Negro Renaissance" (Diss., University of Kentucky, 1976). Not one of these dissertations is devoted entirely to the novels of a Black woman.

Harper includes Louise Meriwether's *Daddy Was a Number Runner* among four other novels by Black men in his discussion of the disunity theme; Melhem includes Brooks's *Maud Martha* as a piece of poetic prose in a study focusing primarily on Brooks's poetry; Mootry includes only Nella Larsen's novels among those of five Afro-American Black pastoral writers; Ramsey includes only the novels of Fauset and Larsen in her study spanning two centuries of "passing" novels; Sylvander includes extensive biographical information and information on Fauset's essays in her study; and Youman includes the novels of Jessie Fauset and Nella Larsen in her study of the middle-class novel.

23

Black Women Playwrights from Grimké to Shange: Selected Synopses of Their Works

JEANNE-MARIE A. MILLER

Early in American drama, white playwrights used misshapen Black images to help justify slavery; in the post–Civil War period, they used them to rationalize this nation's unfair treatment of Blacks. Consequently, slaves were often portrayed as living in an idyllic state; free Blacks were seen as wretched in their freedom; the comic shenanigans of Black servants on stage indicated their happiness in the role of servitude; Black men, by nature, were brutes; and Blacks of both sexes were exotic primitives. Since white playwrights had fashioned their own "truths" about Blacks, it was against such distortions as these that Black playwrights militated, out of necessity, in many of their plays. Black humanity, for the most part, had to be proved to whites.

But the "proving" has not been easy. Theatrical producers, who are usually white and male, are interested in scripts that promise commercial, if not critical, success. While many scripts by white playwrights may not meet this criterion, plays about the Black experience, articulated from a Black point of view that is alien to traditional, middle-class, and usually white theater audiences, have not been welcomed.

Black playwrights have suffered from this neglect, as well as from a lack of adequately equipped stages, and a paucity of talented directors, technicians, actors and actresses, and audiences. It has been mainly in community and university theaters catering to Black people, theaters reflecting a general consensus about the Black experience, that Black playwrights have been given a chance to grow.

While neither Black men nor Black women have had any real clout in the American theater, Black women playwrights have had to contend with the additional onus of sexism, since playwriting has been regarded as a profession for men. With all the barriers of racism and sexism arrayed against them, some Black women writers, nevertheless, have chosen drama as the form in which to express their creative talents and, when given the opportunity to mount their plays, have offered a unique insight into the Black experience.

As early as 1916, Angelina Weld Grimké offered to the public a full-length protest drama entitled *Rachel*,[1] produced in Washington, D.C., by the Drama Committee of the National Association for the Advancement of Colored People (NAACP).

Rachel is set in the early 1900s in the home of the Lovings, a struggling, genteel Black family living in the North, but with its origins in the South, where Rachel's father and half-brother were murdered by a lynch mob. In the North, the Lovings are still not free from oppression, though its form is more subtle. Because of their color, Rachel and her brother Tom, both well educated, cannot find the jobs for which they are qualified. Profoundly affected by an environment that seems to offer no hope and distressed at the thought of an unjust God who permits such conditions to exist, Rachel vows never to marry or to bring children into the world.

A pioneer work, this early protest piece employs an almost unvaried declamatory style. The speeches are, at times, too long, and some of the coincidences are not altogether convincing. *Rachel* succeeds, however, as a protest drama, with an arrow-straight message.

Many early Black women playwrights used the one-act-play form to explore a variety of subjects, a few of them still surprisingly contemporary. One-act plays, often the initial efforts of beginning dramatists, were encouraged in the 1920s, when *The Crisis* and *Opportunity* magazines offered prizes for the best short plays treating the Black experience. The plays—many of them written by Black women—that thus found their way on to the pages of these publications could not have been published had they been full-length works. In some cases, however, the one-act play may also have been the most suitable form for the author's style or purpose.

Like Grimké's *Rachel*, many of the early plays by Black women treated racial injustice. Marita Bonner, in *The Purple Flower* (1928), published in *The Crisis*, employed allegory to suggest the necessity of revolution as a means of effecting change in the demeaning situation of Black people in America.[2] The White Devils, artful creatures who dwell on all sides of the high hill of Somewhere, successfully prevent the Us's, who live in the valley, from reaching the purple Flower-of-Life-At-Its-

Fullest that grows on the top of the hill. Georgia Douglas Johnson, perhaps best known as a poet, turned to Black folk characters and the Black idiom in writing a protest drama entitled *A Sunday Morning in the South* (c. 1925).[3] In this work the principal characters are an old Black woman and her nineteen-year-old grandson, who wants to study law. Shortly after the grandson is taken by the police to be questioned about the rape of a white girl, a crime of which he is innocent, he is lynched by a mob of whites. In *Mine Eyes Have Seen* (1918), Alice Dunbar-Nelson questions the loyalty that a Black man owes a country that has spewed hatred on him.[4] In the end, love of humanity and pride in the history of the Black race's contributions to the preservation of that humanity are shown to be more important than personal considerations.

Problems of special concern to women were also dramatized. In *They That Sit in Darkness* (1919), Mary Burrill wrote about the right of women to have access to information about birth control.[5] This one-acter, set in the South, focuses on a thirty-eight-year-old poverty-stricken Black woman, six of whose eight children sleep in a single bedroom. When the woman dies and her daughter must forfeit her chance for an education at Tuskegee Institute in order to assume the mother's role, the poverty cycle is continued. Though the father does not appear in the play, he is characterized as hard-working and responsible. It is the state laws forbidding the dissemination of birth control information that shackle this family to a life of want.

Miscegenation, a popular theme for American playwrights, was the subject of a short play by Myrtle Smith Livingston. In contrast to other early plays on the subject, *For Unborn Children* (1926) treats a Black man–white woman relationship rather than the more frequently portrayed Black woman–white man relationship.[6] The grandmother of the young Black lawyer who is romantically involved with a white woman disapproves of his choice. An emerging theme is Black women's feeling of rejection when a Black man marries a white woman. Before giving himself up to a white mob that has come for him, the lawyer tells his fiancée to marry a man of her own race; he is now prepared for death. Although the play is interesting, it is weakened by this implausible ending.

Lighter themes, too, were treated by these pioneer women playwrights. Church politics was the focus of Ruth Gaines-Shelton's *The Church Fight* (1925), which uses allegorical names for its characters.[7] This little play unintentionally points out the importance of the church in Black life and at the same time depicts an experience that transcends race. Eulalie Spence, whose plays won several prizes in the middle and late 1920s, wrote *The Starter* (1926), a comedy about a Harlem romance.[8]

The play is about an elevator starter who wishes to withdraw his proposal of marriage to his sweetheart when he learns that her views on marriage differ from his.

Other early-twentieth-century plays by Black women display their varied interests and the breadth of their talents. Georgia Douglas Johnson's *Plumes: A Folk Tragedy*, first-prize-winner of the 1927 *Opportunity* Magazine play contest, makes use of the superstitious background of its Black characters.[9] Charity Brown must choose between the doctor's advice about her young daughter's chances of surviving an illness and the advice of a friend who prophesies by reading coffee grounds in a cup. Obsessed with the desire of giving her daughter a "decent" burial, Charity hesitates, because the funeral and the operation cost exactly the same. While she pauses, the child dies.

An early attempt of a Black woman playwright to employ an African setting and theme was Thelma Duncan's *The Death Dance* (1923), set in a Vai village on the West Coast of Africa.[10] The story concerns Kamo, who is accused of a crime he did not commit and eventually acquitted. Tribal drugs and dancing lend authenticity to the work. In 1929, May Miller [Sullivan] wrote *Graven Images*, a mythological work with an ancient Egyptian setting.[11] Its central character is Eliezer, a brown offspring of Moses and his Ethiopian wife.

Not the least important of these early works were those whose purpose was to show the achievements and contributions of the Black race to humanity. Among these were Dorothy C. Guinn's *Out of the Dark* (1924), a pageant chronicling the history of Blacks in Africa before American slavery, the enslavement, and the contributions of the slaves to American culture.[12] In Frances Gunner's *The Light of the Women* (1930), Ethiopia celebrates Black women of the past—the Slave Mother, symbolic of the mothers of the race, Sojourner Truth, Harriet Tubman, and others—as well as contemporary women who served both their race and their country.[13]

The history plays written by Black women were not restricted to a particular period or place. Maud Cuney-Hare, in *Antar of Araby* (1929), for example, dramatized the bravery, love, and chivalry of Antar, the Black warrior poet of the sixth century and one of the founders of Arab literature.[14] May Miller's *Christophe's Daughters* (1935) was set in Haiti.[15] Both Miller and Georgia Douglas Johnson dramatized aspects of the lives of Black American historical figures, such as Frederick Douglass, Harriet Tubman, Sojourner Truth, and William and Ellen Craft.[15]

The efforts of these Black women forerunners helped to light the way for later playwrights, and the civil rights movement of the 1950s and 1960s and the Black consciousness movement of the late 1960s and early

1970s sensitized some members of the white theater audience to dramas by and about Blacks. Not to be discounted, however, is the increase in Black theater audiences who expected to see authentic dramas about Black life. One of the first Black women playwrights to attract attention during this period was Alice Childress.

Like her predecessors, Childress, in her first published play, *Florence* (1950), used the one-act form.[17] In the waiting room of a railroad station in the South her principal character, a Black woman of low economic circumstances, undergoes a change of mind through a chance encounter with a white woman. Instead of going to New York City to bring Florence, her fledgling actress daughter, home, the Black woman sends her travel money to the young woman so that she can remain in the city, continue to pursue her career, and, perhaps, succeed.

In *Trouble in Mind* (1955), a full-length work, produced in an off-Broadway theater, Childress again focuses on a strong Black woman, a veteran of show business named Wiletta Mayer.[18] Wiletta objects to the unrealistic role she has been assigned to play in "Chaos in Belleville," a melodrama with an antilynching theme articulated from a white point of view. She knows that taking such a stand will result in her termination from the production, but she feels the freedom of giving vent to her long-repressed feelings about prejudice in the American theater.

Trouble in Mind is a mixture of humor and sadness, in which Childress displays her ability to combine teaching and delighting—a combination which characterizes another full-length play, *Wine in the Wilderness*, first presented on television in Boston, Massachusetts, in 1969.

Wine in the Wilderness, which sprang from the Black revolutionary period of the 1960s, brings together inner-city and middle-class Blacks who learn about their identities with the help of a ghetto heroine named Tomorrow Marie.[19] She is sensible, warm, and unpretentious, in contrast to the middle-class types who equate Blackness with such superficial trappings as rhetoric, use of the Black idiom, and African *objets d'art*, but who, in reality, are empty and artificial. What really matters, they learn in the course of the play, is what is *inside* a person.

Other plays by Childress include *Mojo* (1971) and *String* (1971). In *Mojo*, a two-character play whose theme is Black love, a serious illness motivates a divorced woman to visit her former husband, who is now involved with a white woman, and they rediscover each other.[20] In *String* (1971), a short play based on Guy de Maupassant's story entitled "A Piece of String," an innocent man with odd habits is accused falsely of theft at a Black Neighborhood Association picnic in New York City.[21] Again interspersing comedy and sadness, Childress treats the timeless subject of dignity and a man's feeble and futile attempts to hold onto it. And in *Wedding Band* (1973), a full-length play set in South Carolina in 1918, she focuses on a romance between two quite ordinary people, who are, however, forbidden by law to love, because one is white and the other, Black.[22]

Undoubtedly, the best known Black woman playwright is Lorraine Hansberry, whose *A Raisin in the Sun* burst forth on Broadway in 1959 and won critical acclaim and the New York Drama Critics' Circle Award as the best play of the 1958–59 theater season.[23] With this production Hansberry became the first Black woman to have a play presented on Broadway, and *A Raisin in the Sun* is perhaps the most famous play written by a Black American.

Lena Younger, who has presided over her Chicago household since the death of her husband, hopes to bring to fruition her family's long-deferred dream of purchasing a home with light and space enough for everyone. Her husband's legacy—his insurance money—acts as a catalyst, projecting the family into a situation that not only causes dramatic conflicts but tests their characters. The Younger children—Walter, Jr., now thirty-five years old, and Beneatha, a young woman in college—have dreams of their own. Walter, tired of chauffeuring and barely making ends meet, wants to own his own liquor store, a dream that his mother cannot share, partly because of her religious beliefs. Beneatha, a liberated woman interested in her African heritage, wants to be a doctor. Ruth, the daughter-in-law, a bit worn from life's struggles, wishes to help her husband gain the "manhood" or self-respect he is seeking. She also acts as a peacemaker between the generations. Joseph Asagai, Beneatha's friend, dreams of a Black-ruled Africa. *A Raisin in the Sun* is a drama of affirmation.

Structurally, *A Raisin in the Sun* is a conventional realistic, well-made play, with emotional tension throughout. The work builds piece by piece, alternating laughter and tears, until the main crisis is reached when Walter, who has blamed his wife, his mother, and himself for his failure, comes to realize that outward forces, in the form of the American dream, have driven him. As the play ends, Walter, with a boost from Lena Younger, has moved in the direction of "being a man." He has asserted himself.

Five years after *A Raisin in the Sun*, Hansberry's *The Sign in Sidney Brustein's Window* (1964) appeared on Broadway.[24] In this work, Hansberry treats the private woes of Sidney, who has yet to find the right dream, and Iris, who is struggling to be liberated from the confining role that her husband has required her to play. The sign in Sidney's window indicates that he has been persuaded to campaign for a friend who is running as a reform candidate. A number of characters enter the home of Iris and Sidney; one of them, a Black man, eloquently articulates the pains of his race. At the end of the play, despite the dishonesty of the candidate he has supported and his gloom at the suicide of his sister-in-law, Sidney is moved to make something strong of this latest sorrow. Again there is affirmation and hope.

In *The Sign in Sidney Brustein's Window*, Hansberry created a framework in which her characters could comment on the disorders and agitations of contemporary life. It is a drama of ideas rather than of action.

Hansberry, who died of cancer in 1965, while *The Sign in Sidney Brustein's Window* was still running, left several works in progress, as well as some completed plays that had not been produced. Among these was *Les Blancs*, whose final text was adapted by her literary executor and former husband, Robert Nemiroff, and produced on Broadway in 1970.[25] Set in a Mission compound—a hospital established in Africa by a European minister, seemingly suggested by Albert Schweitzer—and in the hut of a tribal elder, the play involves conflicting ideas during a period of change in Sub-Sahara Africa. The Blacks who once asked peacefully for freedom from the colonialists are now staging a revolution. The play focuses on three Black African brothers, who espouse different attitudes about Africa.

In a sentimental, unproduced fable, *What Use Are Flowers?*, Hansberry has an old hermit who has lived away from civilization for twenty years find some wild children, who, before an unnamed holocaust, were brought to the edge of the forest by someone who wanted the human race to continue.[26] The hermit sets about the uneasy task of teaching the children the rudiments of civilization. Before he dies, one of them invents the wheel.

Of Hansberry's unproduced plays, the most interesting is *The Drinking Gourd*, which was commissioned by NBC.[27] While the work reveals the horrors and cruelties of slavery, it is, in Hansberry's own words, "a serious treatment of family relationships by a slave-owning family and their slaves."[28]

Continuing the tradition of writing in a straightforward, realistic manner about the Black experience, especially as that experience has affected women, is J. E. Franklin, whose *Black Girl* was produced off-Broadway in 1971.[29] Franklin concentrates on a Black girl on the threshold of womanhood whose aspirations conflict with the lack of ambition of her two older half-sisters who have succumbed to their suffocating environment. She also meets with the opposition of her mother. The grandmother, who lives in the home, enables the girl to take advantage of an opportunity to leave home, finish her education, and fulfill her dream of being a dancer. The mother eventually confesses her fear that her daughters' lives might turn out like her own.

The middle 1960s produced a Black woman playwright who strayed from the straightforward method and did not use, generally speaking, the conventional techniques employed by the majority of her predecessors, as well as her contemporaries. Instead, Adrienne Kennedy's writing is that of a poet, using image, metaphor, and layers of consciousness. She is a gifted writer with a unique dramatic imagination. Her major dramatic creations, all one-act plays, are, seemingly, autobiographical projections of her inner state, surreal fantasies based on the central character's problems with identity and self-knowledge. Kennedy's technique includes a single character—represented, at times, by more than one performer—and imagery used in kaleidoscopic fashion.

Kennedy's *Funnyhouse of a Negro* (1962) is about the pressures of being Black in America.[30] Sarah, the central character, is a young, sensitive Black woman troubled with problems about love, God, parents, color, and, most of all, identity. The dominant symbol is kinky hair. Unable to accept her hair, her skin color, and the problems surrounding them both, the young woman destroys herself in the end.

In *A Rat's Mass* (1965), Kennedy conveys impressionistically the attractive, powerful white world symbolized by the character Rosemary.[31] Rosemary entices Blacks (Brother and Sister Rat, who were once two pale Negro children), who too easily and innocently fall in love with her and all that she represents. Because of their unhealthy relationship with her, they destroy themselves while she supervises the destruction.

In *The Owl Answers* (1969), one of a duo of plays collected under the title *Cities in Bezique*, a young mulatto woman cannot find her place in either the Black or the white world.[32] The symbol of hair is again dominant—the kinky hair of the Black mother and the long, silky hair of the dead white father. Birds are also symbolic, the dove perhaps representing the soul of the dead father, and the owl, the destruction into which the troubled woman is careening. The second of the two plays, *A Beast Story*, does not emphasize relationships between the Black and white races, but suggests, through images, a young woman's turmoil involving sex, family relationships, and Christianity, among other things.[29]

The most representative of the Black revolutionary women playwrights is Sonia Sanchez. Sanchez, also a well-known poet, has used the one-act-play form almost exclusively, following closely the Black agitprop method of short play forms, simplistic action, and direct language, designed to convey the message of the play to Black people as effectively as possible. Sanchez's plays can be described as Black moralities.

In *The Bronx Is Next* (1968), a Black woman, abused by Black men in the past, plans to teach her two sons to love the women of their race.[34] The Black woman and the white policeman who pays her for sexual pleasures die in a fire set by Black militants.

The Bronx Is Next was to be the first part of a trilogy by Sanchez, who felt that one solution to the problem of Blacks packed into the ghettos of cities like New York was for them to get back to the land. Each succeeding play was to be longer than the previous one, culminating in Blacks' settling some place.[35] The planned trilogy has not been completed, and Sanchez's ideas about the mass movement from the cities to the land may have changed. One of the subjects alluded to, however, in *The Bronx Is Next*—the problems peculiar to Black women—became the theme of other plays, such as *Sister Son/ji* (1969) and *Uh, Huh; But How Do It Free Us?* (1974).

Sister Son/ji has a single character, a Black woman in her fifties, who, in flashbacks, reveals "what i was/shd have been and never can be again."[36] The flashbacks first reveal a young woman who has walked out of her class at Hunter College because she felt that the white teacher did not respect the three Blacks in the class. During the age of Black Consciousness, she and her husband are driven apart, for he is out all week organizing and spends the rest of his time unwinding—without her. Her thirteen-year-old son, a warrior, is killed during the revolution. At the end of the play, the major character is again an old woman who has her "sweet/astringent memories becuz we dared to pick up the day and shake its tail until it became evening. a time for us. blk/ness. blk people."

In *Uh, Huh; But How Do It Free Us?*, a long play with several parts, Sanchez courageously focuses her attention on the Black man–Black woman relationship: the self-centered Black man with two wives; the Black petty criminals who prey on their own communities and do not respect their women; and the Black militant who neglects his own woman for a white woman.[37] The message to be derived from the play is directed at both sexes: Black men must rid themselves of these undesirable qualities, and Black women must patiently help to bring about this change.

Like Sanchez, Martie Charles is best categorized as a playwright in the Black revolutionary traditon. The heroine of *Jamimma* (1972) is a decent, shy, and intelligent young Black woman who is devoted to an unfaithful young man, Omar Butler I, a Black radical and mostly unemployed musician.[38] Jamimma's older sister, a no-nonsense, self-supporting woman, does not share Omar's revolutionary ideas; drugs also enter the picture.

More didactic in tone than *Jamimma* is Charles's *Black Cycle* (1971), which is concerned with the problems of a young woman who revolts against the white-oriented desires of her mother in quest of her own identity.[39] In *Job Security* (1970), the playwright turns to the community problem of teachers who are more committed to preserving their jobs than to teaching their students.[40] *Job Security* depicts the effects of such a system on a bright, sensitive, but troubled, girl.

A very original, brilliantly conceived work by a Black woman playwright made its debut on Broadway during the 1976–77 theater season, and achieved both critical and commercial success. Ntozake Shange's *For Colored Girls Who Have Considered Suicide/When the Rainbow is Enuf* consists of some "twenty odd poems," each a playlet, which form a single statement, a choreopoem.[41] The characters are seven nameless Black women, each identified by the color of her dress. Shange sets out to "sing a black girl's song. . ." that celebrates being both Black and a woman, a song whose theme is the courage of women who have experienced, among other things, rape, unrequited love, and the murder of their children, but who have come through it all. Shange's work is ironic, bitter, humorous, and brutal. It also shows the loyalties of women to one another and ends on an affirmative note: "i found god in myself/ & i loved her/ i loved her fiercely."

Black women playwrights, then, have proved to be multidimensional and not easily defined. Their plays, whether one-acters or, as many of them were after 1950, full-length, have taken various forms: protest, dramas, comedies, tragedies, melodramas, dramas of ideas, moralities, surreal fantasies, choreopoems. Like Black male playwrights, they have written almost exclusively about the Black experience in a realistic manner. Their themes and their treatment of Black women characters, however, have differed from those of other playwrights. Often in plays by Black men, the happiness of Black women or their "completeness" in life depends upon strong Black men. In contrast to white-authored dramas, where Black women have usually appeared as devoted servants to white families, as matriarchs, or as dumb, incompetent people, Black women playwrights have told the Black woman's story—from slavery to freedom —from her point of view. The plays have focused on her tragedies; her struggles; her dreams for herself, her family, and her race. Their images of Black women are usually positive, and their female characters, for the most part, have great moral strength.

It is particularly important that Black women playwrights, in promoting humanistic values, have contributed to the moral growth of society. Often earning their living as educators, writing in other genres as well, and sometimes receiving grants and college or university posts as writers-in-residence, Black women playwrights, handed the torch from preceding generations, have continued to move forward, to develop, to expand, and to contribute to the literature of the American theater.

BIOGRAPHICAL-BIBLIOGRAPHICAL NOTES

Marita Bonner, born and educated in Massachusetts, attended Radcliffe College. She taught English in Washington, D.C., and was, for a time, a frequent contributor to *The Crisis* and *Opportunity* magazines. *The Purple Flower* (1928), published originally in *The Crisis*, has been anthologized in *Black Theater, U.S.A.*, edited by James V. Hatch and Ted Shine (New York: The Free Press, 1974). *The Pot Maker* appeared in *Opportunity* (February 1927), and *Exit, An Illusion*, in *The Crisis* (October 1929).

Mary Burrill taught English in Washington, D.C. Her play, *They That Sit in Darkness* (1919), which appeared first in the *Birth Control Review*, has been republished in *Black Theater, U.S.A.*

Martie Charles (Martha Evans Charles), born and raised in New York City, was an actress and writer for the New Lafayette Theatre in Harlem, which attempted, from 1966 to 1972, to create a Black theater involved in and contributing to the Black community. Charles's play *Black Cycle* (1971) was published in the *Black Drama Anthology*, edited by Woodie King and Ron Milner (New York: New American Library, 1971). *Job Security* (1970) may be found in *Black Theater, U.S.A.*

Alice Childress, born in Charleston, South Carolina, began her career as an actress, director, and writer at the American Negro Theater in Harlem. *Florence* (1950) was published in *Masses and Mainstream 3* (October 1950). *Trouble in Mind* (1955) has been anthologized in *Black Theater: A 20th Century Collection of the Work of Its Best Playwrights*, edited by Lindsay Patterson (New York: Dodd, Mead & Company, 1971). *Wine in the Wilderness* (1969), published in New York by the Dramatists Play Service, Inc., has been anthologized in *Black Theater, U.S.A. Mojo* (1971) and *String* (1971) were published together by Dramatists Play Service, Inc. In 1973 *Wedding Band* was published in New York by Samuel French. Other published plays by Childress include *The World on a Hill* (1968), in *Plays to Remember* (New York: Macmillan, 1968); a scene from *The African Garden*, in

Black Scenes, edited by Alice Childress (Garden City, N.Y.: Double-day, 1971); and *When the Rattlesnake Sounds* (New York: Coward, 1975).

Maud Cuney-Hare, born in Galveston, Texas, and best known as a musician, studied at the New England Conservatory in Boston, Massachusetts, and became Director of Music for the Deaf, Dumb, and Blind Institute of Texas. In Boston she established the Musical Art Studio and sponsored a Little Theatre movement that involved Blacks. Her play, *Antar of Araby* (1929), was published in *Plays and Pageants from the Life of the Negro,* edited by Willis Richardson (Washington, D.C.: Associated Publishers, Inc., 1930).

Alice Dunbar-Nelson was born in New Orleans, Louisiana, and was educated in the public schools of that city and at Straight College, as well as at several universities in the North. She taught school in New Orleans; Brooklyn, New York; and Wilmington, Delaware. In addition to poetry and fiction, she wrote a column in the *Pittsburgh Courier.* She was the wife of poet Paul Laurence Dunbar. Her short play *Mine Eyes Have Seen* (1918), originally published in *The Crisis,* may be found in *Black Theater, U.S.A.*

Thelma Duncan, born in St. Louis, Missouri, had her play *The Death Dance* produced by the Howard University Players in 1923, during a period (1921–24) when a special effort was being made to encourage the writing and producing of plays treating the Black experience. She was educated at Howard University and Columbia University and later taught music in North Carolina. Duncan's *The Death Dance* (1923) was published in *Plays of Negro Life,* edited by Alain Locke and Montgomery Gregory (New York: Harper, 1927). Another play, *Sacrifice* (1930), was published in *Plays and Pageants from the Life of the Negro. Black Magic* (1931) was anthologized in *The Year Book of Short Plays,* 1st series, edited by Claude Merton Wise and Lee Owen Snook (Evanston, Ill.: Row Peterson and Company, 1931).

J. E. Franklin, in addition to being a playwright, is an essayist, a writer of short fiction, and an educator. A native of Houston, she received her B.A. degree from the University of Texas. Among the honors she has received are the Media Workshop Award (1971), Drama Desk Award (1972), a New York State Council on the Arts Public Service Award (1972), and special recognition at a national Afro-American writers' conference held at Howard University in 1974. *Black Girl,* her best-known play, was published in 1971 by Dramatists Play Service, Inc., and in 1977 by the Howard University Press.

Ruth Gaines-Shelton won second prize for *The Church Fight* (1925) in *The Crisis* magazine contest of 1925. This play has been antholo-gized in *Black Theater, U.S.A.*

Angelina Weld Grimké was born in Boston, Massachusetts, and was
educated at various schools, including Girls' Latin School and the
Boston Normal School of Gymnastics. She taught English in
Washington, D.C. Grimké also wrote poetry and short stories. *Rachel*
(1920), originally published by Cornhill, may be found in *Black
Theater, U.S.A.* For a discussion of *Rachel* and Grimké's unfinished
play *Mara*, see my own "Angelina Weld Grimké: Playwright and
Poet," *CLA Journal* 21:4 (June 1978).
Dorothy C. Guinn wrote *Out of the Dark* (1924) to tell the romantic story
of Blacks; the play was published in *Plays and Pageants from the
Life of the Negro.*
Frances Gunner was Secretary of the Y.W.C.A. in Brooklyn, New York.
Her discovery that Black women knew little about their achieve-
ments encouraged her to write *The Light of the Woman* (1930). This
play was anthologized in *Plays and Pageants from the Life of the
Negro.*
Lorraine Hansberry was born in Chicago, Illinois. At age twenty-nine she
became the youngest American, the fifth woman, and the first Black
playwright to win the New York Drama Critics' Circle Award for the
Best Play of the Year (1959). Published in 1959 by Random House,
and in 1961 by the New American Library, *A Raisin in the Sun* has
also been widely anthologized. Some of the publications in which it
appears are: *Black Theater: A 20th Century Collection*, edited by
Lindsay Patterson (New York: Dodd, Mead, 1971); *Contemporary
Black Drama: From* A Raisin in the Sun *to* No Place to Be
Somebody, edited by Clinton F. Oliver and Stephanie Sills (New
York: Charles Scribner's Sons, 1971); and *A Raisin in the Sun and
The Sign in Sidney Brustein's Window* (New York: New American
Library, 1966). *(The Sign in Sidney Brustein's Window* was first
published by Random House in 1965.) *The Drinking Gourd* (1969),
Les Blancs (1970), and *What Use Are Flowers?* (1969) may be found
in *Les Blancs: The Collected Last Plays of Lorraine Hansberry*,
edited by Robert Nemiroff (New York: Random House, 1972;
Vintage Books, 1973). *The Drinking Gourd* also appears in *Black
Theater, U.S.A. Les Blancs* was published by Samuel French in 1972.
To Be Young, Gifted and Black (1969), composed of scenes from
Hansberry's plays as well as excerpts from her speeches, letters,
journals, and diaries, is available in several editions (Englewood
Cliffs, N.J.: Prentice-Hall, 1969; New York: New American Library,
1969; New York: Samuel French, 1971). For a contemporary
appraisal of Hansberry's legacy by writers, scholars, and artists, see
Freedomways 19:4 (1979), which also contains a comprehensive
bibliography on Hansberry.

Georgia Douglas Johnson, born in Atlanta, Georgia, and educated at the
Atlanta High School and Oberlin College, was a published poet as
well as a playwright. A long-time resident of Washington, D.C., she
made her home a center for Black literature gatherings. Her play
Blue Blood (1926) was published in *Fifty More Contemporary One-
Act Plays*, edited by Frank Shay (New York: Appleton, 1928).
Plumes, which was anthologized in *Plays of Negro Life*, has been
published in *The New Negro Renaissance: An Anthology*, edited by
Arthur P. Davis and Michael Peplow (New York: Holt, Rinehart and
Winston, 1975). *Frederick Douglass* (1935) and *William and Ellen
Craft* (1935) were published in *Negro History in Thirteen Plays*,
edited by Willis Richardson and May Miller (Washington, D.C.:
Associated Publishers, 1935). *A Sunday Morning in the South* (1925)
has been published in *Black Theater, U.S.A.*

Adrienne Kennedy, the daughter of a school teacher and a social worker,
lived in Cleveland, Ohio, and attended Ohio State University. In
1962 she joined Edward Albee's workshop. In addition to the Obie
Award that she won for *Funnyhouse of a Negro*, performed off-
Broadway in 1964, she has received grants from Rockefeller,
Guggenheim, and the National Endowment for the Arts. Kennedy
has also written novels, short stories, and poems. Her plays *A Beast
Story* (1969) and *The Owl Answers* (1969) were published together
under the title *Cities in Bezique* (New York: Samuel French, 1969).
Both plays were also published in *Kuntu Drama: Plays of the African
Continuum*, edited by Paul Carter Harrison (New York: Grove Press,
1974). *The Owl Answers* has been anthologized in *Black Theater,
U.S.A. A Rat's Mass* was published in *New Black Playwrights: An
Anthology*, edited by William Couch, Jr. (Baton Rouge: Louisiana
State University Press, 1968). *Funnyhouse of a Negro* was published
by Samuel French in 1962 and may also be found in *Contemporary
Black Drama*. With John Lennon and Victor Spinetti, Kennedy
wrote *The Lennon Play: In His Own Write* (New York: Simon and
Schuster, 1968). Kennedy's *Lesson in a Dead Language* (1967) was
published in *Collision Course*, edited by Edward Parone (New York:
Vintage, 1968); and *Sun* (1969) was published in *Spontaneous
Combustion*, edited by Rochelle Owens, *The Winter Repertory #6*
(New York: Winter House, 1972).

Myrtle Smith Livingston, born in Holly Grove, Arkansas, attended
Howard University and taught school in Colorado and at Lincoln
University in Jefferson City, Missouri. *For Unborn Children*,
published in *The Crisis* in 1926, may be found in *Black Theater,
U.S.A.*

Sonia Sanchez was born in Birmingham, Alabama, and was graduated from Hunter College. She has taught at San Francisco State College and Rutgers University, and has written and published poetry, plays, and short stories. *The Bronx Is Next*, published originally in *The Drama Review* 12:4 (Summer 1968), has been anthologized in *Cavalcade: Negro American Writing from 1760 to the Present*, edited by Arthur P. Davis and Saunders Redding (Boston: Houghton Mifflin, 1970). *Sister Son/ji* (1969) may be found in *New Plays from the Black Theatre*, edited by Ed Bullins (New York: Bantam, 1969). *Dirty Hearts* (1971) was published in *Scripts* (November 1971), and *Malcolm Man Don't Live Here No More* (1970) was published in *Black Theatre*, No. 6 (1972). *Uh, Huh; But How Do It Free Us?* (1973) has been anthologized in *The New Lafayette Theatre Presents*, edited by Ed Bullins (Garden City, N.Y.: Anchor Books, 1974).

Ntozake Shange received a B.A. degree from Barnard College and an M.A. degree in American Studies from the University of Southern California. She has written for numerous publications including *Black Scholar, Yardbird Reader*, and *Third World Women*. Her play *A Photograph: A Still Life with Shadows/A Photograph: A Study in Cruelty* (1977) was produced by the Public Theatre in New York City. With Jessica Hagedorn and Thulani Davis, she wrote and performed in *Where the Mississippi Meets the Amazon*, presented by Joseph Papp at the Public Theater Cabaret. Shange's *Spell #7* was produced at the Public Theatre in 1979. To date, only *For Colored Girls Who Have Considered Suicide/When the Rainbow Is Enuf* (1976) has been published (New York: Macmillan, 1977; Bantam, 1980).

Eulalie Spence, born in the West Indies, came to the United States as a child. In 1937 she received her B.A. degree from Teachers College and in 1939, her M.A. degree from Columbia University. *The Starter* (1927) was published in *Plays of Negro Life. Fools Errand* (1927) and *Foreign Mail* (1927) were published separately by Samuel French. *Undertow*, which appeared in *Carolina Magazine* in April 1929, has been anthologized in *Black Theater, U.S.A.*

May Miller [Sullivan] was born in Washington, D.C., graduated from Howard University, and taught speech and drama in Baltimore, Maryland. With Willis Richardson, she edited *Negro History in Thirteen Plays* (1935). Among her published verse are several volumes of poetry: *Into the Closing* (1959), *Poems* (1962), and *The Clearing and Beyond* (1972). One of her plays, *Scratches*, was published in *Carolina Magazine* (April 1929). *Riding the Goat* (1929) and *Graven Images* (1929) were published in *Plays and Pageants from the Life of the Negro. Graven Images* may also be found in *Black Theater, U.S.A.* Several of her plays, *Christophe's Daughters*

(1935), *Harriet Tubman* (1935), *Samory* (1935), and *Sojourner Truth* (1935), were anthologized in *Negro History in Thirteen Plays*.

NOTES

¹*Rachel* (Boston: The Cornhill Company, 1920).

²*Black Theater, U.S.A.: Forty-Five Plays by Black Americans, 1847-1974*, ed. James W. Hatch and Ted Shine (New York: The Free Press, 1974), pp. 201-7.

³Ibid., pp. 211-17.

⁴Ibid., pp. 173-77.

⁵Ibid., pp. 178-83.

⁶Ibid., pp. 184-87.

⁷Ibid., pp. 188-91.

⁸*Plays of Negro Life: A Source Book of Native American Drama*, ed. Alain Locke and Montgomery Gregory (1927; rpt. Westport, Conn.: Negro Universities Press, 1970), pp. 205-14.

⁹Ibid., pp. 287-99.

¹⁰Ibid., pp. 321-31.

¹¹*Plays and Pageants from the Life of the Negro*, ed. Willis Richardson (Washington, D.C.: Associated Publishers, Inc., 1930), pp. 109-37.

¹²Ibid., pp. 305-30.

¹³Ibid., pp. 333-42.

¹⁴Ibid., pp. 27-74.

¹⁵*Negro History in Thirteen Plays*, ed. Willis Richardson and May Miller (Washington, D.C.: Associated Publishers, Inc., 1935), pp. 241-64.

¹⁶See May Miller's "Harriet Tubman" and "Sojourner Truth" and Georgia Douglas Johnson's "Frederick Douglass" and "William and Ellen Craft" in *Negro History in Thirteen Plays*, pp. 265-88, 313-33, 143-62, and 163-86.

¹⁷*Masses and Mainstream* 3 (October 1950):34-47.

¹⁸*Black Theater: A 20th Century Collection of the Work of Its Best Playwrights*, ed. Lindsay Patterson (New York: Dodd, Mead & Company, 1971), pp. 135-74. *Trouble in Mind* won the Obie Award for the best original off-Broadway play of the 1955-56 theater season.

In 1952 Childress's *Gold Through the Trees* had been presented off-Broadway at the Club Baron in Harlem. This unpublished work depicts the Black experience in Africa, the United States, Haiti, and other places where Blacks have been enslaved, and its theme is the Black liberation movement.

[19]*Wine in the Wilderness* (New York: Dramatists Play Service, Inc., 1969).

[20]*Mojo and String* (New York: Dramatists Play Service, Inc., 1971), pp. 3–22.

[21]Ibid., pp. 25–50.

[22]*Wedding Band* (New York: Samuel French, Inc., 1973).

[23]*Black Theater: A 20th Century Collection of the Work of Its Best Playwrights,* pp. 221–76.

[24]*A Raisin in the Sun and The Sign in Sidney Brustein's Window* (New York: New American Library, 1966), pp. 186–318.

[25]*Les Blancs: The Collected Last Plays of Lorraine Hansberry,* ed. Robert Nemiroff (New York: Vintage Books, 1973), pp. 47–186.

[26]Ibid., pp. 323–70.

[27]Ibid., pp. 187–313. *The Drinking Gourd* was never produced by NBC.

[28]Ibid., p. 193.

[29]*Black Girl* (New York: Dramatists Play Service, 1971).

[30]*Contemporary Black Drama: From* A Raisin in the Sun *to* No Place to Be Somebody, ed. Clinton F. Oliver and Stephanie Sills (New York: Charles Scribner's Sons, 1971), pp. 187–205.

[31]*New Black Playwrights,* ed. William Couch, Jr. (Baton Rouge, La.: Louisiana State University Press, 1968), pp. 61–69.

[32]*Cities in Bezique* (New York: Samuel French, Inc., 1969), pp. 3–29.

[33]Ibid., pp. 31–43.

[34]*The Drama Review* 12 (Summer 1968):78–83.

[35]*The New Lafayette Theatre Presents,* ed. Ed Bullins (Garden City, N.Y.: Anchor Press/Doubleday, 1974), pp. 161–63.

[36]*New Plays from the Black Theater,* ed. Ed Bullins (New York: Bantam, 1969), pp. 97–107.

[37]*The New Lafayette Theatre Presents,* pp. 161–215.

[38]The typescript for *Jamimma,* which to date has not been published, can be found in the Hatch-Billops Archives, 491 Broadway, New York, NY 10012. For critical reviews of *Jamimma,* see Jean Carey Bond, "Love and the Black Woman Explored in 'Jamimma,'" *The New York Amsterdam News,* June 10, 1972, and "Jamimma," *Variety,* May 31, 1972 (NYPL, Theater Collection, Lincoln Center Library and Museum for the Performing Arts, Collection of Newspaper Clippings of Dramatic Criticism, 1971–72).

[39]*Black Drama Anthology,* ed. Woodie King and Ron Milner (New York: New American Library, 1971), pp. 525–51.

[40]*Black Theater, U.S.A.,* pp. 765–71.

[41]*For Colored Girls Who Have Considered Suicide/When the Rainbow Is Enuf: A Choreopoem* (New York: Macmillan, 1977).

24

American Black Women Composers: A Selected Annotated Bibliography

ORA WILLIAMS, THELMA WILLIAMS, DORA WILSON, and RAMONA MATTHEWSON

One very positive result of Black and women's studies programs has been a heightened awareness, especially among Black women, that the cultural contributions of American Black women are being ignored or forgotten. Among those neglected are American Black women composers. When I began looking for their compositions nine years ago, I encountered great difficulty. For one thing, I was interested in all musical styles: classical, romantic, twentieth-century, arrangements of folk songs, jazz, blues, and popular works. However, whenever I asked librarians for help in tracing the works of Florence Price, Margaret Bonds, or Philippa Schuyler, I was sent to the "Jazz" or "Spiritual" references. The self-assured librarians seemed to be saying, "Poor dear, she hasn't yet learned that Blacks have only made a contribution to Jazz and Spirituals."

At that point I realized how important this research was, because involvement in all forms of music has been an American Black tradition. In fact, a look at the biographies of Black musicians shows that hundreds aspired to be classical performers but were discouraged from becoming "serious" musicians. Despite the many obstacles, which included being denied entrance into music schools in the North and South, many Blacks persevered and became concert singers, composers, classical pianists, and violinists.

Fairly soon, my persistent research paid off. Within three months, I had the names of 360 Black women composers and the complete bibliographical data for sixty selections in my hands. This work has resulted in an extensive music bibliography included in *American Black Women in the Arts and Social Sciences: A Bibliographical Survey,* the revised edition published by Scarecrow Press, 1978. Nevertheless, the struggle to make these compositions accessible is not yet over, because music publishers have discontinued printing many of the works, and some of the music companies have merged, folded, or moved.

There are also other complications involved in making the works of American Black women composers available to the public. Although many of our Caucasian sisters still struggle for recognition and attempt to make the public aware of "serious" contributions by white women composers, they tend to try to force invalid criteria for recognizing Black artists on Black women. For instance, there is the effort to discredit what is considered elitist or "bourgeois." However, for a Black person, becoming a trained musician—one who could read and write music—has always been an antiestablishment act.

Some segments of the feminist movement further stereotype Black women as they highlight only the very deserving Bessie Smiths, Mahalia Jacksons, and current young Black popular singers. Although the celebrated eighty-five-year-old Dr. Eva Jessye, composer, educator, conductor of many *Porgy and Bess* choruses, lives on the Pittsburg (Kansas) State University campus, a few hours away from Lawrence, Kansas, the site of the 1979 National Women's Studies Convention, she was neither invited to be a part of the convention nor mentioned at it, except by me. Nowhere were there the albums of Marian Anderson— praised for having "the voice heard once in a hundred years"—Shirley Verrett, Martina Arroya, or for that matter such Caucasian classical artists as Beverly Sills and Lily Pons, who by the very nature of their profession have had to surmount overwhelming difficulties.

It goes without saying that Black women musicians have pursued their careers under even more trying conditions. Generally, there was no one to underwrite the considerable expense; and if they were financially able, music school doors were routinely closed to them. Like other Black composers, Black women composers were obliged to earn a living from other activities. Some had to teach in public schools or colleges in addition to giving private lessons, presenting concerts, or directing church choirs. Furthermore, they often sandwiched composing in between their working, caring for a family, and being involved in many community activities. The obstacles they encountered are indicated in this wonderfully ironic statement by Florence Price: "I was able to snatch a few precious days in the month of January in which to write undisturbed. But, oh, dear me, when shall I ever be so fortunate again as to break a foot?"[1] More recently—during the 1960s—Black female composers have been further obscured as a trend developed to highlight a small group of Black male composers.

This brief bibliography focuses almost exclusively on vocal and choral music for a number of reasons. First, this music has been the easiest to obtain from publishers. Secondly, as a performing soprano, I have sought works to incorporate in the annual programs I give. Preparing concerts, I attempt to make them so diverse that the audiences will be very conscious of the wide range of talent among American Black women composers and arrangers. Also, in this research, we found that Black women have composed more vocal and choral music than instrumental. They were probably creating that which would most likely find an audience and be performed.

The songs included in this article are diverse and date back to a 1918 publication; some are secular, while others are religious. There are folk songs, and also traditional religious songs, spirituals, and gospel selections. Although most of these compositions were published during the last sixty-one years, the spirituals and Creole songs go back to the Colonial period. In fact, Camille Nickerson writes that the Creole songs were sometimes older than the spirituals.

Not surprisingly, the subjects and lyrics are as diverse as the music. There are lyrics by the composer and by Black and white poets, both men and women. Langston Hughes's work has been especially popular for settings; while two of the poems are those of Georgia Douglas Johnson, poet, teacher, mathematician, and housewife.

The bibliography is arranged alphabetically, and the annotations describe both the music and the lyrics.

Ora Williams

Bonds, Margaret. *Ballad of the Brown King*. Wds., Langston Hughes. New York: Sam Fox, 1941.

A Christmas cantata, this work in A-flat major and 4/4 time consists of nine movements—solos, choral numbers, duets, and divided choral selections. The opening movement, "Of the Three Wise Men," suggests some technique patterns used by Bonds throughout. It begins in the key of A-flat major and ends in F-major. The first section is initiated with an eight-measure piano introduction, with the piano playing dancelike rhythms in support of the jubilant and joyous moods which parallel the lyrics:

> Of the three wise men who came to the king,
>   one was a brown man, so they sing.
> Alleluia! Alleluia!

The biblical movement titles give both performers and listeners a common basis for understanding, e.g., "They Brought Fine Gifts" and "Mary Had a Little Baby."

Bonds, Margaret. "Dream Variation." Wds., Langston Hughes. In *Anthology of Art Songs by American Black Composers*. Comp. Willis C. Patterson. Melville, N.Y.: Edward B. Marks Music Corp./Belwyn Mills, 1977.

In C-sharp major and 12/8 meter, this tranquil art song in andante for medium voice and piano has difficult intonation and a challenging piano accompaniment. The intonation in the first two measures, in an ascending, then descending, melodic pattern, is in E-natural, B-natural, and A-natural. The chords in the piano accompaniment in measure 12 are in D-minor in the left hand and A-major in the right hand, thus contributing to the unusual intonation and the impressionist style.

The lyrics and music contain affirmation and racial protest. The speaker dreams of flinging her/his arms wide in some place of the sun, and whirling and dancing until the day is over and night comes. The progression is from day to evening to night, with accompanying contrasts of color and movement.

Bonds, Margaret. "I, Too." Wds., Langston Hughes. In *Anthology of Art Songs by American Black Composers*. Comp., Willis C. Patterson. Melville, N.Y.: Edward B. Marks Music Corporation/Belwyn Mills, 1977.

This patriotic and Black nationalistic solo begins in D-minor and 4/4 time, modulates in and out of near-related keys, and uses modern harmonies. Both the words and the music are dramatic, with the accompaniment providing an appropriate setting for the militant message in the song. As the lyrics become more emphatic, the rhythm of the melody adjusts to the emphasis.

Cleaver, Esther A. "Can You See God?" Newark, N.J.: Savoy Music Company (5837 Corning Avenue); Los Angeles: Dex-es Publishing House, 1973.

Both the lyrics and the music of this gospel song written in the key of F-major and a moderate 9/8 meter were composed by Esther A. Cleaver. The song is divided into two parts—the first focusing on the question posed in the title, "Can You See God?"; the second being the answer to the question. Both sections are written so that a soloist and chorus or two choruses could perform them.

The lyrics are suggestive of pantheism in that they ask if one can see an omnipresent God in the trees, in the thunder riding the breeze, and in the valleys. With the answer, God becomes a personal God who is a refuge, strength, deliverer, redeemer, and friend to the speaker.

Douroux, Margaret. "I'm Glad." Musical arrangement by Albert Denis Tessler. Los Angeles: Rev. Earl Pleasant, 1970.

A gospel song, this selection in the key of C-major and in 6/8 time has a short introduction which foreshadows the three closing measures of the song. The song, marked *moderato*, is in AB form, with two verses and a chorus. The accompaniment, quasi through-composed, is chordal. The lyrics juxtapose human and divine behavior. Because God has been responsible, generous, and protective, the speaker is exceedingly glad.

Douroux, Margaret. "We're Blest." Los Angeles: Rev. Earl Pleasant, 1971.

In the key of A-flat major and in 4/4 meter, this gospel song for solo, chorus, and piano or organ begins with the chorus singing the refrain, followed by the verse-singing solo voice. The rhythmic patterns in the chorus are fairly even, in contrast with the syncopated rhythmic pattern in every measure of the verse. The mood, which can be determined ultimately by the musicians and/or the choral director, counterpoints gratefulness with ingratitude, misfortune, and admonition.

Evanti, Lillian. "Dedication." Wds., Georgia Douglas Johnson. New York: Handy Brothers, 1958.

For solo voice and piano, this moderately slow secular song in the key of D-major and 4/4 time has a difficult piano accompaniment which features arpeggios containing thirty-second and eighth notes. It is twenty-seven measures in length, with the composer modifying the melody of the first four measures twice within the composition.

"Dedication," a love song, speaks to an unidentified person and describes the eight ways in which this person affects the speaker. "Life is good to look upon" because the lover can take away solitude and mingle dreams with ecstasy.

Evanti, Lillian. "Hail to Fair Washington." Wds., Georgia Douglas Johnson. Copyright, Lillian Evanti and Georgia Douglas Johnson, 1951.

This patriotic song in B-flat major and 6/8 and 4/4 meter has an AB form. The rhythm swings in twos, giving a brisk marchlike tempo, while the patriotic lyrics celebrate Washington the President and the city of Washington, D.C., a place of parks, avenues, cherry trees, and congressional halls.

Evanti, Lillian. "High Flight." Wds., John Gillespie Magee, Jr. New York: Handy Brothers, 1948.

This religious soprano solo in 4/4 meter is through-composed and has an intricate piano accompaniment. Although it begins in C-minor, the selection ends dramatically in D-major. Again, Evanti's work concludes on a brighter note, philosophically and musically, than when begun, in keeping with the lyrics: "I've trod the high untrespassed sanctity of space, put out my hand and touched the face of God."

Evanti, Lillian. "I'm Yours for Tonight." Washington, D.C.: Columbian Music Company.

In D-minor and cut time, this surprisingly simple love song is in AB form, having a verse-chorus, verse-chorus pattern, and rhumba tempo and rhythms. The verse resembles a recitative in an aria. This song associates a romance with nature—the stars, night, spring, and the moon. Because she is in love, the speaker sees all things in a new way. Everything is aglow.

Evanti, Lillian. "Speak to Him, Thou." Wds., Alfred Lord Tennyson (from *The Higher Pantheism:* dedicated to Marian Anderson). New York: Handy Brothers, 1943.

This religious solo, which begins in A-minor and 6/8 meter, ends in the key of C and makes several meter changes—to 12/8, then to 6/8, and back to 12/8. Resembling a Handel pastorale, the work almost seems to be a piano solo with a dramatic vocal part. In formal language, there is a repeated insistence that someone speak to God. Not only does God finally hear, but "He is closer than breathing, nearer than hands and feet."

Hackley, Emma Azalia. "Carola." New York: Handy Brothers, 1953.

This lullaby for piano and voice is in F-major and ABA form. The verse has four phrases, with phrases 1, 2, and 4 being melodically similar. The chorus consists of two phrases—the first, four measures long, while the second, a repeat of the first, is extended into seven measures by repeating the words "of love" twice. Although the habanera accompaniment containing the melody is a simple folk one, it is fluid. The works are typical of those used for a serenade, with many natural, tender, and joyous images.

Jessye, Eva. "I'm a Po' Lil' Orphan." Ed. and arr., Eva Jessye. New York: Robbins-Engel, Inc., 1927.

This solo spiritual in the key of E-minor and 2/4 time has a single-chord introduction. The three verses consist of varied repetitions of one statement, "I'm a po' lil' orphan in dis worl'," followed by the assertion, "Good Lawd, I cannot stay heah by mah-self." The tonally-tragic lyrics are in the folk idiom of dialect, and the strophic setting goes from E-minor to E-major *(Tierce de Picardie).*

Jessye, Eva. "Three Tears." Ed. and arr., Eva Jessye. New York: Robbins-Engel, 1927.

In the key of F-major and 2/4 meter, this dramatic song has a four-and-a-half measure piano introduction and three verses. The melody is carried by the chorus, while the accompaniment is in syncopated rhythms underscored with a drone bass. In the folk tradition, this solo spiritual contains three simple statements: "Sometimes I feel lak I nevah been bawn again; Sometimes I feel lak the Lord has need of me; Sometimes I feel lak I'se on a my journey home."

King, Betty Jackson, arr. "Nobody Knows the Trouble I See." Unpublished; can be obtained from the arranger.

This solo for medium voice and piano captures the mood intended by the title and lyrics through intonation, accompaniment, and rhythm. It is in G-major, 4/4 time, and ABA form. Part of the four-measure introduction is later used as an interlude interrupting the lyrics and thought in the last refrain.

Depicting the "trouble I see," the chords thicken the texture in the accompaniment by playing consecutive seventh chords in syncopated rhythms. The chords in the right hand alternate minor ninths with major sevenths. Then those in the left hand, doubled at the octave, omit the third of the chord, a performance practice of the Renaissance era.

McCanns, Shirley Graham (DuBois). "I Promise." Wds., Lorenz B. Graham. (Dedicated to Ruth Graham.) New York: Handy Brothers, 1934.

A love song, this work in the key of F-major, with chords for the ukulele as well as the piano accompaniment, has a simple lyric melody line supported by the piano. The setting consists of chords, chord rolls, octaves, and arpeggios. The lyrics were written by Lorenz Graham, educator, lecturer, and author, for his prospective bride. The language is formal ("Thou wilt always be of me a part.") and expresses the depth of the speaker's love.

McLin, Lena. *Free at Last! A Portrait of Martin Luther King, Jr.* Park Ridge, Ill.: General Words & Music Co., Neil A. Kjos, Jr., 1973, GC43.

For SATB chorus, soprano, baritone, or mezzo soprano, piano accompaniment, and narrator, this cantata-like work is biographical, historical, and political. In the first selection in 4/4 meter, the sopranos in unison introduce the themes of freedom and slavery. Then the soprano solo continues the narrative, which highlights the characteristics of American slavery. Interspersed throughout are melodic patterns from spirituals, such as "Sometimes I Feel Like a Motherless Child." As the story unwinds in this through-composed section, other voices are introduced.

The next major section for the chorus, also through-composed, is written in A-minor and represents the Emancipation period.

Against the background of racial unrest and injustice, Martin Luther King, Jr., "a leader sent from God," is introduced. The cantata continues with additional solos, choral numbers, interludes for the piano, and lines for a narrator. In some sections the voices are in unison; in others they are in four-part harmony. Depending on the event being depicted, the setting is spirited and vibrant, or slow and sad.

McLin, Lena. "Gwendolyn Brooks, a Musical Portrait." (SATB and piano.) Park Ridge, Ill.: General Words & Music Co., 1972.

This choral selection in the key of G-major and in an "easy waltz tempo" has a short chordal introduction. The four voice parts sing a sustained "oo" for ten measures. With some rhyme, the lyrics describe the obstacles to writing poetry and also those experiences which enable us to appreciate such a poet as Gwendolyn Brooks.

Moore, Dorothy Rudd. *From the Dark Tower* (for Mezzo, Cello, and Piano). New York: American Composers' Alliance (170 West 74th Street), 1970.

From the Dark Tower consists of eight songs in modern harmonies, related by theme and tempo. The texts, written by such poets as James Weldon Johnson, Arna Bontemps, Langston Hughes, and Countee Cullen, review Afro-American experience from the early "Black and unknown bards" to twentieth-century protests. Contrast is achieved through the change of meter, melodies, accompanying styles, and lyrics.

Moore, Undine. "Love Let the Wind Cry.... How I Adore Thee." Wds., Sappho, rendered by Bliss Carman, based on the prose translation of H. T. Wharton. In *Anthology of Art Songs by Black American Composers.* Comp., Willis C. Patterson.

The fact that the lyrics of this art song for soprano and piano are from a poem by Sappho suggests the complexity of its musical setting. The song begins with a passionate love statement that resembles an aria, while the very dramatic middle part is recitative-like. There are numerous meter changes, and the accompaniment is chordal and sometimes harmonized.

The lyrics contain an apostrophe, and visual and auditory natural images. The four pleas for the elements to proclaim the speaker's love are climaxed by a plea that the loved one express how much she is loved.

Moore, Undine. "When Susanna Wears Red." Wds., Langston Hughes. (Dedicated to Dr. Carl Harris and the Virginia State College Choir.) New York: Warner Bros., 1975.

Susanna Jones wearing red "maked her face like an ancient cameo turned brown by the ages." For SATB chorus and *a capella*, this lively choral number repeats the major strain and then has a long codetta. Although there are some antiphonal parts, most of the work combines all four voices.

Nickerson, Camille Lucie, arr. and har. "Chere, Mo Lemme Toi" ("Dear, I Love You So"). Boston: Boston Music Company, 1947.

In an expository statement about this Creole love song, Nickerson says that "Chere, Mo Lemme Toi" is a sprightly song often sung on Mardi Gras Day, when a suitor, otherwise timid but now masked, finds the courage to declare his love. The contrasting second part of the strain is a melody the Creoles borrowed from American bands. There is a long, rhythmic piano introduction which anticipates the contours of the melody.

Nickerson, Camille Lucie, arr. and har. "Danse Conni Conne!" ("Dance, Baby Dance!"). Boston: Boston Music Company, 1947.

A Creole nursery song, "Dance Conni Conne!" has a long piano introduction in the bolero rhythm which establishes the lively mood of the piece. In the key of A-flat and in 2/4 meter, the work, taken from the folk tradition, repeats the main melody and lyrics: "Dan-se Conni Con-ne la Nu-nut-sie, Dan-se Con-ni, Pa-pa." Nickerson says this selection is typical of what a nurse sang when amusing a baby with "whatever happened to come into her mind at the moment."

Perry, Julia. "How Beautiful Are the Feet." New York: Galaxy Music Corporation, 1954.

This song is based on Isaiah 52:7. It is in C-major and ABA form, with the A sections solely devoted to treatment of the words, "How beautiful are the feet of them that preach the gospel of peace." There is a close correspondence between the vocal melody and accompaniment patterns. For the most part, the accompaniment is chordal and quite appropriate for the andante tempo indicated by the composer. The interludes repeat melodies previously heard in the vocal line.

Price, Florence B. "An April Day." Wds., Joseph F. Cotter. New York: Handy Brothers, 1949.

In the key of E-flat and 4/4 moderato meter, "An April Day" celebrates being alive in April. A through-composed song, its accompaniment is very pianistic, often arpeggiated, and generally not with the melody. The work concludes with a cadenza in octaves.

Price, Florence B., arr. "I Am Bound for the Kingdom." (Arr. for and dedicated to Marian Anderson.) New York: Handy Brothers, 1949.

The pattern of this solo spiritual is a repeated refrain, verse, refrain, verse, and refrain. In G-major and 4/4 meter, the song has a martial rhythm which accommodates the lyrics, "I am bound for the kingdom, I am bound for the kingdom," with emphasis on each of the twelve "bounds." The accompaniment is largely a chordal rhythm with a few measures of accompanying melody.

Price, Florence B. "Night." Wds., Louise C. Wallace. In *Anthology of Art Songs by Black American Composers.* Comp., Willis C. Patterson. For piano and voice, this melodic art song is in C-major. The rather complex accompaniment, which consists of broken chords, is a through-composed arrangement. The lyrics, which juxtapose night and day, are a romantic celebration of the night.

Taylor, Maude Cummings. "The Day Is Nearly Done." New York: Handy Brothers, 1964. For medium voice and piano, this ABA-form solo spiritual is in the key of G-major and in 4/4 meter (with a work-song rhythm). The accompaniment consists of modern chordal structure supporting the simple spiritual melody and lyrics:

> I must work for the Master,
> I must work for the Master,
> I must work for the Master,
> The Day is nearly Done.

NOTE

[1]Barbara Garvey Jackson, "Florence Price, Composer," *The Black Perspective in Music* 5 (Spring 1977):36.

REFERENCE

Patterson, Willis C., compiler. *Anthology of Art Songs by Black American Composers.* Preface, George Shirley. Introduction, Wendell P. Whalum. New York: Edward B. Marks Corporation, 1977.

25

A Listing of Non-Print
Materials on Black Women

MARTHA H. BROWN

Given the lack of readily available materials on Black women, the following selective list of non-print materials is designed to familiarize students and teachers with what *is* available. The lists of items are inter-disciplinary and should prove helpful not only for specialized studies dealing with Black women but for film courses as well. Items have been culled from a variety of sources and are descriptive rather than evaluative. In some instances when several entries appear concerning the same person or item, I have selected for publication the title I felt most appropriate for high school and college classroom use. The listings are divided into seven principal parts: (I) Instructional or Documentary Films; (II) Major Studio Films; (III) Videotapes; (IV) Filmstrips; (V) Records or Phono-Discs; (VI) Cassette Tapes; and (VII) Slides and Prints.

Most of the scholarly audiovisual material on Black women is buried under the heading of Black Studies. Production of such efforts peaked during the sixties, and the materials are presently in need of updating and revising. In the seventies, most of the scholarly studies on Black women have appeared in conjunction with Women's Studies. One explanation is the fact that in the seventies private philanthropy and federal grants were more disposed toward financing research on women than on Blacks. So

Author's Note: The author wishes to acknowledge gratefully the research assistance of Joyce A. Bleecker, an enthusiastic student of the history of the cinema, women, and Blacks. The editors would also like to thank Margaret Lazarus for her additional suggestions.

in many instances research and interest in Black Women's Studies has migrated from Black Studies to Women's Studies. In the early 1970s many college classes in Black History faced dwindling enrollments while Black Women's History enjoyed a new surge of popularity along with American Women's History. By far the greatest number of Black women gaining recognition in American society have been entertainers. To date, however, only one major film has appeared on the life of a Black woman, *Lady Sings the Blues*. Based on the life of Billie Holiday, this film starred another singer, turned actress, Diana Ross.

Of all media, Hollywood-type films have had by far the greatest impact in shaping images of Black women. These films have depicted Black women primarily as sanctimonious church members, devoted servants, or sensuous mulattoes. Historically, Black actresses have won their greatest acclaim as maids. Hattie McDaniels, who won an Oscar as best supporting actress for her role in *Gone With the Wind*, is a case in point. In the forties, Blacks crashed the Hollywood scene as entertainers, usually appearing in night club or similar scenes irrelevant to the main plot. Thus the audiences occasionally heard songs sung by Lena Horne, Billie Holiday, Ella Fitzgerald, Hazel Scott, and other artists. The two all-Black musical extravaganzas which in 1943 culminated the era of Black entertainers portrayed women performers in the familiar stereotyped roles and contrived situations. These widely publicized films were *Cabin in the Sky* and *Stormy Weather*. Ethel Waters starred in the former, and Lena Horne in both.

In order to acquaint readers with the more popular films delineating Black women, a list of "Representative Films Featuring Black Actresses" is here presented which includes portrayals of Black women in stereotypic roles, as well as in more realistic and positive roles. Since these films have been chosen with the classroom in mind, the lengthy *Gone With the Wind* and recent "blaxploitation" films are not included. Readers are also reminded that a few independent Black filmmakers operated during the 1920s and 1930s. Their works were intended solely for Black audiences. By far the most outstanding producer of such films was Oscar Micheaux, whose works usually probed the problems and achievements of the Black middle class. He produced "uplift" and "assimilationist" films from 1919 to 1948. The best known today is *God's Stepchildren*, a film about "passing" (for white).

For those especially interested in the careers of Black actresses, a special chronological listing by titles takes up a major part of the entire compilation. The concluding film section lists titles of films dealing with African women.

Since the original preparation of this bibliography of sources, a comprehensive book has been published that lists films in which Blacks have appeared, and the dates of their production. Phyllis Klotman's *Frame by Frame* is an excellent reference for those seeking information on films in which Blacks have performed since the beginning of motion picture productions.

A highly selective sampling of disc recordings by women musicians and other instructional tapes are listed at the end of this compilation. Both the artists and their selections represent suggestive samplings.

INSTRUCTIONAL FILMS—16mm

Family Life

Losing Just the Same. 60 min. B/W. The story of a Black mother and her ten children who live on welfare while dreaming of prestige and status. Originally produced for the NET Journal Series. 1966. Dist: IU.

With Just a Little Trust. 15 min. Color. Presents the struggle of a young Black widow with three children who has fallen into financial problems. Three generations, including her mother, struggle to survive in the inner city. 1975. Dist: ROA Films.

Struggle and Achievement

Angela Davis: Like It Is. 60 min. B/W. Includes a discussion with Angela Davis in prison and comments on her case by defense attorneys and others. 1970. Dist: ADF.

Angela Davis: Portrait of a Revolutionary. 60 min. B/W. Portrayal of Angela Davis as teacher, friend, and individualist. 1971. Dist: PYR.

Aretha Franklin Soul Singer. 25 min. Color. Shows the musicians on stage and in less formal settings. 1969. Dist: MGH.

Black Woman, The. 52 min. B/W. Presents Nikki Giovanni, Lena Horne, Bibi Amina Baraka, and other Black women discussing their role in contemporary society and the problems they confront. Includes singing by Roberta Flack, a dance by Loretta Abbott, and poetry by Nikki Giovanni. 1970. Dist: NET; INUAVC.

Chicago Maternity Center Story. 45 min. Documents the struggle of Black, Hispanic, and white women to prevent the closing of a maternity center that provides home births. 1977. Dist: Haymarket Kartemquin Films, 1901 West Wellington, Chicago, IL.

Chisholm/Pursuing the Dream. 42 min. Color. A documentary film about Congresswoman Shirley Chisholm along the campaign trail for the 1972 presidential nomination. 1974. Dist: NLC.

Clorae and Albie. 25 min. The film traces the friendship of two Black women in Boston from high school through the process of making decisions about marriage, school, and childrearing. 1975. Dist: Educational Development Center, 55 Chapel Street, Newton, MA; Attn: Film Rental.

Felicia. 13 min. B/W. A Black high school student searches for answers as she tries to cope with life in a segregated community. Dist: UC.

Flashettes, The. 20 min. Story of a young Black women's track team. 1977. Dist: NDF.

Harriet Tubman and the Underground Railroad. 52 min. B/W. Tells the story of Harriet Tubman's first journey into Maryland and shows her escorting four relatives and another escaped slave to Pennsylvania. Features Ruby Dee and Ethel Waters. 1966. Dist: CBSN/MCGH.

I Am Somebody. 28 min. Color. Relates the story of how fifty-five unskilled hospital workers staged a successful strike for decent wages in Charleston, South Carolina. 1970. Dist: MGH.

Lincoln Hospital. 15 min. Community group, primarily women, try to make Bronx hospital responsive. Dist: Third World Newsreel, 26 West 20th Street, New York, NY 10011.

Phyllis and Terry. 30 min. B/W. Story of two teenaged Black girls who live in New York City. 1964–65. Dist: FC.

Tale of Two Ladies, A. 30 min. B/W. Dr. Thomas Pettigrew reviews the history of Negro protest against racial discrimination. From the "Epitaph for Jim Crow" series. 1961. Dist: IU.

This Is The Home of Mrs. Levant Graham. 15 min. B/W. This film was made in the home of a Black family in Washington, D.C., and edited by them. 1970. Dist: PYR.

Tribute to Malcolm X, A. 15 min. B/W. Discusses the influence of Malcolm X upon the present Black Liberation Movement. Includes an interview with his widow, Betty Shabazz. 1969. Dist: IU.

Veronica. 28 min. Color. A documentary portraying the inner struggles of a Black teenager who is president of her class in a predominantly white high school in New Haven, Connecticut. Dist: JAS.

Where Is Jim Crow (series)—A Conversation with Lena Horne. 30 min. B/W. Lena Horne discusses herself as a symbol of the Negro pinup, the representative of Negro woman, or "this year's Negro," and tells how she had to conquer this image for her own sake and that of other Negro women. From the "Where Is Jim Crow" series. 1964. Dist: UCEMC.

Where Is Jim Crow (series)—A Conversation with Nancy Wilson. 30 min.

B/W. Discusses Civil Rights and the Negro in show business. From the "Where Is Jim Crow" series. 1964. Dist: UCEMC.

Individual Artists

Fine Arts

Black Artists, The. 28 min. Color. Shows how three Black artists are motivated and then return to their studios to complete their work. Includes Samella Lewis painting an abstract in oil. (The other two artists are men.) 1969. Dist: AFRO.

Performing Arts

Black Music in America: From Then Till Now. 29 min. Color. The history of the Black contribution to American music is chronicled in filmed performances of great Black musicians, including Nina Simone, Mahalia Jackson, and Bessie Smith. 1971. Dist: IU.

Body and Soul, Part II: Soul (of Black America Series). 29 min. B/W. Ray Charles comments on the experience and insights of Black performers. His characterizations of soul music are illustrated with performances by Billie Holiday, Mahalia Jackson, Aretha Franklin, and others. 1968. Dist: IU.

Harlem in the Twenties. 9 min. Color. Portrays the Black cultural movement in Harlem during the 1920s. Includes Ethel Waters, Josephine Baker, and others. 1971. Dist: IU.

Lady from Philadelphia. 60 min. B/W. Depicts Marian Anderson's tour of Southeast Asia. Includes her singing approximately fifteen songs. 1958. Dist: MGHT.

Lady in the Lincoln Memorial. 28 min. Color. Depicts the early career of Marian Anderson. Dist: NYT.

Marian Anderson. 26 min. B/W. Presents Marian Anderson singing a program of songs in rehearsals and on the concert stage. Dist: IU.

Writers

Gwendolyn Brooks. 30 min. B/W. An informal look at the life and works of the Pulitzer Prize–winning poet. Set in Chicago, which forms the background for most of her works. Dist: UC.

Harlem Renaissance: The Black Poets. 20 min. Color. Includes excerpts from the works of Georgia Douglas Johnson along with those of male poets of the Harlem Renaissance. Also includes dramatic vignettes of the period. From the "Tell It Like It Was" series. 1970. Dist: WCAITV; CARSL.

To Be Young, Gifted and Black. 90 min. Color. Presents in the form of a play a compilation of Lorraine Hansberry's letters, diaries, and scenes from her works which trace her life and development as a writer. 1972. Dist: IU.

Writers and Artists of the New Era. 30 min. B/W. A college professor discusses four pre–World War I artists, including Edmonia Lewis, sculptor. From the Black History Section II, W. E. B. DuBois, and The New Century series. 1969. Dist: HRAW.

Additional Documentaries

Growing Up Female: As Six Become One. 50 min. B/W. Describes the socialization of the American woman through a personal look into the lives of six females ranging in age from four to thirty-five. Two of the six major subjects are Black. 1971. Dist: NDF.

With Babies and Banners. 30 min. B/W. Story of the women's emergency program that grew out of a workers' strike in 1937 in Flint, Michigan. Includes recollections of the women during picketing and other supportive efforts. Nearly half of those interviewed are Black. Dist: NDF.

Union Maids. 60 min. B/W. Film based on oral interviews and action pictures of the struggle to unionize women in the 1930s. One of the three subjects is Black. Dist: NDF.

Representative Films Featuring Black Actresses

These films present highlights in the film history of Black women and Black family life. They are included primarily for their historical value, rather than for artistic or dramatic considerations. Many of the films, however, were highly acclaimed by both critics and audiences.

Hearts in Dixie (Fox, 1929). One of the first all-Black Hollywood films and one of Fox's earliest talkies. A musical drama of a Southern family, replete with stereotypes.

Hallelujah (MGM, 1929). A pioneer all-Black musical in which a country boy succumbs to the wiles of a bad woman.

Imitation of Life (Universal, 1934). With Louise Beavers, Fredi Washington, and Hazel Washington. Beavers plays both the faithful servant and the rejected mother of the "tragic mulatto" who elects to pass for white.

Autobiography of Miss Jane Pittman (ABC-TV Film, 1974). Starring Cicely Tyson. Dramatizes problems of Blacks in obtaining civil liberties from Reconstruction through the 1960s by unfolding one woman's adventures.

Cabin in the Sky (MGM, 1943). A musical fantasy with an all-Black cast, including Lena Horne and Ethel Waters.

Claudine (Fox, 1974). Starring Diahann Carroll in the title role. Depicts a Harlem welfare mother's aspirations for her children, her struggle with bureaucracy, and her mercurial romance.

The Learning Tree (Warner Brothers-Seven Arts, 1969). Based on Gordon Park's autobiographical novel. Recreates Black family life in a small Kansas town during the 1920s.

Nothing But a Man (Independent, 1965). With Abbey Lincoln and Gloria Foster. Prize-winning film depicting the pressures on the material life of a proud Black man who refuses to accommodate himself to racism.

A Raisin in the Sun (Columbia, 1961). Traces the moral dilemma of a Black family as they seek to move into a white neighborhood. Also offers interesting insights into Black family relationships.

Saint Louis Blues (Warner and RKO, 1929). The only film ever made by Bessie Smith. Features a blues singer troubled by her man's unfaithfulness.

Scar of Shame (Colored Players Film, 1927). Deals with intraracial color prejudices. The ill-fated marriage of a dark-skinned woman and her talented light-skinned husband ends in her suicide.

Sounder (Twentieth Century Fox, 1972). Starring Cicely Tyson. Reveals warm and tender Southern family relations as a mother holds her family together while the father serves a prison term.

Stormy Weather (Twentieth Century Fox, 1943). All-Black musical, including Lena Horne and the Katherine Dunham Dancers. Based in part on the life of Bill "Bojangles" Robinson.

MAJOR STUDIO FILMS

Films Based on Black Women's Works

Georgia, Georgia. Maya Angelou. Cinema Releasing.
The Landlord. Kristin Hunter. United Artists.

A Bright Road. Mary Elizabeth Vroman. MGM.
Uptight. Ruby Dee. Paramount.

Chronology of Pictures Made by Individual Actresses

Pearl Bailey

Variety Girl (Paramount, 1947); *Isn't It Romantic?* (Paramount, 1948); *Porgy and Bess* (Columbia, 1949); *Carmen Jones* (Twentieth Century Fox, 1954); *That Certain Feeling* (Paramount, 1956); *St. Louis Blues* (Paramount, 1958; also Eartha Kitt and Ella Fitzgerald); *All the Fine Young Cannibals* (MGM, 1960); *The Landlord* (United Artists, 1970); *Norman—Is That You?* (MGM and United Artists, 1976).

Louise Beavers

Annabelle's Affairs (Fox Films Corp., 1931); *Girls About Town* (Paramount, 1931); *Sundown Trail* (Producer unavailable, 1931); *Bombshell* (MGM, 1932); *What Price Hollywood* (RKO Radio, 1932); *She Done Him Wrong* (Paramount, 1933); *Imitation of Life* (Universal, 1934; also starring Fredi and Hazel Washington); *Shadow of the Thin Man* (MGM, 1941); *Dubarry Was a Lady* (MGM, 1943); *The Jackie Robinson Story* (Eagle-Lion Production, 1950); *The Goddess* (Columbia, 1958); *All the Fine Young Cannibals* (MGM, 1960); *Facts of Life* (United Artists, 1961).

Dorothy Dandridge

The Harlem Globetrotters (Columbia, 1951); *Tarzan's Peril* (Producer unavailable, 1951); *Carmen Jones* (Twentieth Century Fox, 1954); *Island in the Sun* (Twentieth Century Fox, 1957); *Porgy and Bess* (Columbia, 1959); *Tamango* (Hal Roach, 1959).

Ruby Dee

The Fight That Never Ends (Alexander Productions, 1947); *That Man of Mine* (Associated Producers of Negro Motion Pictures, 1947); *The*

Jackie Robinson Story (Eagle-Lion, 1950); *No Way Out* (Twentieth Century Fox, 1950); *The Tall Target* (MGM, 1951); *Edge of the City* (United Artists, 1957); *Take a Giant Step* (United Artists, 1960; also Beah Richards); *A Raisin in the Sun* (Columbia, 1961); *The Balcony* (Sterling Films, 1963); *Black Girl* (Cinerama Releasing, 1963); *Gone Are the Days* (Trans Flux, 1963); *The Incident* (Twentieth Century Fox, 1967); *Uptight* (Paramount, 1968; script by Ruby Dee); *Buck and the Preacher* (Columbia, 1972); *Countdown at Kusini* (Delta Sigma Theta Sorority, 1975); *It's Good to Be Alive* (Producer and date unavailable).

Katherine Dunham

Carnival in Rhythm (Warners, 1940); *Star-Spangled Rhythm* (Paramount, 1942); *Stormy Weather* (Twentieth Century Fox, 1943); *Casbah* (Universal-International, 1948); *Mambo* (Paramount, 1955).

Lena Horne

Blond Venus (Herald Pictures, 1940); *Cabin in the Sky* (MGM, 1943); *Panama Hattie* (MGM, 1943); *Stormy Weather* (Twentieth Century Fox, 1943); *Swing Fever* (MGM, 1943); *Thousands Cheer* (MGM, 1943; with Hazel Scott); *Boogie Woogie Dream* (Negro Marches On, 1944); *Broadway Rhythm* (MGM, 1944); *Two Girls and a Sailor* (MGM, 1944); *Ziegfield Follies* (MGM, 1946); *Till the Clouds Roll By* (MGM, 1946); *Words and Music* (MGM, 1948); *Duchess of Idaho* (MGM, 1950); *Meet Me in Las Vegas* (MGM, 1957); *Death of a Gunfighter* (Universal, 1969); *That's Entertainment* (MGM, 1974).

Hattie McDaniels

Story of Temple Drake (Paramount, 1933); *Judge Priest* (Twentieth Century Fox, 1935); *Showboat* (Universal, 1936); *The Prisoner of Shark Island*, (Twentieth Century Fox, 1936); *Nothing Sacred* (Selznick, 1938); *Gone With the Wind* (MGM, 1939; McDaniels awarded Oscar for Best Supporting Actress.)

Claudia NcNeil

The Last Angry Man (Columbia, 1959); *A Raisin in the Sun* (Columbia, 1961); *There Was a Crooked Man* (Warner Brothers, 1970); *Black Girl* (Cinerama Releasing, 1973).

Butterfly McQueen

Gone With the Wind (MGM, 1939); *Affectionately Yours* (MGM, 1941); *The Great Life* (Warner Brothers, 1941); *They Died With Their Boots On* (Warner Brothers, 1942); *In This Our Life* (Warner Brothers, 1942); *Cabin in the Sky* (MGM, 1943); *Duel in the Sun* (MGM, 1947); *Song of the South* (RKO-Disney, 1947).

Diana Ross

Lady Sings the Blues (Paramount, 1972); *Mahogany* (Paramount, 1975).

Cicely Tyson

The Last Angry Man (Columbia, 1959); *A Man Called Adam* (Embassy Pictures, 1966); *The Comedians* (MGM, 1967); *The Heart Is a Lonely Hunter* (Warner Brothers-Seven Arts, 1968); *The River Niger* (Columbia, 1976); *Sounder* (Twentieth Century Fox, 1976); *Autobiography of Miss Jane Pittman* (ABC-TV Film, 1974); *A Hero Ain't Nothin But a Sandwich* (Radnitz Mattel Production, 1977); *Roots* (ABC-TV, 1977).

Ethel Waters

On With the Show (Warner Brothers, 1929); *Cabin in the Sky* (MGM, 1943); *Cairo* (MGM, 1942); *Tales of Manhattan* (Twentieth Century Fox, 1943); *Stage Door Canteen* (United Artists, 1943); *Pinky* (Twentieth Century Fox, 1949); *Member of the Wedding* (Columbia, 1953); *The Sound and the Fury* (Twentieth Century Fox, 1959).

Leslie Uggams

Skyjacked (MGM, 1972); *Black Girl* (Cinerama Releasing, 1973); *Roots* (ABC-TV, 1977).

African Women in Films

Black Girl. 60 min. The story of an attractive West African girl from the slums of Dakar who goes to work for a white French family. Directed by Ousmane Sembane. 1969. Dist: NYF.

Boran Women. 18 min. Stresses women's roles and duties among the cattle-raising people in northern Kenya. 1973. Dist: WER.

Fear Woman. 28 min. Depicts women traders in Ghana marketplaces. 1971. Dist: MCGH.

Malawi: The Women. 15 min. Focuses on three women revealing their feelings about their roles and their ambitions—in their own words. 1972. Dist: CF.

Ramparts of Clay. 85 min. Examines the harsh routine of a young woman's life in a remote village at the northern edge of the Sahara. 1970. Dist: C5.

Sambizanga. 102 min. The story of a poor woman's search for her jailed husband. 1972. Dist: NYF.

West Africa: Two Lifestyles. 17 min. Depicts the lifestyle of a contemporary African woman. 1970. Dist: BFA.

Women of the Toubou. 25 min. Position of women living in a society on the edge of the Sahara. 1974. Dist: PF.

VIDEOTAPES

Soul. A one-hour talk program including Shirley Chisholm and Betty Shabazz. 1969. Dist: WNET-TV Channel 13, 356 W. 58th Street, New York, NY 10019.

Naomi Madgett, Donald Hall, and Dan Gerber Reading Their Poems and Talking to Students. Dist: Michigan Council for the Arts, 10215 E. Jefferson Avenue, Detroit, MI 48214.

Robert Hayden, Naomi Madgett, and Dudley Randall Read the Six Poems They Want to Be Remembered By. 50 min. 8mm. B/W. Dist: Oakland Community College, Orchard Lake, MI 48030.

FILMSTRIPS

Doctor Is a Lady, The. Traces the life of Dorothy L. Brown, a Negro who struggled against her orphan background and discrimination to become a competent and dedicated doctor. 1967. Dist: NEGRHA.

Dream Awake—A Series. Traces the history of Black people from roots in

Africa through slavery to the present day. Includes filmstrips on Africa, Harriet Tubman, and The Martyrs—Bessie Smith and Malcolm X. 1970. Dist: SPA.

Harriet Tubman. Sound (disc). From "The Leading American" series. 1964. Dist: OPRINT.

Harriet Tubman. Sound (disc). Discusses events in the life of Harriet Tubman, a Negro abolitionist who aided slaves in their escape to freedom. From "The Chains of Slavery, 1800–1865" series. 1969. Dist: EBEC.

Lorraine Hansberry. Sound (disc). From the "Black Leaders of Twentieth-Century America" series. 1969. Dist: IBC.

(Dr.) Mary McLeod Bethune—Courageous Educator. With captions. Mary McLeod Bethune helped to found Bethune-Cookman College and was an executive with the National Youth Administration under Franklin D. Roosevelt. From the "American Negro Pathfinder" series. 1966. Dist: BFA.

Mary McLeod Bethune. Sound (disc). Presents a short biography of Bethune. From "The Image Makers" series. 1969. Dist: EGH.

Profiles of Black Achievement. Sound (cassette or disc). Series includes self-narrated portraits of painter Alma Thomas and poet-novelist Margaret Walker. Dist: Guidance Associates, Harcourt Brace Jovanovich.

Rosa Parks—Rush toward Freedom. Eight strips in a series, Rosa Parks among them. 1970. Dist: SCHALT.

Yvonne Brathwaite—Black and White. Sound (disc). Describes Yvonne Brathwaite's fight for equality as a Black and as a woman in the field of law. From the "Black Political Powers" series. 1969. Dist: DOUBLE.

RECORDS OR PHONO-DISCS

General Studies

Burroughs, Margaret G. *What Shall I Tell My Children Who Are Black?* (Sound-A-Rama, SOR 101 2S 12).

Burrows, Vinie. *Walk Together Children: The Black Scene in Prose, Poetry and Song* (Spoken Arts Co., #1030).

Davis, Angela. *Soul and Soledad* (ATCO Records, FD 10141).

Hansberry, Lorraine. *Lorraine Hansberry on Her Art and the Black Experience* (Caedmon, TC 1352 1–12" LP, CDL 51352 cassette).

———. *Lorraine Hansberry: To Be Young, Gifted and Black* (Caedmon, TRS 342 1971).

———. *Lorraine Hansberry Speaks Out: Art and the Black Revolution* (Caedmon, TC 1352 1972).

———. *Lorraine Hansberry: A Raisin in the Sun* (Caedmon, TRS 355 1972).

King, Coretta. *Coretta Scott King Reads from "My Life with Martin Luther King, Jr."* (Caedmon, TC 2050).

———. *My Life with Martin Luther King, Jr.* (Caedmon, TC 9300).

Kitt, Eartha, and Gunn, Moses. *Black Pioneers in American History* (Caedmon, TC 1252, CDL 5152).

Mabley, Moms (Comedian). *The Best of Moms Mabley* (Mercury Records/ Phonograms, Inc., 61139).

———. *Mabley on Stage* (Chess Records, 1447).

———. *Stars of the Apollo* (Columbia, CBS Records, C G 39788).

Sands, Diana, and Gunn, Moses. *Black Pioneers in American History.* Includes reading from the autobiography of Mary Church Terrell (Caedmon, TC 1299, CDL 5124).

Music

Anderson, Marian (Spirituals and Classics). *He's Got the Whole World* (RCA, LSC 2592).

———. *Black Image Makers.* Set of four discs, Disc #2 (Eye-Gate House, Inc., 1969).

Fitzgerald, Ella (Pop Jazz). *Newport Jazz Festival Live at Carnegie Hall* (Columbia, CBS Records, 32557 1973).

———. *Ella Loves Cole* (Porter) (Atlantic Record Corp., SD 1631 1972).

———. *Greatest Jazz Concert in the World* (Pablo Records, 2625704).

———. *History of Ella Fitzgerald* (Verve, ZV-8817).

———. *Billie Holiday and Ella Fitzgerald* (MCA Records, Z-4099).

———. *Ella and Louis* (Armstrong) (Verve, 8811).

———. *Porgy and Bess* (Verve, 2507).

Jackson, Mahalia (Gospel). *The Great Mahalia Jackson* (Columbia, CBS Records, KG 31379).

Jenkins, Ella. *"And One and Two," and Other Songs* (Folkways Records, FC 7544).

Author's Note: One distribution source for schools is Rose Record Stores, Inc., 214 S. Wabash Avenue, Chicago, IL 62523.

————. "My Street Begins at My House," and Other Songs and Rhythms from the "Me Too Show' (Folkways Records, FC 7543).

Makeba, Miriam. Sung by Miriam Makeba (RCA).

————. Miriam Makeba Sings African Folksongs (RCA).

Odetta (Folk Music). Anthology of Folk Music (Sine Qua Non Prod., Ltd., 1102 Vols. I & II).

————. Carnegie Hall (Vanguard Recording SOC, Inc., 73003).

Price, Leontyne (Classical). Five Great Operatic Scenes (RCA, LSC 3218).

————. I Wish I Knew How It Would Feel (RCA, LSC 3183).

————. Verdi's Greatest Hits (Victor Records/Rca Recordings, LSC 5011).

————. Leontyne Price Prima Donna (Victor Records/RCA Recordings, LSC 2898 Vol. I; LSC 2968 Vol. II; LSC 3163 Vol. III).

————. Aida (Verdi) (London Records, OSA 1393).

————. Swing Low Sweet Chariot (Victor Records/RCA Recordings, LSC 2600).

Smith, Bessie (Blues). Any Woman's Blues (Columbia, CBS Records, CG 30126).

————. Empty Bed Blues (Columbia, CBS Records, CG 30450).

————. The World's Greatest Blues Singer. Vocals between 1922 and 1933 (Columbia, CBS Records, CG-33).

Ward, Clara (Gospel). All Time Gospel Hits (Savory Records, 7145).

————. Clara Ward Sings (Savory Records, 14060).

————. Memorial Album (Savory Records, 14308).

Poetry

Brooks, Gwendolyn. Anthology of Negro Poets. Includes "Kitchenette," "Song of the Yard," and "Beverly Hills, Chicago" (Folkways Records, FL 9791).

Giovanni, Nikki. Truth Is on Its Way (Right-On Records, 15001).

Hughes, Langston, and Danner, Margaret. Writers of the Revolution (Black Forum) MoTown Record Corp., H-1725).

Walker, Margaret. Anthology of Negro Poets. Biographies of the poets are included in the album (Folkways Records, 1955).

CASSETTE TAPES

Poetry

Brooks, Gwendolyn. Gwendolyn Brooks Reading Her Poems with Comment (LW 3237). Jan. 19, 1961. Dist: Library of Congress, 109.

————, and Viereck, Peter. A joint reading by the two poets at the YMHA Poetry Center, New York. LWO 2863. Dist: Library of Congress, 110.
Danner, Margaret, and Randall, Dudley. *Poem Counterpoem* (Broadside Press).
Fabio, Sara Webster. *Soul Ain't Soul Is* (WAO*, P-125).
Giovanni, Nikki. *Legacies* (WAO, P-126).
————. *Nikki Giovanni Reads Re: Creation* (Broadside Press).
Jordan, June. *Things I Do in the Dark and Other Poems* (WAO, P-143).
Sanchez, Sonia. *Reading Selected Poems* (WAO, P-153).
————. *Sonia Sanchez Reads Her Own Poetry* (WAO, P-113).
————. *Sonia Sanchez Reads "Homecoming"* (Broadside Press).
Walker, Margaret. *For My People* (WAO, B-4).
————. *Prophets for a New Day* (Broadside Press).
————. *The Poetry and Voice of Margaret Walker* (WAO, P-120).

Lectures, Speeches, and Interviews

Black Woman, The. Interviews with Lena Horne, Verta Grosvenor, Jean Fairfax, Martha Davis, and Bibi Amina Baraka (WAO, DC-3146).
Black Women in America: 1. The History of Oppression from the Distaff Side (WAO, DC-3111).
Black Women in America: 2. The Civil War Ends and Another War Begins (WAO, DC-3112).
Carson, Josephine. *The Emotional Attitudes of the Southern Negro Woman* (WAO, DC-3125).
Chisholm, Shirley, and Gertner, Carol. *Congress and the Political Woman* (WAO, DC-3126).
Contemporary Black Women Writers. Pat Exum, lecturer. 5509. Dist: EE.
Davis, Angela. *Angela Davis Answers Questions about Her Political Ideas* (WAO, DC-3103).
————. *If They Come in the Morning* (WAO B-40).
Dee, Ruby. *What If I Am a Woman?—Black Women's Speeches (1833-1908)* (WAO, DC-3129).
Excerpts from the Lives of Famous 19th-Century Women. Narrated by Dorothy Washington (WAO, DC-3107).
King, Coretta Scott. *My Life with Martin Luther King, Jr.* (WAO, PR-1108).
Washington, Portia. *Booker T.'s Child Portia/Booker T. Washington Address.* Narrated by Roy L. Hill (WAO DC-3153).
*WAO — Women's Audio Exchange, 49 West Main Street, Cambridge, NY 19131.

Drama and Dramatic Reading

Burrows, Vinie. *Vinie Burrows* (Production Listening Library, Inc.).
Hansberry, Lorraine. *A Raisin in the Sun.* With Claudia McNeil, Ruby Dee, and Diana Sands (WAO B-29).
Morrison, Toni. *Song of Solomon* (WAO, B-21).

Music

Jackson, Mahalia. *The Life I Sing About.* MU-4102. Dist: WAO.
———. *Movin' On Up.* MU-4109. Dist: WAO.
Williams, Mary Lou. *Mary Lou Williams Plays Her Music.* MU-4105. Dist: WAO.

SLIDES AND PRINTS

Slides

Black Women Artists. Forty slides illustrating the works of America's most outstanding and prolific Black women artists. The set documents the unique contributions of Black women to our contemporary culture and surveys a great variety of techniques. Contemporary Crafts, Inc., 5271 W. Pico Blvd., Los Angeles, CA 90019.

Prints

Catlett, Elizabeth (Artist). Prints listed come from the *Elizabeth Catlett* catalogue, Studio Museum, Harlem.
"Black Maternity," 1959. Lithograph. 16x21½ in.
"Habla la Mujer Negro (The Black Woman Speaks)," 1960. Lithograph. 27½x18¾ in.
"Mujeres de America (Women of America)," 1963. Woodcut. 13¾x18¾ in.
"Rebozos," 1968. Lithograph. 20x13 in.
"Malcolm X Speaks for Us," 1969. Linocut. 37½x27¾ in.
"The Torture of Mothers," 1970. Lithograph. 13x20 in.

SELECTED BIBLIOGRAPHY

Books

Bogle, Donald. *Toms, Coons, Mulattoes, Mammies and Bucks: An Interpretive History of Blacks in American Films.* New York: Viking Press, 1973.

Cripps, Thomas. *Slow Fade to Black: The Negro in American Film, 1900-1942.* New York: Oxford Univ. Press, 1977.

Hughes, Langston, and Meltzer, Milton. *Black Magic: A Pictorial History of Black Entertainers in America.* Englewood Cliffs, N.J.: Prentice-Hall, 1967.

Klotman, Phyllis. *Frame by Frame—A Black Filmography.* Bloomington, Ind.: Indiana Univ. Press, 1979.

Leab, Daniel J. *From Sambo to Superspade: The Black Experience in Motion Pictures.* Boston: Houghton Mifflin, 1975.

NICEM (National Information Center for Educational Media). *Index to Black History and Studies* (Multimedia). Los Angeles, 1971.

Noble, Peter. *The Negro in Films.* London: S. Robinson, 1948; reprint ed., New York: Arno Press, 1970.

Null, Gary. *Black Hollywood: The Negro in Motion Pictures.* Secaucus, N.J.: Citadel Press, 1975.

Patterson, Lindsay. *Black Films and Film-Makers: A Comprehensive Anthology from Stereotype to Superhero.* New York: Dodd, Mead, 1975. Includes "Black Women in Films: A Mixed Bag of Tricks," by Edward Mapp, pp. 196-205.

Pines, Jim. *Blacks in Films: A Survey of Racial Themes and Images in American Film.* London, 1975.

Williams, Ora. *American Black Women in the Arts and Social Sciences: A Bibliographic Survey.* Metuchen, N.J.: Scarecrow Press, 1978.

Articles

Hall, Susan. "African Women on Film," *Africa Report* 22, No. 1 (January-February 1977):15-17.

Mapp, Edward. "Black Women in Films," *The Black Scholar* 4, Nos. 6-7 (March-April 1973):42-46.

324 Bibliographies

DISTRIBUTORS CODE

Non-Hollywood Films and Filmstrips

ABCN/MCGH
ABC News/McGraw Hill
1221 Avenue of the Americas
New York, NY 10036

Ames Documentary Films
336 West 84th Street
New York, NY 10024

AFRO
Afrographics
P.O. Box 8361
Los Angeles, CA 90008

BFA
BFA Educational Media
22111 Michigan Avenue
Santa Monica, CA 90404

CBSN/MCGH
CBS News/McGraw Hill
1221 Avenue of the Americas
New York, NY 10036

CF
Churchill Films
662 North Robertson Boulevard
Los Angeles, CA 90069

C5
Cinema-5
595 Madison Avenue
New York, NY 10022

CLA
Larry Clark
3535 11th Avenue
Los Angeles, CA 90000

DOUBLE
Doubleday Multimedia
1370 Reynolds Avenue
Santa Ana, CA 92705

EBEC
Encyclopedia Britannica
  Educational Corp.
425 N. Michigan Avenue
Chicago, IL 60611

EE
Everett/Edwards, Inc.
P.O. Box 1060
DeLand, FL 32720

EG
Eye-Gate House, Inc.
Subs. of Cenco Instrument Corp.
146-01 Archor Avenue
Jamaica, NY 11437

EGH
See EG

FC
Filmmakers Coop.
Address Unobtainable

HRAW
Holt, Rinehart and Winston
757 Third Avenue
New York, NY 10017

IBC
International Book Corp.
7300 Biscayne Boulevard
Miami, FL 33138

Author's Note: Distributors' addresses are subject to change. For rental purposes many university media centers can be helpful.

IU
Indiana University
Audio-Visual Center
Bloomington, IN 47401

JAS
Jason Films
2621 Palisade Avenue
Riverdale, NY 10463

LON
London Records
539 West 25th Street
New York, NY 10001

MGH
McGraw Hill
110 15th St.
Del Mar, CA 92014

MGHT
See MGH

MSUAC
Michigan State University
Audiovisual Center
East Lansing, MI 48824

NDF
New Day Films
P.O. Box 315
Franklin Lakes, NJ 07417

NEGRHA
Negro History Association
51 Herkimer Street
Brooklyn, NY 11216

NET; INUAVC
National Educational Television
2715 Packard Road
Ann Arbor, MI 48104

NLC
New Line Cinema
853 Broadway, 16th Floor
New York, NY 10003

NYF
New Yorker Films
43 West 61st Street
New York, NY 10023

NYT
New York Times
Off. of Ed. Activities
229 West 43rd Street
New York, NY 10036

OSUMPD
Ohio State University
  Motion Picture Division
Film Dist., 1885 Neil Avenue
Columbus, OH 43210

PF
Phoenix Films
470 Park Avenue South
New York, NY 10016

PYR
Pyramid Films
Box 1048
Santa Monica, CA 90400

ROA Films
1696 N. Astor
Milwaukee, WI 53202

SCHALT
Warren Schloat Productions, Inc.
Palmer Lane West
Pleasantville, NY 10570

SPA
Spoken Arts
59 Locust Avenue
New Rochelle, NY 10801

SQN
Sine Qua Non Prod., Ltd.
1 West Street

TIMLIF
Time-Life, Inc.
Time and Life Building
Rockefeller Center
New York, NY 10020

UC
See UCEMC

UCEMC
University of California
Ext. Media Center
2233 Fulton Street
Berkeley, CA 94720

WCAITV; CARSL
City and Monument Avenues
Philadelphia, PA 19131

WNET-TV/EBC
WNET-TV Channel 13
Educational Broadcasting Corp.
356 W. 58th Street
New York, NY 10019

WER
Wheelock Educational Resources
P.O. Box 451
Hanover, NH 03755

Additional References and Resources

See also articles, bibliographies, and course syllabi.

GENERAL

The Afro-American Woman: Struggles and Images. Ed. Sharon Harley and Rosalyn Terborg-Penn. Port Washington, N.Y.: Kennikat, 1978.

Another Voice: Feminist Perspectives on Social Life and Science. Ed. Marcia Millman & Rosabeth M. Kanter. New York: Octagon, 1975.

The Black Woman. Ed. La Frances Rodgers-Rose. Beverly Hills, Cal.: Sage, 1980.

Christian, Barbara T. *Black Women Novelists: The Development of a Tradition, 1892-1976.* Westport, Conn.: Greenwood, 1980.

Class and Feminism. Ed. Charlotte Bunch & Coletta Reid. Oakland, Cal.: Diana Press, 1974. Available from Diana Press, 4400 Market St., Oakland, Cal. 94608.

Cliff, Michelle. *Claiming An Identity They Taught Me to Despise.* Watertown, Mass.: Persephone, 1980. Available from Persephone Press, P.O. Box 7222, Watertown, Mass. 02172.

Conrad, Earl. *Harriet Tubman: Negro Soldier and Abolitionist.* New York: International Publishers, 1942, 1973.

The Diaries of Alice Dunbar-Nelson. Ed. Gloria T. Hull. New York: Burt Franklin, 1982.

Female Studies, Vols. I–XI. Available from The Feminist Press, Box 334, Old Westbury, N.Y., 11568.

In the Memory and Spirit of Frances, Zora, and Lorraine: Essays and Interviews on Black Women and Writing. Washington, D.C.: Institute for the Arts and Humanities, Howard University, 1979. Available from The Institute for the Arts and Humanities, Box 723, Howard University, Washington, D.C. 20059.

Malcolm, Shirley Mahaley; Hall, Paula Quick; and Brown, Janet Welsh. *The Double Bind: The Price of Being a Minority Woman in Science.* Washington, D.C.: American Association for the Advancement of Science, 1976. AAAS Publication 76-R-3, available from American Association for the Advancement of Science, 1515 Massachusetts Ave. N.W., Washington, D.C.

Midnight Birds: Stories of Contemporary Black Women Writers. Ed. Mary Helen Washington. Garden City, N. Y.: Anchor, 1980,
Noble, Jeanne. *Beautiful, Also, Are the Souls of My Black Sisters: A History of the Black Woman in America.* Englewood Cliffs, N. J.: Prentice-Hall, 1978.
Rich, Adrienne. *Of Woman Born.* New York: W. W. Norton, 1976.
Sisterhood Is Powerful: An Anthology of Writings from the Women's Liberation Movement. Ed. Robin Morgan. New York: Vintage, 1970.
Smith, Barbara. "Doing Research on Black American Women." *Women's Studies Newsletter* 4, no. 2 (Spring 1976): 4-7. Reprinted in *The Radical Teacher* 1, no. 3 (1976): 25-27. Available from *The Radical Teacher*, P. O. Box 102, Kendall Square, Cambridge, Mass. 02142.
Smith-Rosenberg, Carroll. "The Female World of Love and Ritual: Relations between Women in Nineteenth-Century America." *Signs: Journal of Women in Society* 1, no. 1 (1975): 1-29.
Sturdy Black Bridges: Visions of Black Women in Literature. Ed. Roseann P. Bell et al. Garden City, N. Y.: Anchor, 1979.
This Bridge Called My Back: Writings By Radical Women of Color. Ed. Cherríe Moraga and Gloria Anzaldúa. Watertown, Mass.: Persephone, 1981. Available from Persephone Press, P. O. Box 7222, Watertown, Mass. 02172.
Wallace, Michele. *Black Macho and the Myth of the Superwoman.* New York: Dial, 1979.
Women: A Feminist Perspective. Ed. Jo Freeman. Palo Alto, Cal.: Mayfield, 1975.

BIBLIOGRAPHIES

The Black Family and the Black Woman: A Bibliography. Ed. Phyllis Klotman and Wilmer H. Baatz. New York: Arno, 1978.
Black Lesbians: An Annotated Bibliography. Comp. J. R. Roberts. Tallahassee, Fla.: Naiad, 1981. Available from Naiad Press, P. O. Box 10543, Tallahassee, Fla. 32302.
The Black Woman in American Society: A Selected Annotated Bibliography. Comp. Lenwood G. Davis. Boston: G. K. Hall, 1975.
The Lesbian in Literature: A Bibliography. Ed. Barbara Grier et al. Tallahassee, Fla.: Naiad, 1981. Available from Naiad Press, P. O. Box 10543, Tallahassee, Fla. 32302.
A Resource Guide on Black Women in the United States. Comp. Arlene B. Enabulele and Dionne Jones. 1978. Available from the Institute for Urban Affairs and Research, Howard University, 2900 Van Ness St. N.W., Washington, D. C. 20008.

WEECN Resource Roundup: Black Women and Education. Available
from Women's Educational Equity Communications Network, Far
West Laboratory for Educational Research and Development, 1855
Folsom St., San Francisco, Cal. 94103.
Women, Ethnicity and Counseling: A Resource List. Comp. Emily A.
Carey, Oliva M. Espin, and Doris Munos. 1977. Available from
Womanspace: Feminist Therapy Collective, Inc., 636 Beacon St.,
Boston, Mass. 02215.
Women Loving Women. Ed. Marie J. Kuda. Chicago: Womanpress, 1975.
Available from Womanpress, Box 59330, Chicago, Ill. 60645.
Women and Literature. Comp. Sense and Sensibility Collective. Cam-
bridge, Mass.: Women and Literature Collective, 1976. Available
from Women and Literature Collective, Box 441, Cambridge, Mass.
02138.

FEMINIST/WOMEN'S STUDIES PERIODICALS

These periodicals publish creative writing and helpful work in general
feminist/women's studies theory and practice. They occasionally contain
writing by and about Black women.
Aphra: The Feminist Literary Magazine. Box 893, Ansonia Station, New
York, N.Y. 10023. (No longer publishing.)
Azalea: A Magazine by Third World Lesbians. Box 200, Cooper Station,
New York, N.Y. 10003.
Chrysalis: A Magazine of Women's Culture. 1052 W. 6th St., #330, Los
Angeles, Cal. 90017. (No longer publishing. Back issues still
available.)
Conditions: A Magazine of Writing by Women. P.O. Box 56, Van Brunt
Station, Brooklyn, N.Y. 11215.
Feminist Studies. Women's Studies Program, University of Maryland,
College Park, Md. 20742.
Frontiers: A Journal of Women Studies. Women Studies Program,
Hillside Court 104, University of Colorado, Boulder, Colo. 80309.
Heresies: A Feminist Publication on Art and Politics. Box 766, Canal St.
Station, New York, N.Y. 10013.
Matrices: A Lesbian/Feminist Research Newsletter. Julia P. Stanley,
Dept. of English, University of Nebraska, Lincoln, Neb. 68588.
Off Our Backs: A Women's News Journal. 1724 20th St. N.W.,
Washington, D.C. 20009.
Psychology of Women Quarterly. Human Sciences Press, 72 Fifth
Avenue, New York, N.Y. 10011.
Quest: A Feminist Quarterly. P.O. Box 8843, Washington, D.C. 20003.
The Radical Teacher. P.O. Box 102, Kendall Square, Cambridge, Mass.

02142. [No. 6 (December 1977) is a special issue on women's studies.]
Signs: Journal of Women in Culture and Society. Univ. of Chicago Press,
11030 Langley Ave., Chicago, Ill. 60628.
*Sinister Wisdom: A Journal of Words and Pictures for the Lesbian
Imagination in All Women.* P. O. Box 660, Amherst, Mass. 01004.
Sojourner: A Third World Women's Research Newsletter. Dandelion
Publishing Co., P. O. Box 35-198, Detroit, Mich. 48235.
Truth: Association of Black Women Historians Newsletter. c/o Sharon
Harley, Afro-American Studies Program, University of Maryland,
College Park, Md. 20742.
University of Michigan Papers in Women's Studies. Women's Studies
Program, University of Michigan, Ann Arbor, Mich. 48104.
Women: A Journal of Liberation. 3028 Greenmount Ave., Baltimore, Md.
21218.
Women's Studies: An Interdisciplinary Journal. Dept. of English,
Queens College, Flushing, N. Y. 11367.
Women's Studies Abstracts. Box 1, Rush, N. Y. 14543.
Women's Studies Quarterly. The Feminist Press, Box 334, Old Westbury,
N. Y. 11568.

LESBIAN FEMINISM
The Black Lesbian Bibliography. Ed. J. R. Roberts. Tallahassee, Fla.:
Naiad, 1981. Available from Naiad Press, P. O. Box 10543, Talla-
hassee, Fla. 32302.
Brown, Wilmette. "The Autonomy of Black Lesbian Women." Paper
read July 24, 1976, Toronto, Canada. Available from Black Women
for Wages for Housework, 21 Stengel Ave., Newark, N. J. 07112.
Bunch, Charlotte, "Not For Lesbians Only." *Quest: A Feminist Quarter-
ly* 2, no. 2 (Fall 1975): 50–56.
Davine. "The Housework of Heterosexuality." Available from Black
Women for Wages for Housework, 21 Stengel Ave., Newark, N. J.
07112.
Lesbianism and the Women's Movement. Ed. Charlotte Bunch and
Coletta Reid. Oakland, Cal.: Diana Press, 1975.
Lorde, Audre. "Scratching the Surface: Some Notes on Barriers to
Women and Loving." *The Black Scholar* 9, no. 7 (April 1978): 31–35.
New York Radicalesbians. "Woman-Identified Woman." *Lesbians Speak
Out.* Oakland, Cal.: Women's Press Collective, 1974.

RACISM AND THE WOMEN'S MOVEMENT
Bulkin, Elly. "Racism and Writing: Some Implications for White Lesbian
Critics." *Sinister Wisdom* 13 (Spring 1980): 3-22.

Hoffman, Nancy. "White Women, Black Women: Inventing an Adequate Pedagogy." *Women's Studies Newsletter* 5, nos. 1 and 2 (Spring 1977): 21-24.

Pratt, Minnie Bruce, "Rebellion." *Feminary* 11, 1&2 (1980): 6-20. Available from *Feminary*, P.O. Box 954, Chapel Hill, N.C. 27514.

Racism and Sexism: Special Issue. Off Our Backs 9, no. 10 (November 1979).

Rich, Adrienne. "Disloyal to Civilization, Feminism, Racism, Gynephobia." *On Lies, Secrets and Silence: Selected Prose 1966-1978.* New York: W.W. Norton, 1979. Also in *Chrysalis: A Magazine of Women's Culture* 7: 10-27.

Smith, Barbara and Laura Sperazi. "Breaking the Silence: Two Women Take a First Step." *Equal Times* 2, no. 35 (March 13-25, 1978): 10-12. Available from *Equal Times*, 235 Park Square Building, Boston, Mass. 02116.

Top Ranking: A Collection of Articles on Racism and Classism in the Lesbian Community. Ed. Sara Bennett and Joan Gibbs. Brooklyn, N.Y. 11238.

"Violence Against Women and Race." Special Issue. *Aegis: Magazine on Ending Violence Against Women* (March-April 1979). Available from *Aegis*, c/o F.A.A.R., Box 21033, Washington, D.C. 20009.

THE WRITING OF WOMEN IN PRISON

These are only a few of the many publications produced by incarcerated women throughout the country. Check in your own region for additional resources.

I Used To Be Sweet and a Little Sour But Now I'm Sour and a Little Sweet. Women's Correctional Institute Arts Workshop, 1977.

Inner Feelings: First Poems from the Women's Correctional Institute. Women's Correctional Institute Arts Workshop, 1976. Available from W.C.I. Arts Workshop, c/o Joyce Brabner, 2 West Fifth St., Wilmington, Del. 19801.

Muske, Carol. "The Art of Not Bowing: Writing by Women in Prison." *Heresies* 1, no. 1: 30-35.

No More Cages: A Bi-Monthly Women's Prison Newsletter. P.O. Box 90, Brooklyn, N.Y. 11215.

Shakur, Assata [Joanne Chesimard]. "Women in Prison: How We Are." *The Black Scholar* 9, no. 7 (April 1978): 8-15.

"Voices from Within: The Poetry of Women in Prison." Ed. Ann McGovern. *The Radical Teacher* 6 (December 1977): 45-47. Available from *The Radical Teacher*, P.O. Box 102, Kendall Square P.O., Cambridge, Mass. 02142.

Voices from Within: The Poetry of Women in Prison. Ed. Ann McGovern. Weston, Conn.: Magic Circle Press, 1975. Available from Magic Circle Press, 10 Hyde Ridge, Weston, Conn. 06880.

Women Behind Bars: An Organizing Tool. Ed. Resources for Community Change. Washington, D. C.: n.d. Available from Resources for Community Change, P. O. Box 21066, Washington, D. C. 20009.

PERIODICALS: SPECIAL ISSUES ON BLACK WOMEN

The Black Collegian: The National Magazine of Black College Students. Special Issue on Black Women (May–June 1979). Available from Black Collegiate Services, Inc., 1240 South Broad St., New Orleans, La. 70125.

The Black Scholar: The Black Woman. 3, no. 4 (December 1971).

The Black Scholar: Black Women's Liberation. 4, nos. 6-7 (March-April 1973).

The Black Scholar: The Black Woman 1975. 6, no. 6 (March 1975).

The Black Scholar: Blacks and the Sexual Revolution. 9, no. 7 (April 1978).

The Black Scholar: The Black Sexism Debate. 10, nos. 8-9 (May–June 1979).

"Black Women Image Makers." *Black World* 23, no. 10 (August 1974).

"Women Poets, A Special Issue." *Callaloo* 2, no. 5 (February 1979). Available from Charles H. Rowell, Dept. of English, University of Kentucky, Lexington, Ky. 40506.

"The Black Woman's Issue." Ed. Lorraine Bethel and Barbara Smith. *Conditions: 5* 2, no. 2 (Autumn 1979). Available from *Conditions*, P. O. Box 56, Van Brunt Station, Brooklyn, N. Y. 11215.

"Lorraine Hansberry: Art of Thunder, Vision of Light." Ed. Jean Carey Bond. *Freedomways* 19, no. 4 (1979). Available from *Freedomways*, 799 Broadway, New York, N. Y. 10003.

"Third World Women: The Politics of Being Other." *Heresies* 2, no. 4 (1979).

"The Black Women in America." *New Letters* 41, no. 2 (Winter 1974). Available from *New Letters*, University of Missouri, Kansas City, Mo. 64110.

" 'Ain't I A Womon' Issue: By and About Wimmin of Color." *Off Our Backs* 9, no. 6 (June 1979).

"Sexism and Racism." *Off Our Backs* 9, no. 10 (November 1979).

"Generations: Women in the South." *Southern Exposure* 4, no. 4 (Winter 1977). Available from *Southern Exposure*, P. O. Box 230, Chapel Hill, N. C. 25314. (Although not all of these articles are specifically focused on Black women, a significant number of them are.)

BLACK WOMEN IN THE ACADEMY

Epstein, Cynthia Fuchs. "Positive Effects of the Multiple Negative: Explaining the Success of Black Professional Women." *American Journal of Sociology* 78 (1973): 912–35.

Gleaves, Francelia. "Minority Women and Higher Education #1." Available from The Project on the Status and Education of Women, 1818 R Street N.W., Washington, D. C. 20009.

National Institute of Education (N. I. E.), *Educational and Occupational Needs of Black Women: A Compendium,* Vols. 1 and 2. 1978. Available from Women's Research Program, Educational Equity Group, National Institute of Education, Washington, D. C.

Parrish, Dorothy. "A Question of Survival: The Predicament of Black Women." *We'll Do It Ourselves: Combatting Sexism in Education.* Ed. David Rosen et. al. N.p.: 1974, pp. 31–53. Available from Nebraska Curriculum Development Center, Andrews Hall, University of Nebraska, Lincoln, Neb. 68588.

"Recruiting Minority Women—#1," and "Recruiting Minority Women—#2." Available from The Project on the Status and Education of Women, 1818 R Street N.W., Washington, D. C. 20009.

Rickman, Geraldine. "The Doctorate." *Comment* 9, no. 4 (Fall 1976). Available from *Comment,* American Council on Education, Office of Women in Higher Education, 1 Dupont Circle, Washington, D. C. 20036.

Students sorting collars and cuffs, Tuskegee Institute.

Section Seven

Doing the Work: Selected Course Syllabi

General/Social/Interdisciplinary

AFRO-AMERICAN WOMEN IN HISTORY
Bettina Aptheker
San Jose State University, Women's Studies Program
Fall 1978

Beginning with consideration of the Black woman's experience under slavery, this course will examine the role of Black women in the shaping of United States history, including their efforts as industrial, domestic, and agricultural workers, as doctors, lawyers, teachers, journalists, orators, and political activists in the nineteenth and twentieth centuries. Thematic emphasis will be given to historical and contemporary issues in the women's movement, as viewed from a variety of Black perspectives, including the abolitionist movement, woman suffrage, temperance, settlement house work, childcare, lynching, rape, abortion, the family, sterilization, etc.

Required Texts

Gerda Lerner, ed. *Black Women in White America: A Documentary History* (1972).

Alfreda M. Duster, ed. *Crusade for Justice: The Autobiography of Ida B. Wells* (1970).

Akosua Barthwell, *Trade Unionism in North Carolina: The Strike Against Reynolds Tobacco, 1947* (1977).

Supplementary Texts

Joyce Ladner, *Tomorrow's Tomorrow* (1971).

Bert J. Lowenberg and Ruth Bogin, *Black Women in the Nineteenth Century Life: Their Words, Thoughts and Feelings* (1976).

Eleanor Flexner, *Century of Struggle* (1957; Revised edition, 1976).

Herbert Gutman, *The Black Family in Slavery and Freedom: 1750-1925* (1977).

Sept. 6   Introduction

Sept. 8, 11, 13, 18

    I. The Legacy of Slavery

    Lerner, Part 1. "Slavery"

    Angela Y. Davis, "Reflections on the Black Woman's Role in the Community of Slaves," *The Black Scholar*, December, 1971.

    Joyce A. Ladner, "Black Womanhood in Historical Perspective," Chapter I in *Tomorrow's Tomorrow* (1971).

    Robert Staples, "The Myth of the Black Matriarchy," in *The Black Woman in America: Sex, Marriage and the Family*.

    W.E.B. Du Bois, "The Damnation of Women," in *Darkwater, Voices From Within the Veil* (1920).

Sept. 20   The Colonial and Revolutionary Era

Sept. 27, Oct. 2, 4, 9, 11
 II. Abolitionism and Woman's Rights
    Herbert Aptheker, "The Abolitionist Movement."
    Gerda Lerner, "Black and White Women in Interaction and Confrontation," in Jack
    Salzmann, ed. *Prospects: An Annual of American Cultural Studies* (1976), pp. 193-
    208.
    Anne Firor Scott, "Women's Perspective on the Patriarchy, *Journal of American
    History*, LXI (June, 1974), pp 52-64.
    Harriet Beecher Stowe, "Sojourner Truth, The Libyan Sibyl," *Atlantic Monthly*, XI,
    (April, 1863), pp. 473-78.
    Earl Conrad, "I Bring You General Tubman," the *Black Scholar*, I (January/February,
    1970).
Oct. 16, 18, 23, 25
 III. The Civil War, Reconstruction and the Split in the Feminist Movement
    Suzanne Lebsock, "Radical Reconstruction and the Property Rights of Southern
    Women," *Journal of Southern History*, XLII (May, 1977), pp. 195-216.
    Eleanor Flexner, "The Emergence of a Suffrage Movement," in *Century of Struggle*,
    Chapter X, pp. 145-158.
Oct. 30, Nov. 1
 IV. Black Women in Education and the Professions Prior to 1920
    Lerner, Part 2. "The Struggle for Education."
    Lerner, Part 6. "In Government Service and Political Life."
Nov. 6, 8
 V. The Post-Reconstruction Era and the Struggle Against Lynching
    Ida B. Wells. *Crusade for Justice*.
    Lerner, Part 3, "A Woman's Lot."
    Lerner, Part 7, "The Monster Prejudice."
Nov. 13
 VI. The National Association of Colored Women
    Wells, *Crusade* . . . . . .(continued).
    Lerner, Part 8, "Lifting as We Climb."
Nov. 20, 22, 27
 VII. Domestic, Agricultural and Industrial Workers
    Lerner, Part 4, "Making a Living."
    Barthwell, *Trade Unionism in North Carolina*.
Nov. 29
 VIII. The Modern Civil Rights Movement
    Lerner, Part 10, "Black Women Speak of Womanhood."
Dec. 4
 IX. Angela Davis Trial in Historical Perspective
Dec. 6, 11, 13
 X. Feminism and Black Liberation
    Diane K. Lewis, "A Response to Inequality: Black Women, Racism and Sexism,"
    Signs 3 (Winter 1977).
    Angela Y. Davis, "Racism and Contemporary Literature on Rape," *Freedomways*,
    First Quarter, 1976, pp. 25-33.
    Brenda Eichelberger, "Voices on Black Feminism," *Quest: A Feminist Quarterly* 3
    (Spring 1977), pp. 16-28.

HERSTORY OF BLACK WOMEN
Betsy Brinson
Fall 1979

Seminar Assignments:

I. October 9 "Black Women and Slavery"
Readings: G. Lerner, *Black Women in White America*, pp. 5-72.
Questions for discussion:
1. How did slavery affect the Black family?
2. What kind of educational opportunities were available to slave women?
3. How did Black women handle sexual abuse?
4. How did slavery affect the way Black women feel about themselves as women?

II. October 16 "The Struggle for Education"
Readings: *Black Women in White America*, pp. 73-146.
Assignment: Research and prepare brief one-page history on Rosa Bowser for whom the new Open High School building is named. Who was she? What did she contribute to the Black community?

III. October 23 "Black Women as Sex Objects"
Readings: *Black Women in White America*, pp. 149-193.
Questions for discussion:
1. How have Black women been treated sexually over the ages?
2. How has abusive treatment affected the Black woman's feelings about herself?
3. How are Black women viewed sexually today?

IV. October 30 "Black Women Organize for the Welfare of Others"
Readings: *Black Women in White America*, pp. 193-215; 433-477; 497-520.
Research Frances Ellen Watkins Harper, Ida B. Wells Barnett, Jamie Porter Barrett and Maggie Lena Walker in *Notable American Women* (3 volumes—also Richmond Public Library).
Questions for discussion:
1. What motivated women to become involved in anti-lynching campaigns?
2. What motivated women to become involved in interracial activities?
3. How did Black women choose to work for self-improvement of themselves and for others? Were they successful? What were their accomplishments?

V. November 6 "Black Women in Government Service and Political Life"
Readings: *Black Women in White America*, pp. 316-357.
Margaret Rose Gladney, "If It Was Anything for Justice," *Southern Exposure*, pp. 19-23.
Assignment: Make a list of Black women and Black men who are active in politics. What qualities do Black women need to succeed in politics?

VI. November 13 Field trip to Washington, D.C. to visit the National Archives for Black Women's History.

VII. November 20 and 27 "Black Women as Workers"
Readings: *Black Women in White America*, pp. 216-284.
Xeroxed articles to be distributed in class.
Questions for discussion:
1. What jobs were open to Black women in this country prior to the twentieth century?

2. Were Black women discriminated against on their jobs? In what ways?

3. What kinds of paid work did your grandmother do? Your mother?

4. What jobs are open to Black women today?

VIII. December 4 and 11   "Black Women and Racial Prejudice"

Readings: *Black Women in White America*, pp. 359-431; 521-558.

Sara Evans, "Women's Consciousness and the Southern Black Movement," *Southern Exposure*, pp. 10-18.

Questions for discussion:

1. How did Black women challenge racial prejudice prior to the twentieth century civil rights movement?

2. What role did Black women play in the civil rights struggle?

3. Is racial prejudice still a problem for Black women today?

IX. December 18 and January 8   "Black Women Organize to Meet the Needs of Women"

Readings: *Black Women in White America*, pp. 559-614.

Alice Walker, "In Search of Our Mothers' Gardens," *Southern Exposure*, pp. 60-70.

Wendy Wentress, "It's Something Inside of You," *Southern Exposure*, pp. 76-81.

Pauli Murray, "The Fourth Generation of Proud Shoes," *Southern Exposure*, pp. 4-9.

Questions for discussion:

1. What are the concerns of Black women today?

2. Should Black women be concerned with the Equal Rights Amendment? With reproductive freedom? With employment discrimination? Are there other social issues important to Black women today?

3. How do your attitudes on these issues compare with those of your mother and grandmother?

THE BLACK WOMAN
Marsha Darling
Wellesley College, Black Studies Department
Spring 1980

The historical and socio-political experiences of Black Women have often gone unrecorded and unrecognized. Where these experiences have been noted our understanding of the phenomenon of her essence in being female as well as Black has often been obscured. The Black Female has been shaped by the necessities of the historical moment. She has been oppressed because of her gender, race, class, and age. Yet, she has emerged as the cornerstone of the Afro-American community. Without her strength and perseverance in giving birth, nurturing and educating successive generations of little people, there would be no Black community, active and vibrant as it is, to speak of in contemporary terms. The basic economic relationship of Black Women in the world economy—one of working women— has marked the nature of the interface between Black Women, the Third World community and the larger society.

Key institutions have evolved from the environment and experience of Black Women. The course seeks to develop an analysis of the economic, social, political, and cultural role of Black Women in American society from an interdisciplinary perspective, blending historical linkages through chronology (African background, slavery, Reconstruction, agrarian experience, urban migration) with social systems and institutions (family, church).

Importantly, one looks to Black Women's literary, philosophical, and artistic expressions for the substance of self-imagery. Myths and realities will be explored through a combination of sources (fiction, non-fiction, visual, and audio). Inherent in the conceptual framework of this course is the thematic nexus for viewing Black Women as nurturers, educators, protectors—by and large women-identified women, forming as they have the core of a humanistic feminism.

It is hoped that this course will assist students in achieving three major goals:
1. develop a general chronological overview of the history of the Black Woman in America;
2. develop an analysis of the historical context of contemporary problems and phenomena, and an appreciation for comparative and interdisciplinary approaches to issues in the experience of the Black Woman;
3. develop reading, discussion and writing skills used in gaining insights into the key events, issues, and themes in Afro-American history.

The class meets twice a week with occasional review sessions when thought needed by the instructor or requested by the students. Class sessions will be balanced between lectures and discussions. Student progress will be evaluated by means of a midterm or oral presentation and final examination, a short paper (10-page essay, double spaced) or an oral history project and classroom participation (each accounting for one-fourth of a student's course grade).

Reading

In addition to the required reading two bibliographies are indispensable reference books for working in subject areas related to Black Women:

Lenwood G. Davis, *The Black Woman in American Society: A Selected Annotated Bibliography.*

Ora Williams, *American Black Women in the Arts and Social Sciences: A Bibliographic Survey.*

Required Reading

Roseann P. Bell, Bettye J. Parker, and Beverly Guy-Sheftall, eds. *Sturdy Black Bridges— Visions of Black Women in Literature* (New York: Doubleday, Anchor Press, 1979).

Zora Neale Hurston, *Their Eyes Were Watching God* (Urbana, Illinois: University of Illinois Press, 1978).

Joyce A. Ladner, *Tomorrow's Tomorrow—The Black Woman* (New York: Doubleday, Anchor Press, 1971).

Gerda Lerner, ed. *Black Women in White America—A Documentary History* (New York: Random House, Vintage Books, 1972).

Toni Morrison, *Sula* (New York: Alfred A. Knopf, 1976).

Jeanne Noble, *Beautiful, Also, Are The Souls Of My Black Sisters—A History of the Black Woman in America* (Englewood Cliffs, New Jersey: Prentice Hall, 1978).

Barbara Smith and Lorraine Bethel, eds. *Conditions: Five—The Black Women's Issue* (1979).

Robert Staples, *The Black Woman in America—Sex, Marriage, and the Family* (Chicago: Nelson-Hall Publishers, 1973).

Alice Walker, *Meridian* (New York: Pocket Books, 1976).

I. Black Women in Historical Perspective

Hertha Pauli, *Her Name Was Sojourner Truth.*

Billinglsey, *Black Families in White America*, Chapters 6 and 7, Appendix.

Philip S. Foner, ed. *Frederick Douglass on Women's Rights.*

Bert J. and Ruth Lowenberg, eds. *Black Women in Nineteenth-Century American Life: Their Words, Their Thoughts, Their Feelings.*

Martin E. Dann, ed. *The Black Press: The Quest for National Identity.*

Feb. 19   Twentieth Century
Feb. 21   Lecture: Socioeconomic Status and the Black Woman; Black women as members of the rural poor, urban poor and working class, emerging middle class.
Required   Alice Walker, *In Love and Trouble: Stories of Black Women.* Lerner, *Black Women in White America,* pp. 227-275, 437-459.
                 Cynthia Neverdon-Morton, "The Black Woman's Struggle for Equality in the South, 1895-1925," in Sharon Harley and Rosalyn Terborg-Penn, eds. *The Afro-American Woman: Struggles and Images,* p. 58.
Recommended   Joe R. Feagin, "Black Women in the American Work Force," in Charles V. Willie, ed. *The Family Life of Black People,* pp. 23-35.
                 Sheila Rowbotham, *Woman's Consciousness, Man's World.*
                 Alice S. Rossi, ed. *The Feminist Papers: From Adams to de Beauvoir.*
                 Karl Marx, Frederick Engels, V.I. Lenin, Joseph Stalin, *The Woman Question.*
Feb. 26   Contemporary
                 Lecture/Discussion: Today's Black Woman: Issues of Selfhood
Required   Jeanne Noble, *Beautiful, Also, Are the Souls of My Black Sisters,* Chapter 6.
                 Michele Wallace, *Black Macho and the Myth of the Superwoman,* pp. 89-117.
                 Lerner, *Black Women in White America,* Chapter 10.
                 Frances M. Beal, "Slave of a Slave No More: Black Women in Struggle," in *The Black Scholar: Journal of Black Studies and Research,* Vol. 6, No. 6, March, 1975, pp. 2-10.
Recommended   Eleanor Flexner, *Century of Struggle: The Woman's Rights Movement in the United States.*
                 Gerda Lerner, *The Female Experience: An American Documentary.*
Discussion of Term Papers or Presentations

II. Definitions of Womanhood
Mar. 4   Becoming a Black Woman
                 Lecture: Significance of Growth Stages: Childhood
Required   Ladner, *Tomorrow's Tomorrow: The Black Woman,* chs. 2-5.
                 Robert Staples, *The Black Woman in America: Sex, Marriage, and the Family,* pp. 1-34.
Recommended   Helene Deutsch, *The Psychology of Women, Vol. I-Girlhood, Vol. II-Motherhood.*
                 Eugene Perkins, *Home Is a Dirty Street: The Social Oppression of Black Children.*
Mar. 6   Lecture/Discussion: Adolescence, Education, Work, Peer Groups
Required   Alice Walker, *Meridian.*
                 Ladner, *Tomorrow's Tomorrow: The Black Woman,* pp. 177-282.
Recommended   Stephanie L. Twin, *Out of the Bleachers: Writings on Women and Sport.*
                 J.E. Franklin, *Black Girl: From Genesis to Revelations.*
Mar. 11   Lecture: Marriage, Motherhood and Kin Networks
Required   Staples, *The Black Woman in America,* chs. 3-5.
                 Lerner, ed., *Black Women in White America,* pp. 296-322.
                 Alice Walker, "One Child of One's Own," and "In Search of Our Mothers' Gardens."
Recommended   Carol B. Stack, *All Our Kin: Strategies for Survival in a Black Community,* chs. 4-7.

Mar. 13   Lecture: Children, Contraception, Abortion
Required   Nikki Giovanni, *My House.*
                Lucille Clifton, *An Ordinary Woman.*
                Lerner, *Black Women in White America,* pp. 414-436; 512-525.
Recommended   Anne Moody, *Coming of Age in Mississippi.*
                Inez Reid, *Together Black Women.*
Mar. 18   Lecture: Black Women in the Work Force
Required   Terry Fee, "Domestic Labor: An Analysis of Housework and its Relation
                to the Production Process," in *Review of Radical Economics,* Vol. 8, No.
                1, Spring 1976, pp. 1-8.
                F.D. Blair, "Women in the Labor Force: An Overview," in Jo Freeman,
                ed., *Women: A Feminist Perspective,* pp. 211-225.
                Alexis M. Herman, "A Statistical Portrait of the Black Woman Worker,"
                in *The Black Collegian,* May/June 1978, p. 30.
                U.S. Dept. of Labor Employment Standards & Administration: Women's
                Bureau, "Facts on Women Workers of Minority Races."
                Joe R. Feagin, "Black Women in the American Work Force," in Charles V.
                Willie, ed., *The Family Life of Black People,* pp. 23-35.
                Charmeynne D. Nelson, "Myths About Black Women Workers in Modern
                America," in *The Black Scholar,* Vol. 6, No. 6, March 1975, pp. 11-15.

Take Home Midterm
Mar. 20   Lecture: Professionalism, Aging
Required   Dorothy Sterling, *Black Foremothers: Three Lives.*
                Ellen Cantarow, "Ella Baker: Organizing for Civil Rights," in *Moving the
                Mountain: Women Working for Social Change,* pp. 54-93.
                Mary McKenny, "Class Attitudes and Professionalism," in *Quest: A
                Feminist Quarterly,* Vol. 3, No. 4, Spring 1977, p. 48.
                J. Fichter, "Career Expectations of Negro Women Graduates," in *Monthly
                Labor Review,* Vol. 90, November 1967, p. 36.
                Julianne Malveaux, "Black Women on White Campuses," in *Essence,* vol.
                10, no. 4, August 1979, p. 78.
Recommended   Barbara Jordan and Shelby Hearon, *Barbara Jordan: A Self-Portrait.*
                Alan L. Sorkin, "Education, Occupation and Income of Non-White
                Women."
                Trellie Jeffers, "The Black Women and the Black Middle Class," in *The
                Black Scholar,* Vol. 4, No. 6-7, March-April 1973, p. 37.
                Lena Wright Myers, "Black Women and Self-Esteem," in Marcia Millman
                and Rosabeth Moss Kanter, *Another Voice: Feminist Perspectives on
                Social Life and Social Science.*
                Monroe A. Majors, *Noted Negro Women: Their Triumphs and Activities.*
                Ernest J. Gaines, *The Autobiography of Miss Jane Pittman.*

III. Black Women in Afro-American Literature
Apr. 1   Lecture/Discussion: Novels
Apr. 3
Required   Zora Neale Hurston, *Their Eyes Were Watching God.*
                Toni Morrison, *Sula.*
                Rita Mae Brown, *Rubyfruit Jungle.*
Recommended   Larry Neal, "Zora Neale Hurston: A Profile," in *Southern Exposure,* Vol.
                1, No. 3 & 4, Winter 1974.
                Mary Helen Washington, "Zora Neale Hurston: A Woman Half in

	Shadow," in *I Love Myself When I Am Laughing...And Then Again When I Am Looking Mean and Impressive: A Zora Neale Hurston Reader.*
Apr. 8	Lecture/Discussion: Poetry and Prose
April. 10	
Required	Roseann P. Bell, Bettye J. Parker and Beverly Guy-Sheftall, *Sturdy Black Bridges: Visions of Black Women in Literature.*

Women Poets: A Special Issue, *Callaloo #5*, Vol. 2, February 1979.

Ntozake Shange, *for colored girls who have considered suicide/when the rainbow is enuf.*

Recommended   Audre Lorde, "Scratching the Surface: Some Notes on Barriers to Women and Loving," in *The Black Scholar*, Vol. 9, No. 7, April 1978, p. 31.

An Anthology of Poetry, Fiction, Essays & Photography by Women, *Freshtones*, Vol. One.

Apr. 15	Lecture/Discussion: Theatre, Short Stories, Diaries, Oral
Apr. 17	Histories
Required	Mary Helen Washington, ed., *Black-Eyed Susans: Classic Stories By and About Black Women.*

Lucille Clifton, *Generations: A Memoir.*

Dick Cluster, "The Borning Struggle: The Civil Rights Movement, An Interview with Bernice Johnson Reagon," in *Radical America*, Vol. 12, No. 6, November-December 1978.

Gayl Jones, *White Rat.*

Robert Staples, *Black Woman in America*, ch. 7.

Jeanne Noble, *Beautiful, Also, Are the Souls Of My Black Sisters*, ch. 7.

Recommended   Herbert Hill, *Soon, One Morning: New Writing by American Negroes.*

Toni Cade Bambara, *The Sea Birds Are Still Alive: Collected Stories.*

Outlines for Term Paper Due

IV. Voices and Images of Black Women

Apr. 22	*Black Women in the Arts: Music*
	Lecture/Discussion
Required	Derrick Stewart-Baxter, *Ma Rainey and the Classic Blues Singers.*

Bernice Reagon, "The Lady Street Singer," in *Southern Exposure*, Vol. 2, No. 1, Spring/Summer 1974.

Jeanne Noble, *Beautiful, Also, Are The Souls Of My Black Sisters*, ch. 8.

Recommended   Sharon Harley and Rosalyn Terborg-Penn, *The Afro-American Woman: Struggles and Images*, chs. 5-7.

Apr. 24	Black Women in Film
	Film/Discussion
Required	Edward Mapp, "Black Women in Films," in *The Black Scholar*, Vol. 4, No. 6-7, March-April 1973.

Jean Carey Bond, "The Media Image of Black Women," in *Freedomways*, Vol. 15, No. 1.

Recommended   Maurine Beasley and Sheila Gibbons, *Women in Media: A Documentary Source Book.*

Apr. 29	Voices of Black Womanhood: Humanism and Feminism
	Lecture/Discussion
Required	Staples, *The Black Woman in America*, ch. 6.

"Generations: Women in the South," *Southern Exposure*, Vol. 4, No. 4.

Jo Freeman, ed., *Women: A Feminist Perspective*, pp. 430-450; 575-588.

Assata Shakur (Joanne Chesimard), "Women in Prison: How We Are,"

The Black Scholar, Vol. 9, No. 7, April 1978.
Brenda Eichelberger, "Voices on Black Feminism," in *Quest: A Feminist Quarterly*, Vol. 3, No. 4, Spring 1977.
Handouts
Recommended   Charnie Guettel, *Marxism and Feminism*.

V. The Black Woman and Expression of Sexuality
May 1   Black Men and Black Women: The Dynamics of Sexism?
               Lecture/Discussion
Required   "The Black Sexism Debate," *The Black Scholar*, Vol. 10, No. 8, 9, May/June 1979.
               Michele Wallace, *Black Macho and the Myth of the Superwoman*, Part 1.
               June Jordan, *Things That I Do in the Dark*.
Recommended   Nikki Giovanni, *The Women and the Men*.
               Handouts
May 6   Black Women, Bisexuality and Lesbianism
               Lecture/Discussion
Required   Lorraine Bethel and Barbara Smith, eds., *Conditions Five: The Black Women's Issue*.
               Rita Mae Brown, *Songs To a Handsome Woman*.
               Audre Lorde, *The Black Unicorn*.
Recommended   *Azalea: A Magazine for Third World Lesbians*, Vol. 2, No. 3
               Handouts
May 8   Summary and Review; Assessment
May 10-14   Spring Reading Period
May 14   Assignment due: final draft of term paper
May 21   Final Examination

PORTRAIT IN BLACK AND WHITE:
THE EXPERIENCE OF BLACK WOMEN IN AMERICA
Virginia Grant Darney
The Open College/Pine Manor Jr. College
1975

Reading List
Shirley Chisholm, *Unbought and Unbossed* (New York: Houghton Mifflin, 1970).
John Hope Franklin, *From Slavery to Freedom* (New York, Knopf, 1974).
Nikki Giovanni, *Gemini* (New York: Bobbs Merrill, 1974).
Ossie Guffey, *Ossie* (New York: Bantam, 1972).
Gerda Lerner, *Black Women in White America* (New York: Vintage, 1973).
———,*The Woman in American History* (New York, Bobbs Merrill, 1977).
Anne Moody, *Coming of Age in Mississippi* (New York: Dell, 1970).
June Sochen, *Herstory* (New York: Alfred, 1974).
Ida (Barnett) Wells, *Crusade for Justice* (Chicago: University of Chicago Press, 1970).

Daisy Bates, *The Long Shadow of Little Rock*.
Gwendolyn Brooks, *Report from Part One*.

Toni (Bambara) Cade, *The Black Woman: An Anthology* (New York: Signet, 1970).
Septima Clark, *Echo in My Soul* (New York: E.P. Dutton, 1962) Out of print.
Elizabeth Davis, *Lifting As They Climb*. Out of print.
Rackham Holt, *Mary McLeod Bethune* (New York: Doubleday, 1964).
Mary Church Terrell, *A Colored Woman in a White World* (Washington, D.C.: Ransdell, 1940). Out of print.

Syllabus

Jan. 20 Introduction and overview.
Jan. 27 Slavery. Lerner, ch. 1; Truth.
Feb. 3 Education. Lerner, ch. 2; Clark; Bethune (Holt).
Feb. 10 Social Reform. Lerner, ch. 3; Wells.
Feb. 17 Social Reform, cont. Lerner, ch. 6; Terrell.
Feb. 24 Women's Organizations. Lerner, ch. 8; Davis.
Mar. 3 Black Women as Artists. Brooks.
Mar. 10 Black Women as Artists, cont. Giovanni
Mar. 17 Social Reform. Moody; Bates
Mar. 24 Social Reform, cont.
Mar. 31 Politics. Chisholm.
Apr. 7 Contemporary Autobiography. Guffey.

THE BLACK WOMAN IN AMERICA
Sharon Harley
University of Maryland, Afro-American Studies
Spring 1980

This course will be a review of the myriad historical experiences of Afro-American women from their African origins to the present, highlighting various aspects of their lives, including marriage, sexuality, and labor force participation.

The major requirement will be a final paper based upon the use of manuscript census records. You will be required to analyze your own findings from the census as they relate to your assigned readings and class discussion.

Required Texts:

1. Sharon Harley and Rosalyn T. Penn, *The Afro-American Woman: Struggles and Images* (Port Washington: Kennikat Press, 1978).
2. Joyce Ladner, *Tomorrow's Tomorrow: The Black Woman* (New York: Doubleday, 1971).

Additional Readings from:

1. Bert James Loewenberg and Ruth Bogin, *Black Women in Nineteenth Century American Life* (Philadelphia: Univ. of Pennsylvania Press, 1976).
2. Carol Stack, *All Our Kin: Strategies for Survival in a Black Community* (New York: Harper and Row, 1974).
3. Michael Gordon, *The American Family in Socio-Historical Perspective*, 2nd edition (New York: St. Martin's Press, 1978).

Course Requirements:
1. Final Paper
2. Typed Summaries of two assigned articles (see **)
3. Written Examinations and Quizzes
4. Class Discussion
Student Grade:
1. Final Paper and Summaries (50%)
2. Written Examination and Quizzes (50%)
Schedule of Lectures and Assigned Readings:
  I. Introduction (Jan. 18-23)
     A. An Overview of Afro-American Women's Historiography
     B. Current Theoretical and Methodological Concerns
 II. Women in Traditional Africa: Religious, Political, and Social Roles (Jan. 25-30)
III. Black Female Slaves (Feb. 1-8)
     "Black Women in the Era of the American Revolution," *Journal of Negro History*, 1976, pp. 276-289.
     Loewenberg, *Black Women*, pp. 37-77.
 IV. Free Black Women (Feb. 11-15)
     Readings: Loewenberg, *Black Women*, pp. 78-88.
  V. Organizational and Institutional Activities of Black Women (Feb. 18-22)
     **Readings: Harley and Penn, *The Afro-American Woman*, pp. 28-42; 97-108.
First Written Summary Due: Feb. 18
 VI. Life Cycles of Black Women (Feb. 23-25)
     Reading: Ladner's *Tomorrow's Tomorrow*
First Written Examination: Feb. 27
VII. Familial Roles of Black Women (Feb. 29-Mar. 1)
     Reading: "Myths of the Afro-American Family," in Gordon, *The American Family*, pp. 467-489.
VIII. Black Matriarchy: Myth or Reality? (March 3-7)
     Readings: "The Myth of the Black Matriarchy," *Black Scholar*, 1970, pp. 9-16
     "Black Macho and the Myth of the Superwoman," *Ms.*, January 1979, P. 45+.
 IX. Black Female Sexuality (March 17-21)
     Reading: "The Politics of Sexual Stereotypes," *Black Scholar* (March 1973), pp. 12-23.
  X. The Black Female Work Experience (March 24-28)
     Readings: Harley and Penn, *The Afro-American Woman*, pp. 5-16.
     "Why Women Work: A Comparison of Various Groups—Philadelphia, 1910-1930,- *Labor History* 17, pp. 73-87.
 XI. Work and Familial Roles of Black Women (Mar. 31-Apr. 4)
     (as revealed in the manuscript census records)
     Reading: "A Mother's Wages: Income Earning Among Married Italian and Black Women, 1896-1911," in Gordon, *The American Family*, pp. 490-510.
XII. Black Women and Women's Liberation (Apr. 7-11)
     Readings: Harley and Penn, *The Afro-American Women*, pp. 17-27; 87-96.
XIII. Images of Black Women (Apr. 14-18)
     **Readings: Harley and Penn, *The Afro-American Woman*, pp. 58-73; 74-84.
Second Written Summary Due: April 14
XIV. Black Women Today (Apr. 21-28)
     Readings: Women's Consciousness and the Southern Black Movement," *Southern Exposure* 4, 1977, pp. 10-18.
     Stack, *All Our Kin*, pp. 45-129.

XV. Final Report Presentations (Apr. 30-May 7)
Final Reports Due: April 30
Final Examination: May 13

THE INSURGENT SISTER—
THE BLACK WOMAN IN U.S.A.
Gloria I. Joseph and Carroll Oliver
Hampshire College
Spring 1978

Course Description:
   The Black Woman will be viewed as an insurgent person, a perspective which is not often associated with the struggles of Black Woman in America. The status and roles of Black Woman will be viewed from two different viewpoints, within the framework of her insurgency: (1) as a member of the larger society; (2) within her own group.
   This course will cover the following topics:
1) Women Rebels—Historical/Literature, i.e., the real and the imagined.
2) Women in Prison
3) The Battered Women
4) The Concept of Work
5) Sexual Prerogatives
6) Sanity vs. "going crazy"
7) Student and Non-Student Insurgency
8) The Wives of Famous Black Men

Course Requirements:
1) Become insurgent in a politically appropriate manner
2) Read, read, read—discuss, digest—read some more and repeat process
3) One short written paper—one term project
4) Attend activities related to course as scheduled, e.g., movies, lectures, conferences, plays—whatever

Required Texts:
Gerda Lerner, ed., *Black Women in White America* (New York: Vintage, 1973).
Zora Neale Hurston, *Their Eyes Were Watching God* (Westport, Conn.: Negro University Press, 1975).
Angela Davis and Bettina Apethker, *If They Come in the Morning* (New York: New American Library, 1974).
Plays by and About Women
Toni Morrison, *Sula* (New York: Knopf, 1973).
Alice Walker, *Meridian* (New York: Harcourt Brace Jovanovich, 1977).
Toni Cade Bambara, ed., *The Black Woman* (New York: Bantam, 1970).

THE BLACK WOMAN
Sonia Sanchez
Univ. of Massachusetts, Amherst, Black Studies
Spring 1975

This course will examine the nature of the Black woman's role in the Black community as it relates to the significant social and historical forces within the American environment that produced the "mammy," bad Black woman, mulatto, and the matriarch. The Black woman in traditional and contemporary Africa will also be discussed.

Required Work:
1. A term paper (last day of class).
2. A taped interview with one of our elders in the Amherst community or at home.

Required Books:
Okot p'Bitek, *Song of Lawino* (to be read aloud).
J. Bracey et al., eds., *Black Matriarchy: Myth or Reality* (Belmont, Cal.: Wadsworth, 1971).
Gerda Lerner, ed., *Black Women in White America.*
Joyce A. Ladner, *Tomorrow's Tomorrow* (New York: Vintage, 1972).
Sonia Sanchez, *A Blues Book for Blue Black Magical Women.*

Recommended Books:
Denise Paulmer, ed., *Women of Tropical Africa* (Berkeley: U. of Calif. Press, 1971).
Chinua Achebe, *Man of the People* (New York: Doubleday, 1971).
Ayi Armah, *The Beautiful Ones Are Not Yet Born* (New York: Collier, 1969).
Colin Turnbull, *Tradition and Change in Africa.*
David Scanlon, *Traditions of African Education* (New York: Teachers College, 1964).
Baba of Koro, *Women in Nigeria.*
Rhonda Dubow, *Women in South Africa.*
Zanile Dlamini, *South African Women and Revolution.*
Philip D. Curtin, *Africa Remembered* (Madison: Univ. of Wisconsin Press, 1968).
N. Higgin et al., *Key Issues in Afro/American Experience*, Vol. I (New York: Harcourt Brace Jovanovich, 1971)
K. Stampp, *Peculiar Institution* (New York: Random House, 1964).

Course Outline:
I. Film—Wednesday, Feb. 12 (Fayerweather)
II. Wednesday, Feb. 19—The Black Woman in Africa (Traditional)
  a) Religion and Philosophy in Africa
  b) Marriage
  c) Family Life
  Guest lecturer: Aminatou Sanga
III. Wednesday, Feb. 29—The Contemporary African Woman
  a) New roles
  b) Stresses on family life/marriage
  Guest lecturer: Aminatou Sanga
IV. The First Plantation (1619-1860)
  (Black Woman in antebellum society)
  March 5—Slave marriages
  March 12—Black Woman as Mother/Matriarch/Mammy
  March 19—Secondary consciousness of Black women (an extension of the Massa's family [called boy and girl]).

April 2—Contention—no Black family—was an extension of white family. The Black woman saw her husband (Black man) through the eyes of the massa.
V. The Second Plantation (1865-1920)
(post-bellum)
April 9—New responsibility of Black woman in light of emancipation
April 16—New images (film strips)
April 23—Freed woman in North
Woman as whore/bad woman
VI. Black Woman as Activist (1935-present)
April 30—Church/Civil Rights
Image/Identity
May 7—Nationalist
Women in Islam
May 14—Women's Liberation
Final due May 15—10 pages.

HISTORICAL AND CONTEMPORARY ISSUES
OF BLACK WOMEN
Barbara Smith
Univ. of Massachusetts, Boston, Women's Studies
Fall 1976

Schedule of topics and readings:
Week of Sept. 13 & 15:   Black Women During Slavery
Chapter 1, *Black Women in White America*, G. Lerner (New York: Vintage, 1973).
Angela Davis, "The Role of Black Women in the Community of Slaves," *The Black Scholar*, Vol. 3, No. 4, 1971, pp. 2-15.
Week of Sept. 20 & 22:   The Abolitionist and the Women's Rights Movement
Sarah Grimke, from *Letters on the Equality of the Sexes* (New York: B. Franklin, 1970)
Angelina Grimké, from *An Appeal to the Women of the Nominally Free States* (New York: Arno, 1960).
Kate Stimpson, article on the connection between the abolitionist movement and the suffrage movement, in *Women in a Sexist Society*, Vivian Gornick (New York: New American Library, 1972).
Week of Sept. 27 & 29:   Black Women During Reconstruction
Gerda Lerner, chapters 2 and 3, *Black Women in White America*
W.E.B. DuBois, "The Damnation of Women" from *Darkwater* (New York: Kraus, 1975).
Weeks of Oct. 4 & 6, 11 & 13:   Black Women and Urbanization, Black Women and Work
Gerda Lerner, chapter 4
Ann Petry, *The Street* (New York: Pyramid, 1969).

Week of Oct. 18 & 20:   Black Women Artists
    Alice Walker, "In Search of Our Mothers' Gardens"
    Interview with Alice Walker
    Michele Wallace, "Art: Daring to Do the Unpopular: Black Women Artists"
Week of Oct. 25 & 27:   What Is Feminism?
    Readings in Feminist Theory, Women's Movement Lit.
Week of Nov. 1 & 3:   How Do Black Women and Men Relate to the Women's Movement?
    Barbara Walker, "Black Feminism, One Woman's View," *Redbook.*
    Reginald E. Gillian, Jr., "One Man's Opinion," *Essence*, Feb. 1973, pp. 68-69.
    Michele Wallace, "A Black Feminist's Search for Sisterhood."
Week of Nov. 8 & 10:   The Myth of Matriarchy -
    Dolores Mack, "Where the Black Matriarchy Theorists Went Wrong," *Psychology Today*, 4 Jan. 1971, pp. 86-87.
    Alice Walker, "Everyday Use," in *In Love and Trouble.*
    Ann Petry, *The Street*
Week of Nov. 15 & 17:   The Sexual Politics of "Personal" Relationships
    Alice Walker, *In Love and Trouble*
    Articles and discussion concerning rape, battering, forced sterilization
Week of Nov. 29 & Dec. 1:   Black Women and Class: Articles and Discussion Concerning Welfare, Work, the Middle Class.
Week of Dec. 6 & 8:   Black Women and White Women: Conflicts and Solidarity

THE BLACK WOMAN IN AMERICAN SOCIETY
Barbara J. Shade
University of Wisconsin/Madison, Afro-American Studies
Spring 1977

Jan. 24   Definitions and Introduction of Issues, Concept, and the Series
Jan. 31   Roles of Black Women: A Historical Perspective
    Professor Diane Lindstrom, Department of History
Feb. 7   Role of Women of Color: A Third World Perspective
    Panel Discussion: Women in the Caribbean African, Asian, and Arab countries.
Feb. 14   Movie: *Black Girl* (1972). Director Ossie Davis. Portrays lives of three generations of Afro-American women.
Feb. 21   Sociological Perspectives of Black Women
    Professor Cora Marrett, Department of Sociology and Afro-American Studies
Feb. 28   Images of Afro-American Women in Art
    Professor Freida High, Afro-American Studies
March 7   Images of Afro-American Women in Poetry and Literature.
    Ms. Patricia Watkins, Director, Undergraduate Orientation
March 14 Images of Afro-American Women in the Visual Media.
    Dr. Pam Johnson, WHA Radio-Television
March 28 Analysis of Women's Roles in *Roots*: "Real or Distorted?"
    A Video-Tape Presentation

April 4   Images of Afro-American Women and Afro-American Publications
           Mrs. Bettie Pullen-Walker, Editor, *MsTIQUE* Magazine
April 11   Images Developed by Afro-American Women Through Dress
           Professor Marion Brown, School of Family Resources and Consumer Science
April 18   Afro-American Women as Workers
           Mrs. Bettye Latimer, Affirmative Action Officer, City of Madison
April 25   Afro-American Women as Socializers
           Dr. Mercile Lee, Assistant Dean of Students.
May 2   Afro-American Women as Activists and Change Agents
           Representative Marcia Coggs, Assemblywoman, Milwaukee
May 9   Black Women, White Women—Some Pressing Issues
           Panel Discussion: Ms. Elouise Addison, Municipal Management Consultant,
           State of Wisconsin
           Ms. Dolores Greene, Assistant to Chancellor, University Extension
           Professor Susan Friedman, Director, Women's Studies Program, University of
           Wisconsin
           Ms. Jacqueline Macaulay, Freelance Writer and Editor
           Moderator: Dr. Pam Johnson
May 17   Black Women, Black Men: Some Pressing Issues

ISSUES FOR THE CONTEMPORARY BLACK WOMAN
Helen Stewart
Brandeis University, Afro-American Studies Department
Spring 1978

This is the second semester of a two-semester course. Credit may be taken for either semester separately. The first semester provided a general survey with an emphasis on history and biography. This semester is topic-oriented with an emphasis on contemporary issues.

Course requirements include one paper, one exam and a final project.

A. Review; sexual politics of being a black woman; trends

B. Body Politics
   1. Color, features, hair, "shape," self-image (Cox; Coleman)
   2. Sex; celibacy (*Bodies*, ch. 3-4; O'Brien, Staples)
   3. Contraception; sterilization abuse; health care (*Brown Sister* #2; *Bodies*, ch. 18; Chesler, *Rap News*).

C. Relationships
   1. The Black Woman and
      a. Black men (Liebow; Baldwin and Gio.; Wilkinson; Cade; Milner)
      b. White men (M. Walker; Hernton; Fanon, Black Skins; Journal)
      c. Other black women (Cade; Sula; Washington)
      d. White women (Cox; Myron and Bunch)
   2. Black men and white women (Cleaver; Milner)
   3. The couple (Lederer; Stack; Liebow)

D. The question of marriage; of divorce; of adultery (Lederer; Handbook Staples)
E. Alternatives to traditional marriage: lovers, collectives, group marriage, communes, polygamy, polyandry (Constantine; Oui; Phoenix; Bodies 68-9).
F. Mothering; postpartum difficulties (*Bodies*, Ch. 15).
G. The single parent: day care, lovers, kinship (Liebow; Stack).
H. The unmarried woman: before 30; after 30 (O'Brien; *Bodies* 65-8).
I. Class and the Black woman (Bunch).
J. Black Lesbianism (*Bodies*, Ch. 5; Shockley; *Brown Sister* #1; Abbot).
K. Black Women in the struggle for black liberation (*Black Scholar*; Cade; Davis).
L. Black women and the Women's Liberation Movement (*Brown Sister* #1; Cox; *Black Scholar*).
M. Third World women (*Brown Sister* # 2 and # 3; *Signs; Asian Reader*).
N. Aging (Jackson in *Black Scholar*).

Reading List:
Abbott and Love, *Sappho Was a Right-On Woman*
Baldwin and Giovanni, *Baldwin and Giovanni: A Dialogue*
Black Scholar
Boston Women's Health Book Collective, *Our Bodies, Ourselves* (1976 ed.)
Brownmiller, Susan, *Against Our Will: Men, Women and Rape*
Brown Sister
Cade, Toni, *The Black Woman: An Anthology*
Chesler, Phyllis, *Women and Madness*
Cleaver, Eldrige, *Soul on Ice*
Constantine, L. and J., *Group Marriage*
Cox, Sue, *Female Psychology: The Emerging Self*
Hite, Shere, *The Hite Report*
Lederer, William, *Mirages of Marriage*
Liebow, Elliott, *Tally's Corner*
Milner and Milner, *Black Players*
Myron and Bunch, *Lesbianism and the Women's Movement*
O'Brien, Patricia, *The Woman Alone*
Shockley, Ann E., *Loving Her*
Staples, Robert, *The Black Woman in America*
Washington, Mary Helen, ed., *Black-Eyed Susans*
Wilkinson and Taylor, *The Black Male in America: Perspectives on His Status in Contemporary Society*
——, *The Mass. Women's Divorce Handbook*
Suggested Paper Topics:
Theory:
    What is Black feminism?
    Impact of imperialism on Black and Third World women.
    Impact of economic crisis on Black women.
    The future of Black people in the U.S. and implications for Black women.
    A theory of liberation for Black women/Black people in general.
    Alternative marriage and family patterns for Afro-Americans.
    An approach to the resolution of class problems among Black women/people.
    The future of the Black family in America
    The future of Black male-Black female relations.
    The future of Black female-Black female relations.
    Alliances and coalitions between Black women and

Black men
White women
Third World women
Working class people in the U.S.
Third World liberation struggles
The Black Church
Applied Research:
Black women and health care delivery; city hospitals, neighborhood clinics.
Family planning for Black women.
Role of Black women in community organizations.
Women in the Black Church.
History, development, problems of the Black feminist movement.
Black women and rape.
Sources of supplemental income for poor Black women: relatives, numbers, reported and unreported jobs, babysitting, drug dealing, prostitution, theft.
Black couples.
Aging and the Black woman.
Black female elected officials, government appointees, businesswomen.

AFRICAN-AMERICAN WOMEN IN UNITED STATES HISTORY
Rosalyn Terborg-Penn
Morgan State University, Department of History
Spring 1980

The purpose of this course is to correct the distortions and to fill the historical gaps about Black women in the United States; to introduce the topics and sources available in the area of the history of African-American women; to indicate ways to integrate the Black female experience into women's history and Black history; and to add a new topic course to our current list of Afro-American history courses in the undergraduate program. The course is designed to meet the needs of both majors and non-majors.

The data will be examined from two perspectives—the chronological and the thematic. A brief chronological study of the antebellum period to the present will focus upon historical personages and events with an emphasis upon group identity and societal pressures upon Black women within the context of a time perspective. The thematic approach will comprise most of the course and will focus upon topics such as reform, activism, employment, education, health, politics, family life, religion, literature, and the arts. The relationship between Black men and Black women and the contemporary issues concerning women's liberation and the future of Black women will be examined within an historical perspective.

Required Readings
Harley, Sharon and Terborg-Penn, Rosalyn, eds. *The Afro-American Woman: Struggles and Images*. Port Washington, N.Y.: Kennikat Press, 1978.

Lerner, Gerda, ed. *Black Women in White America: A Documentary History.* New York: Vintage Books, 1973.
Assigned articles.
Course outline
1. Introduction to the role of Black women in United States history and the current distortions in women's history.
2. Issues and Concerns of:
   a. Black women from the antebellum period through the Reconstruction years.
   b. Black women from the Nadir through the Great Depression.
   c. Black women from World War II to the present. '
3. Themes:
   a. Black women workers.
   b. Black women and education
   c. Black women as reformers and as activists.
   d. Black women in politics.
   e. Radical black women.
   f. Black women in family life.
   g. Black women and religion.
   h. Health and black women.
   i. Feminism and black women.

THE BLACK WOMAN
Margaret Wade
SUNY/New Paltz, Black Studies
Fall 1976

Purpose of the course: to take a historical, interdisciplinary approach to the study of the Black woman;
A. To examine the life situation of Black women as members of an ethnic minority, and as females;
B. To discuss the contributions made by Black women in America in such areas as education, politics, business, and literature;
C. To examine myths about Black women and the Black family in the light of social science and historical findings which reject "pathological" theses; and ,
D. To propose future directions and development for the Black woman.
   The course will be lecture-discussion. Each member of the class is expected to (1) read the texts and other assigned materials; (2) participate in class discussion by making statements or raising questions; (3) write a long paper on a specific subject related to the Black woman; (4) construct an annotated bibliography on the subject of the long paper; and (5) take a mid-term exam. There is also the option of an oral report for those interested in earning extra credit. Asterisks below indicate that the article will be discussed in class.
Textbooks
Gerda Lerner, ed., *Black Women in White America* (New York: Vintage, 1972).
Robert Staples, ed., *The Black Woman in America* (Chicago: Nelson Hall, 1973).

Toni Cade (Bambara), ed., *The Black Woman* (New York: New American Library, 1970). *The Black Scholar*, March-April, 1973 and March, 1975. Recommended.

I. Background on the Black Family

Sept. 2 Introduction to course

Sept. 7 African background and slavery experience. Angela Davis, "Reflections on the Black Woman's Role in a Community of Slaves," *The Black Scholar*, (December, 1971), pp. 3-15.

Sept. 9 The myth of matriarchy and the Black family. E. Franklin Frazier, "The Negro Family in America," in Robert Staples, ed., *The Black Family* (Belmont, California: Wadsworth Publishers, 1971).

Sept. 14 The Black woman and patriarchial societies.

Sept. 16 The Black family—summary. Robert Hill, *The Strengths of the Black Families* (New York: Emerson Hall, 1971).

Sept. 21 Black women in education. Gerda Lerner, "The Struggle for Education," *Black Women in White America: A Documentary History* (New York: Vintage, 1973).

II. Self-Image

Sept. 23 Joyce Ladner, "The Definition of Womanhood," *Tomorrow's Tomorrow: The Black Woman* (New York: Anchor, 1971), pp. 109-176.

III. Sexual Life

Sept. 28, 30 *Robert Staples, "Black Womanhood: Myth and Reality" and "The Sexual Life of Black Women," *The Black Woman in America*, 1973, pp. ix-71.

*Robert Staples, "Bodies for Sale: Black Prostitutes in White America," *The Black Woman in America*, pp. 73-94.

Alvin Poussaint, "How to Tell the Difference between Sex and Love," *Ebony* (July, 1972), pp. 31-41.

On interracial relations. Calvin Hernton, *Sex and Racism in America* (New York: Grove Press, 1966).

Alex Bontemps, "Startling New Attitudes Toward Interracial Marriage," *Ebony* (September, 1975), pp. 144-150

IV. Relations Between Black Women and Men

Oct. 5, 7, 12 Ann Ashmore Poussaint, "Can Black Marriages Survive Modern Pressures?" *Ebony* (September, 1974), pp. 97-102.

*Shirley Williams, "Tell Martha Not to Moan," in Toni Cade, ed., *The Black Woman*, pp. 42-55.

*Toni Cade, "On the Issue of Roles," in Toni Cade, ed., *The Black Woman*, pp. 101-110.

Carol Merton, "Mistakes Black Men Make in Relating to Black Women," *Ebony* (December, 1975) pp. 170-174, and "Mistakes Black Women Make in Relating to Black men," *Ebony* (December, 1975), pp. 89-93, 170-174.

Robert Staples, "Educating the Black Male at Various Class Levels for Marital Roles," in Staples, *The Black Family*, pp. 167-170.

Robert Staples, "The Myth of the Impotent Black Male," *Black Scholar* (June, 1971), pp. 2ff. (also in *Contemporary Black Thought*, pp. 126-137).

*Robert Staples, "Being Married and Black," in *The Black Woman in America*, pp. 95-126.

V. Black Women and Children

Oct. 14 *Robert Staples, "The Joy and Pain of Motherhood," *The Black Woman in America*, pp. 127-160.

Lee Rainwater, *And the Poor Get Children.*

Black Child Issue, *Ebony* (August, 1974).

VI. Black Women and Sterilization/Birth Control/Abortion
   Oct. 19 Mary Smith, "Birth Control and the Black Woman," *Ebony*, March, 1968.
      Toni Cade, "The Pill: Genocide or Liberation," *The Black Woman*, p. 162.
      Joanna Clark, "Motherhood," *The Black Woman*, pp. 63-72.
      Gail Kennard, "Sterilization Abuse," *Essence*, October, 1974.
      Shirley Chisholm, "Facing the Abortion Question," in Gerda Lerner, ed., *Black Women in White America*, pp. 602-607.
VII. Black Women and Welfare
   Oct. 21 Vernon Davies, "Fertility vs. Welfare: The Negro American Dilemma," *Phylon* 27 (Fall, 1966), pp. 226-232.
      Mrs. Charles Johnson, "The Black Community Looks at the Welfare System," *Public Welfare* 26 (July, 1968), pp. 205-208.
      Henry Miller, "Sqcial Work in the Black Community: The New Colonial-' ism," *Social Work* 14 (July, 1969), pp. 65-76.
      Roger R. Miller, ed., *Race, Research and Reason: Social Work Perspective* (New York: National Association of Social Workers, 1969), pp. 25-34.
      Larry Jackson, "Welfare Mothers and Black Liberation," *The Black Scholar* (April, 1970), pp. 31-37.
      William Ryan, *Blaming the Victim* (New York: Random House, 1971).
   Oct. 26 Midterm Examination
VIII. Media Images of Black Women
   Oct. 28 Edward Mapp, "Black Women in Films," *The Black Scholar* (March-April 73), pp. 42-46.
      Liz Grant, "Ain't Beulah Dead Yet?: Or Images of the Black Woman in Film," *Essence* (May, 1973).
      B.J. Mason, "Hollywood's New Bitch Goddess," *Essence* (September, 1974).
      Donald Bogle, *Toms, Coons, Mulattoes, Mammies and Bucks* (New York: Bantam, 1974).
IX. Black Woman in Literature (Contributions/Images)
   Nov. 2 Nance Fischler, *Black Masks: Negro Characters in Modern Southern Fiction* (University Park: Pennsylvania State University Press, 1969).
      Sharyn J. Sketter, "Black Women Writers," *Essence* (May, 1973).
      Catherine Starke, *Black Portraiture in American Fiction* (New York: Basic Books, 1971).
      Ora Williams, *American Black Women in the Arts and Social Sciences: A Bibliographical Survey* (Metuchen, New Jersey: Scarecrow, 1973).
      Darwin Turner, *Afro-American Writers: Bibliography* (New York: Appleton, 1970).
      Pat C. Exum, *Keeping the Faith: Writings by Contemporary Black American Women* (New York: Bantam, 1974).
      "Black Women on Capitol Hill," *Ebony* (June, 1974).
X. Black Women in Law and Politics
   Nov. 4 Barbara Williams, "Black Women in Law," *The Black Law Journal* (1971), pp. 171-183.
      Sylvia Dannett, *Profiles of Negro Womanhood*, Vol. I, 1690-1900; Vol. II, Twentieth Century (Washington, D.C.: Negro University Press, 1964, 1966).
      Marilyn Ainsworth, "Women in the Law," *Essence* (August, 1975).
      Daisy Voigt, "To Be a Lawyer," *Essence* (December, 1975).
      Michael Barone and Ujifusa Grant, eds., *The Almanac of American Politics* (New York: Dutton, 1972), pp. 45, 57, 90.
      "In Government Service and Political Life," Chapter 6, *Black Woman in White America*, pp. 317-357.

National Roster of Black Elected Officials, Washington Based Joint Center for Political Studies, 1972, pp. 42ff.

XI. Black Women in Business and Medicine

Nov. 9 Carol Morton, "Black Women in Corporate America," *Ebony,* (November, 1975).

Women's Bureau, Department of Labor, *Handbook on Women Workers: Negro Women Workers* and *Negro Women in Industry,* 1960.

Jeanne Noble, "The American Negro Woman, in *The American Negro Reference Book,* ed., John P. David (Englewood Cliffs: Prentice Hall, 1966), pp. 522ff.

James Curtis, *Blacks, Medical Schools and Society* (Ann Arbor: The University of Michigan Press, 1971).

Herbert Morias, *The History of the Negro in Medicine* (New York: Publishers company, 1968).

Dietrich Reitzes, *Negroes and Medicine* (Cambridge: Harvard University Press, 1968).

XII. Educational Level/Employment Prospects of Black Women

Nov. 11 C.D. Nelson, "Myths About Black Women Workers in Modern America," *The Black Scholar* (March, 1975), pp. 11-15.

Jacqueline Jackson, "But Where Are the Men," *Contemporary Black Thought: The Best from the Black Scholar.*

A.J. Jaffe, *Negro Higher Education in the 1960's* (New York: Praeger, 1968).

Lynn Sharpe, "Are We Taking Jobs from Our Men," *Essence* (March, 1975).

Christine Clark, "Fighting for Equal Employment," *Essence* (March, 1975).

"New Careers for New Women," *Ebony* (July, 1971).

XIII. Problems and Stresses on Black Women.

Nov. 16, 18 "Stresses and Strains on Black Women," *Ebony* (June, 1974).

Jack Slater, "Suicide: A Growing Menace to Black Women," *Ebony* (September, 1973).

P. Robinson, "A Historical and Critical Essay for Black Woman in the Cities," *The Black Woman,* pp. 198-210.

Frances Beale, "Double Jeopardy: To Be Black and Female," *The Black Woman,* pp. 90-100

Effie Ellis, "The Quality of Life: The Black Child," *Ebony* (August, 1974).

Hamilton Bims, "Why Black Men Die Younger," *Ebony* (December, 1974).

XIV. Black Women and Women's Rights/"Liberation"

Nov. 23, 30 Barbara Sizemore, "Sexism and the Black Male," *The Black Scholar* (March-April 1973), pp. 2-11.

Robert Stables, "Black Women and Women's Literature," *The Black Woman in America,* pp. 161-182.

Linda LaRue, "the Black Movement and Women's Liberation," *The Black Scholar* (December, 1971), and *Contemporary Black Thought,* pp. 116-125.

Shirley Chisolm, "Racism and Anti-Feminism," *The Black Scholar* (January, 1970), pp. 40-45.

Julius Lester, *Revolutionary Notes* (New York: Grove Press, Inc., 1969).

Joyce Ladner, "Black Women 200 Years: Conditions of Slavery Laid the Foundation for Their Liberation," *Ebony* (August, 1975).

"Black Feminist: A New Mandate," *MS.* (May, 1974), pp. 97-100.

XV. Women Internationally

Dec. 2 Genevieve Ekaeta, "On My Own: An African Woman and Women's Liberation," *Essence* (September, 1974).

Sekou Toure, "The Role of Women in the Revolution," *the Black Scholar* (March, 1975), pp. 32-36.

Frederico Touar, *The Puerto Rican Woman: Her Life Evolution Throughout History* (New York: Plus Uthra Eucation Publishers).

Denise Paulme, *Women of Tropical Africa* (Berkeley: University of California Press, 1971).

Ruth Sidel, *Women and Child Care in China* (Baltimore: Penguin 1973).

XVI. Black Women and the Future

Dec. 7 Frances Welsing, "Black Women Moving Toward the Twenty-first Century," *Essence* (December, 1975).

Pauli Murray, "The Liberation of Black Women," in *Voices of the New Feminism* (Boston: Beacon Press, 1970).

"The Equal Rights Amendment," in *Sex Roles in Law and Society*, pp. 528-555.

Maulana Ron Karenga, "In Love and Struggle: Toward a Greater Togetherness," *The Black Scholar*, (March, 1975), pp. 16-28.

XVII. Dec. 14 Summary Session

For other research sources, see the bibliographies in the textbooks for the course and Johnetta Cole, *Black Women in America: An Annotated Bibliography* from *The Black Scholar* (December, 1971), pp. 42-43.

LITERATURE
MAJOR AFRO-AMERICAN WRITERS:
ALICE WALKER SEMINAR
Barbara Christian
University of California/Berkeley,
Afro-American Studies/Women's Studies

The seminar will focus on the development of Alice Walker as one of America's major women writers. We will be discussing and studying her poetry, short stories, essays and novels in an attempt to define her political vision as a Black feminist, a writer of the ongoing Revolution as well as a craftsperson.

The emphases in this course are:

1. the *development* of a writer who uses four literary genres, poetry, novel, short story and essay; who has been writing for the past fifteen years and who continues to write. The class then will focus on her *craft* as it has progressed and continues to progress, and her *vision* as it has changed and deepened.

2. the attempt of a contemporary writer to show the relationship between *personal, social* and *political* forces at work in the modern world through the crafting of literary works without subordinating literature to "political rhetoric." The class then is concerned with *the definition of a political writer.*

3. the relationship of the writer, Alice Walker, to the *traditions* that precede her: e.g., Black women's literature, Black literature, how she draws from these traditions and enhances them.

Texts

Alice Walker: *Once* (poetry)
Alice Walker: *The Third Life of Grange Copeland* (novel)
Alice Walker: "In Search of Our Mother's Gardens" (essay)
Alice Walker: *In Love and Trouble* (short stories)
Alice Walker: *Revolutionary Petunias* (poetry)
Alice Walker: "In Search of Zora Neale Hurston" (essay)
Alice Walker: *Meridian* (novel)

Prerequisites

Images of Black Women in Literature, Parts I and II. The prerequisites for this course are important since one of the emphases in the course is the relationship of Alice Walker as a contemporary Black woman writer to the traditions that precede her. Students must also have done some literary criticism and must be adept at it. In some cases, students who have taken many Black literature courses or women's literature courses may be admitted without the precise prerequisites.

Except for the first week of class, when the instructor will review the content of the two courses on Images of Women in Black Literature, the format of the course will be a seminar, study group. This course is intended for students who are deeply interested in literature and who are advanced in this area. Students then are expected to be as active in the presentation of material as the instructor. The number of students is limited to fifteen so that each student may participate in the seminar, and so that students might share their ideas, research and analyses.

Requirements

1. Students must of course read and study all the required books. They must participate actively in class, demonstrating their knowledge of the material and sharing their analyses and secondary cources on Walker.
2. Each student must present a fifteen minute oral report on an important aspect of the works of Alice Walker so they may receive constructive criticism from other students as well as the instructor. The instructor will also present an oral report.
3. Students must write a final, twenty pages minimum, in which they analyze a major emphasis in Walker's works.
4. Each student must discuss with the instructor the work he or she is doing on the writer, during the course of the quarter.

BLACK WOMEN WRITERS
Frances Foster
Afro-American Studies
Spring 1976

Texts

Linda Brent, *Incidents in the Life of a Slave Girl* (Harcourt Brace Jovanovich, 1973).
Nella Larsen, *Quicksand* (Negro University Press, 1928).
Zora N. Hurston, *Their Eyes Were Watching God* (University of Illinois Press, 1978).
Lorraine Hansberry, *A Raisin in the Sun* (Signet, New American Library, 1961).
Margaret Walker, *Jubilee* (Bantam, 1966, 1975).
Alice Walker, *In Love and Trouble* (Harcourt Brace Jovanovich, 1974).
Sherley Williams, *The Peacock Poems* (Wesleyan University Press, 1975).
Toni Cade, *The Black Woman* (Mentor, New American Library, 1970).
Toni Morrison, *The Bluest Eye*
Mary Helen Washington, ed., *Black-Eyed Susans* (Anchor, Doubleday, 1975).

Course Description

This is an upper division course dealing with writings that were conscious literary expressions. That is, they were written to be published and read as contributions to some artistic tradition. The selections this semester are all works by Black women. Through careful reading, analysis, and discussion we will attempt to discover the similarities and differences in themes, characters and forms utilized by these authors. Further, we will try to ascertain their role in the general area of Black literature.

Course Requirements

1. Read all books on the required book list. Evaluation of this reading is done by quizzes, exams, and class discussion.

2. Keep a journal. The journals are to include reactions/reflections on the books and articles you've read, the things said or unsaid in class, things you meant to say or tried to say or thought about and want to say again. It is not to be a summary or report. It is not the same as "class notes." Emphasis in the journals should be on the "whys" and "becauses" as well as the "whats." (Analysis/Evaluation as opposed to cryptic declarations.) It is hoped that these journals will not consist of regurgitated opinions but rather, reflect the movement of minds, the process of attempting to synthesize, to conclude, to realize. It is also appropriate to include comments, questions, or suggestions about the methods and activities within the class itself. Journals are collected regularly. No letter grade is given, but credit is recorded. It is expected that a minimum of 2 entries per week be made. The length of which is a matter determined by your time, subject and personal preference (though some evidence of "good faith" should be apparent).

3. Write a paper. Everyone will write one 3-5 page paper—the topic and form of which must be discussed with me BEFORE submitting the paper.

4. One additional project. This requirement may be fulfilled in a number of ways including:

    a. planned presentations to class (group or individual)

    b. library project

    c. a second 3-5 page paper

    d. an original contribution which has been described in writing and approved in writing by me.

BLACK WOMEN WRITERS
Gloria Hull
University of Delaware, Department of English
Fall 1976

"You ask about 'preoccupations.' I am preoccupied with the spiritual survival, the survival *whole* of my people. But beyond that, I am committed to exploring the oppressions, the insanities, the loyalties, and the triumphs of Black women.... For me, Black women are the most fascinating creations in the world."

There are two reasons why the Black woman writer is not taken as seriously as the Black male writer. One is that she's a woman. Critics seem unusually ill-equipped to intelligently discuss and analyze the works of Black women. Generally, they do not even make the attempt; they prefer, rather, to talk about the lives of Black women writers, not about what they write. And, since Black women writers are not—it would seem—very likable—until recently they were the least willing worshippers of male supremacy—comments about them tend to be cruel."

—Alice Walker

Texts

Nella Larsen, *Passing*

Mary Helen Washington, ed. *Black-Eyed Susans*

Gwendolyn Brooks, *The World of Gwendolyn Brooks*

Margaret Walker, *Jubilee*

Ann Petry, *The Street*
Toni Cade, ed. *The BLACK Woman: An Anthology*
Ai, *Cruelty*
Toni Morrison, *The Bluest Eye*
Audre Lorde, *The New York Head Shop and Museum*
Dittoed material

Sept. 9 Course introduction; Introductory lecture: "Black Women Writers: Background"
       14 Larsen, *Passing*
       16 Larsen, *Passing*
       21 Hurston, short stories; Smith, "Frankie Mae," "That She Would Dance No More"
       23 Brooks, *A Street in Bronzeville*
       28 Walker, *Jubilee*
       30 Walker, *Jubilee*
Oct.   5 Brooks, *Maud Martha*
       7 Brooks, *Maud Martha*
       12 Brooks, *Annie Allen*, *The Bean Eaters*
       14 Petry, *The Street*
       19 Petry, *The Street*
       21 Hourly examination
       26 Marshall, "Reena"; Williams, "Tell Martha Not to Moan"
       28 Ai, *Cruelty*
Nov.   2 Election Day
       4 Brooks, *In the Mecca*
       9 Morrison, *The Bluest Eye*
       11 Morrison, *The Bluest Eye*
       16 Essays in *The Black Woman* by Brehon, Brown, Smart-Grosvenor and Clark
       18 Lorde, *New York Head Shop and Museum*
Nov.   23 Walker, three short stories; Bambara, "My Man Bovanne"
       25 Thanksgiving Recess
       30 Poetry (from *The Black Woman* and dittoes)
Dec.   2 Hourly examination
       7 Drama (dittoes)
       9 Black feminist theatre presentation
       14 Class presentations
       16 Cade, "On the Issue of Roles"; Course evaluation

Course Requirements
1. Regular attendance and participation in class discussion and other class activities
2. Two hourly examinations
3. One 5-10 page paper on a substantial work not covered in class (For 665 students, one 15-25 page paper, a bibliography and study of a Black woman writer not covered in class)
4. One 1-2 page reaction paper, a personal response to an assigned work—to be shared orally with the class. *Or* if you are a Black woman writer, a brief reading/presentation of your own work.

Collateral Course Activities
1. Presentation—Black feminist theatre
2. Reading(s) by Black woman poets
3. University-wide appearances by Black woman writers

THE BLACK WOMAN IN AFRO-AMERICAN LITERATURE
Theresa R. Love
Southern Illinois University, Department of English

Course Description

This course is designed to give those enrolled therein the opportunity to study the various roles which have been attributed to the Black woman in Afro-American literature. Although the emphasis is on that literature written during the Harlem Renaissance and thereafter, students will be given the chance to read and discuss works pertaining to Black women prior to that time.

Course Objectives

The objectives of the course are as follows:

1. To study poems, novels, short stories, dramas, and expository works which portray Black women in various roles in the family and in society as a whole.

2. To show the extent to which Black women agree or do not agree with the images which have been attributed to them by Black male writers.

More specifically, those enrolled in this course will:

1. Make a contrastive analysis of the image of the Black woman before and after slavery.

2. Study the Black woman as a maintainer of the family structure during slavery and thereafter.

3. Study the Black woman as a victim.

4. Study her as a proponent of the will to survive.

5. Study the Black woman as social and political commentator and as philosopher.

6. Study the Black woman as a bridge between the races, whether as mistress, as maid, or nurse, or as humanist.

Textbooks

I. *Required:*

    A. Richard Barksdale and Kenneth Kinnamon, *Black Writers of America*, New York, Macmillan, 1972.

    B. John Henrik Clark, *American Negro Short Stories*, New York, Hill and Wang, 1966.

II. Supplementary:

    A. William Couch, *New Black Playwrights*, Baton Rouge, Louisiana State University, 1968.

Calendar: Outline of Course Content

First Week

    Theme: The Black woman before and during slavery

    1. Course organization, format, requirements, etc.

    2. Reading and disucssion of excerpt from Gustavus Vassa's *The Interesting Narrative of Olouday Equiano*, in *Black Writers of America*, pp. 7-21.

    3. Reading and disucssing of Chapters in Alex Haley's *Roots* (Dell, 1977) which deal with the Black woman in Africa and during slavery: Chapters 1, 2, 3, 11, 29, 48, 58, 63, 75, 78, 83, 84, 85.

Second Week

    Theme: The Black woman as a maintainer of the Black family

    1. Reading and discussion of Langston Hughes' "Mother to Son," *BWA*, p. 518; and of "The Negro Mother," and "A Negro Mother's Lullaby" (handouts).

2. Reading and discussion of Charles Chesnutt's "The Wife of His Youth," *BWA*, p. 518; and of "The Negro Mother," and "A Negro Mother's Lullaby" (handouts).
3. Reading and discussion of Zora Neale Hurston's *Their Eyes Were Watching God*, University of Illinois Press, 1978.

Third-Fifth Weeks

Theme: The modern Black woman as victim

1. Reading and discussion of Langston Hughes' "Cross," *BWA*, p. 519. Claude McKay's "Harlem Shadows" and "Harlem Dancer," *BWA*, p. 496. "Black Woman," (Blues Folk Song), *BWA*, p. 889.
2. Reading and discussion of the following:
   a. Paule Marshall's "Reena," *ANSS*, pp. 264-282.
   b. Zora Neale Hurston's "The Gilded Six Bits," *BWA*, pp. 613-618.
   c. James Baldwin's "This Morning, This Evening So Soon," in *Going to Meet the Man*, Dell, 1965.
   d. Ann Petry's "Like a Winding Sheet," *BWA* pp. 763-768.
   e. Ed Bullins's *Goin' a Buffalo*, Couch, pp. 155-216.
   f. Langston Hughes' *Soul Gone Home* (handout).
   g. Douglass Turner Ward's *Happy Ending*, Couch, pp. 3-23.
   h. Charlton and Barbara Molette's "Rosalie Pritchett," *BWA*, pp. 825-835.

Sixth-Seventh Weeks

Theme: The Black woman and the will to survive

1. Viewing and disucssion of movie based on Lorraine Hansberry's *A Raisin in the Sun*, New York, New American Library, 1961.
2. Reading and discussion of Richard Wright's "Bright and Morning Star," *ANSS*, pp. 75-106.
3. MIDTERM EXAMINATION

Eighth Week

Theme: The Black woman as a social and political critic: The Black woman as philosopher

1. Small group discussion of (a) the "message" of each of the following; (b) of their relevance ot the various roles played by Black women; (c) their artistic merits:
   a. Charlotte Forten Grimke's *Journal of Charlotte Forten*, excerpts in *BWA*, pp. 305-311.
   b. Elizabeth Keckley's *Behind the Scene*, excerpts in *BWA*, pp. 305-311.
   c. Angelina Grimké's "Grass Fingers," *BWA*, p. 627; Anne Spencer's "Lines to a Nasturtium," and "Letter to My Sister," *BWA*, pp. 627-28.
   d. Reading and discussion of Paule Marshall's "Barbadoes," *BWA*, pp. 774-781.

Ninth Week

Theme: The Black woman as a bridge between the races

1. Reading and discussion of Margaret Walker's *Jubilee*, with close attention to the solution to racial problems as indicated by the novelist.
2. Reading and discussion of Arna Bontemps' *Black Thunder*, Beacon Press, 1968, with close attention to the roles of Juba and of Melody.

Tenth Week

Students will read their research papers during this week

Eleventh Week

FINAL EXAMINATION

Course Requirements

Students will be required to take a midterm examination and a final. They will also be expected to write two short critical papers or two short papers in which they comment on a relevant problem. They will also be asked to read all assigned materials.

References

Black Writers in America has excellent listings of secondary materials. Students will be asked to read one of these which relates to each writer studied.

IMAGES OF BLACK WOMEN
IN THE WORKS OF BLACK WOMEN WRITERS
Patricia Bell Scott and Gloria Johnson
University of Tennessee, Black Studies Department
Winter 1976

Texts
Mel Watkins and Jay David, *To Be a Black Woman.**
Patricia Crutchfield Exum, ed., *Keeping the Faith.*
Mary Helen Washington, ed., *Black-Eyed Susans.*
*The reason that this text was chosen will be discussed in class.

This course is an upper division, special topics seminar, so it will be conducted in seminar fashion. It will be assumed by the instructors and the teaching assistant that each student will exhibit behaviors typical of an upperclass person; e.g., submission of well-written and typed papers which are grammatically correct, regular class attendance.

Each student will be requried to:

1. Complete two "take home" exams, a midterm and a final. These exams will be composed of several essay questions, which must be answered from material in the reading assignments, class discussion, lectures, and guest speakers. Each exam is worth 25 points.

2. Share a learning experience with the class on some image which he/she has discovered or recognized in some material (literature or media) which is not required for class. The experience which is shared must relate to the image which is being discussed in class (at the time it is shared). For example, one might desire to share a poem which is not part of the assigned reading. This poem must relate to or deal with an image which will be dscussed in class, and this poem should be dealt with at the same time that the image which it relates to is discussed. This sharing experience is worth 15 points.

3. Participate in a class project/presentation which focuses upon some image of the Black woman. This image may be one which has been discussed in class, or it may be an image which the student has discovered. Each person will have his/her own project. This project will be presented during the last two meetings of the quarter. Each project will be worth 20 point.

3. Provide meaningful class participation. Your words should reflect that! Class partici- pation is worth 15 points, and will be used to determine grades for those persons on the borderline.

Introductory Readings
Exum, p. 14; Exum, p. 11; Exum, "The Black Writer and His Role"; Washington, p. ix; Watkins and David, p. 9.
The Black Woman as the Backbone of the Black Family: Faithful Servant and Mammy: Exum, p. 234; Exum, p. 256; Watkins and David, p. 81; Exum, p. 51; Exum, p. 80; Exum, p. 204.

The Black Woman as Daughter:
Exum, p. 123; Exum, p. 166; Washington, p. 69; Washington, p. 78.
The Black Woman as Mulatto and Middle Class:
Washington, p. 23; Washington, p. 37; Watkins and David, p. 23; Washington p. 51;
Watkins and David, p. 103.
The Black Woman as Conjurer, Witch, Mystic and Sage:
"Strong Horse Tea," p. 88—Alice Walker; "The Revenge of Hannah Kemhuff," p. 88—
Alice Walker. The materials in this section will be provided by the instructor.
The Black Woman as Free Spirit, Freedom-Fighter, and Revolutionary:
Watkins and David, p. 249; Exum, p. 67; Exum, p. 85; Exum, p. 87.
The Black Woman in Love:
Watkins and David, p. 163; Exum, p. 88; Exum, p. 93; Exum, p. 97; Exum, p. 117; Exum, p.
66; Exum, p. 68; Exum, p. 70; Washington, p. 114; "Roselily" p. 88—Alice Walker.
Miscellaneous:
Watkins and David, p. 113; Watkins and David, p. 115; Exum, p. 66; Exum, p. 72; Exum, p.
73; Exum, p. 74.

BLACK WOMEN WRITERS
Barbara Smith
Emerson College, Department of English
Fall 1973

Readings
Toni Cade, ed., *The Black Woman: An Anthology*, Mentor, New American Library, 1970.
Aphra: The Feminist Literary Magazine, Vol. 2, no. 3, Summer 1971. Out of print.
Margaret Walker, *Jubilee*, Bantam, 1966.
Zora Neale Hurston, *Their Eyes Were Watching God*, University of Illinois Press, 1978.
Maya Angelou, *I Know Why the Caged Bird Sings*, Bantam, 1970.
Toni Morrison, *The Bluest Eye*, out of print.
Alice Walker, *Revolutionary Petunias*, Harcourt Brace Jovanovich, 1972.
Gwendolyn Brooks, *Selected Poems*, Harper and Row, 1963.
Ann Petry, *The Street*, Pyramid, 1946.
Planned Activities
Film: Growing Up Female: As Six Become One. Filmmakers: Julia Reichert
         and James Klein
         "The makers of·"Growing Up Female" focus on the way in which a woman is
         socialized by showing the lives of six women of different ages and
         backgrounds. This powerful documentary is a basic film for women to
         see...."
Talk and Demonstration by Guest Speaker:
         "A History of Black Music." The contributions of women artists and the
         image of Black women in blues lyrics will be a part of the discussion.
Panel Discussion Guest Speakers:
         Women working in various fields will discuss the particular situations—social,
         economic, psychological, and political—that affect Black women's lives.

Suggestions for Further Reading
"Black Women's Liberation," *The Black Scholar*, vol. 4, no. 6-7.
"The Black Woman," *The Black Scholar*, vol. 3, no. 4.
Verta Mae, *Thursdays and Every Other Sunday Off. A Domestic Rap*, Doubleday, 1972. Out of print.
Gerda Lerner, *Black Women in White America: A Documentary History*, Vintage, 1973.

BLAKWOMEN WRITERS OF THE U.S.A.
WHO ARE THEY? WHAT DO THEY WRITE?

Fahamisha Shariat
1979

During the past nine years, I have had occasion to organize and prepare lists, papers, workshops, and courses on literature by Blakwomen, particularly those of the United States. The same nine years have witnessed the development of interest in women's studies in general, and women's literature in particular. At the same time, interest in Black studies and literature in academic settings has peaked and begun to decline. By the time serious attention was being paid to literature by Blakwomen in an academic setting, it was being done in the context of women's studies rather than Black studies.

Without entering into the complexities of departmental turf, I would submit that serious work and study on any aspect of the Black experience, given the prevalence of institutional racism in this country, should occur in the context of Black studies with cross-listings in women's studies. However, because of this society's inability to pay attention to more than one oppressed group at a time, the "action" today, limited as it is, is found in women's studies.

My personal experience, nevertheless, has been that more Blakwomen writers get read in Blakliterature courses, than women in "literature courses" or Blakwomen in "women's literature courses." The usual explanation for this sorry state of affairs has been that "English teachers" and "women's studies teachers" do not know what work Blakwomen have done or are doing. this outline was developed in part as a response to that ignorance— an ignorance still institutionalized in the graduate school curricula of this country.

More important, though, this outline began in the context of Blakwomen's groups to which I have belonged—sisterhoods, committees, and less structured groups of "sisters." In the literature, we found a delineation of ourselves and a validation of what is now being called Blakwomen's culture.

The isolation of a number of writers for particular study presupposes a sufficient body of common elements for those writers to constitute a group or literary school. Blakpeople in the United States exist and have existed as a separate and distinct cultural group. In the literature, we find an expression of that culture and the historical record of its development. Within the larger group, Blakwomen emerge as educators/culture-bearers/agitators for freedom. Fighting to attain literacy, they have used the written word (and the spoken/sung word) as ornament and as weapon. From the beginning, Blakwomen have been in the front lines of a people's struggle for self-definition, self-determination, and freedom. Thus, from the beginning, Blakwomen have engaged not only in a struggle against white racism, but also in a struggle against white patriarchy (and to the degree that Black men have opted for the patriarchal or paternalistic role, they too have been/are being struggled against). The woman in struggle has a strong sense of herself as a person of worth. She also has a strong sense of community with her mothers and sisters in struggle. Within Blakwomen's literature, then, we find Blakwomen's history—not merely a factual record, but an experiential account of what it means and has meant to be Black and female in a society which places its highest value on white maleness. In Blakwomen's writing, we also find a celebration of Blakwomen as Blakwomen—in language, with Blakwomen's ways of relating to each other and the rest of our people; in struggle, against oppressive conditions; and in achievement.

Within Blakculture, there exists a rich and varied Blakwomen's culture. That culture is recorded, described, delineated in Blakwomen's writing. Blakliterature in the United States begins with the women of the oral tradition ("Black and unknown bards" were female too); moves through early writers, such as Lucy Terry, Phillis Wheatley, Charlotte Forten, and others; and continues into the present. No period of that literature is without its women authors. Participants in the affirming spirit of the oral tradition of the blues singer (whether of the holy blues of the spiritual and gospel tradition or of the more secular variety), Blakwomen writers can be profitably studied for insight into the experience of a people.

Because the quest for literacy has been so much a part of the Blakstruggle in the United States, there seems to be a higher proportion of Blakwomen writing here than elsewhere in the Afrikan world. It is interesting to note that as the quest for literacy accelerates in other parts of the Afrikan world, other Afrikan women are discovering the power of the word. In teaching a course on Blakwomen writers, the instructor is faced with several problems. The most obvious of these is selecting texts. In most cases selection is limited by what is available in print, and the instructor very quickly learns that very few of Blakwomen writers' works are in print, with the exception of works by the most contemporary writers.

In Spring 1977, I taught a survey course on Blakwomen writers at the University of Massachusetts at Boston. The following is an outline of that course. The outline is chronological and generic, although the course itself was thematic. I have appended a note indicating some thematic ways of organizing the materials included in the outline. The course was designed to survey Blakwomen writers from Phillis Wheatley to the present: their subjects, themes, and styles. Questions explored through the course included the following: Who are the Blakwomen writers, major and minor? What have they written? Are there preferred genres among the Blakwomen writers? Are there characteristic themes? Are there preferred subjects? Are there common elements of style? Is there a "Black female sensibility"? How do the social concerns of the day, e.g., Black nationalism and feminism, impinge upon the writings?

The course was structured and readings were selected around the theme "From Blakgirls to Blakwoman: Rites of Passage." Included within this theme was an examination of the treatment of individual and group identity, the relationship of the individual to her family (parents, siblings, mates, children), relationships between men and women, relationships between Blakwomen and white women, relationships between the individual and society. Major works that were read included *The Street*, by Ann Petry; *The Bluest Eye*, by Toni Morrison; and *I Know Why the Caged Bird Sings*, by Maya Angelou. I had originally planned to include *Brown Girl, Brownstones*, by Paule Marshall and would have liked to include *Their Eyes Were Watching God*, by Zora Neale Hurston, but these works were out of print.* The assigned texts also included three anthologies: *Black-Eyed Susans*, a collection of short stories and excerpts from novels, edited by Mary Helen Washington; *The Black Woman* edited by Toni Cade; and *Poetry of the Negro: 1746-1970*, edited by Langston Hughes and Arna Bontemps. The poetry anthology was selected because it included a significant number of women poets. To date, there is no adequate anthology of Blakwomen poets.

In addition to the major texts, selections by other authors were copied for class use. Recordings by Blakwomen poets and music by Blakwomen composers and/or performers were also used in the course. (A discography is in preparation). Finally, three written assignments (two short papers and one long research paper) ensured that the students would read several other writers at length. A list of assigned topics with other suggestions is appended to the outline. Authors read in the course are indicated on the outline by a single asterisk (*) for a complete work read, and a double asterisk (**) for selections or excerpts from the writer's work.

Although Blaklesbian writing was not isolated for special study in the 1977 course, it would be almost impossible to teach a course on Blakwomen writers today without considering the vocal presence of the Blaklesbian writer. Audre Lorde used to be included in courses on Blakwomen writers without mention of her lesbianism. The homophobic nature of much of the Black community is in part responsible for the omission of homosexual writers from study as homosexuals. In the past, though, many homosexual writers were reluctant to identify themselves as such. Today, more writers—women and men—are out of the closet besides Audre Lorde and James Baldwin, and their writings reflect that reality; it is a reality that the teacher of literature—straight or gay—must be prepared to confront.

My special thanks go to my students, who have helped to fill in some of the gaps in my listings of Blakwomen playwrights.

Note: The spelling of Blakwoman, Blakwomen, etc., is an attempt to distinguish an identity from a color; the use of the "k" in the spelling of Afrika and Afrikan is my shorthand way of identifying myself as a pan-Afrikan, nationalist woman. To be Afrikan does not necessarily mean to have been born on the Afrikan continent.

*Their Eyes Were Watching God has been reissued by the University of Illinois Press. Brown Girl, Brownstones has been reissued by The Feminist Press.

An Outline of Literature by Blakwomen in the U.S.A.

I. The beginnings of literature in the United States from oral literature to the Harlem Renaissance
   A. Poetry
      1. Oral Poetry—creators unknown
         a. Religious—spirituals, sermons, prayers, testimonies
         b. Secular—work songs, play party songs, story songs, blues, hollers, shouts, cries, moans, toasts, lullabies
      2. Written Poetry—early poets
         a. Lucy Terry (c. 1730-1821)—"Bars Fight"**
         b. Phillis Wheatley (c. 1753-1784)—Poems on Various Subjects, Religious and Moral, 1773**
         c. Frances E.W. Harper (1824-1911)—Poems on Miscellaneous Subjects, 1854; Poems, 1870**
         d. Alice Dunbar-Nelson (1875-1935)**
         e. Anne Plato
         f. Henrietta Ray
   B. Prose
      1. Oral Prose Forms
         a. Animal story, trickster story, hero story, etc.

b. Sermon (blend of poetry and prose)
c. Speech oratory
   (1) Sojourner Truth
   (2) Frances E.W. Harper
   (3) Harriet Tubman
2. Written Prose Forms—early writers
   a. Slave narrative/autobiography
      (1) Ellen Craft—*Running a Thousand Miles for Freedom, or The Escape of William and Ellen Craft from Slavery*
      (2) Linda Brent (Lydia Maria Child)—*Incidents in the Life of a Slave Girl*
      (3) Sojourner Truth—*Narrative and Book of Life***
      d(4) Elizabeth Keckley (1825-1905)—*Behind the Scenes, or Thirty Years a Slave and Four Years in the White House*, 1868**
   b. Fiction
      (1) Clarissa Thompson—*Treading the Wine Press*, 1886
      (2) Mrs. A.E. Johnson—*Clarence and Chlorine, or God's Way*, 1890
      (3) Frances E.W. Harper—*Iola LeRoy, or Shadows Uplifted*, 1892; *Moses, a Story of the Nile*, 1869; *Sketches of Southern Life*, 1872 (short stories)
   c. Miscellaneous Prose: Charlotte Forten (Grimké) (1837-1914)—magazine articles: "Glimpses of New England"; *Journal*
C. Drama
   1. Angelina Weld Grimké (1880-1958)—*Rachel*, 1916
   2. Alice Dunbar-Nelson—*Mine Eyes Have Seen*, 1918
D. Music (recordings of traditional Black music by Blakwomen performers)
   1. Spirituals
   2. Blues
   3. Lullabies
II. Renaissance and Depression, 1919-1939
A. Poetry
   1. Oral Poetry—the rise of gospel music, prison songs, the move from rural to urban blues, Black popular music or "race records" (including recordings by Ma Rainey, Bessie Smith, Florence Mills, Ethel Waters, Ivie Anderson, and others)
   2. Written Poetry—the first flowering (*Caroling Dusk*, ed. Countee Cullen, is a good source of materials by these poets)
      a. Angelina Weld Grimké**
      b. Anne Spencer (1882-1975)**
      c. Jessie Remond Fauset (1882-1961)**
      d. Georgia Douglas Johnson (1886-1966)—*The Heart of a Woman*, 1918; *Bronze*, 1922; *An Autumn Love Cycle*, 1928**
      e. Gwendolyn B. Bennet (b. 1902)**
      f. Helene Johnson (b. 1907)**
B. Prose
   1. Fiction
      a. Jessie Remond Fauset—*There Is Confusion*, 1924; *Plum Bun*, 1929; *Chinaberry Tree*, 1932; *Comedy, American Style*, 1934
      b. Zora Neale Hurston (1903-1960)—*Jonah's Gourd Vine*, 1934; *Their Eyes Were Watching God*, 1938; "Gilded Six Bits" and "Sweat" (short stories)
      c. Nella Larsen—*Quicksand*, 1928; *Passing*, 1930**
   2. Nonfiction
      a. Mary Church Terrell—autobiography: *A Colored Woman in a White World*, 1940

　　b. Shirley Graham (Du Bois)—biography, drama, and children's literature
　　c. Zora Neale Hurston—criticism and folklore: *Of Mules and Men*
　C. Drama
　　1. Georgia Douglas Johnson—*A Sunday Morning in the South*, 1925
　　2. Zora Neale Hurston—*Great Day*, 1927; *Fast and Furious*, 1930
　　3. Eulalie Spence—*The Whipping*; *Undertow*, 1929
　　4. May Miller—*Scratches*, 1929; *Graven Images*, 1929
　　5. Marita Bonner—*Exit, an Illusion*, 1929; *The Pot Maker*, 1927; *Us White People, White Devils*; *The Call to Revolution*
III. World War II and After: Modern Black Writers
　A. Poetry
　　1. Margaret Danner—*Impressions of African Art Forms***
　　2. Margaret Walker (b. 1915)—*For My People and Other Poems*, 1942**
　　3. Gwendolyn Brooks (b. 1917)—*A Street in Bronzeville*, 1945; *Annie Allen*, 1949; *Selected Poems*, 1963; *The Bean Eaters*, 1959**
　　4. Pauli Murray (b. 1910)**
　B. Prose
　　1. Fiction
　　　a. The Novel
　　　　(1) Ann Petry (b. 1911)—*The Street*, 1946**; *Country Place*, 1947; *The Narrows*, 1953
　　　　(2) Gwendolyn Brooks—*Maud Martha***
　　　　(3) Paule Marshall (b. 1929)—*Brown Girl, Brownstones*, 1959, 1981
　　　b. The Short Story
　　　　(1) Ann Petry
　　　　(2) Paule Marshall—*Soul Clap Hands and Sing*, 1961**
　　2. Nonfiction
　　　a. Margaret Just Butcher—cirtical essay
　　　b. Nancy Bullock McGhee—critical essay
　　　c. Marian Anderson—autobiography: *My Lord What a Morning***
　C. Drama
　　1. Zora Neale Hurston—*Polk County*, 1944; *From Sun to Sun*; *Mule Bone*, 1964
　　2. Alice Childress—*Florence*; *Just a Little Simple*, 1950; *Gold through the Trees*, 1952; *A Man Bearing a Pitcher*; *Trouble in Mind*, 1955; *Wedding Band*, 1961
　　3. Lorraine Hansberry (1930-1966)—*Raisin in the Sun***
　D. Music
　　1. Billie Holliday
　　2. Dinah Washington
IV. After El Hajj Malik: Contemporary Black Writers (1965-present)
　A. Poetry
　　1. Oral Poetry
　　　a. Traditional and popular
　　　　(1) Bernice Reagon**
　　　　(2) Nina Simone**
　　　　(3) Camille Yarborough**
　　　　(4) Zulema**
　　　b. Poetry in performance
　　　　(1) Jayne Cortez**
　　　　(2) Ntozake Shange**
　　2. Written Poetry
　　　a. The Elders

(1) Margaret Danner—*Poem Counterpoem*, with Dudley Randall, 1966**; *Images of African Art Forms*; *The Down of a Thistle*, 1977**

(2) Margaret Walker—*Prophets for a New Day*, 1968; *October Journey*, 1973**

(3) Gwendolyn Brooks—*In the Mecca*, 1968; *Riot*, 1969; *Family Pictures*, 1970

(4) Pauli Murray—*Dark Testament*, 1969**

b. The "New Black Poets"

(1) Mari Evans—*I Am a Black Woman*, 1969**

(2) Naomi Long Madgett (b. 1923)

(3) Sarah Webster Fabio (b. 1928) (recordings available)

(4) Johari Amini (Kunjufu) (Jewel C. Latimore, b. 1935)—*Let's Go Somewhere*, 1969**; *Images in Black*, 1967; *Black Essence*, 1968**

(5) Sonia Sanchez (b. 1935)—*Homecoming*; *We a BaddDDD People*; *Blues Book for Blue Black Magical Women*; *Love Poems*; *I've Been a Woman***

(6) Lucille Clifton (b. 1936)—*Good Times*; *Good News about the Earth*; *An Ordinary Woman***

(7) June Jordan (b. 1936)—*Some Changes*; *New Days: Poems of Exile and Return*; *Things I Do in the Dark: New and Selected Poems***

(8) Carolyn Rodgers—*Songs of a Black Bird*; *Paper Soul*; *How I Got Ovah*; *The Heart as Ever Green***

(9) Audre Lorde (b. 1934)—*Cables to Rage*; *From a Land Where Other People Live*; *The New York Headshop and Museum*; *Coal*; *The Black Unicorn*

(10) Nikki Giovanni (b. 1943)—*Black Feelings, Black Talk*; *Black Judgment*; *My House*; *The Women and the Men*; *Cotton Candy on a Rainy Day***

(11) Barbara Mahone (b. 1944)—*Sugarfields*

(12) Alice Walker (b. 1944)—*Once*; *Revolutionary Petunias*; *Good Night Willie Lee, I'll See You in the Morning***

(13) Carole Gregory Clemmons (b. 1945)

(14) Pat Parker—*Child of Myself*; *Pit Stop*; *Woman Slaughter*; *Movement in Black*

(15) Ntozake Shange—*For colored girls who have considered suicide when the rainbow is enuf*; *Nappy Edges***

(16) Sherley Williams—*The Peacock Poems*

(17) Angela Jackson—*VooDoo Love Magic***

B. Prose

1. Fiction

a. The Novel

(1) Margaret Walker—*Jubilee*

(2) Alice Childress—*A Short Walk*

(3) Paule Marshall—*The Chosen Place, The Timeless People*

(4) Toni Morrison—*The Bluest Eye**; *Sula*; *Song of Solomon*

(5) Alice Walker—*The Third Life of Grange Copeland*; *Meridian*

(6) Ntozake Shange—*Sapphire*

(7) Gayl Jones—*Corregidora*; *Eva's Man*

(8) Ellease Southerland—*Let the Lion Eat Straw*

b. The Short Story

(1) Toni Cade Bambara—*Gorilla, My Love*; *The Sea Birds Are Still Alive***

(2) Alice Walker—*In Love and Trouble***

      (3) Gayl Jones—*White Rat***
      (4) Angela Jackson**
      (5) Hortense Spillers**
      (6) Mignon Holland Anderson—*Mostly Womenfolk and a Man or Two*
   2. Nonfiction
     a. Autobiography/Biography and Personal Reminiscence
       (1) Gwendolyn Brooks—Report from Part I
       (2) Maya Angelou—*I Know Why the Caged Bird Sings**; *Gather Together in My Name; Singin' and Swingin' and Gettin' Merry like Christmas*
       (3) Lucille Clifton—*Generations***
       (4) Nikki Giovanni—*Gemini*
     b. Literary Criticism
       (1) June Jordan
       (2) Carolyn Rodgers
       (3) Sarah Webster Fabio
       (4) Barbara Smith
       (5) Alice Walker
 C. Drama
   1. Alice Childress—*Strings* (one act); *Young Martin Luther King; Wine in the Wilderness; Mojo* (one act)
   2. Adrienne Kennedy—*The Funnyhouse of a Negro; A Lesson in a Dead Language; The Owl Answers; A Rat's Mass; A Beast's Story; City of Bezique; The Son*
   3. Sonia Sanchez—*Sister Son/ji*
   4. J.E. Franklin—*Black Girl*
   5. Martie Charles
   6. Barbara Molette
   7. Ntozake Shange—*For Colored Girls...*
 D. Children's Literature
   1. Gwendolyn Brooks
   2. Ann Petry
   3. Mari Evans
   4. June Jordan
   5. Lucille Clifton
   6. Sonia Sanchez
   7. Sharon Bell Mathis
   8. Louise Meriwether
   9. Eloise Greenfield
  10. Virginia Hamilton
  11. Rosa Guy
 E. Miscellaneous
   1. Verta Mae Grosvenor—*Vibration Cooking; Thursday and Every Other Sunday Off***
   2. Octavia E. Butler—*Pattern Master; Mind of My Mind; Survivor; Kindred*

THEMATIC GROUPINGS***

1. Black Girlhood: Toni Morrison, Toni Cade Bambara, Maya Angelou, Paule Marshall, Zora Neale Hurston, Linda Brent
2. Black Woman to Black Woman: Toni Cade Bambara, Ann Petry, Toni Morrison, Audre Lorde, Alice Walker

3. Black women and Black Men: Toni Cade Bambara, Gwendolyn Brooks, Gayl Jones, Ann Petry, Zora Neale Hurston
4. Black Families: Toni Morrison, Margaret Walker, Paule Marshall, Alice Walker, Zora Neale Hurston, Jessie Fauset
5. Black and White: Alice Walker, Ann Petry, Nella Larsen
6. Black Love: Toni Cade Bambara, Toni Morrison, Angela Jackson, Carolyn Rodgers, Paule Marshall, Zora Neale Hurston, Audre Lorde
7. Black Victimization: Gayl Jones, Ann Petry, Toni Morrison, Alice Walker
8. Social Poets: Sonia Sanchez, Nikki Giovnni, Johari Amini, Gwendolyn Brooks, Margaret Walker
9. Lyric Poets: Carolyn Rodgers, Lucille Clifton, June Jordan, Anne Spencer, Georgia Douglas Johnson, Margaret Danner, Gwendolyn Brooks
10. Black Feminism: Frances E.W. Harper, Sojourner Truth, Anne Spencer, Zora Neale Hurston, Toni Cade Bambara, Lucille Clifton, Audre Lorde
  * Complete work read during course
 ** Selected poems, short stories, or excerpts from longer works read during course.
*** Examples by these authors were discussed in terms of these themes ("Black feminism" represented our attempts to trace those aspects of "literature which stressed women affirming women's experiences).

APPENDIX
ASSIGNED TOPICS FOR RESEARCH AND DISCUSSION

1. A thematic analysis of two or more Blakwomen's autobiographies
2. A critical analysis of the work of a Blakwoman writer
3. A comparative analysis of the work of any two Blakwomen poets, novelists, etc.
4. A comparative study of the poetry of post-World War II poets and contemprary poets
5. An examination of the treatment of a single theme by several writers
6. An examination of the relationship between contemporary poetry and folk lyricists: content and structure
7. An historical survey of Blakwomen playwrights
8. The treatment of Black male/female relationships by Blakwomen authors
9. The treatment of Black mother/daughter relationships by Blakwomen authors
10. The treatment of Blakwoman/white woman relationships by Blakwomen authors
11. A critical study of short fiction by Blakwomen

Other Suggested Topics

1. Characteristics of Blakwomen's language and imagery
2. Blakwomen writing for children
3. The cookbook as a literary genre
4. Blaklesbian writers
5. The development of Blakwomen's literary critical tradition
6. The uses of history in Blakwomen's writings
7. The blues motif in Blakwomen's writings

AFRICAN-AMERICAN LITERATURE: BLACK WOMEN WRITERS*
Alice Walker
Univ. of Massachusetts, Boston, Afro-American Studies
Fall 1972

Week I:
"The Humanistic Tradition of Afro-American Literature," by Margaret Walker. On reserve.
"Negro Character as Seen by White Authors," by Sterling Brown, in *Dark Symphony:*
   Negro Literature in America, Emmanuel and Gross, eds. Free Press, 1968. On reserve.
"Bar's Fight," Lucy Terry, 1746.
Folk Poetry, Folk Sermons, "Sorrow Songs," "Blues," in *The Negro Caravan*, Brown, Davis
   and Lee, eds., Random House, Arno, 1969.

Week II:
Slave Narratives: "The Narrative of Olaudah Equiano," in *Great Slave Narratives*, Arna
   Bontemps, ed., Beacon Press, 1969. Introduction and pp. 1-33.
To Be a Slave, Julius Lester, ed., Dell, 1970. On reserve.
Jubilee, by Margaret Walker, Bantam, 1966, 1975.

Week II-III:
Colonial, Revolutionary (1776), and Abolitionist Poetry: The poems of Phillis Wheatley
   (1753-1784) and Frances E. W. Harper (1825-1911):
   "On Being Brought from Africa to America"
   "To the Earl of Dartmouth"
   "The Slave Mother"
   "The Slave Auction"
   "Bury Me in a Free Land"
Jubilee

*This course was also taught at Wellesley College in 1972.

Week III:
Jubilee

Week IV:
Jubilee
How I Wrote Jubilee, by Margaret Walker, Third World, 1972

Week V:
Open

Week VI:
Some problems encountered by women writers:
A Room of One's Own, by Virginia Wolf, Harcourt Brace Jovanovich, 1963.

Week VII:
A Room of One's Own: Independent research into the writings of Black women authors in

America, published or unpublished, prior to 1920. Results to be discussed in class.
Optional Reading: *Iola LeRoy*, by Frances E. W. Harper, 1892, AMS Press, International
Black Studies Library, Panther House. *Clotel, or the President's Daughter*, by William
Wells Brown, 1853. Macmillan, 1970 and Panther House, 1970.
Of special interest, but also optional: *The Awakening*, by Kate Chopin, 1899. Norton, 1977.

Week VIII:
Cane, by Jean Toomer. A poet's view of post-slavery women. Liveright, 1975.

Week IX:
Cane

Week X:
Cane

Week XI:
Cane

Week XII:
Quicksand, by Nella Larsen
            Nella Larsen
            Zora Neale Hurston
            Jessie Fauset
            Dorothy West
            See index, *The Negro Novel in America*, by Robert Bone, Yale University
                Press, 1965.
            The Harlem Renaissance, by Nathan Huggins, Oxford University Press, 1971.

Week XIII:
"The American Comedy," by Jessie Fauset, an excerpt in *The Negro Caravan*, Random
    House, Arno, 1969.
Their Eyes Were Watching God, by Zora Neale Hurston, University of Ilinois Press, 1978.

Week XIV:
Their Eyes Were Watching God
Dust Tracks on a Road, Zora Neale Hurston, Arno, 1970

Week XV:
Optional: *The Living Is Easy*, by Dorothy West, Arno, 1970. *The Street*, by Ann Petry
    (required), Jove, BJ Publishing Group, 1969.

Week XVI:
From *The World of Gwendolyn Brooks*: Selected poems, Harper and Row, 1971, and *Maud
    Martha*, reprint, AMS Press, 1953.

Week XVII:
Maud Martha
"For My People," by Margaret Walker, Arno, 1969.

Week XVIII:
"Reena," by Paule Marshall, in *The Black Woman*, Toni Cade, ed., Mentor, New American
    Library, 1974.

Who Look at Me, by June Jordan, T.Y. Crowell, 1969.

For the reading period, from this list:

Ann Moody, *Coming of Age in Mississippi,* Dell, 1970

Maya Angelou, *I Know Why the Caged Bird Sings,* Bantam, 1971

Okot p'Bitek, *Song of Lawino,* out of print

Sonia Sanchez, *Homecoming,* Broadside, 1968

Nikki Giovanni, *Black Judgments,* Broadside, 1968 or *Gemini,* Penguin, 1976

Toni Morrison, *The Bluest Eye* (out of print)

Bessie Head,*Maru*

Alice Walker, *The Third Life of Grange Copeland,* Harcourt Brace Jovanovich, 1977

Ernest Gaines, *The Autobiography of Miss Jane Pittman,* Bantam, 1972

Or short stories or poems by: Ann Petry, Paule Marshall, Toni Cade Bambara, Alice Walker, Zora Neale Hurston or Gwendolyn Brooks.

About the Contributors

LORRAINE BETHEL has taught courses and lectured on Black women's literature and Black female culture for various institutions. Her literary criticism and reviews have been published in several journals. She co-edited the Black women's issue of the literary magazine *Conditions*, and is currently working as a freelance editor/writer in New York.

MARTHA HURSEY BROWN teaches Black history and American women's history at Central Michigan University. Presently she is co-editor of *The Great Lakes Review*, a journal of Midwest culture. Brown also co-authored a junior high school social studies text, *Faces of America*. (New York: Harper and Row and Philadelphia: J. B. Lippincott, 1981).

CONSTANCE CARROLL is President of Indian Valley College in Navato, California.

THE COMBAHEE RIVER COLLECTIVE is a Boston-based Black feminist collective which has been in existence since 1974. Collective members are active in addressing Black women's political and cultural issues.

TIA CROSS is a white feminist activist from Boston, who works as a freelance photographer and slide-show producer. She also teaches two classes for whites, titled "Exploring Our Racism," and "Combating White Racism," and runs workshops for many different workplace and community groups on issues of racism and class bias.

RITA DANDRIDGE has taught courses in Afro-American literature at Norfolk State University since 1974. Her articles on Afro-American literature have appeared in *College Language Association (CLA) Journal*, *Black American Literature Forum*, *Obsidian*, *Journal of Negro History* and the *Women's Studies Newsletter*.

JACQUELYN GRANT is a Ph.D. candidate in systematic theology at Union Theological Seminary in New York and has been a doctoral fellow at the Du Bois Institute of Afro-American Research at Harvard University. She is also an ordained minister in the African Methodist Episcopal Church and currently teaches at the Interdenominational Theological Center in Atlanta, Georgia.

ELIZABETH HIGGINBOTHAM is Assistant Professor of Sociology at the University of Pittsburgh. Her doctorate is from Brandeis University, where she wrote a dissertation on the strategies for educational attainment of middle class and working class Black women. While continuing research on Black women in the labor market, she is currently studying the upward mobility of women from different racial and ethnic backgrounds.

An Associate Professor of English at the University of Delaware, Newark, **GLORIA T. HULL** (co-editor) has published criticism (predominantly on Black women writers) and poetry in journals such as *Black American Literature Forum, Conditions, American Literature, College Language Association Journal, Chrysalis*, the *Radical Teacher*, and *Obsidian*. She has edited the *Diary of Alice Dunbar-Nelson* and is working on a study of the women poets of the Harlem Renaissance.

FREADA KLEIN is a feminist activist who works with the Alliance Against Sexual Coercion in Boston.

RAMONA BLAIR MATHEWSON of Villa Park, California, pianist and composer, teaches musicianship and piano privately at local colleges. She is also widely known as a vocal coach and accompanist for opera and the art song.

JEANNE-MARIE A. MILLER, Associate Professor of English and an administrator at Howard University, has published widely on Black American drama. In 1972 she won the Amiri Baraka Award from *Black World* for her articles on Black theatre. Presently she is the editor of the *Black Theatre Bulletin* and Associate Editor of the *Theatre Journal*, publications of the American Theatre Association.

ELLEN PENCE is Director of the Domestic Abuse Intervention Project in Duluth, Minnesota.

MICHELE RUSSELL is a freelance writer who has contributed articles to *Heresies*, the *Radical Teacher*, and *Quest*.

PATRICIA BELL SCOTT (co-editor) is a Research Associate and Director of the Black Women's Educational Policy and Research Network Project at the Wellesley College Center for Research on Women. She has been a fellow at the JFK School of Government and held joint appointments in the Black Studies Program and Department of Child and Family Studies at the University of Tennessee, Knoxville. She has written numerous articles on Black women and Black families and is co-editor with Saundra Rice Murray of a forthcoming special issue of the *Psychology of Women Quarterly* on Black women.

JOAN R. SHERMAN has taught American literature at University College, Rutgers University, since 1971. She has published *Invisible Poets: Afro-Americans of the Nineteenth Century* (Urbana, Ill.: University of Illinois Press, 1974) and *Jack London: A Reference Guide* (Boston: G. K. Hall, 1977).

BARBARA SMITH (co-editor) is a Black feminist writer and activist, who has worked on a range of Black women's issues including reproductive rights, sterilization abuse, violence against women, and racism in the women's movement. She is co-editor with Lorraine Bethel of *Conditions: Five, The Black Women's Issue.* Her most recent writing appears in *Lesbian Poetry: An Anthology; This Bridge Called My Back: Writings by Radical Women of Color* (Watertown, Mass.: Persephone Press, 1981); and *Sinister Wisdom.*

BEVERLY SMITH is a member of the Combahee Black Feminist Collective of Boston, Massachusetts, and directs the Black Women Artist Film Series of Boston. She has been active in Black feminist health, political, and cultural efforts and has contributed articles to *Conditions, Common Lives-Lesbian Lives,* and *This Bridge Called My Back: Writings by Radical Women of Color* (Watertown, Mass.: Persephone Press, 1981).

ERLENE STETSON is Assistant Professor of English at Indiana University in Bloomington. She has published articles in *Obsidian, Journal of Afro-American Issues, CLA Journal, South and West,* and *Heresies.* She also serves as an eidtor for *Sojourner: A Third World Women's Research Newsletter.*

ALICE WALKER, the author of many highly acclaimed books of poetry and prose, received a Guggenheim Fellowship for fiction in 1978. She serves as a contributing and consulting editor to *Freedomways* and *MS.* magazines, and recently edited *I Love Myself When I Am Laughing: A*

Zora Neale Hurston Reader (Old Westbury, N. Y.: The Feminist Press, 1979).

MICHELE WALLACE is a freelance writer, born and educated in New York City. She has written for many journals, including *Essence, The Village Voice, MS.,* and *Esquire.* She is also the author of *Black Macho and the Myth of the Superwoman* (New York: Dial Press, 1979).

MARY HELEN WASHINGTON is Associate Professor of English at the University of Massachusetts, Boston. She has been a fellow at the Mary Bunting Institute of Radcliffe College, and is the editor of two books, *Black-Eyed Susans: Classic Stories by and about Black Women* (New York: Doubleday, 1975) and *Midnight Birds: Contemporary Black Women Writers* (New York: Doubleday, 1980).

R. ORA WILLIAMS, who taught English at Southern University, Tuskegee Institute, and Morgan State University, is a Professor of English at California State University, Long Beach, where she has also taught courses on American Black women. She is author of *American Black Women in the Arts and Social Sciences: A Bibliographical Survey* (Metuchen, N. J.: Scarecrow Press, 1978).

THELMA O. WILLIAMS, a former public school teacher in Trenton and Atlantic City, New Jersey, and music teacher in the public and private schools of Englewood, New Jersey, also taught music at Fairleigh Dickinson University. She is now an Associate Professor of Music at Glassboro State College. A composer of children's songs published in the Prentice-Hall Growing with Music series, Williams has served the company as a music editor and consultant.

DORA WILSON is Associate Professor of Music at California State University, Long Beach. She has presented a number of scholarly papers at professional meetings and published several papers.

JEAN FAGAN YELLIN's bibliographic essay—taken from her forthcoming full-length research tool, *Writings by and about Afro-American Women, 1800-1910*—grew out of work on Black and white women for her current study, *Women and Sisters: The AntiSlavery Feminists in Nineteenth-Century American Culture.* Her pertinent publications include *The Intricate Knot: Black Figures in American Literature, 1776-1863* (New York: New York University Press, 1972) and articles in *CLA Journal, Freedomways,* and *The Massachusetts Review.*

Acknowledgments

Grateful acknowledgment is made for permission to reprint the following copyrighted material:

Walker, Alice, "Women." Copyright © 1978 by Alice Walker. Reprinted from her volume *Revolutionary Petunias and Other Poems* by permission of Harcourt Brace Jovanovich, Inc.

Berry, Mary, "Foreword." Copyright © 1982 by Mary Berry.

Hull, Gloria T., and Barbara Smith, "Introduction." Copyright © 1982 by Gloria T. Hull and Barbara Smith.

Hull, Gloria T., Patricial Bell Scott, and Barbara Smith, "Visions: Recommendations for the Future of Black Women's Studies." Copyright © 1982 by Gloria T. Hull, Patricia Bell Scott, and Barbara Smith.

Wallace, Michele, "A Black Feminist's Search for Sisterhood." Copyright © 1975 by The Village Voice, Inc. Reprinted by permission of The Village Voice.

Combahee River Collective, "A Black Feminist Statement." From *Capitalist Patriarchy and the Case for Socialist Revolution*, edited by Zillah Eisenstein. Copyright © 1978 by Zillah Eisenstein. Reprinted by permission of Monthly Review Press.

Walker, Alice, "One Child of One's Own: A Meaningful Digression Within the Work(s)—An Excerpt." Copyright © 1978 by Alice Walker

Pence, Ellen, "Racism—A White Issue." Copyright © 1978 by *Aegis: Magazine on Ending Violence Against Women*. Reprinted by permission of *Aegis: Magazine on Ending Violence Against Women*.

Smith, Barbara, "Racism and Women's Studies." Copyright © 1979 by Barbara Smith. Reprinted by permission. A slightly different version appeared in the *Women's Studies Newsletter* 7, no. 3 (Summer 1979).

Cross, Tia, Freada Klein, Barbara Smith, and Beverly Smith, "Face-to-Face, Day-to-Day—Racism C-R." Copyright © 1979 by Tia Cross, Freada Klein, Barbara Smith, and Beverly Smith.

Stetson, Erlene, "Studying Slavery: Some Literary and Pedagogical

Acknowledgments   385

Dandridge, Rita B., "On the Novels Written by Black American Women; A Bibliographical Essay." Copyright © 1982 by Rita B. Dandridge.

Miller, Jeanne-Marie A., "Black Women Playwrights from Grimké to Shange: Selected Synopses of Their Works." Copyright © 1982 by Jeanne-Marie A. Miller.

Williams, Ora, Dora Wilson, Thelma Williams, and Ramona Matthewson, "American Black Women Composers: A Selected Annotated Bibliography." Copyright © 1982 by Ora Williams.

Brown, Martha H., "A Listing of Non-print Materials on Black Women." Copyright © 1982 by Martha H. Brown.

Hull, Gloria T., Patricia Bell Scott, and Barbara Smith, "Additional References and Resources." Copyright © 1982 by Gloria T. Hull, Patricia Bell Scott, and Barbara Smith.

Fahamisha Shariat, "Blakwomen Writers of the U.S.A. Who Are They? What Do They Write?" Copyright © 1982 by Fahamisha Shariat.

Grateful acknowledgment is made for permission to use the following photographs: Frontispiece, copyright © 1981 by Tia Cross. All other photographs courtesy of Library of Congress Photoduplication Service.

Index

The Feminist Press at The City University of New York offers alternatives in education and in literature. Founded in 1970, this nonprofit, tax-exempt educational and publishing organization works to eliminate stereotypes in books and schools and to provide literature with a broad vision of human potential. The publishing program includes reprints of important works by women, feminist biographies of women, multicultural anthologies, a cross-cultural memoir series, and nonsexist children's books. Curricular materials, bibliographies, directories, and a quarterly journal provide information and support for students and teachers of women's studies. Through publications and projects, The Feminist Press contributes to the rediscovery of the history of women and the emergence of a more humane society.

New and Forthcoming Books from The Feminist Press

Anna Teller, a novel by Jo Sinclair. Afterword by Anne Halley. $35.00 cloth, $16.95 paper.

The Captive Imagination: A Casebook on "The Yellow Wallpaper," edited and with an introduction by Catherine Golden. $35.00 cloth, $14.95 paper.

Fault Lines, a memoir by Meena Alexander. $35.00 cloth, $14.95 paper.

I Dwell in Possibility, a memoir by Toni McNaron. $35.00 cloth, $12.95 paper.

Intimate Warriors: Portraits of a Modern Marriage, 1899–1944, selected works by Neith Boyce and Hutchins Hapgood. Edited by Ellen Kay Trimberger. Afterword by Shari Benstock. $35.00 cloth, $12.95 paper.

Lion Woman's Legacy: An Armenian-American Memoir, by Arlene Voski Avakian. Afterword by Bettina Aptheker. $35.00 cloth, $14.95 paper.

Long Walks and Intimate Talks, poems and stories by Grace Paley, paintings by Vera B. Williams. $29.95 cloth, $12.95 paper.

The Mer-Child: A Legend for Children and Other Adults, by Robin Morgan. Illustrations by Jesse Spicer Zerner and Amy Zerner. $17.95 cloth, $8.95 paper.

Motherhood by Choice: Pioneers in Women's Health and Family Planning, by Perdita Huston. Foreword by Dr. Fred Sai. $35.00 cloth, $14.95 paper.

The Princess and the Admiral, by Charlotte Pomerantz. Illustrations by Tony Chen. $17.95 cloth, $8.95 paper.

Proud Man, a novel by Katharine Burdekin (Murray Constantine). Foreword and Afterword by Daphne Patai. $35.00 cloth, $14.95 paper.

The Seasons: Death and Transfiguration, a memoir by Jo Sinclair. $35.00 cloth, $12.95 paper.

Women Writing in India: 600 B.C. to the Present. Volume I: 600 B.C. to the Early Twentieth Century. Volume II: The Twentieth Century. Edited by Susie Tharu and K. Lalita. Each volume $59.95 cloth, $29.95 paper.

Prices subject to change. For a free catalog or order information, write to The Feminist Press at The City University of New York, 311 East 94 Street, New York, NY 10128.